Life and Letters of the Late Admiral Sir Bartholomew James Sulivan, K. C. B., 1810-1890

LIFE AND LETTERS

OF THE LATE

ADMIRAL SIR

BARTHOLOMEW JAMES SULIVAN,

K C.B.

B. J. Sullivan

LIFE AND LETTERS

OF THE LATE

ADMIRAL SIR

BARTHOLOMEW JAMES SULIVAN,

K.C.B.

1810—1890.

EDITED BY HIS SON

HENRY NORTON. SULIVAN.

With an Introduction by

ADMIRAL SIR G. H. RICHARDS, K.C.B. F.R.S.

WITH PORTRAIT, MAP, PLANS, AND ILLUSTRATIONS.

LONDON:

JOHN MURRAY, ALBEMARLE STREET.

1896.

Printed by Hazell, Watson, & Viney, Ld., London and Aylesbury

PREFACE.

BEFORE attempting a biography of my father, I consulted a distinguished naval officer as to the advisability of adding another to the many existing records of naval men. I desired to seek his opinion as to the general interest likely to be evoked by the work. He urged me to go on with it, saying he considered no one's life would be more interesting or more instructive. Therefore, if I have not fulfilled this expectation, the fault must lie with me, and not with my subject.

I then went to a friend competent to advise me on another point, and asked him whether I ought to give the materials for a biography to a literary man to edit, doubting my own capabilities. He said, " What might be gained in literary merit, by employing some one else to write the book, would be lost in biographical interest Do it yourself."

Thus emboldened, I have attempted the work. I set about it with all the more courage that I had so many of my father's letters and journals, written at the very time the events and actions they describe took place, so that very little original matter remained for me to write. Moreover, I have to thank my publisher, Mr. Murray, for the valuable literary assistance he has rendered me.

There has been unavoidable delay in the publication of these pages. I have had but little time with my other duties for their preparation. The amount of material has been so great that much labour has been required to choose the most interesting parts, and to avoid overloading the work with what would be of concern only to the family. Critics must remember that the letters were dashed off by a very busy man, often late at night, after a day of hard work, and not infrequently of danger and of conflict. Their interest lies, therefore, more in their vividness than in their literary accuracy.

I am fortunate in procuring a letter from the pen of him who is best able to give a picture of my father Admiral Sir G. Richards was his lieutenant in the *Philomel*, and served with him through the striking scenes of the war in the Parana. He was afterwards his colleague in many a deliberation on naval matters, and is himself a surveyor and sailor of eminence.

My father was often desired by us to write out his own history, but he was only prevailed upon to begin it about two years before his death, when his powers were failing. I feel sure, from the few pages of his autobiography I am able to give, my readers will also regret he was not able to write more himself. I give what he wrote at the age of seventy-seven with hardly a correction.

There is no need for me to say very much by way of introduction. His own letters and those of his friends will best show what manner of man he was; but some few remarks may help my readers to form a picture of him.

Bartholomew James Sulivan was born at Mylor, near Falmouth, on November 18th, 1810. His father, then Captain Thomas Ball Sulivan, R.N., was an able man of fine character and sterling uprightness. He had no resources besides his naval pay—too often but half-pay; and as he had a large family, the school in which they were trained was one of economy and self-restraint

When a commodore on the South American station, he was offered promotion from the Companionship of the Bath, which he then held, to the higher honour of the K.C.B. But he had to decline this promotion, not being able to afford the high fees then exacted from the recipients of knighthood. His four sons all entered the navy. The eldest of the family is the subject of this memoir; the youngest and only surviving one is the present Admiral George Lydiard Sulivan.

Thomas Ball Sulivan resided with his family for the latter part of his life at Flushing, near Falmouth. He died in 1857, at the age of seventy-seven, and was buried in the family vault at Mylor. On leaving his grave, the old family friend and medical adviser, Dr. Miller, said, "There lies the best husband, the best father, the best friend."

Distinguished men are often the sons of remarkable women. Sir B. James Sulivan's mother was the younger daughter of a well-known naval officer. Her father, Admiral James,* had brought up his two daughters in luxury, and the younger was married before his large property, derived chiefly from prize-money made in the old wars, had been lost through misplaced confidence and generous liberality.

Mrs. Sulivan had studied music in London under Mozart, and to her old age retained her beautiful touch on the piano. When her father's money had been all spent, she uncomplainingly settled down to the hard work of bringing up her large family on small means.

She made my father promise to read daily the appointed

* The journals of Admiral Bartholomew James, interesting both on account of the remarkable adventures they record and the humorous style in which they are written, are now being prepared for publication by my brother, Commander Sulivan, and will be brought out by the Naval Records Society.—ED.

psalms, and to pray the collect before the communion
service. He said before his death that he had never
omitted that prayer, and hardly ever omitted reading
the psalms. She was certainly a proud woman, but kept
her pride in check by her strong religious feeling. She had
her father's great vein of humour, and could tell a story,
even in old age, with great wit and power, yet in her
quiet, gentle way. All she ever said had the odour of her
truly sanctified spirit. She lived almost in prayer and the
study of the Bible. She was a brave woman of great force
of character, a staff of strength to her husband and
children in all trials, and she always made the best of
everything.

Her sufferings during the last twenty years of her life
were often great, but she bore them unmurmuringly. She
died in 1874, at the age of eighty-six.

To return to my father. As a lad he was small, but
grew very rapidly afterwards. At the age of seventeen
he was only five feet two inches ; at eighteen, five feet nine ,
ultimately measuring five feet eleven. He was considered
a remarkably handsome man, of fine presence. He had
large, dark, deep-set eyes, which, like his mother's, never
lost their clearness and brilliancy. Though somewhat bald
in old age, he retained the colour of his hair almost to the
last. His sight was so good he could see the satellites of
Jupiter with the naked eye up to the age of forty-five.

In whatever company he was, his was the pervading
presence. Fond of genial society, he charmed and interested every one with his conversation, intermixed as
it generally was with a wealth of anecdote. It is impossible to describe the personal magnetism he exercised
on all who came near him. To rich and poor, old and
young, he was the same earnest, helpful friend and companion But when there was cause for it, he could be

a stern rebuker of meanness or wrong-doing. His honesty of purpose was so great that no consideration of personal interest would lead him to modify his remarks, when he thought it necessary to speak straight out.

I think that his chief characteristic was his simple and manly piety. Although he had always lived a pure and correct life, his first deep religious convictions commenced about the time of his joining the *Beagle*. It has often been remarked that when a sailor or a soldier is religious, he becomes an "out and out" Christian. In the society of mess-mates no half-and-half faith will do. The life is watched, and any inconsistency of practice with profession is quickly noted.

My father showed his faith by his works. It was said of him that his entrance into the mess-room did more to stop any objectionable conversation than the appearance of the chaplain. He showed great interest in the moral and religious welfare of the men under him. A strict Sabbatarian, he avoided all possible work on Sunday. He would never accept an invitation to dinner on that day, even from his commander-in-chief, and would rarely write a letter home. There being no chaplain in such small vessels as he commanded, he not only conducted the ordinary services himself, but instituted classes as well.

When duty called, he exposed himself fearlessly to danger, with the fullest knowledge of the risk he ran, but with a simple faith in a Divine Providence watching over him. If suffered to fall, he knew the like protection would be over those he left behind. He was confident in his own opinion when his experience had given him an absolute right to pronounce judgment; but I could give many instances to show how modest he was as to matters he had not fully studied, though they might seemingly lie in his own province.

The keenness with which, as will be seen in the following pages, he felt any injustice to himself, and the heart-burnings caused thereby, must not be considered as springing from a desire of self-aggrandisement. In his own case he sometimes felt he was fighting the battle of the whole naval service. He thought that in relation to the recognition bestowed upon their services, naval officers were sometimes at a disadvantage compared with those of equal rank in the army. As Napoleon Bonaparte has observed, the glamour which surrounds the picturesque, ever-present aspect of the army makes that branch of the service receive more constant attention and honour than the sister-service, which, although first in precedence and first in importance in our country, is by the very necessity of its work often kept in the background.

With a sailor's inherited instincts and a sailor's training under such masters in the art as his father and FitzRoy, he at least equalled them. An officer once said to one of my brothers, "I served both with your grandfather and your father. The former was one of the best sailors of his day; the latter the best sailor I knew." His early surveying experience was put to good purpose in war-time, and men wondered at his talent for "smelling the shoals." But in the hard work of surveying the power had been gained of drawing rapid conclusions as to the contour of the hidden ground from the outlines of the shore visible It was Wellington, I believe, who spoke of the power the soldier should possess of guessing "what was on the other side of the hill." Many a lesson have I had from my father in earth-configuration during our walks, and he would illustrate the rules by which he navigated such rivers as the Parana from the stream running through the sand.

His mathematical accuracy stood him in good stead in his examinations and in his surveying work. Of intense quickness of perception and power of work himself, he perhaps expected more from his subordinates than they could always accomplish. As will be seen later, when those around him in the Baltic were dilatory and resourceless, he, by his energy, almost enforced action upon them. Greater caution in utterance would, perhaps, have been an advantage to him. It was said of him that, one day in London, meeting a friend, he stopped him and exclaimed, " Why, you are the man we have just been talking about, and I was saying what a shame it is they have given that appointment to you."

He possessed a most active mind, which was ever at work. Far-seeing in his judgment, he never let an event pass without noting the lessons to be derived from it. It will be seen that he proposed many valuable schemes of naval reform, and lived to see the greater part of his plans adopted. Endowed also with great constructive abilities, his plans of organisation and strategy invariably met with success.

As a friend said of him, " his whole professional career was marked by a happy faculty of organisation and a bold and skilful execution of plans." He possessed the combative temperament in a strong degree. He never rested content, after seeing a defective or unjust arrangement, until he had got the mischief remedied. This led him sometimes into conflict with others, doubtless often to the diminishing of his popularity; but generous-minded men admired the powers which lesser men envied.

The late Admiral Sir A. Cooper Key once stated at a public dinner at Singapore that " Sulivan was one of the most profound authorities on naval matters then living," so it must not be thought I am estimating his opinions at too high a value.

His fondness for children was very great. At first,

perhaps, his habits of discipline were rather too strongly exercised in the home circle, though he modified his views of training later in life   In the present day a little more of this home discipline would be beneficial to the rising generation.   No father was a greater playmate with his boys.   Shooting, fishing, boat-sailing, kite-flying, he was their eager coach, no one enjoying the fun more than himself—all the time teaching by demonstration and by story.

During our usual holidays at Flushing, Cornwall, our time was chiefly spent in·boat-sailing and yachting.   This boating was his greatest delight.   If he could not get afloat, the next best thing was a pond and a boy's boat. When he was on a visit to me at Newcastle-on-Tyne, I took him to the Leases' Park to see the model yacht sailing.   He was soon down on his knees, shifting the gear of the small boys' boats and instructing the owners in the art of sail-handling.

On one occasion, when he was as usual whistling and singing about the house, my mother observed, " Oh, a boy he is, and a boy he always will be."   Indeed, this delightful boyishness was a great feature in his character.   The daughter of a man who had been in. the Baltic in one of the ships of the fleet once spent some days in our home at Bournemouth as nurse to my brother's children.   Her father said to her afterwards, " And does the old admiral keep all his faculties?"   She replied, " The *old* admiral! Why, he is just like a boy—and you have to 'hush him up' when the children are asleep, to stop him running about the house whistling."

In 1837 he married one of the eight daughters of Admiral Young, of Barton End, near Stroud.   Admiral Young's brother was Admiral Sir William Young, G.C.B. ; his father, Admiral James Young ; his grandfather was Secretary to the Admiralty.   Of his four sons, two were in the army, two in the navy.

I trust much will be found in these pages calculated to be useful to officers of the present day, and that naval men, as well as the authorities at the Admiralty, may be led to think more highly of the art of the pilot and of the surveyor, which has been truly said to be "so useful in peace and so terrible in war."

H. N. S.

Oakhurst, Colwyn Bay,
   December 1895.

CONTENTS

PAGES

PREFACE . . . . . v-xiii

REMINISCENCES . . . . . xxi-xxxii

CHAPTER I.

AUTOBIOGRAPHY—YOUTH.

1810-29.

Admiral Thomas Ball Sulivan, C.B.—Wreck of the *Anson*—
War with America—Saving Life—Education—The Royal
Naval College—H.M.S. *Thetis*—A Chaplain acting as
Bishop—Tea *v.* Grog—Salvage Services at Gibraltar—
A Wounded Mid—A Sixty-five-foot Sea—Friend or Foe?—
Amirante Brown—Brazilian Impressment—Lord and Lady
Ponsonby—Jack's Love of Drink—H.M.S *Beagle*—The
Beagle's Ghost—A Pampero 1-35

CHAPTER II.

H.M.S. "BEAGLE," H.M. KETCH "ARROW," ETC.

1831-42.

Lieutenant—H.M.S. *Beagle*—Admiral R. O'B. FitzRoy—A
Somnambulist at Tea—The *Beagle* ships a Sea—Botany—
Rough Boat-work—Healthy Appetites—Darwin fossil-
digging—A Merry Party—Survey of Chiloe—A Christmas
Dinner—Diving—Voyage round the World—The Reception
of the Astronomer Royal—Darwin's Sea-sickness—Admiral
Mellersh and Mr. King on Sulivan's Seamanship—Marriage
—Survey of the Falkland Islands—FitzRoy on Sulivan's
Capabilities—Loss of *Pincher*—The *Arrow*—The Falkland
Islands—Commander—H.M. Brig *Philomel*—Botanising
in the Falklands—Tussac-grass in Scotland . . . 36-51

CHAPTER III.

THE PARANA CAMPAIGN.

1842-46.

PAGES

Cause of the War—General Rosas—Siege of Monte Video—
Garibaldi—Amirante Brown—British and French Inter-
vention—H.M.S. *Philomel*—" The Pride of the Station "—
Seamanship—Commodore Purvis and Amirante Brown—
Anxiety—Besieged—The *Gorgon* on Shore—Up the
Uruguay with Garibaldi—Saving Lives—Paucity of Warlike
Stores—Opening the Parana 52-70

CHAPTER IV.

THE BATTLE OF OBLIGADO.

1845-46.

British and French Squadrons—Drilling Seamen—Opening
Fire—The Ships taken in detail—Gallant Conduct—The
Enemy's Heavy Losses—Hope cutting the Chains—Storm-
ing the Batteries—Spiking Guns—Individual Incidents—
Strategical Inferences—Dr. Niddrie—Captain Tréhouart—
Honouring a Brave Enemy 71-92

CHAPTER V.

ASCENT OF THE PARANA.

Opening up the Interior Country—Arduous Ascent of the Parana
—Paraguayan Politics—The Convoy under Fire—Corrientes
—Intricate Navigation—An Artful Dodge—Home—Dis-
cipline—Promotions—No Medal—On Honorary Rewards—
The Royal Dockyard Volunteer Brigade .   .   . 93-117

CHAPTER VI.

WAR WITH RUSSIA.

1854.

Jingoism reproved—Admiral Sir C. Napier—Manning the
Fleet—Surveyor and Pilot—Admiralty Instructions—H.M.S.
Lightning—Reminiscences by Captain Dyer—The Use of
a Surveying-ship—Sweden—Ships' Individualities—Pilots or
Charts ?—" Boots " to the Fleet—Hango—Time wasted 118-144

CHAPTER VII.

HANGO.

PAGES

The Fleet in Danger—Wormsö—Adverse Influence—Reconnoitring the Forts—Diverse Ways of attacking—Strategical Questions—Action by *Arrogant* and *Hecla*—Finnish Peasants 145-163

CHAPTER VIII

RECONNOITRING BOMARSUND.

Comrades' Testimony—Examining Channels—Viewing the Forts —The Governor asleep—Making Friends—Sulivan's Plan —Cholera—Napier's Plan—Why not attempted—Decision of British and French Governments 164-184

CHAPTER IX.

RECONNOITRING CRONSTADT.

British and French Fleets before Cronstadt—*Lightning* leading the Squadron in—Situation of the Russian Fleet—Strength of the Position—Napier goes close in—Biörkö Sound— A Mare's Nest at Koivasto—From " Boots " to " Pioneer " —Cholera increasing—Baro Sound—Sweaborg seen at last— The Bomarsund Secret—A Defence of Napier—Ships *v.* Forts—Why Cronstadt was not attacked—What were Nelson's Tactics ? 185-207

CHAPTER X.

THE FALL OF BOMARSUND.

Lightning leads—An Official Prisoner—Arrival of French Troops—Puffing—A Target of Admirals and Generals— Preparations for Attack—Selection—Landing—*Hecla* on Shore—Sounding under the Fort—The French open Fire— Sulivan's Escape—Ramsay's Battery—The Towers fall— Bomarsund surrenders—Promotions—Wood or Iron for Ships' Bottoms ? 208-241

CHAPTER XI.

THE LAST OF BOMARSUND.

PAGES

Revel viewed—Heavy Gale—A Russian Frigate—Congratulations—Blowing up the Forts—Cholera Mortality—Dirt and Disease—A Gale at Nargen—Newspaper Criticisms—Promotions—Jovial Prisoners—Revel—Napier's Firmness—Napier nearly caught—Press Attacks—Nelson's Tactics—Ships *v.* Forts—Home—Various Schemes against Sweaborg 242-271

CHAPTER XII.

RECONNOITRING CRONSTADT—INFERNAL MACHINES.

1855.

Sulivan's Plans for 1855—Cronstadt—Adequate Means not provided—Urging on the Unwilling—Sea clear to Sweaborg—Peeps at Revel, Sweaborg, and Hogland—Biörkö Sound—Prizes—Cronstadt seen—Its Strength—Surveying on the North Side—The *Merlin* explodes Infernals—The Effects—A Sad Misunderstanding—War Policy . . 272-297

CHAPTER XIII.

INFERNAL MACHINES—A RUSSIAN COUNTRY HOUSE.

Sweaborg—A Flag-of-truce—Cronstadt—Insufficient Means—An Infernal Machine—Accident to Admiral Seymour—The Strength of Cronstadt—Spare Helsingfors—A Russian Baron—Criticisms on our Conduct—A Country House—Preparing for Sweaborg—Russian Gun-boats—Companion of the Bath 298-317

CHAPTER XIV.

BOMBARDMENT OF SWEABORG.

Helsingfors—Plan of Attack on Sweaborg—A Disclosure—Making a Mess of it—A Second Bungle—The Lessons taught therefrom—A Successful Attack—Accurate Ranges—A Series of Explosions—The Second Day—One Fort beats Three Ships—Bad Mortars—Extensive Conflagrations—A Plea for Helsingfors—Congratulations—*Merlin* Ashore—Effects of Mortar Fire—Dundas and Penaud's Despatches—Vertical Fire 318-343

CHAPTER XV.

AFTER SWEABORG.

PAGES

Revel—Russian Losses—A Seaman's Letter—A Patriotic
Baroness—A Unique Surveying Trip—Random Firing—
Tall Talk—Prince Leiningen—A Russian Cutting-out
Scheme—Windy Despatches—Fancied Glory—Nargen
Anchorage—Overworked—Return Home—Cronstadt—A
Compliment from the Enemy—Honours—Seniority, not
Service—A Choice of Appointments—A Sub-marine Experi-
ment 344-374

CHAPTER XVI.

THE BOARD OF TRADE.

1857-65.

Professional Officer and Acting Harbour Engineer—Naval Reforms—Holidays—Overwork—Resignation—Reminiscences
by Lord Farrer, Sir J. H. Briggs, and Bishop Stirling—Flag
Rank 375-390

CHAPTER XVII.

RETIREMENT.

1865-90

Life at Bournemouth—Not Idle—Consulted by Admiralty—
K.C.B —Loss of a Son—Old Chums—"Crossing the Bar" 391-395

APPENDICES.

A. Royal Dockyard Volunteers (1848) Too Successful—
Mechanics Good Gunners 397

B Life in the Falkland Islands (1848-51): Wives at a Premium
—Farming—Improving the Breeds—Mutiny on Board . 400

C. Proposed Strategic and Refuge Harbour at Filey (1859) . 402

D Coast Defences and Vertical Fire (1859): Badly constructed
Forts at Plymouth—Spithead Defences—Ships v. Forts—
Battery Construction—Barrier and Boom Defences—Vertical Fire—Pilotage—The Ram suggested—Foreigners
using Howitzers 404

PAGE

E Navigating and Surveying Officers (1846-63): Abolition of the Master Line—Pilotage in Intricate Waters—Practice *v.* Theory—The Surveying Service—Pioneer Officers . . 411

F. Origin of the Naval Reserve (1846-60) Manning . 418

G The Board of Admiralty (1861): A Commander-in-chief of the Navy. 419

H Navy· Titles of Officers—Flag Rank 423

I Merchant Shipping (1860) Coast Lights, who should pay for them—Compulsory Pilotage 424

J The Army Volunteers (1852): How they originated . . 426

K Fleet Actions (1860): The Chief to direct, not to fight— Large *v.* Small Guns 427

L. Admiral Sulivan's Remarks on Passages in Mr G. Butler Earp's Work on the Campaign of 1854—The Handling of the Russian Fleet. 428

LIST OF ILLUSTRATIONS.

Portrait . . . . *Frontispiece*

Rear-Admiral Chads' Squadron on the way to Bomarsund
To face p 210

Ruins of Fort Tzee, Bomarsund . . . . ,, 230

Fort Nottich, Bomarsund . . ,, 248

LIST OF SKETCHES.

A Principle of Gunnery . . . . . *On p.* 157

The Forts at Bomarsund . . . . ,, 169

The Main Defences at Cronstadt . . . . ,, 190

An "Infernal Machine" . . . . . ,, 302

PLANS AND CHARTS.

Rio Parana and Adjacent Country . . . . *Facing p* 55

Obligado—Plan of Attack . . . *On p.* 74

Hango Bay . . . . . ,, 153

Cronstadt—Main Channel . . . . . ,, 188

Bomarsund and the Channels leading thereto . . ,, 222

Sweaborg Roads . . . . . ,, 268

Cronstadt—General Chart . . . . ,, 288

Sweaborg—Plan of Attack . . . . . ,, 330

PERSONAL REMINISCENCES OF

ADMIRAL SIR B. JAMES SULIVAN.

BY

ADMIRAL SIR GEORGE HENRY RICHARDS,

K.C.B, F.R.S

WHEN it was suggested to me that I should write a brief introductory notice to the memoirs of the late Admiral Sir Bartholomew James Sulivan, K.C.B, then being prepared by his son, I could not but feel that at any rate it would be a grateful task to one who had been a follower, admirer, and life-long friend. At the same time, when I asked myself whether the life of a naval officer extending over a period which offered but few opportunities of distinction for the naval service would attract public interest, and when I called to mind that the life of but one admiral, and he a very distinguished one, had been published within my own recollection, I confess that I felt doubtful whether the public would feel sufficient concern in such a work to justify its appearance in print.

The answer which came to me was that the biography of any man of eminence and high character, in whatever walk of life he had moved, and especially of such a man as the subject of this memoir, could not fail to be interesting as well as instructive, not only to many of his own profession, but also to that large class of English men and women who are connected with the naval service. It would thus have a fascination from the every-day life and personal incidents of some fifty years ago, in the days of wooden ships and masts and sails, and the quaint habits of thought and speech now fast falling into disuse—days when men lived on the sea for months together, when the sea was their world, and their ship was their pride and their home for years. All this is now changed in many respects, and in how comparatively brief a period. But the sea does not change, and the characteristics of the seaman can scarcely do so. Promptitude and action, self-denial and discipline, must ever be the watchwords of the navy, in some respects, perhaps, even in a greater degree now than of old. Whether sailing in ships, or steaming in the ponderous iron-cased machines of the present day, those whose business lies in the great waters must be seamen still.

All these qualities were possessed in the highest degree by the subject of this sketch, though the chief interest which may be looked for in the following reminiscences must doubtless be due to the character of the man himself

He was generous and genial in disposition, simple and modest in his tastes and habits, yet lofty in all his conceptions, while a high moral tone pervaded his life from early boyhood. His professional qualities were perhaps unrivalled—a born seaman and strategist, instinctively a pilot in the most unknown and difficult waters, never at fault, keen to see, and as swift to execute. He, in my opinion, had a greater instinctive knowledge of real pilotage, strategy, and the art of war than any man I ever knew or read of. He was never intrusive, and always loyal. Knowing well his own powers, he merely wished them to be admitted, not to be ignored. He was hasty and impulsive to a degree, it is true, when it rested with others to carry out a service which he felt must be done with promptitude and decision; and this cost him,

perhaps, some friends, for the time; but it was soon
forgotten, for in action or in any difficulties he was cool
and collected, with an unerring judgment in all professional
matters.   None withheld their admiration for qualities
and gifts which were perhaps unequalled.

My first service connection with Sir James Sulivan, then
commander of the surveying-vessel *Philomel*, was in the
year 1842, when I served with him for four years on
the surveys of the Falkland Isles, the river Plata, and the
upper waters of the rivers Paraguay and Parana   From
the fact of my having been brought up as a surveying
officer, his own branch of the naval profession, I had the
privilege and the advantage of a close connection with him,
and it was during these years that I was able to form the
opinions of his character which I have already expressed.
It may perhaps be thought by the profession generally that
the command of a surveying-vessel with a hundred men
is scarcely the test by which to judge of the capabilities
of an officer for high command and great responsibilities.
My experience does not bear out such views; but if I am
wrong, Sulivan, at any rate, was the exception, as was
proved in his after-career.   He had served an apprentice-
ship of six years as a lieutenant in the *Beagle*, under
FitzRoy, in the tempestuous regions of Magellan Straits
and Cape Horn, such as few men had experienced   He
had, moreover, a peculiar fitness for the command of men.
According to the custom in those days, he was permitted
to choose his own crew, and a finer set of seamen
was rarely collected together, most of them from his
native place, Falmouth.   No man had a stricter idea of
discipline than he, but his strong sense of justice and
his unremitting consideration and care for every one
under his command gave him a moral influence such as
is, perhaps, rarely met with, and rendered punishment in

any shape almost unknown. Every man was a seaman, but every man knew that the captain was the best and the boldest among them. His activity of mind and body were equally remarkable. One moment he could be seen at the mast-head with his sketch-book, carrying out the duty of the survey; at another he would be in the chains, showing the leadsman his duties when the ship was in some critical position.

The operations in the Parana in 1845 by the English and French squadrons against the Dictator Rosas gave him ample opportunities for the exercise of his special abilities as a strategist and a pilot, and here he occupied the position which in similar cases had not infrequently been filled by the surveying commander in time of action, viz. strategical adviser to the commander-in-chief; and he performed the duties with brilliant success.

This is not the place to narrate events which will, doubtless, appear in these memoirs from his own journals. Sufficient to say, that he safely piloted the ships, mostly sailing-vessels, for several months, in difficult and altogether unknown waters, for many hundred miles into the interior of South America with skill and success, to the admiration of the fleet. The gallant French captain, Tréhouart, who commanded the French division, may be said to have almost worshipped him.

There was no more modest man than Sulivan on all points but the one of which he knew himself to be the master-hand; and on this he never hesitated to give his views with promptitude and decision, and, perhaps, with more haste than was always agreeable Possibly, this lost him much of the credit which was unquestionably his due; but he always retained the respect and admiration of such men as James Hope, Cooper Key, and many others who knew and appreciated the value of his services

At the close of this campaign, which opened the waters of those great rivers to the shipping of all countries, Captain Sulivan, with the surveying-ship, returned to England; and from that time our ways lay apart for many years. Correspondence was always, however, kept up, principally on professional or technical subjects, in which he knew that I placed the highest value on his opinion and advice.

Some time after Captain Sulivan's return from the Parana expedition, it was determined by the Government to create a defensive force of volunteers from the dock-yards and other like establishments, and he was selected by the Admiralty to organise and drill the force. These dockyard-battalions, as they were termed, were, however, disbanded after a few months of existence, principally on account of financial reasons, so that in 1848 he again found himself unemployed. He devoted his energies for some time to the consideration of many professional reforms, some of which were subsequently carried out; but about this period his health suffered, and he was recommended a change to a southern climate. He resolved, however, with his characteristic determination, that, if he made any change, it should be to the far south, and the same year he embarked with his whole family in a hired ship, and proceeded to the Falkland Islands, where, and also in the adjacent desolate regions of Patagonia and Tierra del Fuego, he had already passed many years of his professional life on the work of the Admiralty surveys. He always considered that, although wanting in most of the comforts of civilised life, the Falklands were really health resorts. These treeless and desolate islands always had a peculiar charm for him. His idea was that they were specially fitted for farming purposes, and for the rearing of cattle and sheep. He accordingly

took with him the necessary farming implements, as well
as some high-class animals for improving the breeds, and determined to make the experiment.   He persevered for some
years, not without encouraging results, though others who
followed his example later were perhaps more successful

By the end of 1851, on the expiration of his leave of
absence, hearing rumours of possible hostilities in Europe,
he could not withstand the temptation of once more seeking
active service in the profession for which his tastes and
abilities best fitted him.   He therefore gave up his farming
speculation and returned to England, where he used every
effort to obtain employment afloat.   He had not realised,
however, that when a naval officer severs his connection
with the sea for ever so short a time, by the traditions of
the service his career is generally considered at an end;
and probably that would have been his fate, but for the
breaking out of the Russian war, when his well-known
abilities could not be dispensed with.   He was unhesi-
tatingly selected by Sir Francis Beaufort, the Hydrographer
of the Admiralty, as the surveying officer to the Baltic
fleet, in command of a small steamer suitable for reconnoitring purposes.

On my return to England at the close of the year 1854
from the arctic regions, and after the first Russian
campaign, I lost no time in seeing him and hearing his
views on the war.   His great grief was the entirely
unprepared state we were in as regarded the proper style
and draught of vessels for making an effective attempt
on the strongholds of Cronstadt or other fortified points
in the Baltic; but great efforts were made during that
winter, though with inadequate results, for the campaign
of 1855, and a more efficient steam-vessel was provided for
him personally.   I was not an eye-witness of any of the
operations of that campaign, but I saw Captain Sulivan

again on his return at the close of 1855. There had been some fair successes obtained, chiefly, I believe, owing to his own exertions, but he seemed depressed generally at the barrenness of the operations. Almost the first thing he said to me was, "My head won't stand another campaign like this ; you must take my place." I fancied I knew him better than he knew himself on some points, and I said, "Wait a little ; you won't want to give up your place when the time comes" Soon after preparations were being made on a gigantic scale, which would probably have given us Cronstadt during the following year had hostilities continued. No one was more heart and soul in these preparations than he, nor had the heads of the Government a more valued and abler adviser.

The truth was, he felt that he had not received the encouragement or hearty support of his chiefs in operations which his sanguine mind and his tried experience and judgment led him to believe could be accomplished. Officers and men would work heartily with him, but his opinion decidedly was that there was no very cordial feeling on the part of the higher authorities towards the surveying branch of the service, of which he was perhaps the universally acknowledged leader. His views, I confess, were and are to a certain extent shared in by myself, although I gratefully acknowledge that I have met with some brilliant exceptions. As I have said, I am unable to write of Sulivan's Baltic services from any personal knowledge, but I have read papers connected with this memoir from men of eminence who knew him well ; and I am so much impressed by their views of his character, coinciding as they do so exactly with my own, formed years before, that I cannot refrain from making this brief reference to them. They will doubtless find a more suitable place in the text.

While he held the office of naval adviser to the Board of Trade, many questions arose between us, on which he often had to suggest or decide, such as the position and nature of sea-lights, sites for docks, defensive positions, etc., in the Colonies. On such points his decisions were always eminently practical, although formed without any local knowledge. On one occasion, I remember, when hostilities seemed imminent with a neighbouring power, I received from him by post a plan showing how he would attempt the capture of a strongly fortified port with a very inferior naval force. The scheme was a bold and ingenious one, drawn up without any information beyond that derived from the English charts, and with a very imperfect knowledge of the defences. But on visiting them in a friendly way some months afterwards, it occurred to me that, even if the designer himself had been the executor of the attempt, the operation would have been an extremely doubtful one. The incident, however, served to show the readiness of the strategist

Soon after his return to England from the Falklands in 1851, he learnt of the untimely end of Captain Allen Gardiner, R N, who with his companions had died of starvation in the inhospitable regions of Tierra del Fuego, where they had gone with an inadequately equipped expedition for the purpose of missionary work among the degraded natives. Had Sulivan received the letter sent him on the subject before he left the Falklands, he might have saved the party. He and other friends of Gardiner revived the mission and raised money enough to fit out a mission schooner and establish headquarters in the Falkland Islands. The work of the mission, which has now spread to the whole of South America, has been attended with wonderful results among the savages of Tierra del Fuego. Sulivan continued to be an active and enthusiastic supporter of the South American Missionary Society, and its nautical adviser to the end of his life.

This brief sketch, principally of the professional side of his character, would certainly be considered incomplete by the younger generation of his time who knew him well without some allusion to what may be called the peculiarities of the characteristics of his ordinary social life.

Impulsive and enthusiastic he was, no doubt, on points in which he took a deep interest—and they were many. For argument on any subject he was always keen and ready, though rarely, if ever, convinced against his own preconceived opinions On politics and religion, like many men of his temperament, he held very strong views, and was always most serious on them. In politics, as the word was understood half a century ago, it need scarcely be said he was extremely liberal. But nothing would ever have induced him, for power or for party, or for personal reasons, to swerve from the high standards of honour and truth which were inherent in him. He used to say in his earlier days that it was his ambition to represent his native place in Parliament; but he, after all, contented himself with devoting all his energies to reforms in his own profession, to the amelioration and improvement of the seamen's position, the modification and uniformity of punishment, and, above all, to the raising the moral tone of the navy. In all these matters he took a deep interest and an active part. Few will deny that the improvements which have been gradually carried out in the naval service, owing to the exertions of such men, have scarcely been equalled in any other great community. He was a strong advocate of justice and of the recognition of individual merit, and was never tired of endeavouring to redress grievances, no matter who the subject might be, sometimes overlooking the fact that in a great service there must be certain hard-and-fast rules, and that cases of individual hardship cannot but occur sometimes, however meritorious the man may be.

In Church matters he certainly was what is termed extremely low, and perhaps not very tolerant, but was always indefatigable in forwarding the interest of those who thought with him. Whatever might be the subject of dispute, he was always ready for argument with the other side, and I have more than once been present at a scene, not without its comic aspect, as, for instance, when he was threatened with excommunication by a High Church dignitary on whom he had forced a controversy at the corner of a street. These things, however, never caused anything beyond momentary irritation, for it was impossible to quarrel with a man without guile.

I remember, too, when he was leaving his ship the *Philomel* in the Parana for an absence of some months, with the leading members of the expedition on a political and exploring mission to the upper republics, some hundreds of miles into the interior, in giving me his last instructions he said, " I have only one cause of anxiety. You will not let my practice of the Church service be altered ? " I assured him that there was no fear on that head He added, " Don't increase the scraping and polishing work, and good-bye." It was one of his hobbies that there should be no addition to the men's work by brass-polishing, which was a good deal in vogue in those days. His great desire, however, was that his ship should always be smart and efficient, and ready for any service at a moment's notice. He took a great pleasure in beating the fleet at evolutions; but as his taking part in them was purely voluntary—a surveying-ship being exempt from these duties—nothing would induce him to do so on Sundays. We all differed from him in this; but he steadfastly maintained his position, saying, "I never will work on Sundays, except to save the ship, or in action." This, not unnaturally, cost us some good-will in the squadron.

When he returned from his mission in the Upper Parana and rejoined his ship, hostilities being in a fair way of ceasing, he was ordered to leave the river and return to his regular duties. The ship, on descending the river, had for some miles to run the gauntlet of the enemy's field artillery, which was placed on the high cliffs in the neighbourhood of the old battle-field of Obligado, and annoyed all passing ships. Sulivan said to me with much glee: "I have a plan which will puzzle these fellows. There must be deep water close under these cliffs. We will pass so close under them that they will not be able to depress their guns on us." He had a barricade of hammocks made about the steering-wheel, and sent all hands below. He took the helm himself, and said, "You keep here by me in case of accidents" The sails were trimmed, and with a light wind aft we passed close under the cliffs in silence. No shot did more than pass some six or eight feet above the deck, several going through the main-sail. This was cleverly done, but some others did not escape so free.

Thus I have touched upon some of the salient points in the character of a unique and highly gifted man. It has been said, and perhaps with some truth, that these strange combinations frequently go together. It is certain, however, that Sir James Sulivan was the type of a thoroughly just, upright, and strictly religious man. One of the first things he gave out when he commissioned the *Philomel* was, "Profane language and intemperance I never will suffer," and one of the remarkable points in his character was that his presence was alone sufficient to forbid the possibility of any conversation of a loose or questionable kind in any society where he might be. He was essentially a domestic man, never caring for club life. Nor did he often attend the meetings of the learned societies (although he was a member of the Royal Geographical and the Meteorological Societies), though a more intellectual and more intelligent man, or a more brilliant conversationalist, perhaps, could not often be met with Though he was not very well known generally among his own brother-officers, from these causes, and from his retiring disposition, yet when troublesome times brought him to the front, his name became a household word among those with whom he was associated.

Those who knew Sulivan well must also have known his wife. I have always regarded her character as one of the most beautiful I have ever met with. Perhaps there never were two people more different in their temperaments, and yet so entirely suited to one another,—he impulsive and enthusiastic in all he undertook, she calm, amiable, and gentle, sharing all his feelings, and never opposing his pursuits, whatever direction they took. Knowing them both well from my early days, I went when I could to see them in their retirement at Bournemouth in the latter years of their lives. She, long an invalid, generally passed her days lying on a couch in the drawing-room, and he rarely left her. If he found it difficult when he met a friend of olden days to refrain from his old habit of referring to past adventures, though he had been strictly enjoined to avoid all exciting topics, a word or a look from her always brought the calm which had become so essential to his health. He was the first to be taken, and her last words to him were, " I shall not be long after you."

G. H. R.

The Cottage, Fetcham,
Leatherhead, December 1895.

LIFE AND LETTERS

OF

ADMIRAL SIR B. J. SULIVAN,

K.C.B.

CHAPTER I.

AUTOBIOGRAPHY—YOUTH.

1810-29.

"I WAS born at Tregew, in the parish of Mylor, on the banks of Falmouth Harbour, on November 18th, 1810. My father was then Commander Thomas Ball Sulivan, R.N., who, after serving from 1793 throughout the whole war as midshipman and lieutenant, was first lieutenant of the *Anson* (Captain Lydiard) at the capture of Curaçao by Captain Charles Brisbane, on January 1st, 1807. For this he was made commander with the two other first lieutenants. On returning in the *Anson* to England, and not being immediately employed, his former commander, Captain Lydiard, asked him to take a cruise, as his guest, in the *Anson*, about to be stationed in the Channel. The *Anson* went into Falmouth on the morning of Christmas Day, 1807, and my father landed with Captain Lydiard. On shore they met the captains of some other ships-of-war in the harbour, and were asked where they were going to dine. Captain Lydiard answered, 'On board'; the others replying, 'Come with us to dine at Woodlands with Captain James.' 'We do not know him.' 'No matter; all the captains in the harbour are expected to dine there.' And they went. This led to the first meeting of my father and mother, the daughter of Captain James, who was then nineteen years of age. The *Anson* sailed next morning for her station on the western part of the Channel, and on December 27th was embayed with a southerly gale in Mount's Bay. Failing to work out against the gale, she anchored off the eastern shore of the bay, and, parting two cables, Captain Lydiard consulted the officers as to the expediency of running her on shore before dark on the Love Sand (a small patch of sand on an iron-bound coast), as it was certain the remaining cables would not hold her through a long winter's night, and if she drove on the rocky shore every soul would perish. This plan was adopted.

" She had been a two-decked, sixty-four-gun ship, and cut down to a forty-four-gun frigate, but with a poop. There was the surf of the heavy southerly gale on the short beach, and directly she struck the next sea threw her broadside on. The poop had been crowded with officers and men, as the highest, and probably the safest, place, but all were swept off the poop, and I have heard my father say he doubted if one there was saved. The masts went at the same time, but providentially the main-mast fell in such a position as to form a bridge from the ship to the shore above the reflux of the surf, and the men had only to watch the wave round both bow and stern, and run along the main-mast before the return of the next one. This formed such a means of escape that six men's wives who were in the ship were saved by it ; one, who had broken her thigh by a fall, was carried on shore by men. Captain Lydiard and my father were lashed to the stanchion of the wheel, and were witnesses to a painful scene. The surgeon of the ship had a son on board, a very young midshipman ; they were lashed to the gun-tackles on the weather side of the ship, near the wheel. The poor boy said to his father, ' What would mamma say if she knew our position now ? ' The next sea dashed him across the ship between two guns, with such force as to kill him The father, letting go his lashings, tried to cross the deck to his assistance, when the next sea dashed him also against the lee side, killing him as well. When apparently all had left the ship, Captain Lydiard said, ' Sulivan, it is our turn now—you go first.' They watched the sea receding, and then ran On reaching the main-mast, they saw one of the ship's boys clinging to the gear round the stump. My father, seeing a wave coming, dropped cross-leg on the mast, and clung to the ropes. Turning round, he saw that the wave had swept away both the boy and Captain Lydiard. When the wave receded, he ran on and reached the beach. To those on shore it seemed that Captain Lydiard was trying to get the boy to go on at the time the sea struck them. Some idea may be formed of my father's feelings as he stood on the beach, and realised the fact that his kindest friend for many years was gone. I can well recollect as a boy how he felt whenever he spoke on the subject.

"The news reached Captain James the next day—Innocents' Day—which was his birthday; and, according to his custom, he had a large party dining at the Woodlands. (I have now by me his journal, containing a list of all his guests on those days, and I find among them Israel Pellew, James Saumarez, Sir Peter Parker, Horatio Nelson, George Cockburn, Thomas Freemantle, James Macnamara, Isaac Coffin, and Edward Hamilton.) As soon as Captain James heard the sad news, he went to the wreck, and brought the surviving officers back to his house. Thus the acquaintance between my father and mother was renewed. This ultimately led to their engagement, and on March 19th, 1808, they were married at Mylor Church, and went to reside in a cottage at Tregew, new Flushing.

"Early in 1809 my father was appointed chief agent of transports, with an expedition from Cork to take reinforcements to the Peninsular army. After his return he for a few months commanded the *Eclipse* on the Plymouth station. In February 1813 he was appointed to the *Woolwich*, a forty-four-gun ship of two decks, to take Sir James Yeo and his officers and seamen to man the Lake flotillas in Canada. On his way from Halifax to the West Indies the *Woolwich* was wrecked in a hurricane on the island of Barbuda, but every soul was saved. The court-martial honourably acquitted the commander and officers, and complimented the commander on there being no loss of life. On March 25th, 1814, my father was appointed to the *Weser* troop-ship. The *Weser* and *Trave*, French frigates, had been captured on their way from Holland to a French port, and then fitted as troop-ships. Captain Money was appointed to the *Trave*, and both ships were fitting out to join a squadron proceeding to Bordeaux, to embark a brigade of the Peninsular army for service in America.

"My father had three brothers in the service; one, Samuel Hood Sulivan, was then first lieutenant on the *Trave*, the sister-ship to the *Weser*. The *Weser* and *Trave* embarked the 4th Regiment (Colonel Faunce), the head-quarters and one wing being in the *Weser* They sailed for Bermuda, where they were joined by some other ships and regiments.   Vice-Admiral Sir Alexander Cochrane took command of the fleet, which then proceeded direct for the Chesapeake.   The first service there was the destruction of Admiral Barney's flotilla in the Patuxent, before the army could attack Washington.   My father commanded the first division of boats on this service.   Afterwards, the army having taken Baltimore, he served with a battalion of seamen, as the senior commander under Captain Crofton, at the battle of Bladensburg, where the seamen are reported in the despatch ' to have behaved with a gallantry and steadiness which would have done honour to the ablest troops, and which attracted the admiration of the army.' *

" I must mention the singular coincidence, that though my father and his three brothers had never all met before whilst in the service, they did so in the fleet in the Patuxent, the youngest being then twenty-one (Daniel Hunt Sulivan).   When the expedition against New Orleans had arrived at the mouth of the Mississippi, the troops had to be taken about eighty miles through the shallow waters of Lake Borgne in boats to a landing-place at its head, separated from New Orleans by a few miles of wooded country.   The Rev. G. R. Gleig, the late chaplain-general (author of 'The Subaltern in the Army,' and 'America'), after dwelling on the hardships of the army, in which he served in the 85th Regiment, says, 'On the part of the navy all these hardships were experienced in a fourfold degree.'

* I will here add a story of Admiral T B. Sulivan, illustrating his high sense of duty, which was also ever the guiding principle of the subject of this memoir   As captain he was appointed to the *Stag*, as wing commodore to the Pacific squadron.   The merchants of Chili exported a large quantity of silver in ingots   There being a heavy duty on this, they used to smuggle it off to H M 's ships for conveyance to the river Plata, paying a large freight for the same   A former commodore, instead of first attending to the duties of his station, had used his ship to earn freight, leaving his station even when a critical state of affairs demanded his presence there   Commodore Sulivan, on his arrival on the station, issued an order that no man-of-war was to take smuggled silver, deeming it wrong for naval officers to assist the Chilians in breaking the laws of their country   On one occasion, when anchored with a squadron off the coast, a canoe came off to his ship after dusk, and a black man placed on the deck a number of bars of silver.   He was followed by the merchant.   " What is this for ? " said the commodore   " For you to take to the Plata," was the merchant's reply.   " Has duty been paid on it ? "   " No "   "Then I

For these services my father was promoted to post-
captain. Not having heard of his promotion, he was, as
the senior commander, attached to a brigade in command
of Colonel Thornton, which was composed of the 85th
Regiment, the Marines, and a party of seamen under my
father. They shared in the desperate attack made on the
leading division. The plan was for Colonel Thornton's
brigade to cross the river, for the purpose of carrying a
battery and turning the guns on the lines of New Orleans
when the main attack was made. Before this two generals
had landed to command the army sent out after the news
had reached England of General Ross being killed With
these came my father's promotion, and the admiral brought
over Commander Money, the next in seniority to my
father, saying, 'Sulivan, as you are a post-captain, we
must give Money a chance ; he will relieve you in command
of the seamen, and you will return and take his duty at
the landing-place as beach-master.' This probably saved
my father's life or a dangerous wound. After the division
had crossed the river and advanced to the attack of the
battery, the seamen were leading, all the principal officers
being in front, going up a lane. At the head of this lane
the enemy had masked field-pieces. Suddenly opening
fire, one round of grape-shot killed or wounded the leading
files. Colonel Thornton, Captain Money, and the officer
in command of the Marines were severely wounded
Captain Money had his ankle smashed ; and though he
escaped amputation, he was lamed for life, and never served
again. He was a very religious man, which in those days

cannot take it." The merchant explained that he had not heard of
the new regulation. He said that, difficult as it had been to smuggle
if off, it would be far more difficult to get it on shore again without his
being caught, so he begged that an exception might be made in his case.
At length the commodore said, "Well, take it to the vessel astern of
me ; but mind, no more silver is to be brought off that has not had the
duty paid on it."
   During the five years the commodore was on that coast, he never
once used his ship for earning freight (whilst much was made by
other vessels of his squadron), although to a man with a family of
fourteen and no private means some extra earnings would have been
acceptable. At the end of his commission, when the merchants heard
that he was about to leave the station, they passed the word along the
coast towns that for months all the silver possible should be saved up
to send by Captain Sulivan's ship on her way to England, in order that
he might have one chance of a good freight. Thus did the very
merchants against whom his former order had been issued show their
appreciation of his conduct.—ED.

led to his being called a 'psalm-singer', and when he was serving under General Ross, before Bladensburg, the general said publicly he wished all his army were psalm-singers, if Money was a specimen of them'

"My father's two younger brothers, James and Daniel Hunt, were made lieutenants for this service; but the elder of the three, Samuel Hood, was never promoted, though he had served as midshipman in the *Achille* at Trafalgar, and went through the whole of the service in the Chesapeake as first lieutenant of the *Trave*, and commanded a boat under Captain Lockyer on the occasion of the gallant capture of the American gun-boats on Lake Borgne. When, after the long war, the Order of the Bath was extended to three classes, my father, in common with many officers who had been promoted to the rank of post-captains for service as commanders, received the C.B He returned home soon after the peace with the United States in March 1815

"One of my earliest recollections, when I was nearly five years old, is of my father taking me one day to Falmouth. On our return, while waiting on Falmouth Quay for the ferry-boat between Flushing and Falmouth, a voice shouted from a window of the Green Bank Hotel, 'Pick up the child in the water!' The tide was running out, and the next moment we saw a very small child float round the end of the quay. My father took off his coat, placed it at my feet, jumped in the water to the rescue, and in a few minutes he was slowly swimming to the steps with the child under his left arm I mention this from its connection with an extraordinary coincidence which occurred nearly fifty years afterwards. My mother was then living at Flushing, and my brother, [then] Commander George Lydiard Sulivan, who had recently been promoted from the royal yacht, was at the top of her steep garden, which rose behind the house. It was a still starlight evening in the month of June 1863. He heard the rattle of oars in a boat, then a splash, and a cry for help, followed by a dead silence, which showed that no assistance was at hand. He ran to the quay at Flushing (about two hundred and fifty yards away), and the tide being very high he was able to step from the quay to a boat. Telling the waterman there was a man overboard at the quay on the other side, they each took an oar, and pulled rapidly across the harbour. When they reached the quay, they found two men discussing the exact spot where the man sank. My brother pulled off his coat and waistcoat, and dived, searching the bottom all round where they thought the man had gone down, but without success. He then got on the steps, and asked one of the men to pull his shirt off, as it was impeding his progress ; as he did so the man said, 'Your father saved my life off this very spot nearly fifty years ago.' On diving the second time he recovered the body, but life was extinct. The man was a navvy, returning from work at the Falmouth Docks.

" My father told my sons, when boys, that I could do a rule of three sum when I was six years of age as well as he could. I attended during the day a school kept by the curate of our parish. My father was never satisfied with the arithmetic taught at school, and I had in addition to do my sums at home of an evening. My mother was fond of poetry, and made us learn many short pieces by heart out of a book called 'The Speaker.' I am sure that this exercised the memory and improved it ; and with the aid of repeating them in night watches as a midshipman, to pass away the time, I have never forgotten them. After two years and a half there I was sent to Mr. Eyre's school at Penryn ; that required a walk of two miles each way, and, as the classical classes were only in the forenoon, I returned home as soon as they were over. But I have forgotten another part of my education for the navy. My father kept two boats, one a rather large sailing-boat, and the other a small thirteen-foot boat for rowing, with a small sail. I was often with him in both boats I remained more than two years at the Penryn school, during which time I went through Ovid and Cæsar, and began Virgil ; but we were hurried through them in classes so fast that I only learnt some of the amusing stories in Ovid and some of the battles in Cæsar, accounts of crossing rivers, etc We also had to go through the Eton Latin grammar periodically till I knew it by heart ; and for many years afterwards, if any one had started me on a line, I could have gone on for pages. Mr. Eyre attached great import- ance to a clear pronunciation, and before the midsummer holidays we had a speech day in public. The first year I chose Pyramus and Thisbe for my Latin speech, and to my astonishment was awarded the Latin medal by several clergymen, presided over by Canon Howell, rector of the parish. He walked a short distance with my father and

mother, and expressed a hope that I should be sent to a
public school, with a view to going to Oxford ; but my
career had been settled long before, and I was to go to the
Royal Naval College at Portsmouth, where many naval
officers' sons received a free education, I believe to the
extent of half the number, the remaining half of seventy
boys paying £70 a year. There was also a chance of
winning a medal at the college, which gave a prospect of
promotion on passing for lieutenant. This was more
important then, when mates (now sub-lieutenants) without
interest were sometimes ten, eleven, and twelve years after
passing before they were promoted, while they saw every
one with interest, or, as the saying was then in midshipmen's berths, 'with handles to their names,' promoted as
soon as they had passed their examinations. A son of
Captain Pellew had won the second medal at this college,
and this was always held up to me as an example. My
father had a large family ; therefore it was a great object
to him and to all poor naval officers to get so good an
education for the navy free of cost.

"On our removing to Feock parish, my father continued
my education at home until I went to the Naval College,
the age for entering which was from twelve and a half
years to thirteen and a half. I went to it when I was
twelve years and three months old. During our residence
at Tregew, my uncle, Lieutenant Daniel H. Sulivan, had
lived with us nearly one year ; afterwards the three uncles,
all lieutenants R.N., and two Lieutenants Loney, R.N.,
owned a large Cawsand Bay boat, called the *Sweet Poll*,
of Plymouth, in which they attended all the regattas on
the south coast. She carried off the first prize of her
class for three years in succession, after which the committees would not allow her to compete. I used to look
forward to their coming to Falmouth with much interest.
My father also encouraged me in the use of carpenters'
tools, of which he had a large box. I have mentioned
these facts because they bear on a question now discussed,
'technical education,' and because I have all my life felt
the value of this early training in the use of tools.

"I now come to my leaving home for the Royal Naval
College. There were no steam-vessels on the south coast
in those days, and the only way to go from port to port by
sea was in smacks, one line from Falmouth to Plymouth,
and another from Plymouth to Portsmouth. My father

took me there, and we stopped for a few days on the way
at Plymouth.   Sir Alexander Cochrane—under whom my
father served in America—was then the commander-in-chief
at Plymouth Dockyard.   One day he asked me what I
looked forward to.   I replied, ' To living in this house one
day, sir, as commander-in-chief.'   He said a few words
in praise of my ambition.   We went on in a smack to
Portsmouth, arriving there three or four days before the
time for the examination.   Lieutenant John Wood Rouse
(my godfather) was the senior of two lieutenants of the
college.   He had lost his leg as a midshipman in one of
the ships of Sir John Duckworth's squadron in the passage
of the Dardanelles, and was, after being made a lieutenant,
appointed   staff-officer   to   my   grandfather,   then   commander of the Cornish district of 'sea fencibles.'   We
stayed at Mr. Rouse's house during the few days we were
at Portsmouth, until I passed in.   My father was very
anxious about my passing, and expressed doubt on the
subject to the lieutenant-governor, Captain John Went-
worth Goring, C.B.; but the questions were all in arithmetic,
excepting the definitions of Euclid, which I had learned
by heart the previous week.   Thanks to my father having
taught me arithmetic so well, I passed first of twelve.

"The head of the studies was the Reverend Professor
James Inman, D.D., author of the work on navigation,
under whom were three assistant-masters for mathematics :
first, Peter Mason, M.A. ; second, Charles Blackburn, M.A. ;
and third, Mr. Livesay.   The preceptor, the Rev. W.
Tate, M.A., took the classical classes, history, geography,
and English.   French was taught by M. Creuze, a French
émigré.   We were also taught fencing and dancing.   The
forenoons were given to mathematics, the afternoons to
French and drawing, the latter taught by a very superior
master, Mr. J. C. Schetky.   There were also classes for
naval architecture, which were taken by Mr. Fincham, the
master-builder of the dockyard.   We began geometry with
Mr. Livesay ; but no boy could get on unless he studied
in his own cabin and at the dining-room tables in the
evenings.   This some of the senior boys tried to prevent
by watching the steps of the junior class, and if the junior
boys showed any intention of studying they were sure to
have their books knocked out of their hands and scattered
about the yard.   Fortunately the one who passed in second
to me—Baugh—was one of the strongest and biggest boys

in the college; he was also one of the studious ones, and often protected me from this bullying. Once the books were in the boys' cabins they were safe, as we were forbidden to enter one another's cabins. I was content so long as I kept with the senior boys of my own batch; and it was a fortunate thing for me that three months after I entered Dr. Inman's son, Richard Inman, joined us. He had learnt the first three months' work or more before he entered, and I had nearly completed in three months what we were allowed six months for. Inman passed in the studies that made him equal with me within a week of entering, and then we went on competing each month. Nothing could be fairer than Dr. Inman was to me throughout this rivalry. He urged me to take my books home at Christmas and midsummer, and work every day, adding, ' I shall keep Richard at work.' He awarded me the junior mathematical prize on December 16th—a splendidly bound book on naval gunnery. The time allowed for going through the whole mathematical studies was two years: ' time ' was allowed only for the studies completed.

"On my way back to college after the holidays, the coach broke down, and I was exposed for some hours of a night of intense cold, the inside passengers not allowing me to squeeze in among them for shelter. In consequence, a week after my return to college, I was taken ill with inflammation of the lungs, and was in the infirmary five weeks. Inman got ahead of me during my illness, but I caught him up again before the midsummer holidays, and it then became a neck-and-neck race. I was awarded another mathematical prize on June 22nd, and to my great astonishment a prize in French The collegians were often taken round the dockyard, and shown the ships building and in dock, and if the boys liked they could attend the rigging-loft to learn to strop-blocks and do many other useful things There were also large barges to cruise about in, to visit ships, and to take us to Haslar Creek on Saturday afternoons for cricket. Our ground was between the Haslar Hospital ward and the sea. From the time I entered the college I received the greatest kindness from Sir George and Lady Grey. He had been flag-captain to Sir John Jervis in the *Boyne*, when my grandfather was first lieutenant of her, and afterwards in the *Victory*. I spent every Sunday afternoon there with two other collegians named Ramage and Coppinger.

" The idea was held in the college that the one who got through the course in the shortest time obtained the first medal, and the next the second medal.　On these grounds Edmonstone—now Admiral Sir William Edmonstone— had won the first medal the previous year, and Allen, who as captain commanded the Niger expedition, the second medal.　I heard when we returned to Portsmouth after my first voyage that Dr. Inman had applied to the Admiralty to grant two first medals, one for Inman and one for me; but their lordships refused, on the ground that it would be creating a precedent, and that he must decide which should have the first medal and which the second, but that it should make no difference when we passed our examinations.　The first medal ensured promotion after passing, and the second medal gave a strong claim to it.　Dr. Inman nominated his son for the first medal and me for the second, which was perfectly fair, as I have explained before.　I had always out of school hours taken to the rigging-loft, and in the latter months of my time was one of six selected to rig a block-model of a frigate, for which a shed was erected in the yard in the rear of the Naval Architectural College.　It remained for many years as a specimen of rigging.　One boy had the bowsprit with the gear of the jib-booms, two had the fore-mast, two the main-mast (one on each side), and the mizzen-mast was allotted to me.

" Inman passed out of the college a few days before I did, as his father was very anxious to get him into the *Cambrian* with Captain Hamilton.　When I passed out of the college I was appointed to H.M.S. *Thetis*, Captain Sir John Phillimore, C.B., Kt., who, going round the college a short time before, had told Dr. Inman, and I believe Captain John W. Loring, C.B. (the lieutenant-governor), that if they sent him any collegians he would refuse to take them.　When I went on board I found the captain was on leave.　The first lieutenant, Drew (who had been promoted for the first Ashantee war), and the second, Cotesworth, were on board.　The latter was the son of Captain Cotesworth, of Falmouth, a friend of my grandfather, and well known to my father and mother.　He told me the captain had a strong prejudice against collegians, but that he would do all he could to keep me in the ship. When the captain returned from leave he sent for me to his cabin in the hulk, and told me that he had never known a collegian worth his salt, and he used strong language against the college and all connected with it. I forgot he was the captain, and spoke hastily in reply ; he ordered me out of the cabin, and followed me quickly to the door. In a short time he sent for me again, and told me that the ship was going out for about two months with an experimental squadron, and that he would try me. He went on shore, and told Captain Loring that he liked the way I stuck up for the college and the spirited way in which I spoke to him, and that he should try me. When the senior midshipmen passed at the Royal Naval College for lieutenants, the senior class of collegians had to work the same paper in the same room. The last time I did so Dr. Inman said to me, ' There was a collegian passing yesterday who won the first medal—his name is FitzRoy ; and he did what has never been done before : in passing for a lieutenant he got full numbers, and I hope when you pass for lieutenant you will do the same.' * He, FitzRoy, was promoted to lieutenant immediately, and two or three weeks after I joined the *Thetis* he was appointed to her as junior lieutenant,—to that I attribute much of my future success in the service.

" Sir John Phillimore, when he commissioned the *Thetis* early in 1823, feeling that the large allowance of rum was the cause of much drunkenness in the service, proposed to the Admiralty that it should be reduced one-half, from half a pint of rum to a quarter of a pint. Their lordships replied that ' if the *Thetis's* ship's company would try it first they would allow it.' The consent was given and the reduction ordered. When I joined the ship it had been tried for more than a year, during which time the *Thetis's* ship's company had to undergo the most bitter persecution from other ships' companies. Whether she was at Plymouth or Portsmouth the liberty-men of the other ships combined to attack the ' tea-chests,' as they called them. This continued after I joined, and men were sent from the *Thetis* to Haslar Hospital with serious injuries from the fighting which ensued. Shortly after the *Ganges* returned from her first commission in the Mediterranean. She had a full crew as an eighty-four-gun ship, whereas the guardships at Plymouth and Portsmouth had only frigates' ships' companies. The crew of the *Ganges* gave notice to the other ships that if they continued to treat the *Thetis's* crew

* This he actually did.—Ed.

in the way they did they would land in a body and take
the part of the *Thetis's* men, because the latter were
instrumental in bringing about the most beneficial change
that had ever been made for the seamen of the royal
navy. They had more than a year's experience of the
advantages given in exchange for the quarter of a pint of
rum. Before the change there were two days a week
when no meat was served out, called 'banyan days.'
These were done away with. Then for breakfast they had
only 'burgoo,' or, in other words, thick water-gruel, and
for their evening meal butter and cheese with their biscuits,
which were said to be often rancid and mouldy. Instead
of these they now had cocoa in the morning and a good
allowance of tea in the evening, with ample allowance of
sugar. In addition to these they had two shillings a month
more pay. Before the change they could not draw any of
their pay abroad, and had no money to spend on leave,
unless they sold their clothes for the purpose, which led to
punishment ; but one of the advantages accruing from the
change was that they were allowed to draw four shillings
a month of their pay abroad. Later, when on detached
service from the *Beagle*, and in boats for many weeks,
while sitting round the fire at night, smoking and drinking
quantities of tea, one of the oldest seamen in the ship, a
petty officer, whom I always selected for my coxswain in
those boat expeditions, used to tell the men that he
looked back with shame and sorrow to the days when he
helped others to attack the *Thetis's* ship's company because
they consented to try reducing the allowance of rum one-
half, and he used to explain to the other men the great
advantages of the change.

"When Lieutenant Drew was promoted, the captain
applied for Lieutenant William Cotesworth as first lieutenant, but was refused, because he had not been ten years
a lieutenant. He was of eight years' standing, and had
been promoted for gallant boat service when in the
Endymion on the coast of North America. Lieutenant
Henry Jellicoe, three years his senior, was appointed as first
lieutenant. While still alongside the hulk we experienced
that terrible storm of November 28th, 1824, one of the
heaviest that has ever been known in England. . . .

"In the same storm nearly all the vessels in Plymouth
Sound were wrecked, and a gap was broken through
Plymouth Breakwater, which was not then finished. One

large schooner was off the Eddystone in the storm ; before daylight she capsized and turned bottom up. The watch on deck were drowned, but the watch below managed to climb into the hold (she was in ballast), and there was air enough in to keep them alive. After some hours they felt the shock of the masts being carried away by their striking the ground, and after that she was thrown bottom up on the top of the breakwater : they cut a hole with their knives in the bottom large enough to wave a shirt from for a signal ; it was seen from the breakwater vessel, and she sent a boat and saved them. I suppose there never was such an instance of men being saved when in such extreme danger.

"But we must return to the *Thetis* alongside the hulk in Portsmouth Harbour. The lieutenants were Henry Jellicoe, William Cotesworth, J. Jervis Tucker, and Robert FitzRoy.

"I have often been asked if it is true that a captain in the royal navy once made a bishop of his chaplain, and I have replied : 'Not only is it true, but the ship I first served in as a midshipman was the ship in which it took place, though I joined her afterwards. Her last voyage had been to take an African regiment to the first Ashantee war, and she landed some officers and men to share in the defence of Cape Coast Castle and the detached forts. On her way home she touched at St. Michaels, one of the Azores. In Roman Catholic countries in which there were no Protestant cemeteries their dead had to be buried in gardens. The Protestants of St. Michaels had purchased a piece of ground about half a mile outside the town, and had enclosed it by a wall. When the *Thetis* arrived, a deputation called on Sir John Phillimore and asked him to take two petitions home for them,—one to the Archbishop of Canterbury, requesting him to send a bishop to consecrate their ground ; and another to the First Lord of the Admiralty, asking him to provide a ship to take out the bishop. Sir J. Phillimore assured them that it was quite unnecessary, because his chaplain should consecrate it for them. They replied that it *must* be a bishop. He then said he would give his chaplain an acting order as bishop. I have seen that "acting order." It ran as follows :
" You are hereby requested and directed to take on your-self the office of Bishop of St. Michaels, for the purpose of consecrating a Protestant cemetery, and for so doing this

shall be your warrant. Given under my hand this day of —— 1824. (Signed) John Phillimore, Capt. N. Royse, Chaplain H.M.S. *Thetis*." The cemetery was thereupon consecrated with full naval honours,*—the Protestants used it, and the feuds between them and the Roman Catholics ceased.'

"Sir John Pillimore had been very kind to me, notwithstanding his prejudice against collegians, and as I had only a quadrant he lent me an excellent sextant. On our return to Portsmouth, he asked Captain Loring to recommend him two more collegians, and he advised him to take my friend Baugh and G. Wodehouse, who were passing out at the time. Before the days of steam-vessels, there was a frigate kept on the Plymouth station to take an ambassador where required, or, in case of an emergency, for other duty. Her first service was taking an ambassador to Mexico ; her second, taking a regiment to the first Ashantee war ; and when not required otherwise she was supposed to cruise on the Cornish coast to look out for smugglers. We sailed from Plymouth again on the 24th, and the same evening anchored in Falmouth Roads. It was a great pleasure to me being so often in Falmouth, as I spent all my time at home. On March 2nd we sailed again, and the next day anchored in Plymouth Sound.

"I have omitted to state that the boys were all in the mizzen-top, with three small but very smart seamen as captains of the top. We had three watches instead of, as usual, two ; so that the officers had the same men with them on the watches. I was mizzen-top midshipman all the time ; and, what was never seen in other ships, the *Thetis* had mizzen-topgallant studding-sails, to train the boys for topmen. Lieutenant Charles Nash was appointed to the ship as fourth lieutenant ; he had been promoted out of the royal yacht, and was a very smart officer. I suppose few ships had all four lieutenants as good as Cotesworth, Tucker, FitzRoy, and Nash. Cotesworth was an excellent first lieutenant, whom the men delighted to work for, and they proved themselves a smart crew by beating every ship they competed with. Another good officer was Lieutenant J. Jervis Tucker.† Lieutenant FitzRoy was one of the best officers in the service, as his subsequent career proved. He was one of the best practical seamen in the service, and

---

* The ship's band, sailors, and marines attending, and the "bishop" being saluted with nineteen guns on his landing.

† Tucker and Sulivan afterwards married two sisters

possessed besides a fondness for every kind of observation useful in navigating a ship. He was very kind to me, offered me the use of his cabin and of his books. He advised me what to read, and encouraged me to turn to advantage what I had learned at college by taking every kind of observation that was useful in navigation.

"After another short cruise in the Channel we were ordered to Lisbon. The *Thetis* then had several short cruises   One of her consorts was the *Aurora*, forty-six guns (which had been captured from the French after a severe action with the *Europas*, forty-six), commanded by Captain John Maxwell   She had rather the advantage in sailing, but we beat her hollow in reefing   The poet of the *Aurora* had a specimen of his poetry published in a Plymouth newspaper. As I recollect every word of it, though I never had a copy, I will give it here :—

> " 'The change in our diet doth grieve our hearts sore ;
> 'Twas first introduced by Sir John Phillimore
> It's a new regulation you plainly may see,
> For they stopped half our grog to give us Bohéa

> " 'As we crossed the briny ocean the eighth day of June
> We fell in with the *Thetis* at four in the afternoon ;
> To beat us in sailing she did do her best,
> But soon the *Aurora* she beat the " *Tea-chest* "

> " 'And soon, my brave boys, if united we keep,
> To beat us in reefing she won't be the ship ;
> To each other we're strangers, as you understand ;
> So *Aurora* for ever, and the " *Tea-chest* " be hanged ! '

" The following answer was published in the same paper :—

> " 'You backbiting rascals who run down our ship,
> And whose backs are well used to the boatswain's mate's whip,
> You had better be easy, or mind what you say,
> Or we'll give you coffee in lieu of Bohéa.

> " 'With regard to our duty, we do it with ease ,
> Every ship in the fleet we can beat if we please ;
> We are happy, contented, good-humoured, and free,
> And we don't see the harm in a good cup of tea.

> " 'So keep your tongues quiet, or take what may follow,
> For in reefing and furling we can beat you all hollow ,
> You had better be easy, those rows don't begin,
> For on board of the *Thetis* you'll find we're all men.'

" After a cruise in the Mediterranean we sailed from

Naples on November 24th, homeward bound.   After taking refuge from a gale in the bay of Alchuda, in Corsica, and experiencing a very heavy gale from south-west to the eastward of Gibraltar, we anchored off the Mole-head on December 16th.   We found that more than a hundred and forty vessels had been driven ashore in the late gale. The largest number of them were coasters and feluccas that had gone on the neutral ground, where they were smashed up.   But the larger vessels, which had driven from their anchors farther out in the bay, had all gone on Spanish territory to the westward of the Spanish lines, and the Spanish authorities had taken possession of these to make them pay the duties on their cargoes, and they had landed a portion of the ships' cargoes on the sand-hills for security.   Directly Sir J. Phillimore heard this he called on the Governor of Gibraltar, Sir George Don, and asked him whether he was going to interfere   He said he was not, as a military interference would probably have led to war with Spain.   Sir J. Phillimore then decided to use all naval means to get the vessels off the beach of the Spanish territory.   Before returning to the ship he had arranged with the dockyard authorities for all the assistance in the shape of anchors and cables, and lighters with capstans in them, and the next day we sent all the boats under Lieutenant Cotesworth to commence work.

"The first thing we had to do was to get the 'Guarda Costas' out of the vessels.   They were in uniform and armed with carbines, and there were three or four in each vessel, of which only one was English, a schooner, the *Lovely Cruiser*, of Portsmouth.   The easternmost vessel, the *Mary*, of Boston, Captain Stikney, was abreast of the guard-house at the end of the Spanish lines.   A junior officer was stationed in each vessel.   The officers of the garrison were anxious to see what went on, and about fifty of them, following the lead of Lieutenant W. L. M. Tupper, of the 23rd Royal Welsh Fusiliers, all mounted, and armed with swords and pistols in holsters, drew up two deep in front of the Spanish guard-house.   These formed our cavalry !   The crew of the brig *Mary* had a musket for every man, and they were full of fight ; they also had two small signal-guns on board, which were pointed through two bow ports into two windows of the guard-house, and were well loaded with canister-shot. These were our artillery !   When the crisis arrived, an officer rode up to the sergeant's guard of the neutral ground and brought them up, forming them on the left of the mounted officers on the beach, close to a Portuguese schooner. These were our infantry! The next thing we did was to bring on board that portion of the cargoes which had been placed on the sand-hills. The vessels were more than their own lengths from the water, and were all many feet in the sand. We had to dig channels to them, the men working up to their necks in water, every form of scraper that our means allowed us to make being used to help. There was a grass-flat in the rear of the sand-hills, and early in the afternoon we saw advancing across it a brigade of Spanish troops, composed of two very small battalions, headed by mounted officers They advanced until they were a quarter of a mile from the Spanish guard-house and about half that distance from the sand-hills, where they were halted : the officer in command, with his staff, rode forward to the guard-house. I was in the best position to see what took place, for the bows of the *Mary* were within about seventy yards of the guard-house. When the leader, attended by his staff, passed between the beach and the guard-house, they found themselves immediately in front of Tupper with his two lines of mounted officers. The colonel—as we called him—rode up to Tupper, and, halting less than a horse's length in front of him, began gesticulating violently, speaking loudly in Spanish, every word of which Tupper understood : he said afterwards he was using threats. Then I saw Tupper take a pistol from his holster and point it at the colonel, who pulled his horse round, and, followed by his staff, rode back to his troops Tupper shouted to us to land, and, as previously arranged, line the sand-hills Then were seen our men from all the vessels jumping down on the beach, and running up to the sand-hills, by which we got on the flank of the enemy. But, directly the officers returned to them, they went to the right-about, going back the way they came About 9 p m., when quite dark, I was hailed by the coxswain in the officers' galley, asking me where the first lieutenant was to be found, as he had a note for him from the governor. I directed him to the vessel. The note was to tell him that they had heard from Algéciras that an attempt would be made in the night with a larger force to drive us off, and that gun-boats would probably be used ; also that he should send

the 42nd Highlanders to bivouac on the neutral ground
in case we wanted assistance.   The coxswain, after finding
Lieutenant Cotesworth, volunteered to pull up along shore,
where the road ran close to the beach, and bring us notice
of their approach.   About half-past eleven he returned and
reported that a large body of troops was marching along
the road, and shortly after we saw them approaching in
the rear of the sand-hills.   It was a clear night, and they
were halted about where the former columns halted, a
few officers advancing to the Spanish guard-house.   But a
different sight met their view, for where the small party
of mounted officers stood in the morning a strong regiment
was drawn up in line.   As soon as the officers rejoined
the column it retired.   This occurred on December 17th.
On the 18th we hove off the Maltese brig *Providentia* ;
on the 22nd the English schooner *Lovely Cruiser*, and that
night the U.S. brig *Mary*, of Boston.   On the 28th a
deputation of merchants and others of all nations came
on board to read a letter of thanks for what we were
doing, and some consignees brought bags of money, which
they wished to distribute among the men, but which the
captain refused.   On December 29th the boats returned,
having got off the three remaining vessels, the Portuguese
schooner *Felix de Mar*, the Danish brig *Grandilo*, and the
Genoese vessel *La Pace*.   On January 21st the boats
returned with all the gear borrowed from the dockyard.

    " On February 2nd we sailed from Gibraltar to try to
beat the frigate out of the Straits against the strong current,
which was said to have been done before.   We succeeded in
doing it as far as Tarifa Lighthouse ; but when standing
across to the Morocco coast a heavy squall struck the ship,
carried away the fore-tack, obliging us to haul the courses
up and lower the topsails, and in a very short time we were
at anchor off Gibraltar again.   On the 3rd the merchants
and consignees gave us a very grand dinner at the Crown
Hotel.   Our captain took two or three midshipmen with
him, but made us promise that we would leave the table
when he and the governor left it, which we did.   But when
we got to the Ragged Staff landing-place we found it was
blowing a heavy gale.   There were no boats to take us on
board, so the captain took us back to the hotel for the
night.   The officers senior to us who attended the dinner
were obliged also to sleep on shore.   In front of the
president at the dinner was a model of Gibraltar, made

of cake, which Lieutenant C. Nash carried off for the youngsters on board who had not shared in the dinner. The gale was so heavy in the night that two or three more vessels went on shore farther to the westward than the former ones. We got under way and anchored off them to cover the boats, which we sent armed and manned as before. They had gone on a rocky point, and we only saved one, the U.S schooner *James Monroe*. On the 14th we sailed again; but after going about under Ape's Hill, and standing towards the Spanish coast, the next time we went about, just as the after-yards swung round, we ran on the Pearl Rock; and as the head-sails twisted her round a large piece of the false keel floated, and the next moment we were off and ran back to Gibraltar. During the digging out of the vessels on the beach we sent several men back to the ship with various forms of pulmonary complaints, and one of the best first-class petty officers died of inflammation of the lungs. On the 16th we finally sailed from Gibraltar. I was ill on the passage with my old chest complaint. On the 30th we anchored at Spithead, and the captain went on shore, but two custom-house officers came on board and put the ship in quarantine, and under their directions we got under way again to anchor at the 'Mother Bank,' the quarantine-ground. When my kind friends Sir George and Lady Grey heard that I was ill on board, Sir George sent his barge to take me to their house, where I remained till the *Thetis* sailed for Plymouth. This was on March 8th. We reached it on the 9th, and the same day made sail into the harbour, and came alongside the *Diadem* hulk.

"I have omitted to state that another collegian, making the fourth, joined us from the *Seringapatam* He had been at the Naval College with the other three, but his mother asked our captain to take him in the *Thetis*. His name was Robert N. Hamond, and he had greatly distinguished himself in an attack on two Greek pirates by the boats of the *Cambrian* and *Seringapatam*.

"We remained at Hamoaze until March 16th, preparing to take Lord Ponsonby(appointed ambassador to the Argentine confederation at Buenos Ayres) to Rio Janeiro, with Lady Ponsonby. A steam-vessel then towed us into the Sound, where we lay until March 29th, when we sailed, having, in addition to two side-cabins in the captain's fore-cabin, several others on the main-deck for the *attaché*, Mr. Scott, and the

servants. It was decided after our arrival at Rio Janeiro that
Lord Ponsonby should go to Buenos Ayres in the *Doris*,
Captain Sir John Sinclair, Bart., which was going round Cape
Horn to the west coast, then under one command, and that
the *Thetis* should return to England   This necessitated the
removal of the cabins to the *Doris*, and fitting them there.
But before this the mates and midshipmen were allowed to
take one boat, a ten-oared cutter, for a trip up the harbour
of Rio Janeiro, to see its beautiful islands.   We only took
six oars with us, intending to sail, as a fine sea-breeze blew
every afternoon.   We were at an island about twenty miles
from the ship, and were all in the water bathing, when
George Wodehouse saw a flock of humming-birds round
the flowers of an orange-tree.   He loaded a single-barrel
gun with dust-shot to shoot them, and, putting on his
shirt, ran towards the orange-tree.   We in the water
heard a shot, and directly after saw Wodehouse running
towards us, his shirt covered with blood.   He had come to
a rock too steep to allow of his jumping down on the sandy
beach with the gun in his hand ; so he took it by the
muzzle in his right hand, and in putting it down he must
have touched the cock against the rock.   It went off, tearing
everything away from the palm of his hand to the elbow,
inside the arm, which was streaming with blood.   Not one
of our party understood that a tourniquet placed above the
elbow was the right thing to stop the bleeding.   The excuse
for us was that none of us had been taught it   Afterwards,
when officers and men were going on service where some
might be wounded, a certain number of their party were
provided with tourniquets, and shown how to apply them
(I am glad to see that the cadets in the training-ship are to
go through the work of the ambulance classes)   We tore
our shirts into bandages, and bound up the fore-arm as well
as we could.   We were twenty miles from the ship, in the
hottest harbour in the world, and we had only five oars to
row a ten-oared boat.   We took one oar to throw the
mizzen over, so as to protect Wodehouse from the sun, and
we had only pulled ten miles, to an island owned by an
Englishman named Lane, whom we were going to ask for
the loan of his boat, with a crew of black men, to take
Wodehouse to the ship, when we saw Sir John Phillimore's
gig coming round the point of the island.   On discovering
what had happened, he took the wounded man into the
gig.   He had, providentially, intended to bring us a week's

provisions, and remain with us another week. He had suffered from a dangerous wound himself in the action between the *Eurotas* and *Clorinde*, a grape-shot having shattered his left shoulder-joint, and caused him to faint three times on deck before he consented to go below After seven months in Plymouth Hospital he left it with a stiff joint, and never afterwards recovered the use of it

"When the cabins were sent to the *Doris*, Sir John Phillimore retained Lady Ponsonby's cabin for our wounded messmate. The captain slept in a cot outside the cabin door, and the midshipmen took it in turns to nurse Wodehouse, but we were not allowed to touch the injured arm—the captain said that that should only be done by one who knew the value of careful handling ; and when our wounded messmate was suffering in the night we had to call the captain. I have known him sit an hour by his bedside, holding the arm in his two hands, trying to ease the pain.

"We sailed homeward bound on August 14th ; and as was then the custom with sailing-ships, the boats of the squadron towed us out before the light land-breeze. Wodehouse got so much better after we sailed that he was soon able to join the other collegians in working with the rope-maker, which we four had always to do when the other midshipmen were at school ; but instead of joining us in spinning spun yarn and nettle-stuff for the ship's use, and taking it in turns to turn the winch, as he had but one sound arm we kept him at the winch. This did not interfere with our regular use of the table in the captain's fore-cabin for our working observations. We, the collegians, had to take sights in the morning for the longitude, and at noon for the latitude, with occasional lunars, which we worked in the fore-cabin

"I have omitted to mention that when a separate class was established for the ' master' line, Alexander Burns Usborne joined us at Plymouth as ' master's assistant.' He was the son of an old naval officer, and was educated at Greenwich School under Riddell. When he left that he bound himself as an apprentice to the Enderbys, and was for three years in one of their whalers in the South Seas. On his return he joined the *Thetis* as ' master's assistant' Greenwich School gave him one of the best mathematical educations, and his service in the whaler made him a thorough seaman. There being no schoolmaster on board, he acted as one to the youngsters who were not collegians, for which he was well qualified.

"Sir John Phillimore gave all the midshipmen a thorough practical training aloft. Every afternoon when the weather permitted it, the officer of the watch had to assemble the midshipmen an hour before the evening meal; and when we had taken in the lighter sails—flying royal and mizzen-topgallant studding-sail—if they were set, we had to take the first reef in the topsail, and come down and hoist it; then the second reef, and come down and hoist it; then the third reef, doing the same; and then shake out the reefs singly. So we had to come on deck six times and hoist the topsails, and, if required, set the light sails above; and if the officer of the watch was satisfied with the way we had done it he sent us down to our tea. If the first or second reef was in, we were saved so many trips to the deck.

"Leaving Rio, we had a fair passage until September 29th, when we were about four hundred miles from the Scilly Islands; then we had a furious storm from the S.S.W., drawing to the westward. When the sea was at its height and we were running with the wind on the quarter, the lee-quarter boat nearly touched the water every roll. Two men were sent into her to get ready for hoisting the davits higher; a very heavy lurch unhooked the foremost tackle I saw the men try to clutch the span between the two davits; one did so, but the second missed it by a few inches. The boat dropped forward, and hung a few moments by the after-tackle; the man fell, and we saw him going astern It was too heavy a sea for a boat to live in, or even to let go the life-buoy; so the man was drowned, and the boat was so smashed by the sea that orders were given to cut the after-fall, and she was lost. We then set storm stay-sails and try-sails, and brought her to the wind; a sea struck her on the starboard side, and stove in two main-deck ports, and the water flooded the main-deck, pouring down every hatchway on the lower deck Such was the storm that Lieutenant Cotesworth, who had a powerful voice, could not make himself heard in the main-top, so he sent me up with the message. As soon as I was in the top I was struck with the fact that when the ship was upright in the hollow of the sea the height of the sea hid the horizon My eye was then sixty-four feet above the hollow. Directly I was sure of it I came down and told Lieutenant FitzRoy, who went into the main-top. His eye was sixty-five feet above the hollow. He states the fact in his account of the *Beagle's* voyage, and expresses his belief that it was the highest sea ever measured. We passed during the height of the storm H.M. packet *Goldfinch*, one of the old ten-gun brigs (or coffins, as they were called, because so many were lost). H.M. sloop *Beagle* was one of them; and on her first voyage, which lasted five years, she went through the most stormy region of the world with perfect safety Like all small vessels, they required careful handling and management of sails.

"On October 3rd we anchored off Spithead once more, having run through the Needles passage. I have omitted to mention the number of times we worked in or out of the same passage, under the skilful pilotage of the master, Mr. William Gowdy On the 28th Commissioner Shields came on board and paid off the ship's company. The next day the pennant was hoisted again for another commission, and Lieutenant Robert FitzRoy was re-appointed to her Sir John Phillimore had very kindly written to Sir Edward Codrington, K.C.B., who had hoisted his flag in H.M.S *Asia*, eighty-four guns, for the Mediterranean command, asking him to take all four collegians with him. Had it not been for Lieutenant FitzRoy's re-appointment to the ship, we should all have accepted the offer, and should have been in the battle of Navarino. Baugh and Wodehouse accepted the offer, but Hamond and I preferred to remain in the *Thetis* with Lieutenant FitzRoy. On December 5th Captain Arthur Batt Bingham's commission was read to the officers and ship's company, on his taking command of the ship. Afterwards he made a speech to the men to the following effect: 'You shall have every indulgence the service can allow; but there are three things I never forgive—drunkenness, disobedience, insolence. Pipe down" He kept his word; he never forgave drunkenness on duty, and especially in a boat on duty—the worst offence a seaman can be guilty of, for it may lead to the drowning of many men. He kept his word also that they should have every indulgence the service allowed: extra time for meals, ·leave when other ships did not give it.

"We were fitting out in Hamoaze until February 3rd, 1827, when we anchored in the Sound. We were under orders to proceed to the South American station, but to go first to Bermuda to take Colonel Cockburn and suite. They embarked on the 7th, and we sailed the next day. We anchored off Funchal on the 17th, but so far off that the anchor was let go in forty-five fathoms, and when we had eighty fathoms of chain out we drifted off the bank, and to add to the weight we had an anchor of forty-six hundredweight at the end of it. We were obliged to use tackles in aid of the capstan, to get the cable in link by link.

" I ought to have stated that our captain was generally known in the service as ' Little Belt ' Bingham, from having commanded that vessel of twenty guns when she fought an action with the *President*, an American frigate of forty-four guns, before the war of 1812.

"When we were fitting out, an order came for fitting out all the guard-ships, for the purpose of embarking ten thousand troops, including the Guards. It was well known at the time as the celebrated ' Canning expedition,' when Canning was Prime Minister. The guard-ships at all the ports were ready for embarking the troops in a week, and they made a quick passage of another week to Lisbon. In these days of steamers could it be done better? When we left England there were rumours of war with France, in consequence of the Canning expedition being directed against the French occupation of Spain. On the evening of April 19th we fell in with a large ship with two lines of ports, which we took to be a line-of-battle ship. Our courses were converging, and at length we were alongside each other. She would not answer our hail, 'What ship is that?' She only replied, 'What ship is *that*?' And so we each went on alternately repeating the question. At length our captain said, 'What ship is that? If you don't answer I will fire into you.' (We could see her double line of ports lighted up with the men at her guns.) Then our captain said, 'Are you ready with the guns on the main-deck, Mr. FitzRoy?' Fortunately she was so close to us that this aside was overheard, which showed them we were English, and they immediately answered, 'The Honourable East India Company's ship *Fairley*, from China to London.' Both ships then shortened sail and hove to, and we sent a boat on board, and then learnt that she had called at St. Helena, heard rumours of war with France, and thus the whole mistake arose ; for in those days they only got news from St Helena through the round-about way of the Cape of Good Hope. She had feared to give her name, lest we, being French, might fire into her. She had besides her crew six hundred soldiers and women and children, so it would have been a terrible thing had we fired.

"On or about July 31st I was most mercifully saved from losing my right arm. A signal was made from the flag-ship for a midshipman; I was sent to answer it in one of the ship's cutters; it was near sunset; we had to go to the side, where there was no accommodation-ladder. I gave the boat rather too much way, and she shot ahead of the gangway about a boat's length. I was standing on the stern-sheets, assisting to pull the boat astern; I had my right arm in the port before the gangway, when the sentries fired their muskets at sunset. (I need not say that a lower-deck port of an eighty-four-gun ship, fitting into its rabbet, would crush off a strong man's arm) It was usual in a line-of-battle ship to let go suddenly the tackles of all the lower-deck ports. I was a youngster, and very thin for my age. I felt the port on my arm; it stopped shutting, so much so that I had some difficulty in drawing my arm out, when it was found that the side man-rope had jammed between the port and the after-sill of the port-hole, and saved my arm If it had been in the next port forward, which had been the case a minute before, where there was no man-rope to jam it, all my prospects in the service would have been ruined. No one would have taken an officer into the surveying service who had lost his right arm It was the first of the wonderful providences of God which have followed me through life. It had been a stand-ing joke against me that I was to be a commander at thirty years of age and a captain at thirty-five. It arose thus: Lieutenant Cotesworth was made a commander when the *Thetis* was paid off at Plymouth; he was just thirty years of age. This led to my saying, 'Promotion would only be worth having if one were made a commander at thirty and a captain at thirty-five.' [This happened to him]

"On August 26th we anchored in St. Catherine's, and sailed again on the 29th for the river Plata. Arriving at Monte Video on the evening of September 3rd, we anchored in company with H.M. ships *Forte*, forty-four, and *Cadmus*, ten-gun brig. We found the town occupied by Brazilian troops, and a strong Brazilian squadron, under an admiral, in the bay.   The Brazilians were at war with the Argentine provinces, and both parties coveted the fine province of Uruguay, with its capital Monte Video, thus carrying on an old dispute between the Spaniards and Portuguese before they were independent of their mother-countries.   The Brazilians held Monte Video, and as far around it as their guns could throw a shot; but the Argentines held the country, and probably a large number of the inhabitants of Uruguay assisted them, for they hated the Brazilians.   One day a party of officers from the *Thetis*, of whom I was one, hired horses and went for a ride.   We were returning to the town by a road or path along the crest of a ridge ; it sloped down on our left to a valley, in which ran a rivulet. Suddenly we saw what looked like a small party of cavalry in extended order.   They leaped the rivulet, cantered up the slope, and when within one hundred yards they all fired their carbines at us, but the balls whistled over our heads.   We sailed from Monte Video on September 26th for the purpose of watering, which consisted in going up the river till the water became fresh, and pumping it in with the wash-deck pump, anchoring as we did so.   Before daybreak the next morning we saw two vessels standing towards us ; one of them fired a shot at us, which cut away our stay-sail stays and tricing-lines.   We immediately got under way and followed them   They were a brig, brigantine, and two schooners ; we believed them to be a Buenos Ayrean squadron that had mistaken us for a Brazilian frigate.   One schooner nearly ahead fired at us —probably with a pivot-gun—a charge of round and grape-shot.   The round-shot tore a large hole in one of our lighter sails; one grape-shot lodged in the main-mast. Directly the shot was fired one old quartermaster who was at the helm said, ' There was grape in that.'   We did not fire a shot, but we sent a boat to the brig, and found, as we expected, that they were a Buenos Ayrean squadron commanded by their celebrated Admiral Brown.   They had mistaken the *Thetis* for a Brazilian frigate.   Admiral Brown had been in the Buenos Ayrean service since the War of Independence.   There was a squadron of Spanish frigates at anchor at Monte Video.   The government of Buenos Ayres fitted out several vessels, manned them with English and Americans, and gave the command to Mr. Brown, then mate of an English merchant-vessel. As soon as they were ready he sailed for Monte Video, and, choosing a dark night for it, ran the Spanish frigates on board, and carried them by boarding. We followed his squadron to Monte Video; and in the afternoon, in broad daylight, we saw the same four vessels that had fired at us in the night standing out of Monte Video in line ahead, Brown's brig the sternmost of them, three Brazilian frigates following, and the headmost firing bow-guns. They looked upon Brown as a madman, who would not hesitate to run his brig alongside any enemy's ship, and then set fire to his own vessel, or even blow up the two, even if he had to fire the magazine with his own hand The object of running this risk was that a corvette of eighteen guns had recently arrived at Monte Video, having been fitted out in France, and they wanted to give her a chance of escaping from Monte Video to Buenos Ayres. This was fully accomplished, for we saw her standing out, and she was afterwards manned and fitted out at Buenos Ayres.

"December 11th, 1827, was the day on which I first saw the *Beagle*, in which I served so long afterwards. I find on that date in my log: 'Exchanged numbers with H.M. barque *Beagle*: 10 40 a.m., anchored near H.M.B. *Beagle*.' On the 12th we sailed in company with H.M.S. *Cadmus*, ten-gun brig, for a cruise off the coast of Patagonia. When off Cape Corrientes we experienced a pampero from S.S.W., which brought us under a close-reefed fore-topsail and fore-topmast stay-sail We ran before it, with *Cadmus* on our larboard beam, under similar sail. The lightning was streaming down round *Cadmus*, so that it was a wonder neither vessel was struck. These were the days before Harris's lightning-conductors, when every man-of-war was supplied with a conductor of long links in a box, supposed to be triced up by signal-halliards, and long enough to reach from the main-truck to the water; but in practice the box and conductor remained in the store-room, and even in a lightning-storm of this nature they were not triced up. The thunder was incessant all round us. It was the heaviest thunder-storm I ever witnessed, even in the Plata, where during pamperos they are very heavy.

"[The *Thetis* was struck by lightning, the fore-topmast being badly splintered.]

"One day at Rio Janeiro, when the liberty-men returned, they reported having seen in a crimping-house four or five

of our men lashed up in hammocks, having been made
drunk first.   The captain immediately selected a dozen
men, and sent them on shore under the command of
Lieutenant Martin and the senior midshipman, Hamilton
They were armed with cutlasses and broomsticks, with
strict orders not to use their cutlasses if broomsticks would
do.   They found the men, and brought them on board
They had no intention of deserting, and would have been
taken on board some Brazilian ship-of-war that night.
On April 9th, 1828, I have it noted in my log that six
men—their names are given—left the boats for duty on
shore.   Having been treated in the same manner, they
were taken on board the frigate *Imperatrix*, Captain Pritz,
a Dane.   It is certain they never volunteered for his ship,
because it was said that when he flogged a man, if he was
an Englishman, he always gave him an extra dozen lashes,
with this remark, 'I shall make you remember Copenhagen.'   They were put in irons on board, and it was
agreed among themselves that one man should pretend to
enter for the ship, and look out for any of the *Thetis's* boats
that might be passing.   They had only to wait a week, for
on the evening of the 16th Captain Bingham had been in
his gig to the head of the harbour, and when returning, on
passing under the stern of the *Imperatrix*, he was hailed
by the look-out man, who said, ' There are several of us
confined on board, sir.'   He at once went alongside, and,
knowing he would want a witness of what would take
place, he sent the gig to the *Thetis* for Lieutenant Bolton,
and on his arrival he went up to Captain Pritz and
demanded his men.   A positive refusal was given.   Captain
Bingham then went to the gangway and sent the gig back
to the *Thetis* with this message to the first lieutenant;
'Send all the boats manned and armed to the *Imperatrix*
directly, with orders to lay off and wait for the captain's
orders.'   I was barge midshipman, but on the sick-list,
so another midshipman was sent in my place, also Lieutenant FitzRoy.   Lieutenant Martin commanded the boats
in the launch.   I could not bear that at such a time I
should not be in my old boat with her picked crew, so I
went in her, and went forward to the head-sheets among
the men, and I heard the words passed aft among the
crew, ' We will make him remember Copenhagen.'   The
position of Captain Bingham and Lieutenant Bolton can be
better conceived than described.   Lieutenant FitzRoy asked

Lieutenant Martin, before we were half-way, if he might go on, as the barge pulled so much faster than any other boat. Captain Bingham went up to Captain Pritz, and said, ' I hear my boat's oars ; you had better give me my men.' They were out of irons and on deck, and he ordered them into the gig, which had returned alongside the *Imperatrix.* Captain Pritz showed the highest kind of courage by giving up the men. He knew he was in the wrong, and gave them up rather than risk a war between the two countries One boy, who was some months absent from the ship, having been crimped and sent on board a Brazilian schooner-of-war, hailed Captain Bingham's boat as she was passing under the stern one day, saying he was confined on board against his will. Captain Bingham went on board and claimed him. He had no idea of deserting the ship. The schooner had been to the coast of Africa and back. It may appear at first sight as if the admiral who was in port should have been consulted before this extreme step was taken, and that it was a case for the English minister. But a previous case had occurred in which all this ' routine ' had been taken ; during the delay the men had been sent to another Brazilian man-of-war, and all trace of them lost.

"We were moored all this time about half a mile below the usual anchorage of the Brazilian ships-of-war, to be near the dockyard, from which we obtained two long spars for sheers to get our damaged fore-mast out We did this on the 11th, and hauled it up in the dockyard.

"It is fair to state that the system of manning the Brazilian ships-of-war was by crimping the men from the English ships, and, in consequence of ours being the only ship that gave leave, they were chiefly obtained from the *Thetis.* But we filled up the vacancies from the English merchant-vessels. It was a common custom for two or three men to come on board to enter, but we had not a single vacancy. We would tell them that such and such ships wanted men, but they refused to go to them ; it was evidently because they did not meet their men on leave. Though our fore-mast was hauled up in the government dockyard, our carpenters did the work. I find in my log : ' Received two of our men from a Brazilian brig-of-war.' On April 21st the dockyard supplied a spar to make cheeks for the new fore-mast, the centre-piece of the old mast being unfit for that purpose, having been struck by lightning. On May 21st we got the fore-mast in and put it in its

place, then got the sheers overboard to return them to the
dockyard.   On the 31st Michael Waters, one of the smartest
petty officers in the ship, fell from the mast-head and died
in ten minutes.   He died with his head on my knee, and
with the doctor kneeling by his side.   He was a native of
Waterford.   It is commonly said in the service that an
Irishman never makes a smart seaman, and it is owing to
this that volunteers for the navy come in batches from
Liverpool, and there are many young Irishmen among
them, or used to be, in my younger days.

"On June 1st, 1828, we sailed from Rio Janeiro in company with the flag-ship.   When twenty-nine miles from
Cape Frio, we parted company with the admiral, for the
purpose of proceeding to Buenos Ayres to embark Lord
and Lady Ponsonby, Lord Ponsonby having been appointed
our ambassador to the Brazilian Government.   We parted
company with the admiral on June 7th.   We anchored at
Monte Video on June 17th, and found there H.M.S. _Heron_
(eighteen guns).   She was commanded by the Hon.
Frederick Grey, of whom it was said that if every Honourable were as good an officer as he was, there would be
more excuse for Lord —— promoting them all as fast as
possible.   We sailed again from Monte Video on the 26th
for Buenos Ayres in company with the _Heron_.   On June
29th we anchored in twenty feet of water off Buenos Ayres.
The next day we were employed in dismounting guns, and
fitting up cabins under the half-deck, and preparing to
embark Lord and Lady Ponsonby and suite.   On July 27th
we sent the barge and pinnace on shore for them.   I was
in the barge.   It blew a gale on shore, and the most that
we could do was to try and reach the _Heron_.   We had
considerable difficulty in getting the party off the mule-
carts, the only way then of reaching Buenos Ayres when
there was a surf on the beach.   (There is now a splendid
pier at Buenos Ayres.)   The _Heron_ was several miles
inside the _Thetis_ and _Sapphire_.   We had previously
received on board the _Thetis_ five horses.   About half-past
five we reached the _Heron_, and Commander Frederick
Grey had to stow us away for the night.   On reaching
the ship she fired a salute, to which the ambassador was
entitled.   The _Heron_ anchored near us the next day, and,
sending the barge to her, we received Lord and Lady
Ponsonby, Mr. Scott (secretary), three female servants,
three men servants, and a child, with a load of luggage by

schooner. I see a notice in my log that the river fell four
feet during the night, with the wind at south-west. There
was a Brazilian squadron blockading Buenos Ayres at the
same time.

  "On July 31st, at 2 p.m, we left Buenos Ayres, the
Sapphire and *Heron* in company. In rounding the tail of
the bank off Port Indio, the *Thetis* signalled to the *Sapphire*
to report depth of water, *Heron* and *Sapphire* having hauled
up to cross it, and the *Thetis* with her draught of water
would have had to go several miles round. The report
was half a fathom less than the *Thetis* drew   It was known
to be a sand-bank   Captain Bingham said to Gowdy, the
master, 'Do you think we should shove her through it?'
We were going ten and a half knots. We hauled up,
following the *Sapphire*. We felt distinctly when she touched
the bank, and dragged through it with the speed reduced
to five knots, and when we were off it we went eleven knots
again. This shows the nerve of the captain and master.
We were under larboard fore-topmast and topgallant
studding-sails. The spars bent like coach-whips.

  " On the afternoon of August 2nd we anchored at Monte
Video   The captain had given orders that we were not to
confine the men to the boats, saying he would not punish good
men for bad, adding, 'If they get drunk in the boat they
know they will be flogged.' (The first time they got three
dozen, and every other time there were six lashes added.)
I was sent to the mole at Monte Video with the barge,
launch, and pinnace to bring off oxen, which was usual in
ships going from Monte Video to Rio Janeiro. So many
men got drunk that we had to lash them to the thwarts.
Immediately they reached the ship the men who were
drunk were put in irons for punishment next morning, and
picked men, none of whom had been punished before,
were to replace them in the boats, to bring off the
remainder of the oxen, as the ship was to sail for Rio
Janeiro the next day. I was senior midshipman, and
Captain Bingham gave me orders to leave the other midshipmen to load the boats, and go to the upper end of the
mole to keep guard over the men, and not allow any of
them to go too near a grog-shop. I had hardly taken my
station when I saw a man named Nicholls at the junction
of the timber structure with the stone-work peeping several
times. I called to him by name, and he came. I said to
him, ' I suppose you want to join those who are in irons,

who you know are to be punished to-morrow morning.' To my astonishment he replied, ' Mr. Sulivan, I'll get away if I can, and I'll get drunk if I can, and I can take my " batty " for it as well as another man.' I replied by ordering him to the boat again, and I walked down the length of the mole with him, knowing him to be one of the best men in the ship. The next morning I was going up as the men for punishment were taken out of irons under the half-deck, and I heard one named Collins, a petty officer and captain of the fore-top, saying, ' I have had twenty-six dozen, and now I am going up to get four more—that will be thirty dozen, even tallies.' The men arranged with each other that they would not ask to be let off, and would bear it without crying out, and the consequence was, Lord and Lady Ponsonby, who were in their dressing-cabins immediately below, were not aware that the men were being flogged over their heads.

"On the afternoon of March 27th we arrived at Rio Janeiro. We found that Lieutenant Robert FitzRoy had been promoted to commander, in the vacancy caused by the death of Commander Stokes, of H.M. sloop *Beagle*. The first thing he did was to ask Captain Bingham if he had any objection to transfer me to the *Beagle*, of course with the admiral's consent, and in a very few days I joined her. I see by my log I joined the *Beagle* on December 15th, 1828, as a midshipman. The *Beagle* was anchored off Hospital Island for the purpose of heaving her down, which was done by hand, to a platform made of four large market-boats. Her bottom was in a shocking state. We found that all the false keel was gone, with the greater part of the main-keel. Unfortunately the summer of that year was the warmest that had ever been experienced in Rio Janeiro. There was a well on Hospital Island, but the water had a bad name, and we had to send miles for better, and then fill our casks from a stream running across the road. The well in the island had unfortunately steps that led down to the water : the result was that I and others could not resist the cool water, but ran down the steps many times a day, dipping up a handful to drink.

"One evening the subject discussed was 'ghosts,' in connection with Commander Stokes having shot himself in the poop-cabin. During the discussion the carpenter was sent for, and he declared that he would never disclose to mortal man what he had seen on board. Soon after

3

this the first lieutenant (Kemp) came into the tent and ordered Sulivan, Stokes, Kirke, to take the whale-boat and our hammocks to the ship, and send the quartermaster on shore, remaining on board ourselves, as he required every seaman to commence rigging the ship. The first salutation we received as soon as we were alongside was, 'Don't go aft, for the ghost is there.' We professed not to believe in ghosts, but we pulled the boat farther ahead, and got in through one of the bow-ports, under the top-gallant forecastle. We had only one duty to do, viz to hail the commander, as he went on shore about eleven o'clock to his lodgings. This done, we retired to rest under the forecastle. It was my first watch The poop-cabin door began to slam, disturbing our rest in the hammocks; instantly there was a cry of 'Sulivan, go aft and shut the door. Take the lantern if you are afraid of the ghost'' they added in a jeering tone The wind blew out the light in the lantern before I had traversed the distance from the fore-mast to the main-mast; I ran forward again, but the poop-cabin door continued to slam, and they continued to jeer. At last I found out that the door would not shut, and that was the reason of its slamming; so I wedged it open. I was in a hammock on the port side, and Stokes, who was on the starboard side, said to me, 'I hear the sound as of some one breathing very loud ahead; you look out of the port bow, and I will look out of the starboard one and listen.' We did hear sounds of heavy breathing, and soon after footsteps overhead. 'The ghost! It is coming down below!' I slipped from my hammock behind the companion, and presently there appeared first one naked foot on a step, then a second I pushed my hands through the open ladder and seized both ankles, when a voice above roared out, 'Oh! the ghost! it has got me!' It turned out to be one of the men, who, having taken too much, had gone to sleep in the larboard head, and so missed the boat which took the other men ashore Rain coming on, he awoke, and thought he would go below, but was in great fear of the ghost!

"We experienced the heaviest pampero any vessel ever did on January 30th, 1829, when the barometer fell to 28.50. We were passing inside Lobos Island, and we had just made out the *Adventure* (Captain King), seeing her higher spars over Goritte Island, off Maldonado. I had been in a cot in the poop-cabin with an attack of dysentery, consequent upon drinking the water on Hospital Island, and the doctor had told the commander when he reported the sick in the morning that there was no chance of my recovery. The water began to rise. We had been waited for by our consort, the *Adventure*, and we should have sailed in company with her for the southward at day-light the next morning, which had an important bearing on my future prospects in the service. The *Beagle* was on her beam-ends several times during the pampero, and at length the water was nearly up to the bottom of my cot, the port side, and I was told that two men whose names I well knew had fallen from the yards into the sea. I thought I might have a chance for my life as well as others. I managed to draw a pair of trousers on and to crawl from my cot. The force of the wind was such as to crush in the weather-quarter boat where she pressed against the davits. I went up the starboard poop-ladder, and then I saw from the mizzen-mast on which I was standing the commander standing on one of the uprights of the poop-rail, and holding on by another upright. She was so much over that the topsail yards blew up to the mast's head, with a man upon each yardarm clinging to the lift, the one upon the lee yard-arm with the help of the brace-block strop, while the one upon the weather yardarm managed to crawl in, and he was seen on the cap, where he was heard to say, 'Thank God, I have got in out of that!' I, from my standing-place, the mizzen-mast, saw that she was standing direct for the rocks and breakers on Lobos Island, and I reported it to the commander. He replied, saying, 'So she is,' and immediately ordered both anchors to be let go. The water was so shallow that she touched the small bower-anchor when passing over it; but the two anchors brought her up, and saved her running on Lobos."

The autobiography breaks off suddenly here. At the time of writing the above my father was asked to con-tribute some reminiscences of his old friend Admiral Sir A. Cooper Key. By the time he had completed these, his failing powers prevented his continuing the history of his own life.

CHAPTER II.

ON the advice of FitzRoy, in view of his approaching examination for the rank of lieutenant, Sulivan only remained in the *Beagle* as midshipman until February 12th, 1829. He then joined the *Ganges*, Captain Inglefield, leaving her on April 12th for the *North Star*, Captain Arabin, evidently for a passage home. On December 8th he passed his examination in seamanship. He was entered as mate of the *Undaunted*, Captain Clifford. His seniority as lieutenant is dated April 3rd, 1830.

I have always understood that my father, having obtained full marks at the Naval College, and also on passing for lieutenant, was given that rank almost immediately, without the usual service as mate, which to many men without interest meant sometimes a period of ten years before becoming lieutenants.

Christmas of this year was spent with the Young family at Barton End. In July 1831 FitzRoy was again appointed to the *Beagle*, for the purpose of undertaking another surveying voyage to the southern parts of South America, and of completing a chain of meridian distances round the world. He took Sulivan as second lieutenant. As descriptions of this celebrated voyage have been given by both Admiral FitzRoy and Professor Darwin, I will refrain from the temptation to reproduce many of the interesting letters my father sent home. The *Beagle* fitted out at Plymouth

in the autumn of 1831.   At that time the family of Admiral
Young were staying there, so my father was often able to
meet my mother.   Although no word on the subject was
spoken, the affection then formed was mutual.

The labour of fitting out, especially towards the end, was
very heavy.   From my father's letters it appears he was
feeling the effects of the overwork, for he mentions more
than once having fallen asleep in the evenings at friends'
houses   The night before the *Beagle* sailed there was a
ball on shore, and Sulivan was hoping to meet Miss Young
there for the last time before the long voyage.   Having
had a hard day's work, at five o'clock he went to his cabin
for a nap, telling the steward to rouse him at half-past
seven, that he might join the gun-room tea before going on
shore to dress.   On awaking, he was astonished to find
it was daylight.   He called the steward, and asked the
time.   "Eight o'clock, sir."   "What do you mean?"
"Eight in the morning, sir."   "What, have I missed the
ball?   Why did you not call me?"   "I did, sir."   "Then,
when I did not appear at tea, why did you not call me
again."   "You did have tea, sir."   Hearing a titter in the
ward-room, he got up, and was told the following tale.   The
officers were at tea, when he appeared in his night-shirt and
night-cap, shouldering a big duck-gun he had hung in his
cabin.   He deposited this in the corner, went to his place
at table, drank the tea they put before him, then rose,
shouldered the gun again, and marched back to bed.   This
was a curious case of somnambulism.   The officers, seeing
he was evidently overwrought, did not like to awaken him,
so he missed the ball.   Owing to heavy gales, the *Beagle*
twice returned after having put out to sea before she
finally sailed on December 27th, so there was an opportunity after all for the farewell to be spoken.

It was the opinion of all on board the *Beagle* that never

had a vessel left England better equipped for the special
service she was to be engaged in.   Captain FitzRoy called
the officers together, and said, " If a man falls overboard,
if we lose a spar or ship a sea, I shall blame the officers of
the watch."   During the whole voyage, part of the time in
one of the most stormy regions of the world, not one
of these events happened, except the shipping of one sea
just after my father had relinquished the deck to FitzRoy.
The captain always had the ports secured, saying that
a ship had no business to be in the position to require
them for freeing ports.   My father never liked this order,
and told the carpenter always to have a handspike handy
for eventualities.   On the occasion in question the vessel
was on her beam-ends.*   On my father reaching the deck
from below, he found the carpenter up to his waist in
water, standing on the bulwark, driving a handspike
against the port, which he eventually burst open.   This
probably saved the ship, for she righted in time to meet
the next heavy sea.   No skill could have prevented the
accident, for the ship was struck by three heavy breaking
seas in succession, and the third came on board.

FitzRoy's orders will repay perusal.   One was that no
one was to go out of sight of the ship except in company
with at least two others.   If one man were hurt, a comrade
could stay with him whilst the third went for assistance.
The only time this rule was broken was at the Falklands,
when Mr. Hellyer, the clerk, who had gone out shooting
alone, was drowned in a lake within sight of the ship's
topmasts.

Sulivan's father had said to him before starting, " Pick
and send home any strange plant you find."   This he did.
The botanist Lindley was a great friend of his father's, and

* See FitzRoy's "Voyage of the *Adventure* and *Beagle*," vol. ii.,
p. 125.

used to examine the plants that arrived. Some of them
having seeds, he cultivated these. In this way the
Tropæolum and another of our now popular creepers were
introduced into England. Although my father did not
attain to the rank of a scientific botanist, the subject
greatly interested him, and the pursuit brought him into
close friendship with Sir William and Sir Joseph Hooker,
as well as with Darwin. The latter has borne testimony
in his books to the correctness of Sulivan as an observer
of scientific phenomena.

Although not receiving the pay of a surveyor, Sulivan
acted as one throughout the entire voyage. It was doubtless to this expedition that he owed his fondness for and
skill in surveying and seamanship. There were no steam-
launches or lifeboat cutters in those days; all the work
had to be done in sailing-boats. FitzRoy replaced the
dangerous dipping lug with two standing lugs, and this
rig Sulivan always adopted afterwards. In the Rio Plata
he boasted of his boats outsailing those of the whole
squadron. Throughout the many years of constant boat-
work in the *Beagle, Arrow,* and *Philomel,* no accident
occurred; this he greatly attributed to the use of this rig.

On the arrival of the *Beagle* at Buenos Ayres, FitzRoy,
anxious to accomplish as much work as he could, purchased and fitted out at his own expense two little vessels
in which to send officers on detached surveys.

Lieutenant Wickham was given charge of one, Mr.
Stokes, the mate, of the other. Sulivan thus describes the
vessels :—

"The cabin in Stokes's craft is seven feet long, seven
wide, and thirty inches high. In this three of them
stow their hammocks, which in the daytime form seats
and serve for a table. In a little space forward, not so
large, are stowed five men. The larger boat carries the

instruments. Her cabin is the same size, but is four feet
high, and has a table and seats."

In these craft did one or other of the officers survey the
coast from the Rio Plata to the Straits of Magellan over
a period of nearly twelve months, whilst the *Beagle* was
engaged farther south.   In the meantime FitzRoy had
added to the "squadron" a schooner-yacht, a much better
vessel, which he named the *Adventure* (after the ship commanded by Captain King), and she was his consort during
nearly the whole of the South American cruise.   In such
vessels and in open boats did he and his officers get
through the immense amount of laborious surveying work
that was accomplished.

Sulivan had his share of ordinary boat work, and during
Wickham's long absences did first lieutenant's duties   In
December 1834 came his turn to undertake a separate
survey. On Christmas Eve he started to survey the east
side of the Island of Chiloe and the islets in the Gulf of
Ancud. With him went Darwin, three officers, and ten
men. They returned on January 7th, but went back to
the same ground a few days later, Darwin not accompany-
ing them this time. On the 17th they rejoined the *Beagle*
in San Carlos Harbour. Some extracts from the accounts
of these trips may prove interesting :—

"Berkeley Sound, *February* 1833

"As we went on the sea became very high, and the
farther we went the worse it was. In the yawl we got on
pretty well. The wind was blowing the water up in sheets
of white spray, flying over the boat's mast-head, and the
only sail we could carry was a close-reefed fore-sail. The
sea was so high that at two cables' distance from each
other it hid the mast-heads of the boats when they were
in the hollow of the sea. Just at this place the whaler
broached to and shipped a good deal of water, but luckily
they got her before it again before the next sea came.

We were at this time about two cables' lengths ahead of her, but had she gone we could not have helped her, as it would have been almost impossible to round to with safety, and if we did we could not have got one inch back. It was a very anxious time—I think more so than I ever yet experienced. As we neared the point the sea got much worse, from the tide forming a race; but the distance through this was very short, and directly we passed the rocks off the point we should be in smooth water. The rocks are about a hundred yards from the shore, and tremendous breakers on them and the shore also, but between these was one small part where it did not break; and as every moment was of consequence, and outside the rocks there was a much heavier sea, we ran for this little opening. Just before coming to it a roller reached us, and carried us on its top right over the ridge without our shipping a drop of water, and the next moment we were round the point in smooth water; but this was by far the most anxious time for me, as we were also out of sight of the whaler, and it was for her safety that I was so anxious. However, just as we went round to stand back under the point we saw her swing round outside the rocks, as they thought it better to run the risk of the sea than to come through the passage inside it. The relief and comfort I felt when she was safe alongside us in smooth water I cannot describe. We got into a snug little cove, where we pitched the tents, secured the boats, and got dinner under way. The weather cleared up a little, so as to enable us to get a few things dry. While dinner was cooking I walked over to the point we had come round with the instruments; but it blew so hard that I could not put one up, not a stand would remain fixed, and we could not stand on the top of the beach ourselves. As it was warm walking and carrying instruments, and the sky being clear, I left my coat behind me at the tents, and on our return it came on to rain, hail, and snow, and I got a complete drenching. The yawlers had now the laugh on their side, as the whalers had had their bags filled with water when the sea came into the boat, and had not a dry stitch of clothes or blankets. However, they got them partly dry before night. We were fortunate to find plenty of wreck-wood on the beach, and we had a glorious fire, round which we sat singing till ten o'clock at night, when a heavy hail-shower drove us into the tents. We all then crowded into one tent, and

went on singing till twelve, and I never under any circumstances saw a more merry party. All the comic songs
that any one knew were mixed up with yarns of English,
Irish, Scotch, and Welsh ; and as we had about an equal
number of each country, it raised bits of laughter against
them all in their turns: neither did the west country
escape."

" RIO NEGRO, September 5th, 1833

"On August 29th I left in the yawl with a mate and ten
men. We started from the ship at 1 p.m. with a strong
breeze but a favourable tide, and we beat up to Punta Alta
in time to have everything landed, the tents rigged, and
the pot under way before sunset. Tea is a great luxury
in cruises of this kind. We always boiled a large boiler
holding four gallons full every morning for breakfast, and
the same for supper, and we never had any left, and, as
there were only twelve of us, we must have drunk one-
eighth of a gallon each meal, or five and a half pints a day.
The same pot full of a mess made of salt pork, fresh beef,
venison, and biscuit was also emptied for dinner, and meat
also of some kind both for breakfast and supper. Such
hardships are hard to put up with, the idea of being among
mud-banks in a boat with nothing but a waterproof awning
to cover her with, and thick blankets to sleep in, with
only two pounds of meat, two-thirds of a gallon of tea,
one pound of bread, and a quarter of a pint of rum each
man per day is dreadful!!!

" In the evening we got all ready for beginning work at
daylight, and then part went on board the boat to sleep. On
the 30th we began at 6 a m, and had finished our work by
breakfast-time, but waited for Darwin to examine the
beach at low water for fossil remains of animals, which
are very plentiful. Besides getting some he had seen
before, he this morning found the teeth of animals six
times as large as those of any animal now known in
this country, also the head of one about the size of a
horse, with the teeth quite perfect and totally different
from any now known, and just at low-water mark he
found the remains of another about six feet long, nearly
perfect, all embedded in solid rock. We started at low
water for the settlement, leaving two hands digging out
the bones.

" After supper we all went on board, and moored the

boat head and stern about four yards from the bushes, to ensure her grounding in the centre where the mud was quite soft. The evening looked very gloomy, with heavy thunder and lightning; but we were quite snug under an awning, which we filled as much as possible with tobacco smoke, to drive away the mosquitoes and sand-flies, which were very troublesome. By filling the upper part of the awning with smoke we kept them all out. I never in my life, I think, laughed in the way I did for about three hours at the stories they were all telling in turns. We had among the men two or three excellent hands for keeping every one alive, and to-night they performed their part to perfection. Such hands are invaluable in a cruise of that kind, particularly if the work is very hard, as they keep men's spirits up in a most surprising manner. I think I never in my life saw people more happy than all our party were; they were in roars of laughter from morning till night, and up to all kinds of amusements when on shore, except when I brought them to an anchor occasionally to prevent their shaking the ground (near my instruments), and then they would find something amusing in that; and when men in those spirits are happy and comfortable, it is astonishing how they make work fly."

"'BEAGLE,' AT SEA, *November* 15*th*, 1834.

"It [Chiloe] will be a pleasant cruise, and all the officers want to go with me. I am to have Usborne, Johnson, and King, the assistant surgeon, and five men, besides the pilot, making a party of ten. We shall have the dinghy with us, so the yawl will be turned into a complete man-of-war. We expect to finish the work as far as Valparaiso by the end of April, when we shall no more return to the south

"*November* 19*th.*—It was declared yesterday by the doctors that if they were to pick out the most robust and healthy person in the *Beagle* it would be me. However, the cruise in the yawl will, I have no doubt, take me down a little, though I never enjoyed better bodily health than I do in these cruises. Still, the work, fag, and anxiety all tend to keep a person from getting too stout. I am to have six men and one boy; and as the best singers and most diverting characters in the ship are among them—and they are all of that kind, and are up to anything—we shall have, I hope, a very pleasant party. We shall have a large bag

full of flour and raisins on purpose for a good plum-dough
on Christmas Day.

"You cannot think how I have enjoyed the society of
Mrs. Miller's and Mrs. Patterson's little children at Valparaiso. I was their chief friend, and they came to me
for everything they wanted. One day I had a large party
of ten children on board, the eldest six and the youngest
two and a half years old, and for four hours all the big
children amused themselves seeing the little ones playing
hide-and-seek and other games about the deck."

"H.M. 'BEAGLE'S YAWL,' SAN CARLOS, *January 9th*, 1835

"It rained every day but one for six weeks, and most of
the days never ceased raining, but by great good luck we
have not had one person unwell.

"I shall amuse you with a few stories For instance, our
foraging on a small island inhabited by Indians, on
Christmas morning, from nine to twelve, in a heavy gale
of wind and tremendous rain, before we could get eggs
enough to make our plum-pudding or a sheep to eat. However, we got into the padre's house attached to the church,
as our tents, clothes, and blankets were wet through, and
by 4 p m. had one side of a sheep roasted, another side
boiled, twelve pounds of English fresh roast beef heated,
and two immense plum-puddings made. No bad quantum
for twelve men! It would have amused you if you could
have seen us in a dirty room with a tremendous fire in the
middle, and all our blankets and clothes hung round the
top on lines, getting smoked as well as dry, while all hands
were busily employed for four hours killing a sheep, picking
raisins, beating eggs, mixing puddings which were so large
that, in spite of two-thirds of the party being west-
country men, we had enough for supper also. However,
we passed a pleasant day in spite of wind and weather,
and it was a holiday to us, as we could only afford to
knock off work when it rained too hard constantly to be
able to move, which happened on Christmas Day and
New Year's Day. Every other day for eight weeks we
were hard at work. It is very curious that I am always
in better health in a boat, for I never have enjoyed such
perfect good health for two months since leaving England."

On one occasion, it being desired to find out the condition of the *Beagle's* bottom after she had struck a rock,

Sulivan dived down under the keel, and, having ascertained things were not very bad, came up the other side, bleeding from several scratches received from the jagged copper. FitzRoy, wishing to make doubly sure, then performed the same action himself.

In May 1835 a Chilian gentleman lent FitzRoy the schooner *Constitucion*, of twenty-six tons. Sulivan was despatched in her to examine the coast near Coquimbo, and that of Chili as far as Paposa. His commander wrote in allusion to this trip, " I well knew that Lieutenant Sulivan would not only make despatch, but do also extremely correct work." This cruise lasted until August 30th. As the *Beagle* was then about to leave for her voyage to the west, Sulivan could not be spared longer, so Mr. Usborne, master's assistant, was sent in the schooner to survey the coast of Peru. Sulivan describes him as one of the best seamen he ever knew.

Sulivan had another expedition in the yawl to survey the centre of the Galapagos Islands. In December 1835 the *Beagle* reached New Zealand, after touching at Ota-heite. The month following she arrived at Sydney, where Mr. King left them to join his father. The *Beagle* sailed for England, calling at Mauritius, the Cape, and other places on her way home for the purpose of observations for meridian distances. She arrived at Greenwich in November 1836.

One story not related by FitzRoy I may now give without offence. On the return of the vessel after such an interesting voyage, so many people came to visit her that the captain gave the order that *respectable-looking persons only* were to be admitted by the accommodation-ladder ; others were to enter by the gangway (where some projections three inches wide against the ship's side afford foothold, there being two ropes to assist the climber).

Sulivan, who was at the time on watch, noticed the sentry wave a boat away from the ladder round to the gangway. Presently the head of a very pretty, stylish woman appeared in it, and Sulivan went forward to assist her. She was followed by a rather plain-looking man, who asked for the captain. After they had been conducted below, FitzRoy came on deck, much put out, and said, "Do you know it is the Astronomer Royal who has been treated with such scant ceremony?" He was paying what was somewhat of an official visit, with his wife. When the captain had retired below, Sulivan rated the sentry for his want of discrimination. The man replied, "Well, sir, he did *not* look respectable!"

Thirty-three years afterwards the nine officers who had been such close companions and friends were all still alive; then the first break began. Now the only survivor is Mr. Philip King, of Sydney. I annex a few remarks written by him and the late Admiral Mellersh, who died only recently. I might add, in relation to Darwin, that he suffered so much from seasickness that whenever the ship was out of harbour he retired to his hammock in the chart-room, the only accommodation afforded him. My father said he believed it was this constant suffering which laid the seeds of the indisposition he was troubled with in later years, and that his patience in persevering with his scientific work, and not abandoning the voyage, was most commendable.

FitzRoy added the following lines to Sulivan's official certificate of service in the *Beagle* :—

"To this usual certificate I am anxious to add a few words expressive of my very high opinion of your ability, integrity, and high-principled zeal I have known you and watched your conduct ever since your entry into the service, and I sincerely believe that a worthier young man is not to be found. Wherever you go, or whatever

may be my lot, remember that among your numerous
friends one of the earliest and not the least sincere is
" ROBERT FITZROY."

From the late Admiral A Mellersh, C.B. —

"HOVE, BRIGHTON, *February* 18th, 1891.

" DEAR MR SULIVAN,—I have not 'the pen of a ready
writer,' but I may say that I have had, in nearly thirty
years' actual sea-service, great opportunities of seeing and
judging of naval officers, and I do not hesitate to declare
my opinion that your father was amongst the 'first
flight.' He was a *perfect* sailor, a first-rate observer and
navigator, a capital gunnery officer, and indeed an 'all-
round man.' As I am writing a scene comes into my
mind. We were near the western entrance of the Straits
of Magellan, in mid-winter, going westward ; it was blowing hard ; treble-reefed topsails and reefed courses ; the
main-sail hauled up, but not furled ; wind from westward.
I (then a mate) was officer of the 'middle watch' (12 to
4 a m.) The captain directed your father to keep with me.
The night was *inky* dark, when about 1 a.m. the look-out
man called out, 'Rocks close on the starboard beam.' As
we were 'land-locked' the water was smooth. Your father
gave the order 'Lower main-sail,' and the watch ran the
'main-tack on board,' and hauled aft the main-sheet so
quickly, that, though so close to the perpendicular rocks,
the lee clew of the main-sail nearly touched the wall-
like cliff. The ship sprang off like an arrow from a bow
A moment's indecision would have been fatal ; but there was
none, and the ship was saved. Though your father was
only a year my senior in years, I learned from him and
Wickham all that made me successful in my own long
service as first lieutenant. In conclusion, I may say that
your father was one of my dearest friends on earth, and
one whom I hope I may meet again in heaven.

" Yours very truly,
" A. MELLERSH."

From Mr. Philip Gedley King :—

"SYDNEY, 1892

" Never shall I forget the kindly welcome he gave us as
we stepped on board after our hazardous absence [in the

small craft, with Lieutenant Wickham]. His was the cheery, open heart which held out the hand of genuine friendship to any one, though of inferior rank in the service. As the voyage proceeded changes were made, and I became not only his shipmate but his helpmate ; and later on he was appointed by Captain FitzRoy to take his share in the small-craft service, which added so much to the real work performed by the officers of the *Beagle*.

"To his craft I had the happiness of being appointed, and the few months spent on board her are full of memories of pleasant relationship with my commander, with whom or from whom I do not ever remember to have had an angry word. Full of zeal for the service, and animated with a somewhat fiery spirit in the prosecution of his duty, he yet had the gentle heart and kindness of disposition which marks so eminently those ' who go down to the sea in ships, and occupy their business in the great waters '— these are they 'who tell out the works of the Lord with gladness,' and offer their hearts to their fellow-men.

"It was at Sir James Sulivan's instance that a portrait was painted of our estimable commander, Robert FitzRoy, now hanging on the walls of the Painted Hall of Greenwich (Hospital that was), a photograph of which has had a place in my library, opposite that of his old senior officer, my father, the late Admiral Phillips Parker King (of H.M S. *Adventure*)—and not far away are the likenesses of Darwin, Wickham, Usborne, Mellersh, and of my lamented friend.

"PHILIP GEDLEY KING."

On the return of the *Beagle* the visits to Barton End were resumed, and the two whose affection had been so well tested by absence without correspondence were married on January 14th, 1837. In December of that year my father was appointed to the schooner *Pincher*, intended for watching the slave-trade on the west coast of Africa. But a few weeks afterwards the Hydrographer, Captain Beaufort, was wanting an officer to undertake the survey of the Falkland Islands. He wrote to FitzRoy, asking about Sulivan's qualifications for the post. The

following is his reply (a copy of which he enclosed to
Sulivan), resulting in the latter's appointment to the ketch
Arrow for the work in question :—

"31, CHESTER STREET, *January 5th,* 1838

"DEAR CAPTAIN BEAUFORT,—In answer to your note
with respect to Lieutenant Sulivan, I will try to put the
truth, the whole truth, and nothing but the truth into
as few words as possible. In my humble opinion (having
known him ever since he got the first medal at the Naval
College) Sulivan is '*up to the business completely.*' He
is as thorough a seaman, for his age, as I know, and he
has been used to the smallest craft as well as to the largest
ships He is an *excellent* observer, calculator, and surveyor, and I may truly say that his *abilities* are better
than those of *any* man who has served with *me*. Besides
these advantages he has the solid foundation of the highest
principles, and an honest and warm heart. Nothing on
earth would induce Sulivan to swerve from his *duty*, even
in the *smallest* degree. Whatever he may have to do, he
will do honestly and as well as circumstances allow.

"Now for his defects—and who has none? Sulivan
is *eager*—often hasty—and wants some of the *reserve*,
and caution towards *strangers*, which sailors seldom have
while young. He *was* fidgety, and never thought he or
those with him were going fast enough ; but this is wearing
off fast. In official minutiæ, forms, letters, etc., he may
at first appear deficient, having undervalued them perhaps
too much. He is not a *neat* draftsman, though his chart
work is *extremely* correct. (His hand is not quick enough
for his mind, or his mind is too quick for his hand.) This
is all that I, or *any man*, can say against him.

"May I now conclude by saying, *earnestly*, that I know
no young man, *of his age*, equal to him in abilities and
high principles?

"Most respectfully and sincerely yours,
"ROBERT FITZROY."

Another officer was sent to take the command of the
Pincher. Both vessels fitted out at Chatham. Sulivan had
been a week with the crew of the *Pincher*, preparing her.
As a good and therefore a cautious sailor, he had taken

4

down all the long spars suitable for the tropics, and fitted
shorter ones.   His successor's first exclamation on taking
her over was, "What has become of her long spars?"
Sulivan replied, "They are stowed below until wanted   I
was not going to take her down Channel with them in the
winter."   "What are you afraid of?" said the officer; "I
intend to have them up."   So they were replaced, with the
canvas belonging to them   The two vessels being ready
for sea at the same time, the *Pincher's* commander suggested
a race round to Portsmouth.   When near Beachy Head,
the schooner of course leading by some distance, a thick
squall came on.   The look-out man said he could not see
the *Pincher*, so it was supposed she had run ahead into
the mist.   But on reaching Portsmouth they found no
Pincher there.   A week afterwards they found her in the
Channel, bottom up, with every sail standing, the sad
result of foolhardiness!   The bodies of the watch below
were all in her, showing she must have capsized instantly.
These Sulivan had to identify.

Although there are many interesting letters concerning
the surveys both of the coasts and of the interior, and
accounts of the life in the islands, I have not space for
them in this volume   Sulivan published his remarks on
the islands in a pamphlet, which was translated into
French.   The climate appears to resemble that of the
west of Scotland.   The high winds prevent the growth of
trees.   When the breeze blows from the mainland of
America, the dryness of the air is remarkable.   To this
and the equable though not genial temperature Sulivan
attributed the great healthiness of the place.

The *Arrow* came home in 1839.   Captain Beaufort was
much pleased with the work done.

In May 1841 Sulivan was made a commander.   In an
official letter to his father the secretary to the Admiralty

said that, as a special mark of their lordships' approbation of his services as commodore on the Brazilian station, they had promoted his son.

In 1842 it became necessary to undertake a further survey in connection with the Falklands and the Rio Plata. Beaufort again selected Sulivan for the task, and he was appointed to the brig *Philomel*. The account of his work in the Rio Plata will be found in the following chapter; that in the Falkland Islands must be dismissed for want of space in a few words. As will be seen, his wife and family accompanied him thither. My mother found time to make a collection of the flora of the islands. The plants sent home were arranged by Miss Warren, a lady botanist who lived at Flushing; Lindley also examined them, and named some plants after the finder.

My brother, Commander James Young Falkland Sulivan, was the first British subject born on the Falkland Islands.

The Falkland plant of greatest value is the tussac-grass, growing six feet in height, and containing, weight for weight, almost as much nutriment as corn, as testified by the Royal Agricultural Society's chemist. Sulivan considered it would thrive well in the western islands of Scotland, or Ireland. He introduced it to the late Sir James Matheson, who planted it at Stornoway, where it answered all expectations. But it was at last destroyed, owing to the neglect of the injunction *not to let the cattle feed on the plant*, but to cut it. A fresh attempt should be made to introduce this valuable plant, but it must be fenced in.

NOTE.—A short account of another visit to the Falkland Islands will be found in Appendix B.

CHAPTER III.

THE PARANA CAMPAIGN.

1842-46.

IT may be well to give an outline of the cause of the disturbances which led to the three years' siege of Monte Video, and to the British interference, resulting in the Parana campaign of 1845-46.

Since the Declaration of Independence in 1816, every state in this part of South America had been in almost a constant condition of anarchy. At length arose a man of great force of character, Juan Manuel de Rosas, who became president of the Argentine Republic. He first drove out the aborigines. Backed up by an army of Gauchos, he obtained unlimited power, and was not scrupulous as to the means of retaining it.* After con-

---

* The following stories I remember hearing from my father illustrate the power Rosas exercised, and the means he did not hesitate to adopt to strengthen that power. Once one of my father's brothers was dining with some friends in Buenos Ayres during Rosas' reign of terror. Suddenly a friend of the family rushed in, saying he heard a domiciliary visit would be paid them that evening. The head of the house said that he had done nothing against Rosas, and that he had nothing to fear. One of the family recollected that a room upstairs was papered in green, the opposition colour. That would be sufficient to damn them. The whole party, my uncle included, left the table, went upstairs, and with every instrument obtainable scraped the walls clean and removed the *débris*. They had not long finished when the domiciliary visit was made, but nothing objectionable was found !

An officer was going up-country, so he asked Rosas if he had any commission for him to execute. Rosas replied, "You will pass Fort —— Will you take this letter to the commandant for me ? " " Certainly," the officer said. Before starting, he met a friend, who said, " Be careful ; I hear your name is on the black list." " Oh no,

solidating his power at Buenos Ayres, he turned his attention to the subjugation of the Banda Oriental, the capital
of which was Monte Video.   In 1842 there were two rival
leaders of the hostile factions in this town—Oribe and
Riviera.   Oribe being worsted, fled to Rosas, by whom
he was supplied with men and money.   Oribe then returned, overran the Banda Oriental, and laid siege to
Monte Video.   His operations were conducted with great
cruelty.   He tried to starve the garrison into a surrender.
The Buenos Ayrean squadron, under the command of an
Englishman named Brown (previously referred to), cut
off the supplies by sea.   Mr. Mandeville, the British
Minister, and Commodore Purvis encouraged the Monte
Videans to resist with hopes of British support.   This,
however, was a great mistake.   When Riviera had been
defeated outside the town, had Oribe been allowed to
enter, the cruel war extending over nearly four years
would have been avoided.   As he was not permitted to
enter, Oribe gave out that neither life nor property would
be respected on the capture of the city.   This raised a
strong feeling among the foreigners against him.   Three

I have just left Rosas, who was very friendly, and asked me to take a
note for him." "Well, don't take it." But he would not listen to the
advice.   On reaching the fort, he handed the letter to the commandant,
who read it, and said, "Do you know the contents of this letter?"
"No," the officer said, "General Rosas asked me to bring it to you."
"Well, look at it!" It read, "Shoot him!" He was shot.
Several conspiracies were formed to put an end to Rosas.   Once,
one of the conspiring party, having undertaken to kill Rosas, actually
obtained the post of guard outside the door of Rosas' room.   He
prepared his pistol, when Rosas appeared.   The mere sight of him
was sufficient to strike terror into the heart of the conspirator, who
dropped upon his knees and confessed his intention.
Rosas' daughter Manuelita was a general favourite.   When a young
girl, she saw from her balcony an English midshipman at the door of
the hotel opposite in difficulties with his horse.   She ran down to the
street, jumped upon the man's saddle, galloped the animal up and
down a few times, and then returned it to the humiliated midshipman
in the sight of his shipmates   Manuelita afterwards resided near
Southampton, where I believe my father once or twice called to see her.

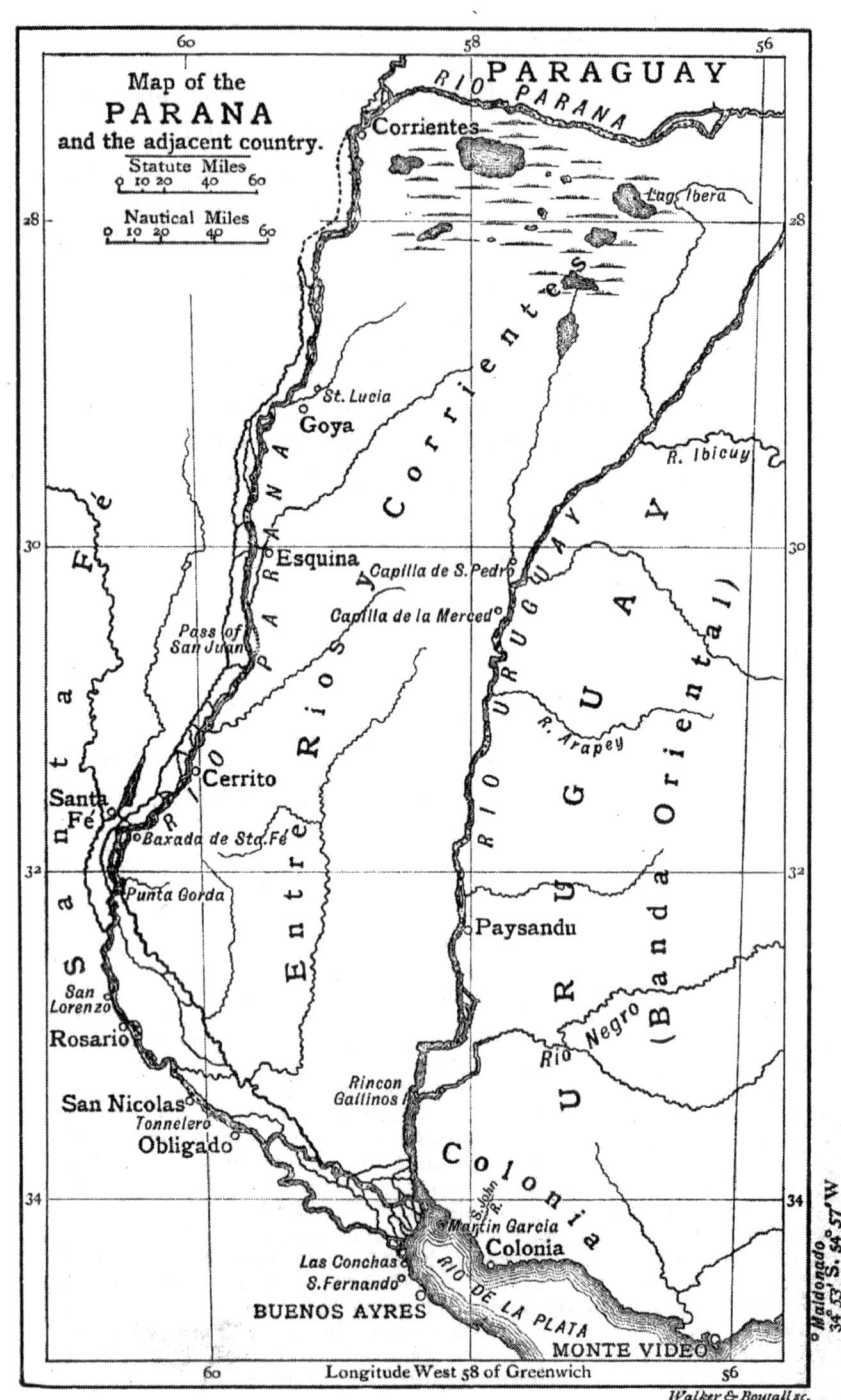

Map of the
PARANA
and the adjacent country.

Statute Miles
0 10 20   40   60

Nautical Miles
0 10 20   40   60

PARAGUAY

RIO PARANA

Corrientes

Lag. Ibera

C o r r i e n t e s

St. Lucia
Goya

R. Ibicuy

P A R A N A

Esquina
Capilla de S. Pedro

Capilla de la Merced

Pass of
San Juan

E n t r e   R i o s

R I O   U R U G U A Y

R. Arapey

(B a n d a   O r i e n t a l)

Santa   Fé

Cerrito

Baxada de Sta. Fé

Punta Gorda

Paysandu

U R U G U A Y

San
Lorenzo

Rio Negro

Rosario

San Nicolas
Tonnelero
Obligado

Rincon
Gallinos

C o l o n i a

S. John R.
Martin Garcia
Colonia

Las Conchas
S. Fernando
BUENOS AYRES

RIO DE LA PLATA

Maldonado
34° 53′ S. 54° 57′ W

MONTE VIDEO

Longitude West 58 of Greenwich

Walker & Boutall sc.

thousand residents (chiefly Basques and Piedmontese) were armed, and a nondescript force was raised by an Englishman named "Cockney Sam." To imitate the uniforms of the British regiments, he dressed them in red shirts. The celebrated Garibaldi, having formerly been taken prisoner and treated badly by Urquieza, one of Rosas' generals, raised a party of five hundred Italian sailors from the coasting-vessels. He adopted Sam's idea of the red shirt, a dress which in later years became still more celebrated in Italy.

Rosas determined to gain possession of both banks of the Rio de la Plata. England and France, having formerly guaranteed the independence of the Banda Oriental, after much vacillation on the part of our authorities, at length actively intervened, and in 1845 summoned Rosas to withdraw his troops. On his refusal, Brown's squadron was captured, and a blockade was proclaimed against Oribe. Admiral Inglefield had succeeded to the command of the British squadron, Admiral Lainé being at the head of the French.

While these events were passing, General Urquieza, a nominee of Rosas, was governor of Entre Rios. The president of the revolted province of Corrientes was General Maderiaga, who formed a league against Rosas with the independent province of Paraguay. These two states had collected an army, over which was placed General Paz, a rival of Rosas.

In 1845 the British and French ships were ordered to reopen the Parana, which had been closed by Rosas, who thereupon concentrated his opposition at Obligado. After forcing the defences at this point, the combined squadrons proceeded to Corrientes, eight hundred miles up the river, convoying a large number of merchant-ships, which were sent for the purpose of taking up manufactured goods and releasing the produce of the inland states, which had been accumulating for some time at Corrientes.

At this conjuncture my father's part in the events on the Parana commences. But as the *Philomel*, which he commanded, worked in the summer on the survey of the Falkland Islands, proceeding during the winter with the surveys of the river Plata, a chronological record would be confusing. I shall therefore not refer further to the work in the Falklands.

H.M.S. *Philomel*, referred to in the previous chapter, was one of the beautiful Simondite brigs, and well upheld the reputation of her builder. She sailed from Plymouth on July 25th, 1842. Sulivan had put thirty tons of ballast in her, in lieu of the customary fifteen. He believed it was want of sufficient ballast that caused the one or two losses that had occurred in this class of vessel, and wrote a few days after sailing :—

"The officers * and crew are all I could possibly wish for. I am delighted with the ship ; I was never in a drier vessel."

He wrote from Rio on September 15th :—

"My men are constantly on shore without officers. There has been no case of drunkenness and no desertion I have had to disrate one petty officer, one of the best men in the ship, who had been five years in the *Beagle*, for disrespect to a lieutenant. I hope to avoid the use of the 'cat' by making them feel certain they will have it if they break rules"

He arrived at Monte Video on October 3rd, and found the unsettled state of affairs already referred to.† As it

---

* The officers were .—*Lieutenants :* Harston, George H Richards (afterwards Hydrographer). *Master :* John F. Rees. *Surgeon :* William Chartres ("one of the best in the service"). *Assistant Surgeon :* M. C. French. *Clerk :* G. W. Pickthorne. *Mids :* W. S. Sulivan and Steveley.

† An invasion of Uruguay by Rosas was expected.

was arranged for his wife to join him with his family at
Monte Video later on, he writes to her :—

"If you come out, it is settled in the gun-room you are
to go too ; but if there is any fighting, you are to be put
in a two-ton tank!"

The *Philomel* left for the Falklands on October 14th, and
returned to the river Plata on April 1st, 1843. Mr. Fegan
there joined as assistant surveyor. The town of Monte
Video was blockaded by land, and the inhabitants were
anticipating a blockade to be declared by Rosas' squadron
by sea also. The marines of the fleet were landed to
protect British property.

By this time, in order, smartness, and discipline, the
Philomel would have borne comparison with the best ships
in the service. On one occasion, having weighed very
quickly from a difficult position in answer to an unexpected
signal from the admiral, as the *Philomel* passed under the
flag-ship's stern, the flag-captain, Captain G. B. Martin, a
well-known and good officer, was standing there with a
number of officers, and hailed her, saying, "Sulivan, we
may well call her the pride of the station." The crew of
the *Philomel* were considered smarter than any of the fleet,
and she was the admiration of both French and English
officers, who would often watch to see what smart thing
she would next do.

Various stories could be told illustrating this. Once,
Sulivan, having to work the *Philomel* out to windward
between two lines of vessels, could not quite weather a
French ship at the head of one line, so he kept her on
until she seemed about to touch the ship, when, putting
the helm down, he shot the *Philomel* up dead in the wind's
eye some distance, until she cleared the Frenchman's bowsprit ; then he paid her off and sailed her clear away. A

French officer went on shore to the club, and, after excitedly
recounting the manœuvre, declared that the devil must
be on board the *Philomel*, or she could not be made to
do what she did !

Later on Sulivan received the thanks of the Lords of
the Admiralty for two years' blank returns of punishment.
This was the secret of his method of discipline :—

" I fear too often blank returns show that offences that
ought to be punished are not : it has not been the case with
us, for I have only had one complaint made to me deserving
punishment, the only case of drunkenness that has occurred
in the ship. I did not like to go from my word, as I
believe that the certainty the men felt that they would not
be forgiven if reported for drunkenness or disrespect to
an officer has been the means of preventing the necessity
for punishment   While other ships complain of not being
able to keep their boats' crews sober with officers in all the
boats, we never send an officer with them, but trust entirely
to the men, and have not yet had a case of drunkenness,
and our men are now daily going on leave, and we have
not yet had one man come off tipsy or a moment after
his time." *

When the *Philomel* returned to Monte Video, Oribe was
encamped two miles outside the town, cutting it off from
the country. But the defenders had so strengthened their
lines that there was little chance of his getting in. The
government of Buenos Ayres then proclaimed a blockade
by sea as well as by land, and " Admiral " Brown, with
a corvette, two brigs, and seven smaller vessels, was off
Monte Video. On the score of there being so many
Englishmen in the town, Commodore Purvis said he
would not permit a blockade by sea, as this would have
resulted in all foreign non-combatants being turned out to
starve, nor would he allow any firing on the town from the

* In a letter to the Hydrographer, Lieutenant Richards says, " We
cannot be other than comfortable with Captain S. Indeed, his chief
study is to make every one in the ship so."

sea. One day Brown ran in with his fleet to the inner harbour, and took possession of an island, on which was a quantity of gunpowder belonging to British merchants. The *Fantôme* and *Philomel* were ordered to go in close up to his ships. The *Fantôme* could not go in as close as the *Philomel*, which was therefore directly exposed to Brown's brig of fourteen guns, and his four vessels with two or three pivot-guns each. Brown was ordered to give up the powder, which he did, and he then ran out. Oribe a day or two after wrote a letter threatening to treat all the foreigners in Monte Video "as rebels and savages." The commodore demanded an explanation, and a guarantee for the lives and properties of British subjects Before an answer came Brown ran in again to the inner harbour.

The *Fantôme* having previously moved out, the *Philomel* alone remained close in. The British ships were cleared for action, but the others were three times as far off as the *Philomel* was ; so, had hostilities commenced, poor *Philomel* would have had to stand the first brunt of the action, and would probably have been sunk the first broadside. As Brown's vessels entered, Sulivan was told to go to the headmost vessel, order her out, and fire into her directly if she refused. He at once made her and the others lay-to Brown had replied to a message from the commodore, " I am going in for fresh meat ; if the commodore wants me out, he must take me out by force." This put the commodore in a great rage. Ordering another signal to be made to prepare for action, he said he would see Brown himself, and went in the *Philomel's* boat with Sulivan on board Brown's vessel What occurred is thus described by Sulivan :—

" Brown was standing abaft a large skylight, with only room for one to pass between it and the bulwark, and, as the commodore was very excited, I slipped in first to get between them, and the following conversation then took place :—

"*Brown.*—'How de do, Captain Sulivan? You don't look quite so much like a billy-goat as you did the last time I saw you.' (I had shaved my beard off since then)

" *Commodore* (putting a gold watch with chain and seals down on the skylight).—' Mr. Brown, if you are not out of this in ten minutes, I will sink you.'

"*Brown.*—' MISTER Brown, commodore ? I would have you to know that I am Brigadier-General Brown, and I hold a higher rank than you do.'

" *Sulivan.*—' No, no, admiral ; commodore and brigadier-general are the same rank.'

"*Brown.*—' Now, commodore, those people on shore are urging you on. Take my advice ; don't let them get you in a scrape. They will not care as long as their own ends are assured.'

" *Commodore.*—' I never got in a scrape in my life.'

"*Brown.*—'Then the more reason, commodore, you should not get in one now. Now, commodore, is it not hard that Garibaldi may come down here with his gunboats and fire on my friends on shore, and I must not come in to prevent him ? '

" *Commodore.*—' Well, I think it is hard '

"*Brown.*—' Now, commodore, to please you, I will only wait to get some beef, and will go out by sunset ; but I hope you will prevent the gun-boats coming down here.'

" *Commodore* (taking up the watch and putting it into his fob).—' Well, I don't want you to go out to-night, if you will be out by nine to-morrow morning.'

"*Brown.*—' No, no, commodore, I will keep to my word and be out by sunset '—which he was.

" All this time I was putting in an occasional word in favour of a peaceful settlement of the dispute ; but if I had not got between them, I fear the commodore and the admiral would have come to fisticuffs.

" Thus ended the battle of Rat Island.

" Brown had said he would not give way to force ; and as he could not himself fire on the British flag, he would leave with the Englishmen on board the brig, and let the others defend their flag as long as they could."

Brown admitted Oribe was in the wrong and must have written in a moment of passion. Later, Oribe wrote, saying he only meant that those foreigners who took up arms against him should be treated like others in arms. Sulivan and some other captains thought the explanation quite satisfactory; but the commodore and one or two others were not of the same opinion, and demanded a more explicit refutation of the first letter.

As previously mentioned, Sulivan was expecting his wife and three children to come out to Monte Video. They were to leave Falmouth by the March packet. Weeks went by after the date the vessel was due at Monte Video, but there was no news of her. Sulivan's anxiety was very great, especially as there had been a great storm. At length the packet leaving Falmouth a month later arrived, but brought no news of the missing ship. Sulivan used every morning to go up with his glass to the top of the cathedral tower to see if perchance she was in sight. The officers used to shake their heads and say, "There goes poor Sulivan again; but it is of no use—the packet must be lost."

At last, six weeks after her due time, Sulivan one day saw from the tower a packet with the agreed-upon signal. She had suffered in a gale, and had put into Madeira, and thus had been delayed.

Once or twice while Mrs. Sulivan and her three children were living in Monte Video, on an alarm being given that the enemy were entering, all the English ladies went off to the ships. On one such occasion, all the rest having gone, my father said he would go to the walls first to make sure there was real necessity to fly, my mother in the meantime putting the children back in bed. After going to the ramparts, he returned to say he thought the enemy were not likely to get into the town. He was astonished at my mother's coolness in putting the children to bed again, but she showed she had done so with their clothes on. So they remained, the only English family who had not fled.

They used to watch the cannonading from the flat top of the house, until one day, an old woman on the next roof to them being cut in two by a round-shot, this amusement was tabooed. Once my mother, having ridden outside the town, accompanied by my father and a French officer on foot, and skirmishing just then beginning, she induced them to take her nearer, until one of the enemy's cavalry suddenly fired at them, the ball going close between the two gentlemen The party then bolted, followed by the man, loading and firing as often as he could. Then my mother's rides were restricted to the beach inside the town. One day, when she was riding ahead of my father, a cannon-ball struck the sand so close in front of her horse that the animal in his very next stride leapt the furrow it made. So her rides came to an end altogether!

The siege still went on. Food was scarce, money still more so.

"Martin tells me they are almost starving in Monte Video. Cats three and sixpence apiece, and Parry's fat dog made into cutlets! Many even of the best families are fed entirely by the daily rations of flour and beans given them by the government It is a dreadful war, and the scenes daily going on are sufficient to make one hate the name of war for ever after Neither side can do anything decisive, so the time is occupied by trying to shoot individuals. The three hundred dismounted Gauchos— who had scarcely ever moved half a mile on foot in their lives—are the finest body of men the Monte Videans have, and they have behaved uncommonly well on every occasion. The Italians also behaved well, having never given way."

Prisoners were never taken, the lance or knife finishing all off.* What was the warfare of the elders may be

* From a letter written by B. J. S. from Paris, 1864· "In the train

imagined from the play of the children. A party of boys would divide themselves into two bands and act pursuers and pursued. Some of the pursued would fall down as if wounded, when it would be the aim of a pursuer to draw his finger across the throat of a fallen one without breaking his stride.

On one occasion (the Monte Videan horses having been all killed by the enemy or by the butcher) a request was made that the merchants would lend their horses, so that a fair show of cavalry might be made at a review in the square. About a hundred and twenty mounted men were thus forthcoming. After a short parade these made a sortie on the merchants' horses by way of the beach; passed the camp of the enemy, four thousand strong, two or three miles to the rear; killed about sixty of the enemy's men; then leisurely recrossed the river with about thirty horses and cattle that they had captured, and eight prisoners, brought in alive, besides two stands of colours.

About September the *Gorgon* got badly ashore. By very great perseverance Captain Hotham at length got her off. Parties from all the men-of-war were sent to assist the *Gorgon's* crew in digging a channel for her through the sand. A great compliment was paid to the *Philomel* in a letter written by Captain Hotham to the admiral, requesting that the men sent from one vessel might be withdrawn in consequence of the trouble they gave, but begging that, as a party of men from the *Philomel* had shown such an excellent example of order and discipline to the others, an additional number of men from that ship

. . . one foreigner turned out to be from Monte Video. He was, when a boy of fifteen, under arms during the siege. Talking over old times, I mentioned the dreadful murder of the prisoners after one battle by Urquieza, the truth of which I was sent to inquire into. I found Colonel Flores in command, and all taken were lanced to death. The poor man was much affected; the tears came in his eyes, and he said, 'Colonel Flores was my father.' Was it not a singular coincidence?"

might be sent. This was done; and after the *Gorgon* was off, Hotham applied for and obtained the promotion of one of the *Philomel's* petty officers.

Not much surveying work could be done in the Plata, owing to the acute state of affairs; but Sulivan did what he could, notwithstanding the difficulties he met with when landing men for obtaining provisions or making observations on the coast of Colonia. On more than one occasion it was necessary for him to display great firmness in facing parties of soldiers who were trying to bully his seamen and some settlers.

Lieutenant Harston left the *Philomel,* and Doyle succeeded him as first lieutenant *

On October 26th, 1844, the *Philomel* sailed again for the Falklands, Mrs. Sulivan and family going in her.

The *Philomel's* surveying expedition had been well timed, for without it the combined fleets would have been at a serious disadvantage. On April 19th, 1845, the *Philomel* returned to Monte Video from the Falkland Islands Sulivan, seeing the probability of our interfering in the local war, told Commodore Sir Thomas Paisley, to the astonishment of the latter, that he could, if necessary, take the steamers *Gorgon* and *Firebrand* up to Martin Garcia.

Up to July Sulivan was occupied in finishing his Falkland Island charts, and in adding to the survey of the Plata. In August 1845 he found a channel of fifteen feet, mean river-level, to Martin Garcia.

---

* Harston—now Captain H —was appointed to a ship on the west coast of Africa. Later on, when every officer and man in her was struck down by fever, he himself being the only one able just to crawl on deck, he shipped a lot of the Krue boys, and with them brought the ship to England in that state—a meritorious performance. Sulivan wrote of him "A correct, gentlemanly officer, setting all a good example, particularly in his method with the men and internal discipline."

On August 28th active operations were commenced by
the combined British and French squadrons operating on
the coasts of the Banda Oriental. Mrs. Sulivan, with her
children, returned to England.

At Colonia the ships had an engagement with the
enemy outside Monte Video. The latter were driven off
by the men of the fleet and the Monte Videan troops who
landed there. They then repaired the lines, so that the
Monte Videans might hold them. Sulivan, having taken a
good share in this encounter, then went across to Buenos
Ayres, and was well received by the Argentine minister
there.

"This very singular state of affairs," he writes to
Beaufort, is "owing to its being understood that we are
not at war with Buenos Ayres, but only want to turn their
troops out of the Banda Oriental. Yet we take their
vessels-of-war, and give them up to the Monte Videan
Government to be employed in direct warfare against the
Buenos Ayrean coasts. If this is not a hostile act, I
cannot think what is."

Sulivan then took the *Gorgon* and *Firebrand* up to
Martin Garcia without touching the ground, except once
where it was necessary to drag the *Gorgon* over the bar,
there being some inches less water than she drew.*

The British and French admirals, with some of the ships,
remained off Monte Video, a few of the smaller vessels
being sent on an expedition to open the Parana. Captain
Hotham, who commanded this detached British squadron,

---

* Captain Bingham, of H M.S. *Acorn*, had gone as far up the Uruguay
as Rincon Gallinos, and had to remain there to protect seven hundred
refugees, placed on the island of Viscano. He was the senior commander, and by this lost his chance of service in the Parana, Though
the service he performed was arduous, and he was frequently engaged,
he was not promoted. The master of the *Acorn*, Mr. Thomas Goss,
had surveyed the river for nine miles. The plan of holding the Rincon,
and getting a supply of cattle from it for the fleet and for Monte Video,
had been proposed by Sulivan to the minister and the admiral.

determined first to take a force up the Uruguay, to assist
the escape of other colonists reported to be hiding. The
vessels taken were the *Gorgon* (s.), the *Philomel, Dolphin,*
and *Fanny.* They were joined at the Rio Negro by the
Buenos Ayrean squadron under Garibaldi—" a regular
mosquito fleet of twenty, from a sixteen-gun brig to a
whale-boat, little more than a party of buccaneers." It
had been supposed that no vessel of more than twelve feet
could proceed for more than a few miles up the river, and
the enemy had sunk vessels in the regular channels But
Sulivan found other deeper ones, up which he took the
ships to within six miles of Paysandu. He had hard 'work
to accomplish this, constantly going ahead in a boat to
sound. Once, when the *Philomel* was ahead alone, a party
of fifteen hostile cavalry rode along the bank watching her.
Sulivan could easily have knocked them over ; but, desirous
of avoiding needless slaughter, he, instead of firing, waved
his cap to them. They returned the salutation and laughed,
seeming to enjoy the fun, and rode by the ship for some
distance, till, coming to a point, they galloped on a little
way and dismounted, as Sulivan noticed afterwards, *the off
side,* and stood apparently leaning over the backs of the
horses. As the ship came abreast of them, they fired a
volley at Sulivan, who was conning the ship from the
forecastle. The shot rattled round him, but he fortunately
escaped unhurt. The men instantly sprang upon their
horses, Gaucho fashion, lying concealed along the farther
side, and quickly disappeared over a ridge. Sulivan
writes :—

" The Monte Videans required as much watching as the
enemy '; but adds : " I am happy to say that a few days
since Garibaldi surprised a town on the Buenos Ayrean
side of the river in the night, and took every soul in it, and,
so far from putting any to death, he gave them their

liberty again when he left, merely putting a forced requisition of clothing on the place. Yet in that very town some years since, Garibaldi, when a prisoner, was tortured by being hung up to a tree for two hours by his thumbs, and then by one arm."

On nearing Paysandu, the Monte Videans, finding that even with the British force they would be far outnumbered by the enemy, refrained from attacking the place The enemy had seven hundred infantry and one thousand cavalry ; the Monte Videans three hundred men and our one hundred and seventy blue-jackets. The ships' guns were ineffectual, owing to the position of the town. Garibaldi then moved his force higher up the river, being escorted past the town by the *Philomel* and *Dolphin*, which then returned with the two other British ships. The river having fallen, Sulivan had great difficulty in piloting them down again. But he safely accomplished the task, and the ships joined the rest of the squadron at Martin Garcia. Thus ended Sulivan's service with Garibaldi, whom he singularly resembled in appearance.

The squadron destined for the Parana then assembled near Martin Garcia.

In October, owing to the breakdown in health of his excellent surgeon Dr. Chartres, Sulivan had to run the *Philomel* to Buenos Ayres. This led to an incident he always looked upon as a providential interposition, a number of circumstances all combining to save the lives of about twenty-five persons. After landing Chartres, Sulivan was delayed two days by his own indisposition. A foul wind drove him to Colonia. Seeing signs of an approaching gale, he anchored near the mouth of the St. John, the coast of which he had surveyed two years previously. A small schooner lay near him. A gale came on of such force that the *Philomel* scarcely rode it out with three anchors down. Next day nothing could be seen of the schooner, even from the mast-head. The wind moderating in the afternoon, the *Philomel* proceeded. One of the officers asked Sulivan if such a spot was not the creek they had surveyed. "No, that one," he replied, pointing his glass at St. John's. To his astonishment, in the field of the telescope appeared the schooner's masts, with a reversed ensign. She was inside the breakers at the bar of a river in the enemy's district Sulivan knew if the Blancos had got the crew, they would all have been murdered. As they got nearer, soldiers were seen on the beach, about seventy yards from her, firing at her. There was a bank of hard sand which Sulivan did not at first like to cross, but, seeing horsemen in the water a few yards from the schooner, and some armed men getting into a launch about two hundred yards from her, he went at the bank, estimating after the gale there would be just water enough for the *Philomel*. The launch was by this time close to the schooner. Another minute, and it would be too late to save the people. A thirty-two-pounder gun on the *Philomel's* forecastle being already loaded, Sulivan gave it all the elevation possible, and fired a chance shot. The ball passed directly over the boat, and hit one of the horsemen full in the chest. At the same moment the crew of the schooner poured a volley into the boat, now alongside. The double incident so frightened the Blancos that they retired. When within half a mile, Sulivan and Richards took the boats, and, crossing the bar, came to the schooner, the forty Blancos in sight not venturing to fire again. On board were fifteen men, five women, and four children. The schooner, breaking adrift in the gale, had been driven over the bar, but had brought up in the smoother water. She had been early discovered by the Blancos, who for

seven hours had been firing at the people and telling
them their throats would all be cut. Having only a few
cartridges, the crew reserved their fire. The poor people
had been all day watching the *Philomel's* masts, hoping
for succour, and had given up all hope when the Blancos
discovered the launch, it fortunately having been overlooked
previously. Then they saw the *Philomel s* signal of assistance. Besides some soldiers' wives, the wife of the commandant at Martin Garcia was on board. Too sea-sick
to remain below, she had lain all day on the deck, protected by a few boxes from the shot. One strapping
woman had shown great spirit, and had collected a pile
of stones from the ballast with which to greet the launch.
The schooner was hauled out, and she returned to Colonia,
the *Philomel* taking the women and children on to Martin
Garcia. The captain's cabin was given up to them, and
they received the first food they had tasted for twenty-
four hours. The rescue could not have been attempted
but for Sulivan's previous survey. He wrote : " It is the
most gratifying thing to me that has occurred."

The *Philomel* then joined the squadrons at Martin
Garcia, and the vessels prepared for the ascent of the
Parana.

" I am afraid," he writes to his father from the entrance to
the river (November 4th, 1845), " what Captain Villio told
you will have made you very anxious, but you will know
how little there was to do at Martin Garcia or anywhere
yet. Rosas knew that if he left a force in Martin Garcia
it must be captured, so he took all the guns up to the point
in the river where he is going to dispute the passage. I
expect we shall have some sharp work there. We know
of about twenty heavy guns and nearly three thousand
men of all arms. This sounds very formidable, we having
only a hundred and fifty marines, a hundred and eighty
English and a hundred and eighty French seamen. It
seems a serious thing to have to land and destroy their

guns ; but it must be done, or the river navigation will not be safe. Certainly I think the authorities at Monte Video have a very serious responsibility resting on them. They know the force there, and yet with six hundred English soldiers and two hundred and fifty marines at their disposal they send only seventy marines, Hotham having suggested at least a hundred. They ought to have sent the two hundred and fifty, and then we should have three hundred marines. They seem to think they want all the force to take care of themselves at Monte Video, forgetting what a serious thing any reverse up the river would be. I do not fear such a thing, but they ought to *guard against the possibility of it*, as they have the means. How the Admiralty can have acted as they have done, knowing the chance of hostilities, I cannot think. Captain Villio's note to you shows they expect it ; yet for shallow rivers the only steam-vessels we have are two of the largest steamers in the service, drawing sixteen and seventeen feet (seventeen and three-quarters feet water) ; not a single store or munition of war have they sent out The ships are even short of their usual Pease powder and shot, and there is not a single Congreve rocket in the squadron, though a few would be just the thing for this kind of warfare. The only field-piece we have to land (except one three-pounder I got and one Hope got from the Monte Videans) is one six-pounder ; and the whole supply of conical case-shot for that is twenty rounds, and not one shrapnel-shell. So much the authorities have provided for our doing the work efficiently. I hope they do not despise their enemies, for these people have during the last two years shown such courage and performed such acts of gallantry as have never been excelled "

CHAPTER IV.

THE BATTLE OF OBLIGADO.

1845-46

ON November 8th the combined British and French squadrons—composed of the ships mentioned at foot *—started on their expedition up the river. The wind was fair. The British squadron, led by the *Philomel*, composed the "port," the French, led by the *San Martin*, the "starboard" division. Owing to the strong current and the occasional grounding of ships, they only made forty miles the first day, and did not reach the ground suitable for exercising the landing-parties. So the next morning, as the wind was then foul, the *Firebrand* took the *Philomel* and *Fanny* in tow, to go on in search of a proper place. This done, on the 11th the training began. While the French sailors

* BRITISH.

	Tons.	Guns	
Gorgon (paddle-steamer) .	1111	6	Capt. C. Hotham
Firebrand (P.S.) . .	1190	6	Capt. J Hope.
Philomel . . .	428	8	Com. B. J. Sulivan.
Comus . .	492	18	Act. Com. E. A. Inglefield
Dolphin . .	318	3	Lieut. R. Levinge.
Fanny[1] (schooner) .	—	1	Lieut. A C. Key.

FRENCH.

San Martin[1]	200	8	Capt. Tréhouart.
Fulton (P.S.) . . .	650	2	Lieut. Mazères.
Expéditive . .	—	16	Lieut. De Miniac.
Pandour . .	—	10	Lieut. Du Paie
Procida	—	4	Lieut. De la Rivière.

[1] Taken from Brown's squadron.

were properly drilled to act on land, there was no such system in the English service, as may be imagined from the following description of the men who were shortly wanted to face large bodies of trained troops. It was only the simplest evolutions that were required of them, yet they were ignorant even of these. Sulivan had to hold some of the lieutenants before he could get them to understand that, as pivot-men when wheeling in line, *they must stand still.* Of one ship's company, it was discovered *not one man had been taught to use a musket* The officers and men of this large ship's company showed such utter ignorance of soldiering, that, fearing a mistake on their part in action might endanger the whole party, it was decided to do without them, there not being thought to be sufficient time to train them. However, a young officer, Lieutenant Brickdale, a supernumerary on board the ship, asked Sulivan to be allowed to try what he could do with the men. Leave being given him, he took the men out of sight of the others, and so drilled them in one week that it was thought well to allow them to join the rest.

To continue with the journals :—

"'Philomel,' forty-five miles up the Parana,
"*November 12th,* 1845.

"The men really make a good show. The orders for landing, etc, came out last night. Marines, commanded by Captain Hurdle, form one column on the right—the seamen-battalion, under Captain Hotham, cne column on the left. The companies of seamen commanded by Lieutenants Woodley, Barker, Levinge, and Brickdale. The *Philomel's* party, commanded by Commander Sulivan and Lieutenant Doyle, will form in front, and precede the columns as skirmishers. The French have been drilling apart from us, but to-morrow we all land together. It is very singular that in the Uruguay, at the mouth of the Parana, we had not one mosquito, and that the moment we enter this river we find them swarming, yet there is very little difference in the land on the banks of the river.

Even among the islands in the Uruguay we had not one.
Is it not a singular thing that all the captains of our
squadron are collegians—Hotham, Hope, Inglefield, myself,
also Lieutenant Key? The latter got the first medal, and
afterwards won his commission at the New System College
It is astonishing how the few days' drill has got the
men on. The naval battalion to-day 'marched past,' and
went through all the exercises uncommonly well, and the
'light company' were complimented on their exercise.
The officers have been laughing at Doyle being such a
good light-infantry man, he being about the heaviest in
the field ; and our 'double quick' to-day, and the constant
four hours' work, with frequent runs to get into our rallying
square, has quite knocked him up. We all feel the benefit
of this daily exercise after being cooped up so long, but
the weather is getting very warm. We are to go on on
Monday. I do hope the *Fulton* will arrive first, as there
is still a probability that she may bring news of peace ; and
however well we may succeed, it would be very sad to
think that we had any loss of life that was not necessary
to gain our object. But the desire to open the trade of this
river will, I fear, prevent the ministers coming to any
terms with Rosas, until they have by force passed up the
river "

" OBLIGADO, RIO PARANA,

" *November* 23rd, 1845

"Through the merciful providence of God I have been
preserved through scenes of bloodshed while many have
been called away. I can only give you a short account of
it, as the letters must be closed to-night. We reached our
anchorage two miles below this on the 18th (my birthday).
We saw the batteries prepared to dispute our passage. They
were certainly more formidable than we anticipated, and
were beautifully built : parapets twelve feet thick (some
more), of rammed clay—the position excellent, a slight
bend enabling them to fire both right down and across the
river. We reached the place too late to do anything on
the 18th. The boats were all sent early that day to bring
some enemy's vessels from under the land ; but on getting
near, they were found to be two miles up a narrow creek,
close under high land, with a force posted along the cliffs
all the way, and out of reach of the ships' guns. Richards,
with two of our gigs, and a French lieutenant, in his boat,

going near the mouth to examine, were fired on, and one
Frenchman was wounded. Two shots came into our gig
close to young Steveley, who was steering her. The
officers all agreed that it would not be right to risk the
loss they must have met with to destroy a few little boats
(for they were nothing more), and very prudently returned,

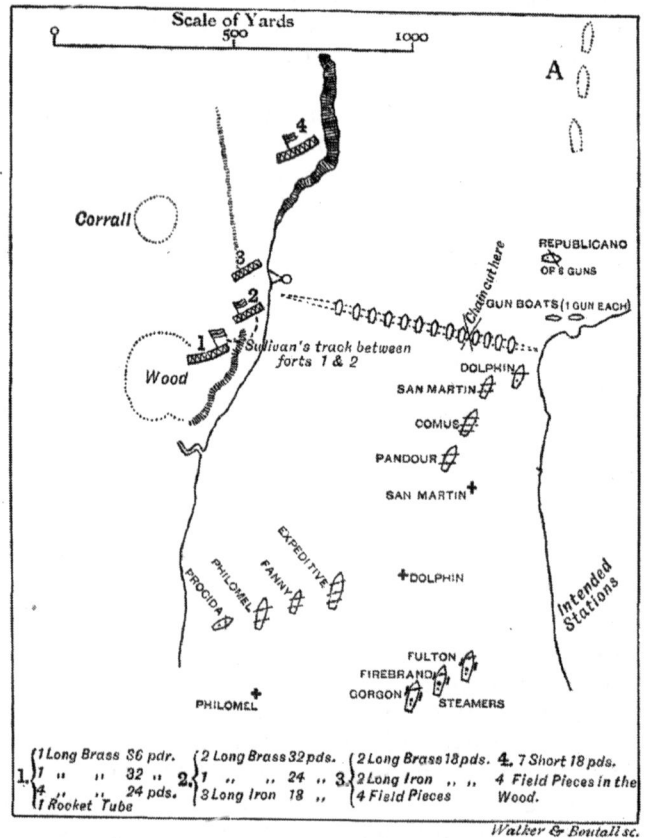

Scale of Yards

A

Corrall

REPUBLICANO
OF 8 GUNS

GUN BOATS (1 GUN EACH)

3

2

Sulivan's track between
forts 1 & 2

DOLPHIN

SAN MARTIN

1

Wood

COMUS

PANDOUR

SAN MARTIN

EXPEDITIVE

DOLPHIN

PHILOMEL

FANNY

PROCIDA

Intended Stations

FULTON

FIREBRAND

GORGON

STEAMERS

PHILOMEL

1.	{	1 Long Brass 86 pdr.	2.	{	2 Long Brass 32 pds.	3.	{	2 Long Brass 18 pds.	4.	7 Short 18 pds.
		1 " " 32 "			1 " " 24 "			2 Long Iron " "		4 Field Pieces in the
		4 " " 24 pds.			3 Long Iron 18 "			4 Field Pieces		Wood.
		1 Rocket Tube								

Walker & Boutall sc.

PLAN OF OBLIGADO.

much to my delight, as I saw the position from our mast-
head, and thought it useless to attempt it.

"On the night of the 18th I went with a French officer,
Lieutenant Mazères (each in our own boat with muffled
oars), and sounded close up to the chain and batteries,
without being discovered, though we heard them talking
on shore. Then a man in the French boat, who interpreted
for us, whispered to me, 'The captain thinks it time to be

off.' I quite coincided, particularly as several lights were shown, and I expected a shower of shot on us. The next day was spent in reconnoitring and planning the attack. I was given command of the left division, and was to lead it —the heaviest vessels (*San Martin*, *Comus*, and *Pandour*) being intended to be more abreast of the batteries, while *Dolphin* was with them to attack the enemy's vessel. It was not supposed that many guns would bear toward the left division, and we should, we thought, rake the batteries, except No. 1. We were therefore to go first, so as to cover the right division in taking their positions. On the morning of the 20th there was a fog with a light breeze ; and as the current, of three or four knots, was against us, we could not go on. At eight it cleared ; and thinking there was wind enough, Hotham made the *Philomel's* signal to weigh. Tréhouart had very handsomely ordered the two commanders of the French vessels in my division to put themselves under my orders, as if theirs were English ships. Hotham had also put our ships of the right division under Tréhouart, who was in *San Martin*. When we weighed, the *Expéditive* could not get on, and anchored again, which obliged me to wait for her. She soon came on, and we proceeded *Procida* was close to me—*Fanny*, *Expéditive*, just astern ; but we only got over the ground about half a mile an hour, so light was the wind and strong the stream. As we got near, I saw Nos. 1, 2, 3, batteries could point all the guns at us, and we saw them turning them towards us. I confess I wished all the other ships were up to share it ; but the right division were some way astern, except *Dolphin* (Levinge), who, being anchored farther up, did not wait for her division, but weighed as soon as we came abreast of her, and ran up the middle of the river. Levinge's doing so saved us from a dreadful loss. We had got within three or four hundred yards of our station, only just making headway against the stream, when a thirty-two-pounder in No. 1 fired at us (9.50 a.m.). The shot passed inside our rigging, a few feet above the ship, and cut the ensign halliards and brought down our ensign ; it was soon rehoisted, and we fired one of our bow-guns in return (we had two on the topgallant forecastle), and the next moment every gun opened on us, and a hail of shot and rockets flew past us, all either a few feet over or on one side. As young Steveley described it, they were like large cricket-balls passing us. I had just been

forward to fire a shell with the starboard bow-gun, to try
the range, and then had gone aft to look to the steering
(as we had to anchor by bearings as a guide to the others),
when I saw a crash on the forecastle. A large shot flew
past my head (we were standing straight for the batteries),
and I saw poor Doyle (who had gone to fire the gun I had
just fired before) fall back, and roll nearly off the forecastle,
while two or three other men were knocked down. A shot
had come through the gun-carriage and slide, knocking
them in pieces, and the iron splinters caused all the
damage. I thought Doyle was killed, but was soon told he
was only dreadfully wounded   The shots still came close
past, and in a minute the fore-topmast was cut more than
half through (the only shot that went high), and we were
obliged to lower the fore-topsail below the wound, and at
the same moment the main topsail-tye was shot away, and
down came the main-topsail, and she began to drop astern,
so we let go the anchor about three hundred yards short of
our position. In another moment two more shots came
through our starboard bow   Just as I was going up on the
forecastle to see what damage was done to the gun, one shot
came through under the forecastle, and knocked a fowl-
coop to pieces, the splinters and iron bars flying past in a
way I cannot describe, and knocking down two or three
more men   Our deck aft to the wheel was covered with
splinters of wood and iron. We then got two more guns
through our bow-ports under the forecastle. But all this
that I have described took place in less then ten minutes,
and was only the first burst of the batteries. And beautifully the enemy fired ; they had placed targets to practise
at before, and so knew the range exactly. The vessels in
my division anchored at the same time ; but trying to get
their broadsides to bear across such a strong tide, were all
swept away back some distance, except *Fanny*, with Key,
who kept close to us. At this time the only other vessel
up was *Dolphin* ; and she, not getting the first burst, stood
on, till, seeing her nearer and more abreast of them than
we were, the enemy turned every gun at her, except two of
the No. 1 battery. Had not Levinge been up, I am convinced we should have suffered dreadfully. At this time
there was not a steamer within a mile of us. But poor
Levinge soon began to receive the same treatment as we
had, with this difference, that it lasted longer with him, for
he went on till all his ropes and sails were cut away, and

then anchored, as he could get no nearer. He was exposed within six hundred yards to the fire of every gun, the only return to which was from her three guns, three bow-guns of *Philomel*, and one of *Fanny* In another quarter of an hour, Tréhouart, in the *San Martin*, came up, and got ahead of Levinge, taking all the weight of the fire off *Dolphin* ; but by that time the latter had been terribly handled, having nineteen men killed and wounded. The same treatment was then given to the French brig The *San Martin's* sails were rapidly disabled, but she had nearly shot the short distance to her station when her anchor was let go by a shot cutting the stoppers. *Comus*, following, had been able to reach her station near *San Martin*, where her broadside of heavy carronades would have been most effective ; but trying to use a stern-anchor as a spring, she drifted back, and brought up outside *Dolphin* in an exposed but less effective broadside position *San Martin* was thus left unsupported in her advanced position, as *Pandour* had brought up near her station, below the intended position of *Comus*. When we consider that she was a small brig of about two hundred tons, we may safely assert that no vessel of her size was—few even of any size were—ever exposed to such a trial, and certainly one never behaved more nobly. On her beam, at a distance of six hundred yards, she had a large share of the fire from the three first batteries ; on her port bow, the nearly raking fire of the seven guns of No. 4, at six hundred yards' range ; and, nearly ahead, the raking fire of the eight guns of the *Republicano* and gun-boats. Some idea of the severity of this fire may be had from the following facts : On the port bow, between her figure-head and cat-head, she was struck by thirty-six round-shot. The three shell-guns on her broadside, as well as the bow eighteen-pounders, had been rapidly disabled ; and on shifting one over from the other side, three men who tried to fire it were killed in succession before doing so ; and before another could fire it, it was dismounted, as were the other two guns shortly after they were shifted over. She was thus rendered a passive target for the enemy's guns. *Yet she kept her station !* Her cable being shot away, she drifted down a little, but again brought up in a good position. Though the other vessels were by that time coming up and opening their fire, and the steady fire of *Dolphin, Philomel*, and *Fanny* was evidently beginning to slacken the fire of the batteries, yet they poured such a fire into poor Tréhouart that his vessel became a complete wreck, with forty-four out of his one hundred men killed and wounded The other vessels could not all get up to good positions, the wind getting so light * But the steamers about this time came up, and began to throw their heavy shot and shell; and the French steamer went right on to support her senior officer, and took a very good position, by which she received much damage. Fearing damage to the machinery, it had not been intended that the steamers should go close until the chain was cut, when they were to pass the chain, and flank the batteries from above. But the signal being made by Tréhouart that she was to support him, the French steamer (*Fulton*) went right up in the thick of it near the chain. The cause of the damage to the leading ships was the lightness of the wind, which prevented all getting up to their stations, so that the batteries could take each in detail; and what we had for a few minutes Levinge had for much longer, and the French brig for still longer. But her greater loss is to be partly attributed to this: she was old Admiral Brown's brig, which we had seized with other of Rosas' vessels at Monte Video; and seeing their old vessel brought against them, it made them pick her out for a more particular share of their favours I confess, when I saw *Dolphin* and ourselves under such a heavy fire, and then the French brig and our ships coming up one by one, and also observing the beautiful way the batteries fired, I began to fear we should not pass. About 11.30 the crew of the *Republicano* deserted her in the gun-boats, and, having set fire to her, went to add to the strength of the seamen in No. 4 battery, which, from its high parapet and its position, had scarcely suffered any damage. But No 3 was nearly silenced, and the field-guns had been withdrawn, but were placed in other positions in the wood. Several guns in Nos. 1 and 2 were also silenced, but the remainder were worked as gallantly and as coolly as ever. The cross-fire on these batteries repeatedly cleared the men from the guns, but they were as quickly replaced. Carts full of dead or wounded men could be seen constantly passing to the rear of the woods. One small body of infantry appeared to be retreating, but were

---

* At 10 50 the enemy let loose ten fire-vessels, but they drifted past the ships without doing any harm.

driven back by cavalry. From the shot and shell that passed over the batteries, sweeping the ground in their rear, the slaughter amongst the troops there was also great. But we saw large bodies of cavalry and infantry retreating a little inland, and the batteries were evidently not fully manned. The enemy certainly behaved well; and one man in a white waistcoat was most conspicuous on No. 1 battery, directing the guns, standing on the parapet while the shot ploughed up the clay round him; yet he remained unhurt to the last, and was the admiration of all. But I am sorry to say we afterwards heard he was old Brown's son;* yet, though born of English parents in Buenos Ayres, he is, according to Sir Robert Peel's late decision, a Buenos Ayrean, and therefore, I suppose, has a right to fight us. The other battery that held out so well was commanded by Thorn, an American, and worked by seamen, many of whom were English; and some we have found wounded. But they said if they refused to serve they would have had their throats cut!

"But to proceed. About noon, having repaired our rigging a little, a light breeze enabled us to weigh and get closer. During the rest of the action only an occasional gun was fired at us, and our hull was never struck again. About a quarter past twelve the *Republicano* blew up. But the boats of the *San Martin* and *Dolphin* were destroyed, and they had suffered so much that they could not attempt to cut the chains, on which all now depended. So Captain Hope volunteered to do it. With three boats (calling at *Dolphin* for the armourers, who had previously practised chain-cutting) he pulled for the chain, about the seventh or eighth vessel from the island, and within five hundred yards of the batteries. In a moment there were three sets of saws at work,—one with Captain Hope cutting through the four cables on the deck of one of the vessels; the others with Lieutenant Webb, Mr. Nicholson (mate of *Dolphin*), and Mr. Commerell (midshipman), cutting the six riding-cables of three vessels, the boats' crews in the boats being sheltered by the vessels' hulls. The whole fire of the batteries appeared to be directed on the small clusters of men on the vessels' decks. Yet, though round- and grape-

---

* Afterwards understood to be Colonel Rodriguez; but Colonel Thorn's son has lately claimed the honour for his father. See page 91.

shot were driving splinters from the spars and decks on which they stood, not one man was touched, and in four minutes the ten chain-cables had been sawn through, and three vessels swung out of the line, leaving a gap nearly a hundred yards wide. From prisoners we learnt that the general had ridden to the batteries, and offered fifty ounces (£200) to the men of any gun that would knock Captain Hope down—his tall figure (six feet two inches), standing by the working-parties, making him a conspicuous object.

"The *Fulton* had before this fired away all her shot and shell, and, like *San Martin*, had become only an unresisting target for the enemy. As soon as the passage was made, the French steamer went through, and soon after *Firebrand* and *Gorgon*; then for the first time the two latter were under fire, but there were only a few guns then firing, and they received no loss, only one or two shots and rockets hitting them. Their position above now enabled them to rake the batteries. Soon after Hotham made the signal for the armed boats to go to *Gorgon*, and we all shoved off— Richards and young Sulivan * going with our party, besides myself, leaving Fegan and Brown on board, with men enough to work two guns. When the boats were pulling past the chain to go to *Gorgon*, they fired at them with grape-shot from No. 4, but did not hit any one. When I got on board, I found Hotham in great doubt about landing. We knew there had been at least three thousand men on shore, and we did not then know how much execution our fire had done; but Hotham evidently felt that the thing would be only half done if the guns were not destroyed. Hope had been to the French commandant, who said he was so cut up he could not spare any men, but if Hotham landed, as he was then coming up with two French vessels (into one of which he had shifted), he would lay them close to the batteries to cover us. Hotham asked for my opinion. I felt so much the uncertainty and the responsibility of it, also that if we failed it would give the enemy a victory; and if we left it undone, we should not really succeed in our intentions. What between the anxiety to land, and the fear of the advantage it would give Rosas if he prevented our landing, I hardly knew what to say, and for the first time I said I would rather not give an opinion,

* The late Captain W. Sulivan, his first cousin.

but if he decided on going I should be very glad to go.
Hope had previously asked to go also if we landed, though
it was intended he should command afloat. Hope and
Captain Hurdle of the marines had, I believe, been in
favour of landing. Hotham in a few minutes determined
to land, and bring it to a decisive issue.* The batteries
being flanked by woods, made it impossible to know what
force they had there. And as No 4 battery was then
firing guns, in spite of some beautiful shots thrown into
it, and as our force was reduced by the absence of the
French, and the killed and the wounded of the English,
Hotham certainly deserves every praise for his determination to try and carry the batteries when there was so much
doubt about it. The principal battery being No. 1, it was
determined to attack that first, as Nos 2 and 3 were close
down, and the ships could destroy them at any time. We
landed under these. While we were coming on shore and
forming up, they fired one or two shots from No. 4 at us;
but we were so close under they could not depress the
guns enough to hit us. I then spiked some of the guns in
No. 2,† but unfortunately forgot to haul down the large
flag with all Rosas' mottoes, though I was close to the
staff. When formed, we moved up towards No. 1, which
is on a steep slope forty feet high (I have marked in dots
the way we went up.) I had to lead with a company of seamen under Lieutenant Key of *Gorgon*, and the coverers of the
Philomel under Lieutenant Richards, who were the battery
party. Key went round, while we went right up the slope,
both arriving in the battery at the same moment. There
was not a soul in it, but a number of bodies dreadfully
mutilated by our shot. One of our men hauled the flag
down. We had scarcely shown ourselves when a sharp
fire of musketry was opened on us from the trees within
fifty yards, though we did not see a man. It is perfectly
wonderful numbers of us were not struck; but they fired
high. We poured a heavy fire into the wood, and in a

* 180 seamen and 145 marines were landed. Tréhouart, in spite of
his disabled state, managed after all to land a party of French seamen
to assist our men.

† Whilst the men were forming on the beach, he went alone into
No. 2 battery, which was open to the rear, and spiked five of the guns,
under a heavy musketry fire from the enemy. But with the sixth the
spike bent, but would not break; so, after hitting it several times, the balls
rattling round him, he jumped over the parapet unhurt. In later years
this action would doubtless have won for him the Victoria Cross.—ED.

minute or two their fire ceased. Before the marines, who
were close behind us, could get up it was all over. Key's
men then lined the wood, as ordered, while we laid down
our arms and commenced trying to break the guns'
trunnions. I first spiked the gun that had fired the most
at us, and that had done so much injury to Doyle and
others (myself and Richards, with two men, had a hammer
and a bag of spikes each for this purpose) It was a
beautiful brass thirty-two-pounder, richly ornamented I
hope to show it to you one day mounted in some
public place at home. We had just spiked them all, and
the men were trying to break the trunnions off, when just
at the flag-staff I saw one of our men, as I thought,
examining one of the dead bodies, and told him to come
away, when, to my surprise and grief, I found it was poor
Pollyblank, my coxswain, who had been close to me as
we reached the top of the slope, and must have been killed
at that moment. He was shot through the head, and only
breathed slightly for an hour, dying as we returned to the
ship. You may easily imagine what my feelings were
However, there was not much time to think of it further
than what a mercy it was that his was the only life lost,
for the balls whistled as close past our heads as possible
During this time there was some sharp firing in the wood,
where Hope had two companies of seamen. He had
entered the battery while we were firing, while the marines
stood across the rear of the battery to hold it till we could
dismount the guns. This we soon did, but could not break
off their trunnions (I am now glad of it, as we have them
on board safe as trophies) Out of six only two were
serviceable, the carriages of the others being hit by shot.
One gun was much dented in by a shot; all but one were
struck and slightly dented in. The parapet was scored up,
and the rocket-tube had two shots through it. I should
think every gun and carriage averaged three shot each
that had struck. And when it is considered that we were
at first nine hundred yards, or perhaps a thousand, off,
and never nearer than five hundred, and that the battery
was forty feet above us, it will show how beautifully we
fired: there was not much difference in any ship The
French fired well also; in fact, their countrymen may well
be proud of their behaviour altogether. With half the
number of men we had, they lost about twice as many;
but their loss was nearly all in *San Martin.*

BRITISH.			FRENCH (450 men).		
	Killed.	Wounded		Killed.	Wounded.
Gorgon ...	0	... 3	*San Martin* ...	10	... 25
Firebrand (s.)	1	... 1	*Expeditive* ...	2	... 4
Philomel ...	1	... 6	*Pandour* ...	2	.. 10
Comus ...	2	.. 2	*Fulton* .	1	... 6
Dolphin ...	5	... 14	*Procida* ..	0	... 0
Fanny ...	0	... 1			
	9	... 27		15	... 45

" The French had four hundred and fifty men altogether, and their killed and wounded were sixty, or one in seven and a half. Our loss fell on *Dolphin, Comus*, and *Philomel*, they having between them thirty killed and wounded, out of the thirty-six. Now these three ships had only two hundred and forty men in them, so that the loss in them was one in eight, very nearly the same as the French. Even *San Martin* did not lose many more than *Dolphin* in proportion ; she had thirty-five killed and wounded out of a hundred, and *Dolphin* had eighteen out of fifty-eight ; so there is not a great difference. It is singular that in such a severe contest there is not one marine killed or wounded, the whole of the marines from the ships having been sent to the steamers beforehand to be ready to land. The steamers were under fire only a few minutes in passing the chain, and that from only one or two guns ; and when the landing took place, the skirmish in the fort was over before the marines could get up.

" Perhaps I should add, as you will all be pleased with it, that when I went to Hotham, after the heat of the action was over, before the chain was cut, to suggest something to him about the position of one of the ships, he told me before all hands on *Gorgon's* quarter-deck that the way *Philomel* behaved was the admiration of every one. However, I cannot help giving first place (of the English) to *Dolphin*. The other most meritorious points were Hope's cutting the chains in the manner he did, and Hotham's determination to land and decide the thing at once, rather than risk the chance of their saying we had not entirely succeeded. Then the gallant way in which the enemy fought at first ! They certainly gained great advantage by the damage they did to *Dolphin* and *San Martin*. This would have enabled them to make out a pretty good story, but for our decisive success in landing

When we think that our loss in landing was only two killed and three wounded, it certainly was most fortunate and creditable to Hotham that he decided to try it. I forgot to say that, not liking to separate our forces, we only disabled Nos. 1, 2, and 3 batteries by dark, while their flag was flying in No. 4, and there was a skirmish going on between our boat-guards and men in the wood round No 4. It was there the *Gorgon's* man was wounded One of our boys (Payne) shot one man who was in the act of firing at him. We killed and wounded several by our first fire in the skirmish at No. 1 battery, and found them in the wood as our light company advanced.

"I must give you particulars of *Philomel's* loss Considering the position we were in, and that on board *Gorgon* the officers say that the shot rained round us so the first few minutes that they thought we must be sunk, it is indeed a most merciful interposition of Providence that prevented our loss being greater The only man killed was Pollyblank, my coxswain. Poor Doyle, though, is, I fear, mortally wounded. The fragments of a large cast-iron plate in the gun-carriage entered his side and left thigh in three places, fracturing his hip-bone, while another entered and broke his arm, and another smashed his hand ; so that if he survives the dreadful wound in the hip (which the doctors think impossible), he must lose his arm. He behaved nobly when told they were deserting the batteries , he cheered as he lay in such agony ; and when the fire slackened, and I went below for a moment to see him, he asked if we were driving them out, and seemed delighted when I told him we were. The poor fellow then said he had just been thinking how much better it was for him to be hit than me, as he had no one depending on him, as I had. This was too much for me, and I think I never felt more grief than I did at that moment. To see him so mangled and bleeding, and, as we thought, dying fast, and yet thinking of others! It really showed a noble spirit.

"I believe the enemy will never make a stand again, this has been such a lesson to them But it is dreadful to think of the carnage! In the little space we have walked about in close to the shore, there are above a hundred dead bodies, all most dreadfully cut to pieces by round-shot ; for it is a most singular thing that, notwithstanding the number of shells fired, few men have been killed by their bursting (I could only see one), while both men and horses have been killed by the shot or shell before it burst. Every hut has its proportion of dead, and we hear at first they took numbers away in carts, to prevent others being disheartened. We saw cavalry outside trying to force infantry back; and in one case an officer on horseback tried to send a party of infantry back into the wood, and they shot him and marched on. Every day we have found poor wounded wretches in the wood still alive. To-day three were found who had lain three days with limbs off, and yet alive: they have had their limbs amputated since I fear that in the large wood numbers are still actually dying of starvation, being unable to move on account of their wounds. There are men of all nations among the wounded: we find English, Americans, Spaniards, Russians, etc., and a number of poor blacks. I trust I may never again have to enact a part in such a scene; and yet I am astonished with myself, and rather disgusted at my want of feeling, that the second day I found myself moving among these bodies as unconcerned as if they were not human beings, and examining the effects of our shot. Yet when I thought how many my own hand might have put to death, it certainly made me shudder; for, as we changed our charge of powder with our distance, and the shots were not so good, I fired several myself to get the range. In fact, I fired so many that I wore off the skin of my fingers by pulling the trigger-line, because I saw it was of the utmost importance to fire so as to make them fear every shot. Sometimes we cleared the battery, when a few men would come, fire one or two guns, and either be killed or leave; but their places would be again supplied by others. Yet, with such slaughter, old Brown's son could stand nearly the whole time on the parapet without being hit. Sometimes he went and laid the gun, and whenever he did a shot went into something or another. Both *Dolphin* and we at last got quite a respect for him, and did not wish him to fall. We only hear it was Brown's son from the wounded prisoners, but of course are not certain. One of our shot had an extraordinary effect. There was a large tree with a very thick trunk, and right in a line with us behind it, in the rear of the battery, three officers had evidently placed themselves to avoid our shot, thinking the tree a protection. The ball passed through the tree, and took all three of their heads off, and they were lying in the exact line as they had fallen. The huts and houses had evidently been long inhabited, and things of all kinds were found, plenty of wine and spirits, all of which were started, even to a number of cases of champagne. Unfortunately five marines got too fond of the spirits, and are to be punished to-morrow. Only one of my marines was complained of; and Hotham paid our men a great compliment, particularly for the way we worked at the batteries. As we shoved off from *Gorgon* to land, he hailed us, and said, '*Philomel*, recollect I have picked you out to get into the batteries and disable the guns, because I know you of old, and I am sure you will do it well.'

"The next day we landed early, the French leading up to No. 4 to destroy more guns, but there was no resistance; the seven guns were rolled over into the water. At the same time I had two companies given me to go to No. 1, and try to saw through the trunnions of the guns (we had by this time disabled the carriages); but finding we could not succeed, I asked Hotham to give me a lot of men and let me try and get the guns off; so he gave me a hundred and fifty marines besides my men, while the seamen kept guard and had an occasional shot at the enemy reconnoitring. We had lots of ropes on the guns, and hauled them down to the boat by main force; and by working hard at it all day, we got them all off by half an hour after dark, the marines and seamen relieving each other. We are all delighted at our success, as they are splendid trophies, and a good set-off against our flags in Buenos Ayres. The account of them in the sketch is not quite right, as the guns are larger than we then thought they were—three thirty-two-pounders, five twenty-four-pounders, and two eighteen-pounders, all splendid old Spanish brass guns, one highly ornamented, cast in 1663, and the others about 1780, all at the royal foundry at Seville. I suppose more beautiful brass guns have never been taken We of course give half to the French, but the five we shall get will do very well as trophies.* To show how well they fired, at first, except one, not a shot passed ten feet above us, and the jib that was kept set after we anchored had seven shot through the foot of it, without any higher up but the one shot that cut the topmast.

---

* The Frenchmen's trophies are still to be seen at Paris. Ours were returned, with somewhat of an apology, on the change of government

"And now I think I have told you all except the names of our wounded. Besides Doyle, poor old Raymond, the captain of the forecastle, who was five years in *Beagle*, was dangerously wounded. A piece of iron as large as a thimble was taken out of his head (it cut the temple artery), besides which his elbow-bone is broken, but still I hope he may do well Cummings and boy Williams both severely wounded by splinters, and old Lee slightly in his back and arm, and Templeman in both arms. These are all we return ; but there are two others in the list with contusions. I did not like the idea of swelling the list too much, and therefore would not have them put in. Besides these, there were numbers with blood on the face and hands, from the multitude of slight splinters that flew about One young Scotch boy, that had just joined us out of a merchant-brig, was going up on the forecastle with the powder, as coolly as if it was his every day's work, with the blood running down his cheek Lee and one or two others, after their wounds were dressed, could hardly be kept below five minutes. There seemed more curiosity about watching our shot than fear about the round-shot that were knocking about us. The youngsters did very well ; they both went to their stations in the tops for furling, when we anchored, as eagerly as usual, and Steveley hailed me that the fore-topmast was nearly gone, just as he would to let go a rope. W. Sulivan hoisted the ensign directly after the halliards were shot away ; and as it was hoisted, and the shot went through it, old Hall, the quartermaster, proposed that it should not be repaired, but should be hoisted with the hole in it when we went home. It was very singular that one of the first shots fired at us should nearly have killed Doyle ; and the first fired at *Comus* took poor Lieutenant Brickdale's head off as he was firing the forecastle gun, and it killed the powder-boy, but did not touch the ship One of the first fired at *Expéditive* knocked her thirty-two-pounder off her forecastle, killing the lieutenant who was going to fire it. Only one other officer was killed, and he was a fine young man—G. Andrews, clerk in charge of *Dolphin* She had had her cable shot away, and drifted some way off ; but the firing was then nearly over, and he had just said how wonderfully they had escaped, when a round-shot came through below and killed him in the gun-room, where he was assisting the doctor."

The casualties among the British officers were as follows :—

> Lieutenant C. Brickdale, *Comus*, killed.
> G. Andrews, Clerk, in charge *Dolphin*, killed.
> Lieutenant Doyle, *Philomel*, wounded severely (died)
> R. Warren, 2nd Master, *Dolphin*, wounded slightly.
> J. Gallagher, Assist. Surgeon, *Dolphin* „   „
> T. Ellstob, Assist Clerk, *Dolphin*   „   „
> Lieutenant Key, *Fanny*   „   „

It may be well here to add extracts from Captain Sulivan's evidence before the Royal Commission on Coast Defences, 1860. He used the statements to show how difficult it was to stop vessels passing batteries, also to show how batteries should be constructed, as well as the value of vertical fire over direct fire at forts. His reduced charges really turned his guns into howitzers. Some conclusions may be drawn therefrom bearing on modern warfare.

"They could not sink the vessels, in consequence of the smoothness of the water. The *San Martin* had a hundred and six round-shot through her hull, and the greater proportion in the copper above the water. The nearer the water-line the thicker the shot, which was the only reason a man was left on her deck. They did not strike so much above ; they fired at the water-line. If she had heeled six inches, she would have gone down ; but there was not one shot under water. Yet I believe that as long as there had been a single sail set she could have gone by."

"The batteries were built by a Russian engineer, entirely of rammed clay, with a sixteen-feet parapet ; and so perfect were they, that a cross-fire from vessels even in eight hours could not silence them ; and only those guns that were behind parapets, where the embrasures were not deep enough and the parapets high enough to shelter the men's heads, or to cover the guns sufficiently, could be silenced,—not by injuring the guns, for after eight hours the principal battery had only one gun injured; it was only accomplished by cutting off the men's heads and shoulders by careful parapet-firing from the ship."

"I do not think shell-fire would succeed in stopping a ship going by a battery. I may add that so little effect had a fire on one battery, which had a parapet a foot above the men's heads (the only one of the kind), that, though two of our heavy steamers, after the booms were passed, got very close on its flank, where the guns could not fire on them, and were for three or four hours with four heavy guns flanking it, besides all the direct fire on it, not the slightest impression could be made on it, and hardly a man was hurt."

"We had not concussion-shells then. The fuse-shells were evidently so wasted against the earthwork, that, after I had fired twelve myself carefully at one battery, finding that they either went into the parapet without bursting, or, if they passed the least to the rear, burst beyond the men, and that it was only wasting the shell, I would not fire any more, and I confined myself to shot with reduced one-pound charge, fired as close as possible over the parapet, to drop them into the battery.* There was one remarkable case there to show what a steam-vessel could stand. The French steam-boat *Fulton* (six or seven hundred tons) went up to cover her chief, who was suffering dreadfully, and anchored between him and the batteries The boom not being cut, she was detained there for, I think, three hours. They put fifty-six heavy round-shot into her paddle-wheels and sponsons; they destroyed every particle of the wheel nearest the side, both the wheel and the paddle-beam, so that the shaft only had a mass of broken iron to heave round; and yet, when the chains were cut, she was the first that went through with her one remaining wheel, and she afterwards came down and repassed the batteries, to tow up some other vessel with her one wheel. Though three round-shot went in among her engines, they did not do any damage."

"There were eight hundred men, by their own account, killed and wounded, out of three thousand; but they were nearly all struck by round-shot in the batteries as fast

* He likened it to a boy lobbing stones over a wall, and afterwards always used this incident as an argument in favour of the advantage of vertical over direct fire against such forts.—ED.

as the men were brought in, and we believe from the deserters' accounts that the loss was very much greater"

"*Were any of the guns which you speak of 'en barbette'?*"—"None, though they were all in embrasures; and, with the exception of one battery, the mistake had been made of not raising the parapet enough, which left the men's heads and shoulders showing over it, and left the guns exposed to direct fire, so that we saw the breech of the gun over the parapet very well."

Captain Key: "*Do you know how many guns we had engaged at that time?*"—"Not reckoning one which was disabled, and only fired two shots, we (*Philomel*) were only firing three guns at the batteries; the *Dolphin* fired two; then there was one long thirty-two-pounder in *Fanny*, and the *Comus* had two thirty-two-pounders. One French vessel had six shell-guns (three on one side); and when they were all knocked over, she shifted the other three, and the whole were disabled in an hour. That makes fourteen. There were about sixteen thirty-two-pounder, medium and long guns in the sailing-vessels. In the steamers there were one ten-inch, two heavy sixty-eight-pounders, and one thirty-two-pounder. Those were the most that bore at any one time. And there were about thirty carronades, twenty-four and thirty-two-pounders, on the broadsides of other vessels [almost ineffective]" *

Dr. Niddrie, the surgeon of the *Gorgon*, went in a small gig through the thickest of the fight from ship to ship to aid the surgeons in the ships suffering most. When he found his own ship had later on passed the batteries, he followed her under fire against a four-knot stream His conduct was admired by both French and English, yet, being unmentioned in the despatches, he was not rewarded, in spite of Sulivan's later efforts on his behalf. Twenty-five years after, my father was telling the story to some young doctors in the Turkish baths at Blarney.

* Captain Sherard Osborne wrote in 1861, referring to this action "My argument amounts to this. If you with brigs and corvettes can fight such an action against an enemy firing shot and come off victors, whilst our huge ships were repulsed at Sevastopol without one being sunk, that the only way to account for it is by the moral effect of the shell and hot shot fired at the ships." (Hence the need of armour.)

One of them afterwards, in my presence, went up to a lady visitor at the establishment, and said, "We have been hearing the story of a Dr. Niddrie who was at Obligado. Was he any relation of yours?" "*My husband!*" She told my father that, disappointed at being passed over, really because he had bravely spoken out when it was his duty to do so, he retired into private practice soon afterwards, but did not survive his disappointment many years.

Sulivan, in his pamphlet on "Honorary Rewards," speaking also of Captain Tréhouart, says, "His noble conduct was the admiration of all, and the cordial, frank, and thoroughly straightforward manner in which he acted towards his allies throughout the expedition was beyond all praise." For this action Captain Tréhouart was promoted to the rank of admiral. It is a pity our rules do not admit of a similar promotion for special naval service.

Hotham gave Sulivan the flag the latter had hauled down under fire. In 1883 the authorities at Buenos Ayres returned a British flag, supposed to be one of the 71st Highlanders', captured from them in 1807 (but afterwards proving to be one taken from one of our merchant-ships). Sulivan then, through the Argentine consul in London, made a return of his flag. It will be seen, from the following copy of his letter to the consul, he thought the defender of the battery was Rodriguez. But after my father's death Admiral Brown's grandson wrote claiming the honour for his father. It will be seen in these journals that Brown was the name originally mentioned, so there is evidently some uncertainty about the matter.

"BOURNEMOUTH, 1883.

"At the battle of Obligado in the Parana, on November 20th, 1845, an officer in command of the principal battery excited the admiration of those English officers who were nearest to him by the manner in which he encouraged his men and kept them to the guns during a heavy cross-fire, under which that battery more especially suffered. For more than six hours he walked the parapet of the battery exposed to his feet, except when he occasionally left it to point a gun himself. From wounded prisoners of his regiment we afterwards learned that he was Colonel Rodriguez, of the Buenos Ayrean Regiment of Patricios. When all the artillerymen were killed or wounded, he manned the guns with men of his infantry regiment to near the close of the battle, losing five hundred killed and wounded out of the eight hundred men of his regiment. When the English seamen and marines landed in the evening, and first took that battery, he and the remainder of his regiment alone, of all the defending force, held the position in the rear of the battery, notwithstanding the heavy cross-fire of all the ships through the woods in the rear of the batteries, and were the last to retreat. The flag of the battery he had so nobly defended was hauled down by one of the men with me, and was given to me by the English senior officer, Captain Hotham When hauled down, the flag fell on some of the bodies of those who had fallen, and was stained with their blood. I have lately seen a statement that an English regimental flag, that had been in the possession of an Argentine family since the war of 1807, has been restored to the regiment by a member of that family. I am desirous of following that example by restoring to Colonel Rodriguez, if alive—or if not, to the Patricio Regiment of Buenos Ayres, if still existing—the flag that so many of their regiment nobly fell under in the defence of their country. If Colonel Rodriguez is dead, and the regiment does not now exist, I would ask any of the surviving members of the colonel's family to accept it in remembrance of him, and of the very gallant conduct of himself, his officers, and men at Obligado. Those of us opposed to him who had witnessed his self-devotion and gallantry were very glad indeed to hear afterwards that he had escaped unhurt to the end of the action.

"B. J. Sulivan, *Admiral*."

CHAPTER V.

ASCENT OF THE PARANA.

AFTER Obligado, the men of the squadron had been destroying and burning all on shore that was of no use to them. Sulivan, with eighty men, searched the woods and houses, and exchanged a few shots with a party of cavalry. Captain Hope went on with three boats to attack a schooner (the *Chacabuco*), and sent a lieutenant back for more boats and men, who were to come up another channel, to prevent the schooner escaping that way. The French commander, thinking it too hazardous, refused his boats, for the vessel had three pivot twenty-four-pounders and eighty men, and there was another vessel with two guns. Hope had only three boats and forty men, and went with such a strong tide, that, if he failed in his attack, he could not escape, there being a chain of boats across at the spot. Sulivan thought his friend Hope was wrong to go with such a small force, when by waiting a day or two he could have got other boats and the *Fanny*. He wrote, "There may be occasions when, to save an army, or a ship, or to prevent a defeat, it may be right to risk a number of lives against great odds"; but he thought this attempt was not justified. Being anxious, Hotham sent the *Firebrand* and two of the *Philomel's* gigs under Richards, and also Sulivan to take the lead, in case Hope had been defeated. Fortunately Hope, having heard there were two hundred men with the schooner, did not attack. The incident, together with the following remarks, may be recorded for the sake of the lesson they convey :—

"It would be a dreadful thing to have three boats destroyed, and such a number of men with poor Hope and others, when the sacrifice is not necessary. My own mind is made up not to care for what people may say or think ; but if I am sent on service, and have reason to think that, from the position, force, or other causes, the losses are likely to be more than the thing is worth, I will not attempt it, and I do not think that any man with proper prudence and reasoning faculties would.   I hope the breeze will enable me to get on to-morrow, as *Philomel* may be able to get up to the vessels, if *Firebrand* cannot ; and then we might cause the enemy to do what I wish to see, as it would save bloodshed—that is, destroy their own vessels and go on shore.   Our point would then be gained without risk to ourselves or to others.   I never got hold of a Falkland bull by the horns, but by his tail, because I thereby accomplished my purpose with less risk to myself, and this I *think* should be one's object on occasions of this kind."

On December 3rd they were nearing Rosario, where resistance was expected. " We are all living on salt meat, while thousands of head of stock of all kinds are looking at us from the shore." Doyle was doing so well that it was resolved to take off his arm. He bore it wonderfully. Lieutenant Mackinnon, in his book, mentions the wonderful healing power of the Parana air, despite the heat. The *Firebrand* was chasing the *Chacabuco* and two other schooners, which the enemy were trying to save, towing them up-stream with horses. After a long chase, when close to them, the steamer struck on a bar. Not knowing this, the enemy blew up the *Chacabuco*.

" Directly these vessels * are gone, the rest go on up

* *Comus* was returning to Obligado, *Dolphin* and *Fanny* to Monte Video for boats and to convoy merchant-vessels up the river.

the river as fast as possible. When we get a little higher, the French chief goes into the steamer, and *San Martin* remains in the river at that place. A little higher, at Punta Gorda, *Firebrand* leaves us, and she then takes charge of the river, visiting the different ships and places occasionally, so as to keep the river open. Hotham will probably take *Gorgon* or *Philomel* on to Corrientes and Assumption in Paraguay, where no vessel-of-war has ever yet been. It is certainly the most interesting trip ever undertaken. The Paraguayan people have for years been shut out of all intercourse with the world by the tyranny of Dr. Francia, and since Francia's death Rosas has kept the river shut up; so that, except to a few people who reached it, and were imprisoned in the country for years by Francia, it is really a new country. Our only attempt to open diplomatic intercourse with them failed through the folly of the person sent ; and now, if we are able to reach them with the steam-vessels, and give them some idea of what the opening of their river may lead to, it will be a most important event. It is singular this chance should have fallen to my lot. You may recollect I asked before I left England to take the *Philomel* up, and was told it interfered too much with the internal policy of these states   I have often since said that the only thing that should tempt me to serve again would be the command of a vessel to go to Paraguay, should any mission ever be sent there. But I have not finished about our plans. If it is found that there is every chance of getting *Gorgon* up to Assumption, *Philomel* will be left at anchor in the river ; but I go on with Hotham in *Gorgon*, so that the plan of the river and observations, etc., may be carried on all the way up   If anything after all prevents *Gorgon* getting right up, we can go on in the tender ; but I hope *Gorgon* will get up, as she is such a very large ship, that her getting so far up will have a great effect on those who have never seen a vessel larger than a small coasting-vessel. When the Paraguayan envoys were at Buenos Ayres and saw the *Pearl*, they were astonished, and said, 'Why did you not send Mr. Gordon [the British envoy] in a vessel like this, instead of smuggling him across the country in a cart?' and they expressed their wish that such a vessel could be seen at Assumption. What then will they say if they see the *Gorgon* there ? It will be a most interesting thing. We shall be eleven hundred miles from the sea, in one of the most splendid

countries in the world, where the largest population of any
South American state have been shut out from all communication with the rest of mankind, and with whom (if
we can establish commercial intercourse) a trade may be
opened that will materially tempt our manufacturers, and
through them all classes of our people ; in fact, would more
than compensate for any loss our trade may suffer through
the Brazilians not taking our goods, as in that case the
whole of Brazil could be supplied with them through
Paraguay and Corrientes, where the frontiers are so extensive that the Brazilians would find it impossible to
prevent smuggling to any extent.

"*December 4th.*—I am thankful to say that, instead of
meeting with any resistance at Rosario, we found all the
inhabitants—men, women, and children, as well as many
soldiers—outside their houses on the slope, to see the (to
them) wonderful sight of such a squadron passing. From
some people who were in Rosario since our action at
Obligado we have heard many particulars. They lost
four hundred men killed (I suppose this includes wounded)
But the most important thing is that numbers took advantage of the defeat to desert, having probably been
years from their homes, compelled to serve, and, belonging
to the distant inland provinces of Cordova, Tucuman, etc.,
they were glad of the chance to get away. Out of all
the two thousand five hundred to three thousand troops
Mancillia had the day of the action, he has only been
able to collect four hundred under arms ; so that, allowing for the killed and wounded, nearly two thousand
men must have deserted   They went off in large parties
for their homes ; in fact, every one belonging to the
distant provinces that could get a good horse started off
All this will have a great moral effect. And if it is true (as
we hear) that Prudentia Rosas (Rosas' brother), who was
sent against the 'rebels' at Santa Fé, has joined them against
Rosas, why, the thing is up with him altogether. From what
we hear, it is not likely that we shall meet with any more
resistance up the river. We also hear that they knew all
our plans through Monte Video, and they were quite prepared for our landing, and they had still, when we landed,
two large bodies of troops drawn up in the rear out of
fire. When we were landing, the general having, as he
thought, got one body to advance, went to the other to get
them to go on ; but while he did this, the first body had

gone to the right-about; and out of all the force, only the men that resisted us in the battery at first could be kept. There were about two hundred and fifty men. Had they stood well, they would have caused us much loss; for the advance that I took into the battery was not more than fifty-five men. They might easily have overpowered us, and driven us back down the slope, had they come out of the wood and charged us, as our men, having to scramble up a steep slope, arrived in the battery out of all formation, and the marines were then a little way behind. But I suppose that they were panic-stricken at seeing such rushing into the battery, and thought that we were much stronger than we really were."

In a letter written on board the schooner *Obligado*, off Esquina (December 21st, 1845), he describes the ascent of the Parana, the ships struggling with a contrary breeze against a current of three to four knots, the thermometer eighty-eight in the cabin. The rate of progress was about ten miles a day, sometimes the ships being warped at the rate of a mile in four hours, at others being hauled along the bank, when they did a mile an hour. As many of the men showed symptoms of scurvy, they were anxious to press on to Esquina, the farthest point occupied by the Corrientino forces—therefore the first where fresh meat could be obtained. By the giving way of a bank, Sulivan fell into the four-knot stream. He had hold of a twig. A man coming to help him also went overboard, and caught him by the arm, and said he could not swim. Fortunately the twig held until assistance came. The ships soon passed the *Fulton* ashore, and pushed on to Goya, Hotham and Tréhouart having started on horseback for Villa Nueva, the headquarters of Paz. Three Corrientino gun-boats came to meet the ascending vessels.

"It is certainly a satisfaction to be taking up the first British flag—the first vessel-of-war of any nation that has been up the river. The mosquitoes are troublesome . . .

trying to get the latitude by stars, with my head and neck black with the flies, while I held the sextant, which I had to put down every moment to brush away the mosquitoes."

The French steamer coming up, gave them a tow, but ships were constantly touching the ground. They reached Goya, the second place of importance. There being not water enough near the town, they had to go eight miles above it, where they found an encampment of Paraguayan troops

"Most important things have occurred lately, affecting the politics of these countries. The government of Paraguay, having failed on every side to get Rosas to acknowledge their independence, and give them the free navigation of the river, at last have made a treaty with the Corrientinos, by which they assist them in their war against Rosas with all their means, and offer as many men as are wanted The vanguard of their army, two thousand five hundred men, arrived two days before us, and the vessels bringing the second division are daily expected. We are now anchored fifty yards off their tents ; and it is altogether a most interesting subject, when we consider that for thirty years Dr. Francia, the dictator, not only shut up Paraguay, but by a system of terror also shut up the ideas and minds of all the inhabitants, and that till his death occurred four years since no one dared even to express his thoughts on any public question. It is most interesting to observe what the effect of being brought up under such a system has on the character of the people. . . . Paz takes all his Corrientino troops against Rosas ; he has about six thousand that he can advance with, and Lawrence says they are the best he has seen in these countries, some fit to be compared with English troops. Hotham and Lawrence, with the French captain, returned from the army the day we arrived here, and are staying at Goya, which is about eight miles off. . . . The manifesto of the Paraguayan Government declaring war against Rosas is very well and sensibly written. It points out to the world how they had tried for years to obtain from Rosas the recognition of their independence, and the free navigation of their river, the only highway they have for foreign trade. All they could obtain from him was a denial of their independence, and a declaration in which the province of Paraguay was termed one of the Buenos Ayrean states—a thing it never had been, having been independent from the first year the Spanish dominion was overthrown   Having explained all the negotiations which were entered into, and the determination of Rosas to deny their independence and prevent their trade, the manifesto goes on to show that, should Rosas conquer the Banda Oriental, he can assert all his forces against Corrientes, which, though it has held out for so many years against him, may be overpowered, in which case the Paraguayans may feel certain that Rosas would then invade them, to endeavour to force them to become part of the Buenos Ayrean confederation, and that it was better to assist Corrientes—which was the outpost of Paraguay—than risk its being conquered, and then the horrors of war carried into their own country.

"On January 2nd the authorities of Goya gave a grand ball in honour of our visit; and as the thermometer was above a hundred, they rigged up a very nice place under a canvas roof."

Again he writes on January 15th, describing a week's hard work piloting the *Gorgon*, with *Philomel* and *Fanny* in tow, up the Parana. Very hard work indeed it was for him and the master of the *Gorgon*, they having at the least difficulty to go ahead in boats to find the channel—on the paddle-box or in the boat, under a burning sun, from 4 a.m until 7.30 p.m. At one place, after three hours in the boats, he gets *Gorgon* over passes with only one foot under her keel. They were anxious to push on fast; for many men in *Gorgon* —though none in *Philomel*—were down with scurvy, one man having died. They had no lime-juice, and had been three months on salt provisions. Providentially, Sulivan saw and successfully chased two cows swimming in the river, which gave three days' fresh meat to all Captain Hotham then decided to leave the *Gorgon*, and to go on in the schooner with Sulivan as fast as possible, the latter to survey the upper river. Lieutenant Richards, taking command of the *Philomel*, was to go in her to Esquina, a distance of forty miles, to procure the much-needed beef for the *Gorgon*, etc During the time of Sulivan's absence, Lieutenant Richards continued the work of survey and pilotage in the *Philomel*.

Sulivan, in the schooner, arrived at Corrientes from Goya on January 20th, Hotham having gone on in the French steamer to Assumption, the capital. News had come that Paz was retreating before Urquieza. Rosas had sent a large force, and appeared inclined to try the issue of a battle, with the object of gaining possession of the produce before the convoy arrived. If he succeeded, he would upset the policy of our ministers, and make the victory of Obligado useless. This had never been anticipated by our authorities. Numbers of merchants were calculating to make fortunes out of the expedition. But their goods could not be landed if there was any fear of Rosas succeeding. Rosas' force had already got so near Goya that that place had been abandoned. Sulivan feared —as did take place—that Rosas might get possession of the cliffs and intercept the convoy on its way up. He was anxious for Hotham's return, as there were no instructions for the combined fleet to attack Rosas' army. Paz was a prudent general, who had never lost a battle, because he never allowed himself to be drawn into a combat at a disadvantage. The female population of Goya had taken refuge in ships.

"CORRIENTES, *January 25th*, 1846.

"It is really sad to see even here the poor families in terror talking of embarking—large families of females (the males being all with the army) with no one to protect them or assist them, and all knowing what treatment they would receive if taken in the town. There are about ten thousand inhabitants, of whom nearly all are women and children; and even were all the men (six thousand) now with the army at their homes, such has been the destruction in the constant civil wars, that there are in the provinces six females for one male."

The *Gorgon* had been left three hundred miles below Corrientes, above passes with only just water enough for her, and two hundred miles from the squadron off Santa Fé. Above the *Gorgon*, at Corrientes, Captain Hotham and Captain Tréhouart had only a small French steamer, a brig, and a schooner. At this crisis news arrived that the army of Rosas had invaded the province, defeated the army friendly to us, and was marching on Corrientes, having already reached a point on the river nearly two hundred miles above where the *Gorgon* was left among the islands. As it was impossible to leave Corrientes undefended, and also important to get the *Gorgon* down at once, and bring up the smaller steamers expected from England, Captain Hotham was in a very anxious state. Sulivan saw that, unless he went down himself, *Gorgon* could not be moved, and no other vessels could ascend the river until the convoy—all sailing-vessels— worked its way up. He therefore offered to go in the dinghy with two boys, going as much as possible through the islands, and trusting to escape notice in places where he would be obliged to pass the main bank of the river. Captain Hotham at first refused to sanction it, as he thought the risk too great; but eventually he allowed Sulivan to proceed. Sulivan thus describes his adventurous expedition :—

"CORRIENTES, *February* 28th, 1846.

"Hotham returned from Paraguay on January 28th, but determined to remain here till the result of the invasion was known; and yet he wanted *Gorgon* taken down the river before it fell. Having only the schooner with few men, he could not spare any to send down; and

seeing he was pushed how to manage it, I offered to
go down in the *Philomel's* dinghy with my steward and
boy. He was very much pleased. It is three hundred
miles from this to *Gorgon*; but I took advantage of a
small vessel going to Goya, and so saved half the voyage
in the dinghy. From Goya to *Gorgon* was a hundred
and fifty miles: it took us two days and nights in the
dinghy. You would have been amused if you had seen
us start. I had in her all my clothes, instruments, chrono-
meters, tiger-skins, etc. Horn and Worthing composed
the crew. We could not venture to land in the night
for fear of tigers, and, still worse, mosquitoes; but we had
some preserved meat and biscuits for provisions. I was
never more tired of anything than I was of sitting so long
in a boat without moving. We anchored a few hours one
night to get a little sleep. The day after we reached
Gorgon we started in her down the river. It was the most
anxious work I ever had—very narrow channels with
numerous banks, a three- and four-knot stream setting
down, and a heavy ship that took many minutes sometimes to answer her helm. Some of the bars had only
six inches or one foot more water than she drew, with a
very hard bottom; but we got over all these well, and
I began to think we should have no mishap. But at
last, running along a narrow channel in a bay close
to high cliffs, she would not answer her helm, and ran
on shore with all the force of steam and stream, within
fifty yards of cliffs on the enemy's shore—a nice position, had they attempted to molest us. You may fancy
my anxiety for the two days it took us to get off. The
river fell six inches a few hours after we went on shore;
and had it gone on falling, *Gorgon* would have remained
there at least till next year. But the next day it rose
again, and *Dolphin* and *Fanny* arrived with the convoy,
and with their assistance and three bower-anchors out we
got off. Having done this, I took *Dolphin* and *Fanny*
back with me, as I knew then that Hope, who commands
in the river during Hotham's absence, and who was to
have been at the Baxada to station the vessels, was not
coming up, as there were batteries lower down he wished
to pass near, and therefore I had to station the vessels, so
as to provide for this difference in the plans. Rosas had
prepared all the force he could to attack the convoy
coming up; and knowing now that permanent batteries

were of no use, as we were sure to take them, he adopted
the much wiser plan of movable artillery, and had about
twelve heavy field-pieces, with about two thousand men, at
the cliffs of San Lorenzo, which are about four miles long,
about seventy feet high, and the vessels had to pass within
a quarter of a mile of the cliff the whole way.   The ground
behind being quite level, nothing can be seen from the
river but the cliff, so that all the men are safe from the
fire of the vessels, unless looking over the cliff.   There
were sixty vessels.   The *Dolphin* led with the first division
of the convoy, Key in *Fanny* with the next division, while
Hope was behind to cover them   [With a light breeze
they were stemming the tide only at the rate of one or
two knots.]   The guns kept galloping up to the cliff, just
showing the muzzle over, firing, and then withdrawing
again, and, when loaded again, appearing at a new place.
In this way they pounded the convoy for three hours in
passing, hitting every vessel several times.   One merchant-
brig had thirty-four shots in her—*Firebrand* twenty-two,
four through her funnel ; yet providentially no one in all
the sixty vessels was killed, and only two in *Firebrand*
wounded.   Hope had a very narrow escape ; his seat on
the paddle-box was shot away, and the ridge-rope he was
holding on by shot close to his hand.   Yet so well did the
enemy work their guns that it was quite impossible to hit
them, the muzzle only showing for a moment, and then
going to another place ; so that before we could get a gun
trained at it, it had fired and disappeared.   If the ships
fired a foot too low, the shot buried itself in the cliff ; if a
foot over, it went inland over the heads of all the troops.
Though the *Dolphin* and *Fanny* fired fifty rounds a gun,
and the French corvette *Coquette* also, they do not think
they did the enemy the least damage.   At the end of the
cliff the channel veered right away, and the vessels all had
to turn their sterns to the cliff ; and they would have
suffered much there had not there been a little rising
ground behind the cliffs, so the enemy could not bring a
gun to that point without exposing it.   Levinge remained
near that point in the *Dolphin*, and directly they brought
two guns there in sight, one of his shot either struck one
of the guns or went so close to it that they withdrew them,
and did not attempt to bring any more there, which saved
the vessels from the worst fire they would have received.
The enemy fired beautifully, and worked the guns as

smartly as the best artillery in the world could have done
If Rosas adopts that kind of warfare, he may give us great
trouble, as we can do him little damage ; but it costs him
so much in shot and powder, and he is afraid to trust his
guns too far from Buenos Ayres, for fear of the Orivinus
rising, so that this was merely got up for the convoy, Rosas
being bitter at vessels of all nations availing themselves
of our protection to force the trade he has always pro-
hibited, and he has declared the people on all these vessels,
except the French and English, who are only enemies, to
be pirates, and orders all his authorities to treat them as
such.   There are many American vessels among them.
Tom Hamilton is in one, and he does not half like passing
down again ; two young Lafones are also in other vessels,
and many amateurs who never expected such a fire on
them.   One Italian buried himself up to the neck in a
cargo of salt, and a shot nearly took his head off, and he
got so pickled that he has been ill ever since ! At Tonnelero,
a little lower down, they had four guns, and fired a good
deal   One shot took the leg of a French midshipman ; but
that was the only damage,—he is doing well.*

"Having reached the Ianito (?), I left *Gorgon* there, and
took *Dolphin* on to *Philomel* at the Baxada, and you may
fancy our delight when the next morning the *Alecto*
arrived direct from England, and bringing the mails ; but
our pleasure was much damped by hearing of the death of
poor Doyle and of Chartres.   Doyle had nearly recovered,
when, by a mistake either of the surgeon or the druggist,
he was given five grains of morphine at once. enough to
kill three men   The quantity made him vomit it up again ,
but the excitement caused an artery in the stump of his
arm to break out afresh, and put him to the pain of
another operation : the consequence was, he could not stand
it, and, after three weeks more, he sank under it.   We also
heard that both the young officers of Captain Tréhouart

---

* From the Defence Commission evidence, illustrating how ships
can pass batteries· "I may mention one thing, which Captain Key
perhaps would not like to mention—namely, that in his little brig, after
passing with the sixty vessels, mistaking the signal, he repassed the
cliff, and, finding it a mistake, had again to repass alone against the
fire of all these guns which had been pounding the whole sixty vessels ;
and though they hulled him repeatedly, he went by at about two knots
over the ground. Now if that can be done with a light breeze, and
with small vessels, what would not a steamer do passing rapidly, at
the rate of ten knots ? "

had died of their wounds, one from not having his leg cut
off soon enough, every case of amputation from the action
having recovered. We were sorry to hear that, after Martin
had organised a force, and after three months' trouble had
got possession of Maldonado, Flores with the Monte
Videan soldiers against positive orders went outside and
was surrounded and defeated by the enemy, having two
hundred infantry cut off and put to death   This obliged
Martin to give up Maldonado again and embark.   I
had not even time to read my letters before we were
off again in the *Alecto* for Corrientes.   We did not wait an
hour. She was ordered to wait Hotham's coming down at
Liguina ; but I thought, knowing his ideas and wishes, I
had better take on myself to alter this, and take her to
Corrientes, and I was obliged to go in her, for her pilot
would not take charge of her above the Baxada, as she
drew so much water for the upper passes.

"We reached Corrientes in the *Alecto*, having only
grounded once in a distance of four hundred miles : that
once detained us two days.   I sent Lieutenant Mackinnon
on by land with the mails.   He rode the hundred miles
in the afternoon of one day and the forenoon of the
next.   The people of Corrientes were delighted at an
English steamer arriving, and have been flocking on board
her, hundreds of ladies coming and going as fast as possible.
Sometimes the engine-room was so crowded with them
that there was no moving.   I am happy to say we all go
down the river shortly, as Urquieza has returned out of the
province, and there is no more fear of its being conquered.
But I must tell you the further particulars about the
invasion. Paz retired before Urquieza till he was nearly in
the extreme of the province. Unfortunately, through the
rashness of General Madanager, who commanded the rear-
guard of Paz's army, it was surrounded, and had to disperse
to escape, Madanager being taken prisoner. This misfortune injured our cause very much, and broke the confidence of the army—besides which, even among themselves,
there have been intrigues and disputes that have bothered
Paz very much, and no doubt prevented his success.   Still,
he was able to harass Urquieza so much, that at last he
(Paz) drew up his army in a good position and offered
battle.   Urquieza was afraid to attack him, and again
retreated, followed by Paz, each party being afraid of the
other. He is now out of the province, and Paz has again

taken up his quarters on the frontier.   Both parties are so
done up by the month's work (that is, their horses are
knocked up), that it is not likely either can resume the
offensive.   They will spend the coming six months in
making preparations for the next campaign.   I fear there
is so much intrigue and jealousy at work among the
Corrientinos, that we cannot depend on them for a moment,
and I see more strongly than ever the necessity of our
confining ourselves to the independence of the Banda
Oriental, and not mixing ourselves up with the civil wars
of the Buenos Ayrean provinces.   If we do, there is too
much risk of Rosas defeating us, as on shore we have only
to depend on the people of these provinces ; and it appears
almost impossible they can succeed against the power of
Rosas, even if they were united.   But they are not.   Every
leading family hopes to reap the most benefit, should they
succeed ; and each is jealous of the other, and this thwarts
all their plans and makes them dangerous allies."

"H M S 'Alecto,' Goya, March 4th, 1846

"We left Corrientes on the 2nd in the *Alecto,* having
Fanny and *Obligado* lashed alongside us, and the French
steamer following us.   This was anxious work for me, as
I only thought the passes safe for *Alecto,* drawing twelve
and a half feet, or at most thirteen feet, and the *Fulton*
drew fourteen feet, having just filled up with coals and
provisions.   However, we came down a hundred miles the
first day without touching.   Yesterday morning we got
over the worst pass.   *Fulton,* following, got on shore.   As
soon as we were over, I went back to her and got her
through also, but touching all the way.   We arrived here
yesterday ; and as we do not go till to-morrow, I have a
day's rest, and you cannot fancy how much I value that
now.   No school-boy ever enjoyed an extra holiday more.
Yesterday was, I think, the hottest day we have had, and
being from daylight to dark either in a boat or on the
paddle-box was very trying.   However, I have been wonderfully well, considering the work.   I have never been off work
one day.   To-day I have a headache : fortunately it is
a day at anchor.   What tends soonest to knock me up is
the stretch my mind is kept on, and the anxiety for fear
of getting on shore, particularly in coming down, when the
rapid stream would prevent you stopping if going the
wrong way, and when even sounding is of no use, as before

the vessel could stop she must be on shore. I will try and explain the kind of navigation. A multitude of islands, sometimes leaving a channel of a mile wide, sometimes not a quarter of a mile ; in every part sand-banks running off the islands, leaving a narrow channel, winding like a serpent These banks are all under water, and not to be seen, and one has nothing to trust to but the eye and recollecting at which points to cross from one shore to another. Then in the eight hundred miles we have gone up the Parana there are at least eight hundred bends and crossings in the channel, and all the islands are so much alike—very low, with thick wood. This will give you an idea of the constant anxiety as to whether one can be sure to cross at the right spot fifty or a hundred times a day. I could not continue this kind of work much longer ; but the pilots cannot or will not take charge of the large vessels, and they do not really know the deepest channels. I have now two always with me on the paddle-box as pupils—two or three officers besides. But the pilot will not take this vessel up again ; and I have offered, if she goes up, to take her up once more and down again, when the pilots say they will know the channel, and after that trip will take the vessels up. I hope the officers will be able to do so by that time also. At all events, I mean to strike work after that, and I hope we shall go out of the river. They cannot keep *Philomel* out much longer, as her keel came up alongside the other day, and all her fore-foot is off, so that the cables catch in it."

"H.M S 'ALECTO,' CERRITO, *March 9th,* 1846

"We reached the *Gorgon* safely last night—got her over all the bad passes without touching, *Fulton* following us. It is a great relief to me. The three last days have been intensely hot, and I could hardly stand it, so anxious did it make me." *

* This passage of the *Alecto* is thus described in "Steam Warfare in the Parana," by Captain Mackinnon, R N., lieutenant of H.M. steam-sloop *Alecto.* The *Alecto* was one of three lighter draught steamers sent out by the Admiralty in January 1846. She brought out a supply of Congreve rockets :—

"After going up above the town, so as to turn, full power was now put on, and with the *Fanny* alongside, and the *Obligado* astern, she tore down the torrent-like current, and shot round the point with almost the speed of a rocket, once again, and for the last time, in full view of our friends. So sudden and unexpected a reappearance of the *Alecto* came

In a letter, dated June 1845, written to the Hydrographer, Sir F. Beaufort, Sulivan describes his descent of the river and his passing the batteries in the *Philomel* :—

"Shortly after the *Alecto* left, the *Firebrand* came up to the Baxada with the account that they were preparing batteries at San Lorenzo and Tonnelero, to attack the convoy going down. They had fired at the *Firebrand* coming up with field-pieces, hulled her eight times, and killed one man.

"On March 26th the French steamer *Gassendi* arrived from Monte Video. She had not been attacked on the river, but had seen the enemy working at the batteries, and heard from deserters that guns were on their way from Buenos Ayres to mount in them. She brought orders from the admiral to Hotham to send *Philomel* down

upon them as a surprise. With one accord they raised a scream of pleasure, which continued as we flew past them, for about two minutes, when another point shut us out from Corrientes, and we were once more in a perfect desert.

"As the difficulty in ascending the river has been sufficiently explained, it will easily be imagined that the danger was aggravated a thousand times in going down with so rapid a current. A thorough seaman may, from constant practice, have nerves of iron, but it is indeed awful to find several vessels thus in a body, propelled by the full power of mighty steam, in combination with a rapid current, tearing down a river at almost railway speed. Although not on duty, I could not leave the deck, being fascinated by the velocity with which we were threading narrow and tortuous passages. Sometimes, when the channel ran close to an island, the whirl of trees, as the vessels appeared to fly past and the branches brush the paddle-boxes, made me giddy.

"'If we were only to touch the bottom at this pace,' thought I, 'what would become of the *Alecto*? I don't believe the Lords Commissioners of the Admiralty would give much for her safety now, if they had a bird's-eye view of her.'

"All this time the usual routine of the vessel was carried on as if nothing uncommon was going forward. Of course, to descend at this apparently reckless pace with safety, it was necessary to have a good pilot. There was only one person in South America who had either the nerve, knowledge, or ability to do it. It is natural to suppose that this person must have been a native of the country, brought up on the river, and who had spent a long and active life in getting such a thorough and precise knowledge. With pride do I say it, this was not the case. The pilot was a brother-officer, Captain B. J. Sulivan, who coolly stood on the paddle-box, and conned the vessel by a motion of his hand to the quartermaster. The whole of the river, up to Corrientes, is now surveyed by the above-mentioned officer, and better known, by his means, in London than at Rosas' capital, Buenos Ayres."

the river if he could possibly spare her, as he wanted
to see me to get information about the rivers and the
Buenos Ayrean coasts. He had previously sent similar
orders, but Hotham could not let us go then ; but as there
was such a large force assembled, he had no more excuse
for keeping the *Philomel*, particularly as Hope knew the
lower part of the river better than I did, he having gone
up and down it so often. The *Firebrand* had to tow
some vessels as far up the river above the Baxada as she
could go, and Hotham determined that as soon as she
returned (I having to go up in her as pilot) the *Philomel*
should go to Monte Video. We went as far as the pass
of San Juan (about a hundred miles), which is as high
as vessels of the *Firebrand* class can go with a high river.
Above that there is not more than thirteen and fourteen
feet in the passes, while below it there is seventeen and
eighteen feet, and the navigation is not so difficult. In
the *Firebrand* on our return we went eighty miles in six
hours, going ten and eleven knots sometimes through
the water, beside three and four that the stream was
running.

"I returned to the Baxada on March 31st, and on
April 2nd left for Monte Video. The same evening we
reached Lorenzo cliffs I could not see the battery, as
from up the river it is hid by a projecting bluff till you
are nearly abreast of it ; but as there were many soldiers
near, and some making signals, I fancied that they might
have got some guns in it ; and as it is useless attempting
to return their fire when going rapidly past, when by
doing so the men must be exposed by being kept at
quarters, I thought by running close under the cliff, and
sending all but Lieutenant Richards below (for fear of
musketry), they might not be able to depress their guns
to hit us. So we ran round the bluff, going about three
knots (with stream, over the ground six knots), and, as we
opened the first embrasure, saw a gun with a man standing
with port-fire over the touch-hole. But though I could
see the muzzle was down to the ground, we were so close
(about thirty yards) the shot went a few feet over our
heads, and fell about that distance outside us. They had
only three guns, which they had but time to reload once
before we were past. So we only received six shots, all
of which, like the first, passed close over and struck a
little outside us, doing us no damage, but cutting a few

ropes. We were not a cable's length off, and had we been a few yards farther every shot would have told. They have built mounds between each gun, as traverses to protect them from a flank fire ; and at Tonnelero they have adopted a still better plan, and are preparing for placing each gun singly between two mounds, and the guns fifty yards apart. As Tonnelero is not accessible like Lorenzo, I expect to hear that these guns are brought off when the convoy comes down, as the form of the ground there will enable them to sweep it from the ships   We met the *Alecto* going up with three vessels in tow. The Buenos Ayrean papers since state that in passing San Lorenzo she got a good hammering.

"On our arrival at Monte Video, we found that a revolution had just taken place among our friends, the government party, in Monte Video. Riviera had turned out the existing government after some bloodshed. In consequence of this, the ministers wanted to send despatches home as soon as possible, and the *Lizard* was about to start for the Baxada with orders for *Firebrand* to come down to go home with the despatches ; but our arrival altered this, the admiral considering that we could start at least ten days before the *Firebrand*, so that we might get home as soon as she would, and he would then have *Firebrand's* services still for the river ; and as she is the only efficient steamer on the station, she could not well be spared. It was then arranged that we should start directly with the despatches ; and Mr. Turner (our minister at Monte Video) and the French secretary, who take them, being ready to go, we sailed on April 20th.

"We are very much crowded on board, having fifty-five extra people, invalids and prisoners. We also picked up a boat in latitude six south with the crew of the Hamburg schooner *Adler*, that had foundered four days before, as the master said, from springing a leak. But the day after we took them on board the crew accused him of having scuttled her, and said that they were going to report to me. He tried hard to prevent them, offering them money if they would not inform ; but finding that they were determined to do so, directly he saw them come aft to report it he jumped overboard. We were going eight knots at the time   The life-buoy was let go close to him ; but though a very good swimmer, he would not go to it, and before the boat reached him he had sunk. It is evident he sank the vessel to get the insurance on a thousand hides which he said he had on board of his own, and which he had insured for, when he had not one single one"

On the arrival of the *Philomel* at Falmouth, after a voyage quicker than that made by any packet-boat, all the men from that district were given leave for forty-eight hours, with orders for them to join the ship punctually at Plymouth, where she was to pay off. The brig, on entering Plymouth Harbour, owing to the strong tide, over-shot her appointed moorings. Sulivan called out, "Now, my men, as we are all soon going to land, it will be hard if the brig does not have a run on shore too" He turned her instantly into a little pebbly cove, and ran her bow gently up the beach, thus taking the way off her. A rope was got off to the buoy, and all the men were run aft to the quarter-deck. This was enough to cause the brig to float forward, and she was quickly moored. An officer from another ship had previously come on board and told them that all leave on paying off ships had been stopped, owing to the general bad behaviour of the seamen when on shore during the process. Sulivan said at any rate he had not *yet* received orders to this effect. The moment *Philomel* was moored, he told the men to take shore-boats, and get away as fast as they could, but to be back strictly at the hour appointed for beginning work. On his reporting his arrival to the admiral, the latter said, "Mind, there is no leave given now whilst paying off." Sulivan replied that his men were already all on shore! "Then they must not have leave again until the work is completed." After much trouble, and explaining how well his men had behaved during the commission, and that the ship's company had returned after a four years' cruise without a single desertion—a thing almost unprecedented in the days before continuous service—he obtained the admiral's permission to test the men's behaviour. All but one of the Falmouth men returned at the time appointed. This one had been married in the interval, and overstayed his leave a few hours. In consequence, after the work of each day was over, he was put in irons until the next day's work began. The men went ashore every evening, and not one failed to be on board at the appointed time every morning, perfectly sober. Many officers then at Devonport told Sulivan that for weeks afterwards they were constantly meeting the *Philomel's* men, and never saw one that was not perfectly sober and not in his best clothes. This shows that the strict discipline and kind treatment of the men not only affected their behaviour when under the eye of their commander, but influenced their characters for good.

For some months in each year at Monte Video, at their own request nearly all the crew were landed every Sunday afternoon to attend the service in the English Church. No officer was ever sent with them, but they were considered pledged never to enter a house or drink anything on these occasions ; and from what Captain Sulivan heard from some of the men after the ship was paid off, he had every reason to believe that not one man ever broke his pledge.

Captain Sulivan was, on his return, desired by Lord Palmerston to call and give him some information on the state of affairs in the river Plata   In the course of the interview that ensued, the former expressed his opinion pretty freely on the question of our interference

By returning home when he did, Sulivan lost the opportunity of being " gazetted " a second time for the action which ensued on the return of the convoy, when the hundred vessels composing it passed the batteries of San Lorenzo. A judiciously masked rocket-battery, under the command of Lieutenant Mackinnon, formerly of the *Arrow*, placed on the island opposite the forts, so discomfited the Spanish gunners at the right moment that they could do little harm to the ships. As has been stated, the *Philomel* passed these batteries alone; but not wishing to make a despatch of such an event, Sulivan had merely recorded it in a private letter to Captain Hotham.

The French authorities fully recognised the services of their own officers and men at Obligado. Captain Tréhouart was made an admiral (a special promotion of which their regulations admit), and honours were freely given to their other gallant officers engaged. The French share of the captured guns is still to be seen in Paris, and the action is kept in memory to this day by two of their men-of-war being named *Obligado* and *Tréhouart*. At the Louvre is a very good painting of the engagement. But no such fitting recognition of the services of our navy in the Parana can be recorded. Our guns were returned *with an apology*, Lord Aberdeen having publicly declared we had no right to force Rosas to open the rivers. No medal was granted for the eight months' arduous service in the Parana, nor for any of the actions in connection therewith. The commanders were immediately promoted, and I believe one or two first lieutenants; but the other first lieutenants and the officers of other grades were overlooked, presumably owing to the omission of their names in Hotham's despatch, which was much criticised for its brevity.

On his return to England, Sulivan urged at the Admiralty the claims of the first lieutenants of the ships engaged, and of his own junior officers. Poor Doyle had been promoted; but as he died of his wounds, Sulivan put forward the claims of Richards for promotion as senior surviving lieutenant of the *Philomel*, also those of Key, whose services he brought to the notice of the authorities, and after persistent efforts he obtained the promotion of several of these officers, dated back to the day of Obligado. This was done at the final meeting of the then Board, the day before their vacating office.

The fact of their receiving no medal was felt greatly by the officers and men of the squadron. One officer said, "I have two medals I am ashamed to wear, as I was not within a hundred miles of the enemy; but if I get a medal for the Parana, I shall have some pride in wearing it."

In 1869 Sulivan drew up a petition, which was signed by the principal officers then surviving, who had served in the Parana, requesting that a medal might be granted for the work in the river, with a clasp for Obligado In the petition were recorded the main facts of the services performed—the work of the *San Martin* and the *Dolphin*, and the cutting of the chains by Hope and his party, being prominently mentioned. It went on to say, " Yet the men who served in such an action have nothing whatever to show for it ; while they have the mortification of seeing some of their comrades wearing medals for very trifling service—others who had never been under fire—employed only in blockade or transport service, not only during the Russian war, but more recently for Abyssinia "

The request was refused, on the plea that the "duty of the Admiralty was to exercise the greatest caution in granting medals; and if they entertained this application, it would be necessary to consider other cases, and this their lordships were not prepared to do"!

The name "Obligado" is not even to be found in modern maps.

Both Captain Hotham and Admiral Beaufort brought Sulivan's services specially to the notice of the Admiralty,

and asked for the C.B. for him,.Hotham making the statement mentioned below. The reasons for refusing it show
the want of judgment with which honours were then given
and withheld. " They could not give it to Sulivan because,
if they did, they would have to give it to Captain Talbot,
R.N., for his gallant action against pirates in Borneo."
Actions against pirates, however, were not considered
deserving of honorary rewards. Yet at the very time
captains in the army were granted the C.B. for service
in India, although by the rules of the order they were
too junior for it. At the same time, for a single New
Zealand skirmish, a commander R.N. received both
promotion and the C.B., the Board saying " they had to
give way then, because the army majors were receiving
it for the same action." Captain Hotham considered that
by refusing the C.B. to Sulivan, and giving it in the other
instance, a slight had been thrown on Obligado and all
who were there engaged. Lord Auckland said his claims
should be given consideration at the next distribution of
honours. But the death of Lord Auckland prevented this,
the succeeding First Lord not knowing anything of, or not
recognising, the promises of his predecessor.

Captain Hotham recognised in several official letters
the assistance he received from Sulivan :—

" He astonished English as well as French by his energy
and activity. He piloted the *Gorgon* into places hereto-
fore deemed impregnable. In the Parana he in reality
conducted the heavy ships, and trained such officers as
were willing to learn in a system whereby our squadron
was rendered quite independent of local pilots. He took
the principal part on three occasions at the battle of Obligado. He made a plan of the ground, he commanded a
division of ships, and he led the advanced guard of the
landing-party."

Cooper Key, who had so diligently studied the pilotage,

wrote to a relative some months after Sulivan had left :—

"I now flatter myself I am a pretty good pilot for the navigation of this intricate river ... under the auspices and tuition of my friend Captain Sulivan, one of the best surveyors and practical seamen in the service. He is lately gone home ; and I have lost a valuable friend—indeed, a man I have looked up to as a model for my future professional career. . . . To our Parana squadron his loss is irreparable."

Captain Hotham in his despatch (which Beaufort criticises as too meagre compared with the China despatches) says ·—

"I should be unmindful of the ability and continued zeal of Commander B. J. Sulivan did I not bring him especially to your notice   By his exertions we were furnished with a chart which enabled us to complete our arrangements for the attack."

Sulivan returned to England with the rank of post-captain   Naturally he expected to have to wait a short time before being appointed to another vessel.   But he was not idle, as will be seen from the accounts given in the Appendices of his endeavours to improve the badly constructed forts at Bovisand, to establish a system of small-arm drill for our seamen, and to increase the inadequate supply of sailors for manning our fleet, etc.

In 1848 he was appointed Colonel-in-Chief of the Staff of the Royal Dockyard Volunteer Brigades.   A full account of his services in this position will be found in Appendix A.   When his appointment suddenly terminated, he found himself without employment, and without any immediate prospect of obtaining a ship.   His health had also suffered somewhat from continued disappointment. He therefore obtained three years' leave of absence, and went with his family to the Falkland Islands.   In Appendix B will be found a brief narrative of this trip, which was not of a professional nature.

He came back to England in the autumn of 1851, and again endeavoured to obtain employment, but without success. Even one of the several appointments in connection with the sea fencibles, for which he was specially qualified by his volunteer work, was denied him. Yet all turned out well. To this period of enforced inaction is probably due the original idea which started, or at least greatly helped to start, the Army Volunteers.* His eight years of half-pay left him, moreover, free to be selected—if only at the eleventh hour—for service in the great war, the approach of which he had been for some years watching.

* See Appendix J.

CHAPTER VI.

WAR WITH RUSSIA.

1854.

TOWARDS the close of 1853 it became evident that we should soon become involved in a war with Russia. In December Captain Sulivan wrote to the *Times*, cautioning the public against the absurd expectations put forward in the newspapers that the combined British and French fleets would not only quickly destroy Sevastopol, but also the Russian fleet of equal size anchored in the harbour under the fortifications. He pointed out that it was unlikely the admirals would be so foolish as to risk their fleets, and in consequence their naval superiority, by such an attempt. He reminded the public that neither Nelson, Collingwood, nor Exmouth ever thought of attacking a French fleet in Toulon, however inferior in force. The recent improvements in weapons and shells were more favourable to batteries than to ships. He recalled the saying of the Duke of Wellington, that it must not be supposed that ships could contend successfully with stone walls. He explained that at Acre the gunners in the batteries could not hit a line-of-battle ship at eight hundred yards, and the advantages there were entirely in favour of the fleet At Algiers the enemy made the mistake of allowing the ships to come close to the forts before firing. Yet the ships were in no condition next day to contend with a force half their strength Their ammunition was nearly expended, several of the ships seriously damaged, and the loss of men was very heavy. He pointed out the more rapid approach of a screw-ship might enable her to get close up to the fort before being injured, but there was the danger of a mast being shot away and the wreckage fouling the screw (a point, perhaps, not noted previously). Cases cited were the *Amphion* in the Tagus, when only the jib-boom was carried away, and the *Melbourne* of Spain, when her main-top fell and disabled her screw. He concluded by assuring the public that the admirals would attempt as much as any men in their situation would be justified in doing.

These remarks are interesting, read in the light of after-events.

As soon as there appeared a possibility of a war, Captain Sulivan wrote to the First Lord, Sir James Graham, requesting employment in the event of hostilities. He sent copies of the letters he had received from his former superior officers, and pointed out the fact that he had received his captain's commission for special service in action. He was afterwards told by Lord Hotham that Sir C. Hotham had gone to the First Lord and stated that, if he were offered a command for the war, he would make it his first object that Captain Sulivan should be employed under him. What was Sulivan's disappointment and vexation to find ship after ship given away, officers junior to him being given commands, but he himself overlooked. Just as the fleet was ready for sea, the senior Naval Lord said to him, " You have no chance of a ship, for all the frigates are given away, and you are too junior for a line-of-battle ship." On complaining of this to his very kind and warm friend Admiral Beaufort, the Hydrographer, the latter said, " Never mind ; if the fleet goes to the Baltic, there must be a surveying captain, and I will take care no one is appointed but you." So the very neglect of his claims was eventually the cause of his being given exactly the post he could best fill, and in which his ability and energy could have most scope. But it was so long before the Hydrographer could succeed in his efforts that the fleet had sailed before the two surveying-ships granted were ready, and they were not out in time to assist in getting the fleet through the Belt. Thus whatever benefit was derived from the services of the surveying officers was owing, as Captain Sulivan always said, to Sir Francis Beaufort. Yet long before, in China, as well as in the Parana, the great value of their services had been proved and recognised.

There had been lying for some years in the pigeon-holes of the Amiralty Sulivan's scheme of organisation for training seamen to serve on shore, and for the formation of seamen-battalions by a *pro rata* contribution of men from each ship, so that an admiral, on taking command of a fleet, would know at once how many men he could rely upon for a naval brigade This plan lay neglected until war broke out, and then Sulivan received a letter from Captain Hamilton at the Admiralty approving of his plan, giving him a list of the ships that would form the two fleets, and asking him to adapt his plan accordingly. This he did, and a copy was forwarded to the commanders-in-chief in the Baltic and Black Seas.

The command of the Baltic fleet was given to Admiral Sir Charles Napier, an officer of great service and ability. But it is doubtful whether at the age of sixty-eight an officer, however able he may have been, retains the power of prompt decision and readiness to undertake responsibility so necessary in a commander-in-chief. There was no lack of ships to compose the fleet, but seamen to man them were wanting. This has been clearly shown in

the "History of the Baltic Campaign," published under
the authority of Napier himself. I remember my father
saying that the deficiency of seamen was made up by
shipping cabmen and others who had never been to sea
before. The state of the fleet was thus described by him
in his evidence before the Royal Commission for Manning
the Navy in 1858 :—

"While the ships that had been in commission prior
to the war were very fairly manned, some only pretty
well so, the newly commissioned ones were very badly
manned. The whole state of the fleet proved, without
doubt, that we were utterly without any means of fitting
out a war-fleet in an emergency. After a few months, by
great effort on the part of those in command, they were
brought rapidly and wonderfully into a fairly efficient
state, considering the material. He considered that a
newly commissioned British ship was not fit to be got into
action with either a newly commissioned French ship or
a Russian ship of equal size for three months. One
captain told him his ship, in his opinion, would not have
been ready for six months !

"Fortunately we had the French on our side. Had we
had to contend against the French and Russian fleets
combined, there would have been nothing but ruin before
us. Further, had we had to contend against the Russian
ships alone, with their well-trained crews, it was only the
advantage we possessed in having the new screw-frigates
that would have given us the slightest chance of being able
to hold our own. They had twenty-five sail of the line
which had been with their crews training in the Baltic for
years. We had only sixteen sail of the line, five or six of
which were at first scarcely fit to go into action. The
Russians, with their vessels all lying prepared for sea when
the ice broke up, would hardly have allowed our ships to
keep the command of the Baltic, if they had come out to
attack us ; but the advantage of our steam-ships in a
comparatively calm sea secured us against that danger."

In Appendix F "manning the navy" is referred to,
and the danger we are still running from the want of an
adequate reserve of trained seamen pointed out.

Captain Sulivan was commissioned to the *Lightning* paddle-steamer, 100 H.P., three guns, on February 25th. She was the first steam-vessel built for the navy.

It will be well here to give an outline of the plan of operations suggested by the Admiralty, with some remarks upon how this was followed by Admiral Napier, so that the description given in the journals of what was actually done or left undone may be more readily comprehended.

The fleet was ordered first to Wingo Sound The sealed orders, there opened, instructed Napier to take up a good position at the entrance to the Baltic, and to prevent any Russian ship escaping from the Baltic into the German Ocean. After the ice had cleared away, he was to shut up the Russian fleet in the Gulf of Finland (" Napier," p. 51) ; to turn his attention to the Aland Islands (p 57) , not to undertake any desperate work. He therefore wisely disposed his fleet to prevent Russian ships passing the Belt, and yet he in consequence received a reprimand My father makes a note on " Napier," p. 78 : " Sir Charles was perfectly right on this point, and it ought never to have been raked up as an error on his part." The orders further instructed Napier to ascertain the exact strength of Bomarsund and the nature of its approaches ; to report if Bomarsund was open for attack, etc.; to look into Revel and other fortified places. In reply to Napier's request for pilots he was informed, " You must grope your way in your own surveying-vessels " (p. 93).*

---

* In order that the points in question may be looked at in the light of the evidence given in the journals, I here mention that Admiral Napier, on his return home, was severely criticised by the Press and by the Admiralty, being attacked in Parliament by Admiral Berkeley, Sir Robert Peel, etc. Sulivan upheld Napier on most questions, especially for his firmness in resisting the pressure put upon him to attack the Russian fortresses with his ships, the very thing the Russians were hoping he would do ! Also, it is evident the Admiralty blamed him unjustly on many trivial matters. Sulivan, however, held that where Napier was to blame was in his delay in examining Bomarsund

The following are the instructions issued by the Hydrographer, Sir Francis Beaufort, to Captain Sulivan :—

> "HYDROGRAPHIC OFFICE, ADMIRALTY,
> "*March* 18*th*, 1854.

"SIR,—My Lords Commissioners of the Admiralty having
selected you to the command of H.M. vessel *Lightning*,
to join Vice-Admiral Napier for the purpose of assisting
with the important operations of the Baltic fleet, by
making such skilful and rapid reconnaissances, as well as
occasional hydrographic surveys, wherever it may be considered necessary, I scarcely consider myself warranted
in supplying you with any special instructions as to the
service on which you will be employed ; still, for the sake
of preserving that connection which has so long subsisted
between you and this office, and I may add with such
beneficial results to H.M. service, I would exhort you
to keep all our surveying rules and habits always in your
mind, so as to render everything you do more or less
subservient to the great object of improving our charts ;
never to defer to the following day writing the remarks
and observations that you may have collected, as they
may be of lasting value long after the campaign in which
you are engaged has passed away ; to give descriptions
of the characteristic features of the land, or of the leading
peculiarities of the different districts of the Baltic navigation.
Perhaps you will have an opportunity of tracing the usual
course of the changes of the wind, the connection between
those changes and the comparative temperatures of the
air and water, and the prevalence of fogs in the different
bights and gulfs of that mediterranean sea.   All these
are fit subjects for careful attention, if guided by your
experience and love of general knowledge.

" In your partial and desultory surveys take great care
to establish the connection of some one permanent and
conspicuous object with your triangulation or bearings,

and Sweaborg. Had the latter been reconnoitred earlier, there would
have been time to have sent home for mortars, and for the bombardment to have taken place the first year   Again, whilst Napier was
brave enough under fire or in personal danger, he was terribly nervous
about the safety of his ships at sea, etc., and when broken down in
health (chiefly from the attacks made upon him by the Press) owing
to this anxiety, he brought home the fleet earlier than he need have
done.

by which you may subsequently adjust any new work, or by which any new labourers may bring every fragment of fresh information into harmonious agreement with former acquisitions.

"The most immediate service you can do this office will be to keep our charts perpetually under your eyes, correcting their coast-line, inserting soundings day and night, with the nature of the bottom, studying the niceties of the sea-marks, and representing them by drawings, marking convenient landing-places, and in correcting the nomenclature of the places, not only in their orthography, but in their vernacular appellations.

"You will, of course, keep up a regular correspondence with me, informing me of everything appertaining to general surveying proceedings as opportunities may offer, and transmitting tracings not only of those surveys, but also of such as you may have made under the special direction of the commander-in-chief, unless he may have intimated his desire that they should for the present be kept secret.

"Considering you as one of the admiral's eyes, and knowing that through it he will see everything that he ought to see, I feel sure that at the end of the campaign he will exclaim, as Sir William Parker did in the China Sea, 'Without those admirable surveyors I should have done nothing.'

"I am, sir,
"Your obedient servant,
"F. BEAUFORT,
"Hydrographer

"CAPTAIN B. J. SULIVAN,
  "H M.S.V. <i>Lightning</i>, WOOLWICH."

A sketch of Captain Sulivan, sent me by Captain Richard C. Dyer, who served under him as master of the *Merlin* during the campaign of 1855, may be inserted here to convey some idea of his personality at this period of his life.

"STOKE, DEVONPORT, October 5th, 1893

"I am safe in asserting that every officer who had the good fortune to serve under Sir B. J. Sulivan looked up to and appreciated him as the best surveyor of his age, a . most gallant officer and good Christian. Speaking for myself, I was a young and very inexperienced officer when with him ; but during that time he taught me more than I ever knew before, and was the main cause of my own success in that branch of the service to which I belonged.

" In accordance with your request I give you some reminiscences of your late father. To begin with, I may describe his reception of me on joining the *Merlin* at Greenhithe in March 1855, I being then a perfect stranger to him. I arrived on board on a Sunday forenoon. The quartermaster on duty informed me that service was being performed on the lower deck, and I waited until it was over. On Captain Sulivan coming up, I reported myself to him, but to my consternation he received me in the most chilling manner, saying, ' I do not want you ; I asked for and arranged to have another officer appointed, who has been with me before.' This was rather a damper, and left me in a state of uncertainty as to what I should do. It occurred to me that I ought to go to the Admiralty for an explanation, but before doing so I put the question quite blank to him, ' Am I to go up and say it is a mistake ? ' He said, ' Certainly not ; now that you are here you will remain.' From that moment to the paying-off I received at all times the greatest kindness and consideration from him, and had reason to congratulate myself on the mistake the Admiralty had made. Captain Sulivan was impulsive, but it was momentary and in small matters only—his natural kindliness of heart soon overcame these occasional little outbursts ; but, in all affairs of importance and on really serious occasions, no man was more cool or had clearer judgment than he.

" I remember in the Baltic some gun and other boats were running soundings under his immediate direction from the stern of the *Merlin*. Gold bands were worn on the caps in those days, and, in waving to the boats which way to go, the bands went flying in all directions, until he had none left. His brother-captains used to quiz him on this point.

" When the commander-in-chief, with other admirals and captains, came on board for a trip, which was apparently to examine channels and passages which he had surveyed, but really to gain information and experience, Sulivan would become so absorbed in his subject and so energetic in his descriptions as to lose sight of the ship's head. It then became my duty to look out for him and to be on the *qui vive*, watching his every movement to find out what he intended to do or in what direction to go next.

"When surveying coasts I was always struck with his profound knowledge and the rapid conclusions he arrived at Indeed, it was a common remark amongst his officers that he had an instinctive knowledge of the bottom He always knew where to place buoys and beacons long before those around him had completed their calculations. As a pioneer on a coast in time of war he had no equal. . . .

"Captain Sulivan perfectly understood the art of organisation ; and, whilst discipline was firmly and consistently carried out, he endeared himself to the men by his earnest consideration for their comfort, physical and moral.

"The *Merlin* was a thoroughly happy ship, and, from the position and status our accomplished captain took in the fleet with the admirals and captains who were always seeking his opinion and advice, we were all proud of belonging to her. I used to derive much information from him during the night watches on the bridge, when he would discuss our present position and relate many of his former surveying experiences, and also thrilling incidents connected with the river Plata and Parana expedition of 1845. The late Sir James Hope and Sir Astley Cooper Key, who were also in that campaign and had the highest respect for his great abilities, were constantly on board with him when opportunity offered.

"The commander-in-chief, Sir R. Dundas, kept him as much as possible at his elbow, and did nothing without consulting him. At the conclusion of the Russian war the great naval review was held at Spithead, when the *Merlin* took her old Baltic station as leader of the weather line. This was our last service, and to our general regret we were soon after paid off. At this time Captain Sulivan had some idea of going as commodore to the Cape station, and I was under promise to go with him. But the Board of Trade appointment became vacant and was given to him. Thus, to my sorrow and that of many others, terminated his naval career."

From a later letter :—

"Being a surveying-ship, the men had many advantages, and were not at all of the ordinary man-of-war type Everything went on smoothly and without friction of any sort. Discipline was maintained strictly and firmly, and there was a remarkable absence of crime and punishment. The utmost attention was paid to the comfort and well-being of the men in every detail, the result being that our captain was universally beloved and respected.

"I remember many commanding officers coming on board for information, the ship being looked on as a model of comfort and order. Sulivan had great moral weight with officers and men, and seemed to impart his activity and energy to all those around him. Some officers believed that his energy bordered on rashness and would lead to disaster, but the more senior and experienced men were his friends and appreciated him better."

The *Lightning* sailed from Lowestoft on March 25th. The following is a list of the officers who sailed in her :—

Lieutenants—F. A. Cudlip, A. T. A. Bullock.

Master—Fred T O. Evans (afterwards Hydrographer)

Surgeon—J. F. Johnson.

Clerk—E. S. Cooke.

I will now quote from the journals which my father sent home to my mother for circulation among some of the family, with strict injunctions that no remarks made about the fleet, etc., were to be mentioned beyond the family circle. He also sent to my mother private letters containing interesting personal information *for her own perusal only*. Although some might be thought to savour of egotism, they must be understood as having only been intended to interest the wife about her husband's personal doings ; and what more natural than that flattering remarks should have been repeated, without any idea of their being ever published ?

"On the 29th we ran through the Great Belt. .... We had run about half-way across Kiel Bay, when we saw the *Duke of Wellington* through the haze, leading the fleet under sail, standing to the eastward. We then ran to the eastward for two hours, and anchored about 6 p m."

Sulivan went on board the admiral's ship, taking the

despatches and his appointment for "surveying and pilot-age duties."* The admiral thereupon told him before several officers that *he did not know what he had come out for, or what was the use of a surveying-ship, unless to make a fire-vessel of!*

(*Thursday, March 30th.*)—"The fleet is going to Kioge Bay, the admiral fearing that in Kiel Bay he would be less able to watch both passages out of the Baltic .. We were ordered alongside the *Odin* to get some coal. On the 30th it was too thick to see the land. The pilot in the *Duke* would not start, and with a light, fair wind we lost the day at anchor. I assured the captain of the fleet that we could run round the coast by the lead, and this evening it has been decided that, thick or not, we start in the morning, and that I am to lead round the coast of Femern Belt, the fleet following half a mile on our off-shore quarter. The paddle-steamers with Admiral Plumridge had gone on before, to lay at the end of the reef off Giedser Point.

"Some of the ships are a terrible distance off, and they are all sadly out of line and distance I fear there is sad want of regularity and attention on these points. Mind any remarks I make about the fleet or ships for the naval portion of the readers of this must on no account be mentioned beyond our own party, or I should be afraid to say anything on the subject. There has been plenty of practice all day with the guns and Minié rifles."

(*Friday, 31st*)—"We started at daylight, and soon after I saw the low land on the south coast of Femern Belt. We ran all day, the latter part of it the fleet being under steam We passed the steamers anchored off Giedser Reef, Admiral Plumridge joining us in *Leopard*, and we ran on by night, making the light of Moen Head, and getting about three o'clock on Saturday morning near the entrance of Kioge Bay, when a dense fog came on, so thick that at a cable's length we could not see the admiral's light. We ran on a little and heard the admiral anchor. In the morning it cleared, and the fleet were all pretty well up, except one or two stray sheep. *Cressy* had carried away her fore-yard by running into the *Princess Royal*. We then steamed on and anchored in Kioge Bay about 10 a m."

* See Captain Sulivan's evidence as to his advice to Napier to use his ships as rams, Appendix D.

This lead the *Lightning* gave·to the fleet ought to have made the admiral see that there was some use in a surveying-ship after all!

"'LIGHTNING,' KIÖGE BAY, *April 2nd*, 1854

"I was leaving the admiral about three when a steamer hove in sight. Shortly after the vessel signalised, 'Have minister on board with declaration of war.' So all hope of peace is over It was sad to think to-day that the line of beautiful ships surrounded by boats with pleasure-parties of the Danes and with steam-boats from Copenhagen full of spectators, with a most lovely calm day, might so soon be acting such a different part. I believe the paddle-steamers are to start directly for the Gulf of Finland to reconnoitre; but I suppose the admiral will think us so well adapted to act as his despatch-boat that he will keep us here

"*Monday, a.m*—In the middle of the night I was called by an officer of flag-ship to say they had heard a number of guns in the direction of the Copenhagen channel, and the admiral wanted me to go directly in that direction to see what it was. We were away in about ten minutes, as our fires were banked up, and we ran round the light-vessel in the Copenhagen channel, but they had heard no guns at all, so we returned. You may suppose that *Lightning* is improving when I tell you that we ran the ten and a half miles there and the same back in two and a half hours, or more than at the rate of eight knots, and we had to ease several times to prevent running over vessels, and were a few minutes speaking the *Gorgon*, the guard-steamer, so that we must have gone nine knots; but the boilers had just been cleaned well, and the steam was well up at starting—it gradually fell from eight to five pounds on the square inch, so that in another hour we should have been going slow. This shows that if they had put boilers in her that could keep up steam she would be a very fast vessel, considering she was the first steamer built. The admiral sent to say I was to go very cautiously by the lead. I suppose he thought it terrible to be near banks in the night, but I know now the charts are good and the bearings of the light-vessel are quite sufficient to run up the channel with.

"*April 3rd, p.m*—At anchor at Copenhagen with a furious gale. Brought the minister and party, travellers, and

9

every steward of all the messes in the fleet, and all the mails. We coal and hasten back to-morrow to go with Admiral Plumridge and the advanced squadron to the entrance of the Gulf of Finland . . .

" I was in the admiral's cabin this morning with Admiral Plumridge and the captain of fleet, and we were discussing some of the charts. Admiral Plumridge had given me a very cordial reception, and, when the chief asked him if he would like to take *Lightning* with him, I gave him a nod behind Napier's back, so he said he would, and it was settled that I leave all the officers and captains' stewards here for Buckle to take back, and then coal and water and return to join Admiral Plumridge's division before he leaves I believe *Leopard, St. Jean d'Acre, Tribune, Dauntless*, and *Lightning* go to the ice in the Gulf of Finland, to see how open it is and to commence hostilities if we have a chance. This trip will try if *Lightning* is fit for the work, or whether she is a clog on those with her. I fear if there is bad weather we shall never be able to keep company with the large ships without their losing much time. There is no chance of any of their ports being open yet, so that it will merely be a reconnoitring trip, and after this gale we are likely to have fine weather. The moon is also getting well on, so that it is a nice time and the days are getting much longer.

" Directly we returned to the fleet Admiral Plumridge weighed, and we joined him. He took Evans from me to assist as pilot, he having been up in *Munder* to the ice before. We ran with a fair wind past the north end of Bornholm, made the south end of Oland and Gothland, and on the second day (6th) the admiral anchored under the land to complete our coal, and sent me to examine Faro Sound to see if it would do for the colliers, and then to return and report to the commander-in-chief. I found that, instead of having to anchor in an exposed place under an island, there was an excellent inner harbour, to which the charts only gave a passage of nine feet, but we found it had twenty-four feet, and anchorage inside in good depth and muddy bottom. It blew a hard gale the two days we were there, so that I had to sound the harbour in the vessel, and I only landed once. It is a poor, barren place, with a stony soil, thickly covered in most places by woods of dwarf pines, with patches of cultivation here and there. . The Swedes greatly feared that the Russian fleet might pounce on

Gothland before ours got up, as the Emperor had long desired it for winter harbours for his fleet, and tried all he could to get it by money and other means. The Swedes had lately increased the troops on the island to fourteen thousand men, and they seemed very glad our fleet was so near. The officer told me every Swede was with us in heart.

"A great many more ships have joined the fleet this last week, chiefly small ones; but *Boscawen* and *Cæsar* have joined, and the *James Watt* is in the Belt; so we have now, with the French ships, fifteen sail of the line. Our fleet in all musters thirty pennants; but most of the large ships want time to get in anything like order. The admiral and captain of the fleet are not particular enough; they let ships form a bad line anchoring, and do not make them move again; but they work them hard at the guns, and Admiral Chads works ship after ship. At sea they want a great deal of work to get them to move in order; and even with the four frigates with Admiral Plumridge, though he allowed them open order (four cables apart), they seemed afraid to get so close. . . . *Impérieuse*, with Watson, is a beautiful ship, and ran all the time under topsails, and those sometimes lowered. Admiral Plumridge seems most active and fit for work. I am very glad I escaped being off the ice with them in this heavy weather. The fleet is now, I believe, going to lie off Gothland, to be ready for the gulf being clear of ice. The longer it remains closed the better, as it shortens the time of hostilities and shuts the enemy up better than we could."

The *Lightning* returned with the report to Admiral Napier.

"On Tuesday night, April 11th, after reaching the fleet, I was ordered back again to Copenhagen to send up a collier for the *James Watt*, just arrived, and to bring back the master of the fleet. I could not get things arranged to return the same evening, so I started early Wednesday morning The day before, the British minister, with about a hundred people of the first rank, were to have gone in the *Dragon* to see the fleet and to see it sail; but the wind prevented the party going off from the shore, so I had to tell the admiral they were coming on Wednesday at eight;

but at seven, when I reached Kioge Bay, the fleet was under way and standing out."

"We are now getting near Faro Sound, and I thought the fleet would anchor to-night in the bay between it and Ostergarn Island, which we have just rounded, but it has fallen so calm that we are scarcely moving. We came away in such a hurry on Wednesday morning in consequence of the *Dauntless* having returned from Admiral Plumridge, who found up to Helsingfors clear of ice: they counted seven sail of the line there with topgallant-masts struck. I hope it is not clear at Cronstadt yet, for we have only twelve sail of the line with us, and they could send two to our one, which would be too long odds. . . . We had been since noon standing to north-west, till we made the distant land of Sweden about four o'clock and tacked to the southward, the admiral giving Landsort Island as the rendezvous. Besides the *James Watt*, the *Monarch* was there, and we heard of three large ships in the Belt. If they join us, thus making eighteen sail, with the French ship nineteen, we are strong enough to be secure against any force the enemy can bring out; in fact, he will not attempt to come out if we have more than sixteen ships. We sadly want large frigates, for we have not more than five or six, including some small ones, and I believe they have twenty frigates, which, as some of them are heavy ones, would tell against our line-of-battle ships. . .

"The *Duke of Wellington* sails beautifully, particularly off the wind, when the old block-ships have difficulty in keeping up under all sail; but to-day, blowing a good topgallant breeze, on a wind, she did not spare others much canvas, and *Edinburgh* and *Hogue* nearly kept way with her. *St. Jean d'Acre* running free comes nearly up to *Duke*; but on a wind the *St. Jean d'Acre* had to set nearly the same sail as the blocks. *Neptune* is an astonishing ship; though an old 'one hundred and twenty,' like *Britannia* and *Trafalgar*, she sails nearly equally with *Duke*, and is one of the fastest in the fleet, and having *Regent's* old crew is certainly the crack ship of the fleet *Boscawen* is also one of the fastest, and keeps up the credit of the Symondites. I doubt if any ship in the fleet would beat her, judging by the sail she is generally under, and she is very creditable for a new ship, always in her station, and apparently with little trouble. *Cressy*, the ship of Chatfield and Reed, does not, I think, sail equal to several others ; certainly *Duke*, *Neptune*, *Boscawen*, *St. Jean d'Acre*, and I think *Princess Royal*, spare her canvas. *Ajax* and *Blenheim* are the slowest, *Edinburgh* and *Hogue* having a great advantage over them. *Edinburgh* is in good order and does well."

He speaks of *Euryalus* as the most beautiful ship he ever saw (except *Impérieuse*). The first lieutenant, Luckraft (later governor of Lewes Naval Prison), said she was perfection in sailing and steaming. Sulivan calls her "the finest vessel in the world"—Luckraft, "such a good first lieutenant."

"*Hogue* has two or three times had a desire to run over us. The morning we left Kioge Bay, as we were rounding under *Duke's* stern to put the master of fleet on board, she ran up out of her station on the lee quarter so close that I had no alternative but to risk running alongside the *Duke*, or be run right over by *Hogue*. I roared at her to the no small damage of my throat, and she got a sharp hail from *Duke*. So close did she jam us that I had to close *Duke* till our masts were inside her lower yard-arms, and we were nearly striking her lower-deck ports, and I thought we could not possibly save our main-topmast in steering out ; but we never touched a thing in either ship, and they allowed in the flag-ship it was no fault of mine, and that I saved a smash well. The officers of watch in *Hogue* got a reprimand. Their lower yard-arms were very little clear, and poor little *Lightning* between them, *Hogue* going seven or eight knots. If she had given us a crack, they would certainly have had to send me out another vessel or send me home, for there would have been an end of *Lightning*.

"*Monday, April 17th.*—On Saturday we rounded Goth-land and Gottska-Sando, and hauled up for the Swedish coast to rendezvous and meet other ships off Landsort Island ; but when about thirty miles off my signal and Admiral Plumridge's were made, and I found the admiral was going with half the fleet to look into Helsingfors, and I was to go with a Swedish lieutenant, Theorell, who has joined our service, to Stockholm about pilots, and to see Mr. Grey, the *chargé d'affaires*."

The following is from a later note by Captain Sulivan :—

"Sir C Napier's only idea of nagivating the fleet was through pilots ; and, as it was soon found that the Baltic pilots supplied to the fleet in England knew nothing of the shores, harbours, etc, having simply made voyages to and from Cronstadt, he wanted to obtain Swedish ones. On his ordering me to Stockholm to bring down pilots hired there, I pointed out to him that they might be paid by the Russians to run us on shore, and urged him to let the surveying officers and the captains and masters take care of the ships ; but he would not listen to my objections, and ordered me to go for the pilots. When speaking to our minister about the pilots to be engaged, I asked him what security we had that they had not been tampered with. He replied, 'None whatever': and I found that a Russian agent, said to be well supplied with funds, was a near relation of one of the pilots ; so I determined not to take any of them, and returned to the admiral without them   He then seemed satisfied that I was right, and by degrees his confidence in his own officers increased."

In Admiral Napier's book * is shown his great anxiety about pilots. His cry is continually for "pilots, pilots, pilots." Eight pilots were sent for the sixteen ships when in the Downs. Sulivan remarks : "The pilots we had were quite useless, and did nothing but learn the pilotage they were supposed to have learnt before" Yet, notwithstanding the admiral's anxiety, when Sulivan arrived in the *Lightning* with his appointment for "surveying and piloting duties," his services were not made proper use of.

"Again, the charts of the Baltic—chiefly Russian—were excellent, those of the Aland Islands excepted, and the ships ought to have been navigated by these without pilots
"For the passage up the Baltic from Kioge Bay to Revel, pilots were not more necessary than in many of the ordinary passages made by men-of-war. The charts were

* "History of the Baltic Campaign of 1854" (G. Butler Earp).

more to be depended on than many pilots, who would only
have known the direct route to Cronstadt.   They knew
nothing of the inshore pilotage "

I must here reluctantly explain the true cause of the
admiral's disregard of the services of his officers appointed
for surveying duties and of his fatal waste of time in not
having Bomarsund, Sweaborg, and other places surveyed
before the fleet moved up.   The master of the fleet
appeared jealous of the arrival of surveyors, presumably
thinking that it was an encroachment upon the duties of
his department, and he attempted to perform himself the
work for which they had been specially appointed.   Being
the only officer who had served previously under Napier,
and being with him in the *Duke*, he had much influence
with the admiral at first.   It was not until the admiral
learnt to distinguish between the official capacities that he
began to appreciate the importance of the surveyors' work.

The necessity for throwing light on the conduct of the
campaign alone induces me to touch upon this petty
jealousy, and to blame one, now no more, who was a good
officer in his proper capacity.

Admiral Plumridge having taken off Evans and found
him too useful to return, Captain Sulivan had night and
day work alone whilst suffering from sore throat, which
was increased by constantly hailing other ships.   Although
there were other small steamers under commanders and
lieutenants, the senior surveying officer, a post-captain, was
made to run about for all kinds of work, towing boats,
carrying letters and beef, whilst the admiral was complaining of having no pilots.

In "Napier," p. 115, it is stated that the admiral went
with his squadron towards Hango Head, with the intention
of running up to Sweaborg.   He complains of the situation—
" No pilots, no buoys, no beacons "—and he fears for the

safety of his fleet.   So he retired without seeing Sweaborg
or sending any one to reconnoitre.   But he had_ been
informed that the Russian fleet was *outside* Sweaborg in
the ice.   If so, he might have got at them, and therefore
there was no excuse for turning back without setting the
point at rest.

Again, the admiral speaks of the dangers of the fleet
without pilots, yet does not take his surveying-ships with
him   On p 139 the same complaints are made of the
absence of marks and of *there being only two surveying-
ships !*   Yet neither was utilised, nor were the buoys,
specially supplied by the Admiralty for the purpose of
placing on the shoals, etc.

"Off Elgsnabben, April 23rd, 1854

"On returning from Stockholm, when thirty miles only
on our road back, we fortunately heard the fleet firing, and
soon after saw the upper sails of some large ships off our
deck.   The mirage was very extraordinary and distorted
everything on the horizon.   One would have supposed that
nothing could be seen at any distance, but to my surprise
we ran towards the ships twenty-five miles by patent log
after seeing them off deck, they being becalmed all the
time   On joining the flag-ship, I was instantly sent to
tow boats and take admirals to their ships.   The next day
we were near Landsort, the admiral meaning to anchor
in this place.   I was sent on ahead to get pilots, and,
taking five out of the first boat, hurried back, knowing it
was of importance to save daylight, as there is no anchorage
in any part of the channel for miles except at this spot.
But the admiral seemed afraid of going on unless every
ship had a pilot.   I advised him to let two ships without
pilots follow each ship with one, and I offered to take all
the frigates and smaller vessels ; but he would have a pilot
for every ship, and ordered me to put these five on board
his division and go for more.   Knowing the risk, if much
delay took place, I thought it right to tell him this, that
if the last ships waited they might lose their daylight, and
there was no anchorage in the channel for the twenty miles
from Landsort to Elgsnabben.   All I got was a sharp

answer and an order to get more pilots. By some more coming out and meeting the ships, *Gorgon* having a signal flying that pilots were there, we lost little time, and I got in and got four more out, and then the last ships did not reach the anchorage till after dark, which was hardly safe ; while if he would have listened to me and to his own master, who agreed with me, all would have been at anchor an hour before dark, with no risk. Thinking it might be as well to let the admiral know the sort of duties it was considered I was appointed for, I took my instructions from Admiral Beaufort and asked the captain of the fleet to read them, and, if he thought proper, to show them to the admiral. Whether he did or not I do not know, but last night I was ordered to start at 3.30 this morning with the purser of the flag-ship to Dalaro and *wait his directions*—in fact, putting me under the orders of the purser for the time. You will see how thick the islands are near Dalaro ; but we went without a pilot, and the purser, meeting the man about beef coming down in another steamer, returned to the flag-ship with him, and told me he did not require me any more, and I might return, and by eight we were back again. That part of the channel is ten times more intricate than anything the fleet came through, and that proves that I could easily have brought any of the ships here. The *Duke of Welling-ton* might have gone with us to-day among all the small islands in perfect safety, for we never had any shallow water the whole way. We had evening service in the cabin this evening, and about fourteen attended. I merely read a very nice prayer for Sunday evening out of the book Otter sent me, and then one of the nice cottage sermons : they were very attentive. I have asked all who wish to come every evening at eight. . . . Otter has very nice work piloting the French ships through the Great Belt : he has brought one through, and is looking out for the others That would be much better than being ' boots ' to the fleet, and beef-boat also. To-night Admiral Plumridge has joined, and I shall make a row about Evans not coming back.

"I have written a semi-official letter to the Hydrographer, explaining exactly the way I have been employed, the work I am kept at, and the little chance there is of my being able to carry out the intentions of himself and the Board so long as I am in this vessel, which the admiral

finds so handy for a tender, and I have requested, as the
only way of freeing me from it, that they will give me a
larger vessel and leave this one either as tender to the
admiral or as a lieutenant's command; that I cannot
go on receiving pay and nominally holding a position I
am not allowed to do the work of, that it would be unjust
to myself or to the service to do so ; and that, rather than
continue in this way, I would prefer being superseded, even
if I had to return to half-pay, if the Board would not give
me a frigate as a regular ship.   I found last night from a
brother-captain that others have expressed their opinions
respecting the way I am employed and the want of consideration for my rank and position shown by the admiral,
and it has even been remarked on in his presence, for I
am told he said that she ought to have been sent out as
a lieutenant's command, showing that he is utterly unable
to understand the position or use of a surveying officer,
or he would not consider solely her requisite as an admiral's
tender. . . . My own firm conviction is that it has
been a great mistake appointing our present chief; he is
evidently very nervous, afraid of the land, and, I think,
seems weighed down with the responsibility (he always
has a very nervous twitching of his lips and face), and
yet he will not be easily advised by those around him, but
will have his own way.   That he will do any fighting work
when it comes very well I dare say, but others would do
it as well, and perhaps with more judgment and forethought.   Up to this time I have never seen the fleet
perform one single evolution, except tacking when necessary, so that any changes of position from divisions into
line or from line into sailing columns have never been
attempted.   They are well worked at guns   Chads * and
the captain of the fleet go from ship to ship, working them
at quick and horizontal firing, supplying powder quickly,
etc, etc., and there is so much practice that many are
beginning to ask where a fresh supply of powder, shot,
and shell is to come from !"

"ELGSNABBEN, *April* 27*th.*

" Yesterday the admiral returned from Stockholm, and
I had a talk with him about my work ; he was more civil
than usual, and asked me to dinner with him, but he told
me that Admiral Plumridge was going with paddle-

* Described by Sulivan as the best gunnery officer in the service

steamers to the Aland Islands, that he could not send me, as my vessel could not carry enough coal, had no speed to keep up with the others, and would be a clog on them. Unfortunately I could not dispute these facts. I told him I had asked for a larger vessel, and he said he hoped I should get one, but that *Lightning* could not even defend herself against a gun-boat, and that as he could not let Mr. Evans' services be lost also, the latter must remain with Admiral Plumridge till the fleet was up there and I had my work to do, when he should rejoin me. I asked him if he would allow me to go also in one of the other steamers, as I should then be able to acquire knowledge that would be useful by-and-by, and that there could be no necessity for my remaining with *Lightning*. He made some objections about my leaving my ship without her captain. I told him that, when piloting a squadron before, I had hardly been on board my own ship for eight months, and for three months never saw her, but I could not get a decided answer from him ; and we are now, I believe, about to sail, having just got a cargo of bullocks we have been waiting for, and I shall not know if I go till we are outside. Buckle wants me to go with him in *Valorous*. This morning I was going to breakfast with him at seven, and we were going to beat up an island where blackcock, hares, and woodcock were seen, and some shot yesterday ; and just as I was going the signal was made, 'Annul all leave'—so we are done.

"*James Watt* has joined, and now we have fourteen sail of the line. The French *Austerlitz* is outside somewhere, making fifteen   The impression here is that the Russian fleet will come out, if possible, before more ships join and try their fate. We ought to have twenty sail of the line to make us secure, as, besides twenty-seven sail, they have about twenty heavy frigates, while we have only three and two smaller ones. In paddle-steamers we should have the advantage, and in small screws. They have three screw-frigates like *Arrogant*."

The following was the reply from the Hydrographic Office :—

"[*Private.*]
                                            "ADMIRALTY, *April* 24*th*, 1854

"DEAR SULIVAN,—Both Sir F. Beaufort and myself are especially mortified to find that you are running about with messages when you ought to be making yourself acquainted with the Gulf of Finland and buoying its shoals. Sooner or later the running one or more ships on shore will prove that your time has been wasted and your services and knowledge misapplied. Under all the circumstances of the case we think it better not to move officially in the affair, but to give a little more time, feeling convinced that ere long it will be found that you must take your natural position. It is all very well for Admiral Plumridge to dash on to the entrance of the gulf, but directly the fleet gets farther advanced they will find their mistake, regret not having allowed you to do your proper work, and bitterly regret having sent home pilots who had been twenty times at Cronstadt.

"Thus much is certain, that the commander-in-chief must admit that you have been extremely useful to him, although not in the way intended.

"I quite agree with you as to the Swedish pilots, and I hope you will say to Sir C. Napier every word you have written to me. It is of no use blinking the truth; there are times in which one must speak out. There seems to me mighty little wisdom in some quarters in Stockholm; the ridiculous accounts that have come home from time to time would be ludicrous if they did not involve a great stake. The moment I heard the rumour of the evacuation of the Aland Isles I said it was a case of double deceit; not only did the Russians not intend to evacuate, but they meant to throw in more troops, and so it now appears they have done. And this in the face of a British fleet in the Baltic!

"Your pilot has just called on me; he speaks of your kindness to him and of Mr. Cudlip's, and that he would be ready to go round the world with you We have just heard of poor Foote's death; it is very sad, and I hope will be a warning to the officers of the fleet that bar harbours are not to be trifled with in the wretched boats supplied to our ships.

"With best wishes,
"Ever yours,
"JOHN WASHINGTON."

"ELGSNABBEN, <i>Saturday, April 29th.</i>

"We have had great part of yesterday and all to-day a north-east gale, with rain, sleet, and snow mixed, and the thermometer below the freezing-point at night and very little higher by day. It is just like a very bad winter's day at Falklands. The land is patched with white and looking very miserable, and yet this ought to be spring, if they have such a thing here. The people on shore will be very glad, for the weather has been so dry for the last month that they feared their growing crops failing. I have not been sorry to avoid this dirty weather outside, but we should look very foolish if a batch of Russian frigates were to push out while we are here and get through the Sound, dispersing over the Atlantic. We must be very careful now, as the ice must be nearly clear up to Cronstadt. There is a report of our going to attack some batteries at Hango, the north entrance to the Gulf of Finland; but I can hardly fancy it is true, for there is little advantage to be gained; and, though there are only three batteries, mounting less than forty guns, yet before they were destroyed we might have two or three ships crippled in their masts at least, and with only fourteen sail we cannot afford to risk any of them being disabled, when a Russian fleet so superior in number may take advantage of it and come out. We cannot afford to weaken our force either by loss of ships or men, for we have now ships with very reduced crews through sickness. The *Royal George* has sixty short of complement and a hundred and twenty on the sick-list; other ships vary from sixty to forty sick; but all are improving. The lower decks of the large ships must be bitterly cold. Our men with their comfortable stove on the lower deck are, I think, the best off of all, and the officers coming here from the large ships' large ward-rooms with no stove envy our officers their warm, snug gun-room. Yesterday I dined with Buckle in *Valorous*; we had a regular Falkland evening, for the master was there in *Champion*. . . .

 " There are now no less than forty-one captains commanding ships in the Baltic, including those we know are on their way out, and of these I come twenty-second in seniority.

 "There is very little done in the fleet in the way of exercise, except at the guns. The smartest ship in the fleet takes four minutes to take in two reefs and furl, but they work their guns much smarter. Shot are flying among the ships through every opening, and firing goes on nearly all day. I have been trying our shrapnel-shells from our eighteen-pounders, and at eleven hundred yards burst them beautifully at the target; so I would not advise a gun-boat to come as close as that to us. But I believe their favourite range is fifteen hundred yards, and they use ricochet firing, their guns being close to the water, and not elevating much   I saw some similar gun-boats at Stockholm; they mount one eight-inch gun aft and one thirty-two-pounder forward; they can only fire directly ahead or astern, and they point the gun with the oars; but a Swedish officer told me they fire very correctly with them.   The guns are so low that if the water is smooth the ricochet fire would be very effective, but if there is any sea it must be difficult to fire them at all correctly   They carry sixty men each, who are terribly exposed to shell, but, at a distance at which they could strike a large ship every shot, it would be very difficult to hit them if they were spread far apart, each giving only a small object to fire at   If they came close to us, which they would only do if we got on shore, I think our Minié rifles would tell.   Some of our men are getting very good shots with them up to four hundred yards; our best shots are the stokers, and our best shot with the long guns is a man not long in the navy, who never fired a gun before.

"*Sunday, April 30th.*—It seems we are never to have a quiet Sunday.   This morning, about four, our signal was made to get up steam, and shortly after the master of the fleet came on board and gave me verbal orders from the chief to take him with a pilot to examine another channel out; in fact, I was to take a junior officer in this vessel to do the very duty I was sent out to perform, without being consulted or even knowing what channel we were going to till I got there   This is certainly the climax of indignity, and if I could do it I would not remain here an hour longer. Not liking to let my feelings influence my conduct to the master of the fleet privately, or of course to delay for a moment the service, I did everything I could to assist him in the work.   I found that the channel was one that I had mentioned to the chief the last time I dined with him as a better one—I thought—for the fleet to go out by than that by which they entered, and that of course led to his wishing it examined; it was therefore more extraordinary his not sending me.   I had a long talk with Commodore Seymour; he also seemed quite to feel that I have been treated very differently from what my position entitled me. I told him plainly that I could not continue much longer to retain the command if I were treated so that, even in my special piloting duties, a junior officer, who is not a surveyor, was sent in my vessel to do work of the kind without my being consulted in the slightest way or my opinion asked ; in fact, exactly as he would be sent in an admiral's tender or a lieutenant's command. I am not sorry for it, for it must bring things to a crisis, and anything is better than going on as I am. I mean to send the captain of the fleet extracts from Hotham's letters to the Admiralty, asking him to lay them before the chief, in hope that, when he knows how I did similar work before, he may be induced to put more confidence in me, for that if he does not I cannot possibly be the assistance in piloting the fleet that I ought, and that I know the Admiralty expect of me. This is the least I can do, and if that has no effect I must apply to him officially on the subject.

"You may suppose it has not been very much like Sunday, though we had our regular services before dinner and a very attentive congregation. We go on very steadily —no complaints—and I have not heard an oath in her since I spoke to them about it at Woolwich.

"*Monday, May 1st.*—I have just heard the sad news of poor Foote of *Conflict* being drowned with four of his boat's crew off Memel. He is generally lamented, for he was one of the finest fellows in the service. To-day we have had very threatening weather with an exceedingly low glass, and we have wisely kept at anchor. The French ship *Austerlitz* arrived to day ; she is a lump of a ship, not nearly so handsome as our ninety-gun ships ; she looks like one of our block-ships enlarged.

"*May 2nd.*—Still detained by dirty weather. *Arrogant* is watching Gulf of Finland ; *Esperance* off Dager Ort with Archer ; Key with *Amphion* and *Cruiser* off southern entrance to Riga ; *Euryalus* and one or two others somewhere else.

"*Evening, 2nd.*—Buckle in *Valorous* and Glasse in *Vulture* were off early to examine the Aland Islands, reconnoitre Bomarsund, and intercept gun-boats, the very work that Washington in his last letter supposes I have some paddlesteamers doing. Buckle was very anxious to have me with him either in his ship or *Lightning*, as he said such work was quite new both to him and to Glasse. Every officer commanding steamers *but myself* has now been detached on such work, whilst I am the only one appointed for the purpose ! We are the only vessel that has no pilot at high pay "

Captain Sulivan had been supplied by the Hydrographer with information and plans respecting Bomarsund; and had received a letter from him soon after the fleet had entered the Baltic with the expression, " We hope by this time you have found your way to Bomarsund and reported on it." The ships sent were too large for the work, and had ultimately to return without accomplishing anything As mentioned, Captain Buckle had asked the admiral to send Sulivan to pilot his ships. Captain Sulivan told the admiral he had been sent out for these special duties, and tried to explain how useful the surveyors had been in China and in the Parana. But it was all useless. Commodore Seymour's support was likewise in vain Thus, as will be seen, a whole month's valuable time was lost.

"Admiralty, *May 15th,* 1854

" My dear Sulivan,—Your note of the 30th is indeed very grievous : to bear slights of that kind is often more difficult than to bear injustice. Yet I say to thee, Bear on, submit, and do so moreover with a good grace and with a smiling face. It is, I well know, hard to do so, but you must handcuff your feelings whether the cuffs are hard or not. Things will soon come round. Washington and I are on the look-out ; but you must endure. The thought of asking for supersession would in the present position of *la chose publique* be destruction to you. I have a clear second sight that prejudice and dulness will clear away, and allow your light to shine unshorn by either of those misty clouds. But again I say, or rather entreat you, to bear and forbear.

" *May 16th* —Since writing the above Sir James Graham has seen and read your note ; and though, as you must well be aware, he cannot interfere in a direct manner, you may be confident that he will not lose sight of your position.

(*Signed*) " F. Beaufort."

CHAPTER VII.

HANGO.

"OFF GOTTSKA-SANDO, *May* 14th, 1854.

" MY last from Elgsnabben would not have led you to suppose that I should immediately after get into the chief's good graces ; but the vessel had hardly sailed when I was sent for, and the commodore told me the admiral had received a plan of mine for organising seamen-battalions which he was much pleased with, and was sorry it had not come before they did anything of the kind, and told me they wished me to adapt what had been done as well as I could to my plan. It is rather a hobby of the admiral's landing men as soldiers, so I suppose he was pleased to find others were interested in the same thing. He shortly after came out of his cabin, and, in a very different tone from what he had generally spoken to me, told me to go and read the letter from the Admiralty, as it was very complimentary to me, and then, for the first time since I joined him, spoke to me of my proper duties, asked me about buoying the shoals, and said he should soon want me at my work, and actually ordered Mr. Evans back to the ship—all, I believe, through the impulse of the moment, because he was pleased with a thing that had no bearing in any way on my duties here. You will recollect in my last that I had suggested to the admiral to take the fleet out by the wide channel south of Danziger Gatt, where you will see 35 and 31 in the chart. Had he done so he would have saved himself and others plenty of anxiety and his fleet from a great risk that it is wonderful they all escaped from. We sailed, or rather steamed, on the 6th, losing the whole of a beautiful afternoon. After the steam was up, by making each ship's signal separately to weigh, when the one before had got about half a mile off, it took three hours to start the whole ; and just after the last ship had started, and we were all spread over the length of the channel from Elgsnabben to Landsort, where there is either no anchorage or very deep water, one of these Baltic fogs rolled in from sea, and completely hid the ships from each other, with narrow passages between islands and rocks to find their way through. Half the fleet had passed my channel before it came on Had the admiral taken my advice, they would have been out through it safely, instead of being caught in the very worst part with miles to go to Landsort passage. We kept sight of the flag-ship by keeping close on her bow, and when we were abreast of this channel they hailed me to haul out through it ahead of her. I hoped the next ship would see us and follow, and so on the others ; but it was too thick, though *James Watt* and the French ship were close behind us. We were in a few minutes out of all danger and at sea, while the others were all going on through the very worst part, and, to add to our troubles, it came on to blow hard in the night, and at daylight only *Lightning* and *Duke* were together, and it was blowing a gale from S S.E. right in on the passage. The chief has since told me he never passed such an anxious night in his life, as he thought it impossible all could escape ; and so did I. About noon we saw several ships to windward, and the sea got up so heavily that, seeing we were half buried keeping alongside *Duke*, they made our signal, ' Act to the best of your judgment.' I instantly bore up again for the passage, thinking it much better to lie in a comfortable anchorage than knock about outside, and I was also anxious to know if any ships had got on shore. The barometer being very low, I thought the gale would last some time, and, the day following being Sunday, I hoped to lay quiet inside till Monday. We found a tremendous sea running in among the islands and the rocks forming the channel ; but when I got inside I saw that several ships had put back and were lying comfortably in their old anchorage, and I also learnt that not the slightest accident had happened. Out of all the ships only three liners and one steamer failed to get out. How they escaped is most surprising. At the worst point of the channel the steamer towing *Neptune*, the *James Watt*, and the Frenchman found themselves huddled together, yet they kept clear ; *Neptune* and the Frenchman got out safely, *James Watt* getting back to the anchorage. The steamer towing *Monarch* was running right on to a small island, and hauled off so suddenly that she snapped both hawsers ; but the *Monarch* was got under sail quick enough to keep her clear, and she also got back to Elgsnabben. It is most creditable to so new a fleet that in such a trying position all managed to escape accident There was so much sea running at the anchorage that I determined to try a nice little cove inside, and I found it a most excellent place, but so small that we had to moor."

[A later note says :—

"No fleet was ever in a more trying position, and the way every ship was taken care of in such a place in a thick fog shows that the officers were much more competent than the admiral allows. The badly manned *Monarch* was got out of great danger by skill and promptness, Captain Erskine being one of our best officers.]

" We rejoined the fleet in the afternoon of Sunday with most beautiful weather, and the chief ordered me to go and join *Arrogant* off Hango, and to examine the anchorage at Hango and Wormso, the one at the north entrance to the gulf, the other eastward of Dago Island on the south. In the middle of the night, when off Dago Island, we saw a vessel, evidently a steamer, standing to the westward about a mile from us, with three masts, but only a square fore-topsail. Knowing we had no steamer so rigged, and that no merchant-steamer could be coming down the gulf, I really feared she was a Russian on the look-out for us, and my fears were not lessened when I twice made the first portion of the private night signal without her answering it. We were then passing her ; but knowing I could not leave her without ascertaining if she was an enemy's vessel or not, I turned round, took our sails in, and went to quarters. To add to my doubts, though she did not answer the signal, she fired a gun, and afterwards hoisted lights, but not the right ones. When we were quite ready we stood towards her, and in the half-light night, as we neared her, saw that she set a main-topsail, and was one of our own steamers cruising—*Desperate*. She had never noticed our signals, and she was making what she thought the private signal to us, *but for the wrong day!* I assure you I was not sorry to find her a friend, for there can be no Russian steamer that is not four times our force, so that we must have been taken had she

been an enemy.* We joined *Arrogant* with my old messmate Henry (now called Yelverton) in *Undaunted*, Ryder in
Dauntless and Hall in *Hecla*, all off Hango, and we all
dined together with Henry, who is really a most excellent
hand for all the work he has been doing. He has been for
a long time keeping a look-out on the shores of the gulf on
both sides as high as Revel, sometimes alone, occasionally
with a second vessel, and one could not have a more
excellent, pleasant senior officer to serve under. William
Sulivan is gunnery lieutenant of her, and Henry speaks very
well of him. In the evening it was arranged that I should
keep *Dauntless* with me as a body-guard, and also to
assist me in finding the rocks we want to put buoys on, by
anchoring near, so that we could work round her. Henry
(Yelverton), with Hall, was going to try to get into a place
near, where they could stop vessels passing with material
for new batteries at Hango. We spent several hours in
sounding round the rock off Hango, and put a large red
buoy on it. We afterwards got some soundings in the
roads, and then anchored as near to the batteries as we could
venture, to get a sketch of them   We were two thousand
eight hundred yards off, but they did not fire at us, so I
suppose they have no long-range guns. They all seemed in
good order, and had sand-bags on the parapet on each side of
every gun. This the sketch will explain to you ; and if you
look at the plan below, you will see how from our anchorage
we saw the four forts in the position of the sketch   B fort is
new, and I think not yet complete. Of course there is no
strength beyond what a few of our ships could destroy in a
short time, but it is a question whether any advantage is to
be gained by it, worth even the damage done to a few
ships, and the few lives that would be lost. The large fort
could, I think, be destroyed by shell at a long range

"I then landed on an island the other side, and had
a good *shot* at the fort with a *four-inch — theodolite !*
Having seen all I wanted to see there, I left about
10 p m. with *Dauntless*, and ran across for Wormso Sound,
which is the anchorage inside the Stapelbotten bank off
Wormso Island   Sir James Saumarez, with his fleet,
used to lie there and get plenty of supplies from Dago

---

* A seaman of the *Desperate* afterwards told my brother of the feeling
of admiration the men entertained for the behaviour of *Lightning* on
this occasion, the little vessel fearlessly dashing up close to her possible
big antagonist !—Eᴅ.

Island. We spent the next day (11th) in sounding the
banks and putting small buoys on their ends. I feared
to put large ones till our ships go there, as they might
be removed or sunk. In the evening, wishing to see if
the passage by Wormso Island was protected by batteries,
I stood in and saw them working very hard at telegraphs
newly erected on every point; but I could see no guns
or works of any kind, so we ran in close to the shore,
where there is a large village of poor houses, I fear
quite deserted. It was inhabited by a colony of Swedes
There was an officer at the telegraph, with a party of
men who did not appear to be soldiers. I could easily
have destroyed the telegraph, but did not wish to let
them think I was firing at a few men in such a position;
and, did we land to destroy it, we knew they would
instantly remove all but the post and then bolt, as they
did at a place nearer Revel, where *Arrogant's* men landed
They saw one man, whom they tried, by virtue of
showing him a sovereign, to induce to bring two sheep
The man left, and the first lieutenant and doctor went
a little way inland, till, seeing something shining over
some bushes, they found themselves watched by two
dragoons with brass helmets, who were behind the
bushes. They made the best of their way to the boat,
and were not pursued: perhaps a fear of their revolvers
had something to do with it. In the morning Ryder,
with the master of *Dauntless*, came on board before
breakfast, and remained till we anchored with her inside
the banks in the evening, when I dined with him. The
difference between the work I had been at before, and
such pleasant days at my proper work, with such pleasant
men and old friends as Henry and Ryder, you may readily
fancy. It made me wish to remain away altogether;
though we had plenty of work, for with so little night
we were obliged to be up early, and in three nights and
days I only got nine hours' sleep.

"The next morning (12th) being calm, I took *Dauntless*
in tow, to take her out to the Apollon Shoal, which you
will see ten miles outside. We spent all the day in
sounding over it, and found it much longer than in the
charts, the two ends being the worst parts, and three
miles apart. It was very foggy nearly all day, so that
we were delayed a little. We put one of the large cone-
shaped buoys on the north end, with a large A painted

in white on its head. I am going to put all black buoys on the south side of the gulf, and red on the north; and where different colours or marks are necessary, have them white and black on the south, and red and white on the north. I also put a small one on the other end. I think these are too far from the shore for any one to touch them or even find out they are there. Having finished about 5 p.m., I left Ryder to find his way back, when fog and calm allowed him (you must know that the screw-steamers never get up steam except in cases of emergency, and they act quite as sailing-vessels), and steamed through a dense fog back to Hango, guided by occasional guns that I thought must be fired by *Arrogant* as fog-signals. About ten at night I ran alongside *Arrogant*. Henry agreed with me that I had better return to the admiral, as there was no other place I could examine but Revel, or rather the Nargen anchorage off Revel, and it was not safe for me to go so near Helsingfors without a larger force. I think that is the best anchorage for our fleet; and Yelverton was also anxious to go there, and would have taken all four ships, but did not like to do so without the admiral's consent. . . .

"I find the comfort of having Evans back, as now I have a real assistant. The chief would not let me go to Nargen, but said we must go there with a large force He asked me to dinner, and, as I have done before, I remained and dined in a frock-coat, so he is not over-particular"

I here add the following later note on this subject :—

"We (Yelverton, etc.) knew that the ice had long disappeared, and that Sweaborg ought to be reconnoitred, but the admiral had given positive orders that we should not go above a certain point without his permission. I therefore returned to the fleet with a request from Captain Yelverton to the admiral that he would allow me to go up and reconnoitre Sweaborg, if he would not come up with the fleet, but urging him at the same time to bring the fleet up at once to the fine anchorage of Nargen opposite Sweaborg. This would, I am sure, have been done had not the officer to whom I have already alluded prevented it by assuring the admiral in my presence that it was not safe to take the fleet up yet, and that Nargen (which he knew nothing of) was an unsafe anchorage. It was in vain that I mentioned the Hydrographer having told me it was the finest anchorage for a fleet in the gulf, and that my father,* who had been first lieutenant of the brig that led Nelson's fleet into it, had told me the same. The adverse influence was too strong, and thus the chance was lost of reconnoitring Sweaborg in good time to have sent home for mortars and bombarded it that year."

If Admiral Seymour had been allowed to exercise his proper influence as captain of the fleet from the commencement, or had any of such masters as Stokes Moriarty, Bodie, Hill, Allen, Blakey, Scott, or Evans been in the position of master of the fleet that year, working cordially with Captain Sulivan, as any one of them would have done, and as some did on many occasions, and as Mr. Baker, the master of the *Gorgon*, had done throughout the Parana expedition—for which he was made a commander —this loss of time would have been saved. Captain Sulivan said he never forgot the tremulous excitement of Sir Charles Napier, when, after listening to the opposite opinions of his two advisers, he said with trembling lips, " What am I to do when you two, whom I ought to trust to, give me directly opposite opinions?" It was a misfortune for the admiral and the service that he had in such a position an officer who, instead of helping to give him confidence when he was so anxious about the safety of his ships, seemed to delay his movements and to encourage his weakness.

" I have always tried to impress on the commodore, and once I spoke to the chief of, the power we possess of shelling at long range any large space, such as a fortress or mole, with the ships' long-shell guns, heavy sixty-pounders; that our ships would be comparatively safe from their fire, instancing Hope shelling a lamp out at nearly four thousand yards with his two sixty-eight-

* Rear-Admiral T. B. Sulivan, C.B.

pounders. Directly the commodore read the account of Odessa, he turned to me and said, 'This proves the correctness of all you have been saying on the subject' I think we shall be trying something of the same kind."

"My last left us with the fleet off Gottska-Sando. Soon after the screw-steamer left, the chief left Admiral Corry with half the fleet, and with nine sail of the screw-liners, including *Austerlitz* and some paddle-steamers, started for this place. On our way I went to examine an American vessel direct from Cronstadt three days before, and the information we got from him was so important that the chief sent me back to bring him on board, with her owner, who was also there. They left twenty-one sail of the line ready for sea at Cronstadt, four more fitting, some frigates, etc, and thirteen steamers. They took their shot and powder the day before he left At Helsingfors they have fifteen sail of the line and a proportion of other vessels, so that they have in all forty, but every harbour-ship has, I think, been fitted out to make a show, and they say that they are not coming out, as they cannot contend with the English ships, unless we first knock our ships to pieces against their batteries, and then they can finish us. . . .

"We reached this (Hango) three days since, and yesterday (Sunday), very early, I was ordered to go and put buoys down on the rocks outside the entrance, the enemy having cut away the one I put down a fortnight since In going towards one rock we struck against the side of another, not in the chart, with only about five feet of water on it The sun was ahead, so the man at the mast-head would not see the rock. We hit it a hard crack, but glanced off it, heeling over a good deal, at the time the man was hauling in the lead-line, having just had twenty-five fathoms, and we were going very slow.

"On our return from this about midday, the chief said he wanted me to go and try to get in behind the island near the forts, to have a good look at them, and see if any ships could get behind them ; but I must give you

---

* There seems to have been a sketch attached to this letter, showing all the positions referred to. But this having been lost, some of the points mentioned cannot be marked on the plan of Hango Bay —ED.

an idea of the place, so that you may put it before you as you read.

"We went round from the fleet outside the outer islands, and anchored where I have marked +, *Lightning*, and I then went in my gig to try and have a close look at the forts from the rocky islands, behind which the boat could lay out of sight.   Not seeing anything as close as I could wish, I thought I would go on Ryson Island, close to the large fort of thirty-one guns, and as it is wooded I thought I

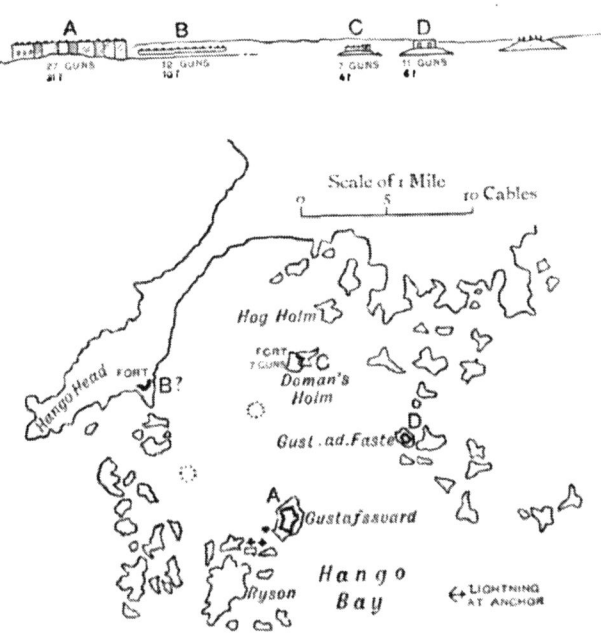

might easily conceal myself from those in the fort.   I thought there might be men watching me from the island, and had doubts about going there, until I saw on one of the highest of the low stunted trees a hawk perched—that made me think no one could be there, and I foolishly pulled round into a channel not fifty yards wide; but just as I was about to land, I felt that perhaps I was wrong, as there might be risk, and I could perhaps see what I wanted from another island. It was indeed Providence watching over me and the boat's crew; for as we went on and pulled out of the narrow channel, we saw a party

of soldiers running along the shore of Ryson Island to
cut us off. You may suppose we pulled hard, and they
ran as hard ; but by the time they reached the point of
the island, we were nearly four hundred yards off. I
feared they were riflemen ; and when I saw them form up,
and their muskets flashing in the sun, I thought they
would give us a volley, and took up a Minié rifle in the
stern-sheets to return it ; but they never fired, so I took
off my cap to them instead. Had we been three minutes
later, we must have been all shot in the narrow channel, as
the rocks quite overlooked it within thirty or forty yards.
I ought to have known better than to put a boat in such
a position Even if I had landed, I ought to have pulled
outside, and not risked the boat in a narrow creek. Had
I landed, I must have been either killed or taken prisoner.
It was indeed a most merciful Providence that made me
turn away at the moment I was going to land My boat
had evidently been seen from the thirty-one-gun fort, and
the men had been sent across : as I saw them go back in a
large boat I counted twenty-two of them.

"I then crossed to an island, where I had a capital look
at the batteries. I crawled along to the summit, and, with
the glass resting on the rock, saw everything beautifully
The soldiers were crowding on every high rock near them,
but they never attempted to fire any of the guns. I took
care to have a good steep rock at hand to get behind when
I saw the flash, had they done so.

"The forts marked 4 and 6 guns I had only seen
that morning from the *Duke's* topmast-head. We had not
known of them before ; so wishing to have a good look
at them, I went to the top of another little island,
from which I saw into the rear of the forts, one pointing
to the eastward, the other to the westward As soon as
they saw me, they shoved off a large boat full of soldiers,
who landed on a small island opposite to where I was,
so I wished them good-bye and got away before they
reached the summit, as it was within musket-shot. I then
returned, sounding as I came out, and we ran round to
the fleet. I reported to the admiral that I could place
four steamers, so that they could shell the thirty-one-gun
battery, at a range of about two thousand two hundred
yards, and that there would be only two guns bearing
that way, while we could take all the chief fronts of
the forts in flank and rear ; that the same ships could

afterwards shell the ten-gun battery; while two others, or two of the same, could move on, and shell the flank and rear of the six- and four-gun batteries, where not a gun would bear on the ship. I also pointed out a position from which the fort could be flanked by two vessels through an opening to the eastward of Ryson Island. He seemed determined to try it, and ordered me to go to the eastward and find *Impérieuse*, with the three paddle-steamers with her, and bring them back with me. Mind, I never gave any advice as to whether this place should be attacked or not—I have all along felt that if we did it most effectually it would be of little use to us, and not worth the risk, the loss, and the ammunition expended. All I have been anxious about is that, if it is to be attacked, care may be taken to do it in the most careful way, so as to have as little loss and damage as possible.

"I returned this morning with the steamers, and was ordered by the chief to go round again and look at the channels and batteries. I took Nugent, the lieutenant of Engineers, with me, as he never gets sent anywhere, and has only got out of *Duke* when I have asked for him to come with me. We went round and anchored just out of shot, and pulled up in the gig under a little island, from which we got a capital look into the six- and four-gun batteries. When we were lying flat on the top of the island, peeping with our glasses over the ridge, we saw them all watching us, and at last turn a gun towards us. I had seen them do it the day before; but they did not elevate it enough to reach me—that I could see distinctly—so I did not move, but this time, while watching them, I saw its muzzle rise quite high enough; so I jumped up and called Nugent to come, and we walked back a few yards, giving them a full view of us, to a nice high over-hanging rock, which we were under before a shot could have reached us; but they did not fire—not I suppose, being ready in time. We were about twelve hundred yards off, and about a thousand yards from the other forts, but looking at their flanks. I wonder they did not try the Minié rifles We then went on, when, to my surprise, I saw *Dragon* come in and anchor only sixteen hundred yards from the large fort, and shortly after begin to fire. I hurried back, supposing I should have to bring in more steamers, as it seemed madness placing one alone at a distance that the forts could so easily hit, and I saw the shot striking her, as we went back a little outside her. I was ordered to take *Magicienne* and *Basilisk* under my orders, and take them where I proposed. I went on in *Magicienne* (as the other had to get her steam up), and anchored her where she saw into the flank and rear of the large fort at two thousand one hundred yards Two guns from that fort and the two on the flank of the ten-gun battery fired at her, but the shot fell a hundred yards short, while her large ten-inch gun threw the shell into the fort They burst a few shells well over *Magicienne*—I think from a mortar; but none struck her. I then went back in my boat to meet *Basilisk*, and found *Lightning* close to *Dragon* She had brought down the master of the fleet, who had first placed *Dragon* there, and certainly made a great mistake, as she was six hundred yards nearer than I proposed to place the shelling-steamers; and though she hit the fort well, her shell made no impression on the stone walls or the earthen parapet. If they had been fired a little farther off, and so dropped into the fort, they would have been more effective. She had then a number of shot in her hull, one man killed and one wounded, and one shot close to her shell-room under water. I waited in *Lightning* till the master of the fleet returned, and then went on in her to meet *Basilisk*; and just as I was taking her close to *Magicienne*, intending to place her so as to flank the six- and four-gun batteries, our signal was made to return, and mine to bring back *Magicienne*, and *Dragon's* to haul out It was a perfect bungle, intended, I believe, only to try the range for shelling; but the *Dragon* having been improperly placed so close made it look like a serious attack I hope it is not going to be attacked, for it is not worth to us the loss and damage the ships would meet with; and, if he sends smaller ships in, they will be beaten, and the large ships will be obliged to join, and so compromise the whole squadron, and then, perhaps, let the fifteen sail of the line from Helsingfors, sixty miles off, come down on us while our ten sail are damaged, and have expended half their powder and shot, etc.

"*Monday*, 23rd.—I have just been hauling a prize (not ours) off the rocks, and I hear the chief is really going to send in the block-ships and smaller ones to silence the batteries I hope not, for the heavy battery has the guns so well mounted, the men out of sight, and a high parapet, that

it may do great damage to several ships, if not beat them.
That we must destroy it in the end is certain, but at a loss
and risk that it is not worth.   I believe the fact of *Arrogant*
and *Hecla* having silenced a battery on the coast and
brought out a vessel makes him anxious to try it ; but they
were small guns badly mounted.   They did it very well,
and only suffered from rifle-balls from numerous troops. . . .

"I only wish the chief would try the effect of shelling the
forts from every large gun in the fleet before putting ships
alongside them.   If we even silence the forts, and do not
take possession and totally destroy them, we only do half
our work, as they will soon repair them ; and as they have
the mainland commanding the inner roads, they may drive
our ships out, even if we have totally destroyed the forts,
by bringing guns on the rise of land thickly wooded, and
firing at long range on the anchorage.

"The great mistake in placing the *Dragon* was, I think,
made by the master of the fleet, from his ignorance of the

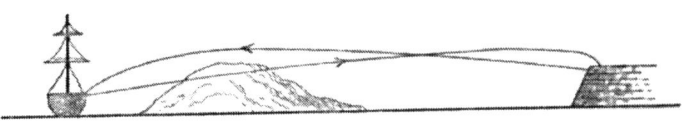

principles of gunnery ; for when I gave the admiral the
report in the morning, and pointed out that I would place
two steamers in that line at two thousand two hundred
yards' range, he said that the master of the fleet had found
a place where a steamer could be sheltered from the fire of
the fort behind an island, and that was the reason he
placed her so near, and did not seem to understand it
till I explained to him that a low island was no protection
against guns on shore when they had the range, while it
might prevent the ship hitting the fort from not seeing it
with the sight, and that as the shot leaves the gun so much
more horizontally than it falls, an island might actually
prevent the ship firing, and yet the fort might hit her
over it. . . .

"I am sorry he has done anything at all here, as it is a
petty kind of warfare for such a fleet."

"HANGO, *May 24th*, 1854.

"The admiral sent for me this morning, and I had a long
talk with him about the forts, etc., and was glad to find

that he had no intention of sending the ships in against them But he seemed inclined still to try shelling at long range on the large fort, and asked me where the block-ships and steamers could be placed, so that he has fallen back on what I first suggested; and had not the *Dragon* been so imprudently placed where she was and so got mauled, it would have been all right, and I believe he would not have fired a shot at all, which is certainly his best plan. The master of the fleet was present part of the time, and said that I was right. I had advised two thousand two hundred yards, and it was entirely his own doing that the distance was altered. The poor chief is really too shaky, nervous, and borne down by the responsibility to have such a charge on him. He has no plans or system, but the impulse of the moment alone guides him, and I trust we may have no serious thing to do, requiring careful plans and system. He is now thinking of Bomarsund; but that is a stronger place, and would be far more difficult to attack.

"I have been again with the chief for some time, and he has been asking me a great deal about attacking the batteries, where to place the ships, etc Shortly after I was talking to the commodore about it, and telling him how I hoped the chief would not risk the ships for such a thing. I said that guns mounted as these were in their batteries would be very destructive to ships before they could be silenced. You recollect my dispute and correspondence about the Plymouth batteries, and my giving a decided opinion that guns mounted in a certain way ought to beat any ships. These guns are mounted exactly in the way I said was the best. They are thirty-three feet above the water, behind a high parapet, the upper part of which is earth, no embrasures, and the men's heads not seen There would be nothing but the muzzles of the guns showing, and from their height the lower guns of the ships could hardly see them,. while the upper part of the ships would get every shot. We could, of course, with our force, destroy them all, but with far greater injury and loss to us than they are worth, as the ships that went alongside them would probably have to go home to repair. The large ship that went against the chief fort could not expect to escape without a hundred killed and wounded, and we want every ship and every man, in case the Russian fleet comes out. The commodore said Admiral Chads' opinion coincided exactly with mine, and he hoped that I had told the admiral so. I said that I had not had a chance, as he had never asked me whether it was worth attacking, or if the ships would be much damaged, but merely where ships could be best placed to attack it, and that I had feared to volunteer an opinion on a point on which he had not asked it. Just after the chief came up on the poop for me to point out more things to him, and he asked me plainly, 'Don't you think this ship would soon knock down that fort?' I said it would be very difficult, as the solid masonry of granite would be difficult to batter, and that I thought the damage and loss to the ships would be of more importance than the place was worth He said that was the real question, and we had a long talk about it. I think he will not do anything more, as he must see that perfect success here can have no bearing on the important points of the war, whilst it might compromise our superiority at sea. We have here only ten sail of the line, and fifteen of theirs are at Helsingfors, six hours' sail off, and the Cronstadt ones, of which fifteen at least are sea-going ships, are only a few hours more with this strong easterly wind; so we certainly ought not to risk our ships. Had there been a squadron here inside, then it would be our duty to destroy the forts to get at them, and they are not too strong to prevent our doing it, if anything like the destruction of a squadron could be secured by it.

"I hope none of you ever speak of anything I say about the admiral or the fleet out of the family. If I were not confident this would be attended to by all, I should be afraid to write one-half I do.

"25*th*.—I have been again for hours with the chief, who is on board the ship, and sends for me every now and then He is still reluctant to give up the idea of attacking this place. He asked me if I thought the large fort could stand out for a moment against the fire of the *Duke*. I said that of course she, with other ships, could soon destroy it, but that she would probably suffer severely first, and other ships also, and perhaps have to go home for repairs, particularly if her lower masts were disabled. He allowed that the fear of the ship's lower masts was the most against it ; but as to going home for repairs, ' Why, no ship had to go home from Acre.' ' No, sir ; but at Acre they could not hit a line-of-battle ship at eight hundred yards ; here they hit the end of a small steamer at one thousand five hundred yards. We must compare it more with

Algiers, where every ship was much damaged.' I then urged him, if he thought fit, to try every heavy gun in the squadron shelling at a long range, and so at least greatly shake it I fear he will not be satisfied without trying it.

"Two deserters came in a punt about twenty miles last night from near Degero, above Hango. The long creek to Baro above it is the place where *Arrogant* and *Hecla* had their fight. I breakfasted with Yelverton and got all particulars. *Arrogant* grounded in the entrance just as she had destroyed the battery of four twenty-four-pounders The Russian horse artillery had been most gallantly galloped down and unlimbered on the open beach under her fire within three hundred yards; but our ships knocked over so many men that they galloped the horses down again to try to limber up under fire, and two guns were upset, one in the water. Several horses were killed, and at last the Russians cut the traces and left the two guns. The *Arrogant* got her anchors out and hove off, keeping the fire of the rifles down with grape. They saw one officer on horseback cut in two by a round-shot, and the deserter says it was the major commanding. They brought out the one vessel; two others were aground, and they could have burnt them; but I was glad to hear Yelverton say that he had not the heart to do so, as it could do them no good, and only perhaps ruin a poor man Ekness was at his mercy, and they saw women and children flying from it and collecting outside, many well-dressed ladies among them, and the people removing their things I said I wished he had sent a flag-of-truce in to say they had nothing to fear, as we should not fire at a defenceless town , and he wishes he had done something of the kind. But I fear the old chief will not approve of any such Christian-like mode of conducting war, for he thinks Yelverton ought to have demanded the vessels on shore, or knocked the town down, if they were not given up; but he agreed with me that nothing should induce him to fire a shot at defenceless houses, women, and children. The deserters are from gun-boats sent down there, and they say that three hundred of their troops were killed (this perhaps included wounded), and the next day all the inhabitants were ordered out of the town, so that they might burn it if a ship came again

"Though several round-shot struck both vessels, no one was hurt, except by rifle-bullets. The man in *Arrogant* (the captain of the gun) was killed by a ball on the main-deck through the port. It seems to have been a well-done thing by Yelverton and Hall. Hall led, and got several shots from the battery in his bows; but when *Arrogant* got up in the narrow channel, and turned round about three hundred yards off, she gave it a broadside that completely silenced it. It was a temporary battery hastily constructed. Hall has certainly opened the business; and having a small but well-armed steamer, he will be in the best position possible He said it was fortunate for us we had not remained with them, as having no bulwarks we must have been terribly exposed to the rifle-balls, which came like hail. It is a hint for us, and I shall take care, if we go near the shore, to have a good barricade of our hammocks, boxes, bags, etc, so as to be as much sheltered as if we had high bulwarks.*

"The deserters also said that on the island sheep and cattle may be bought, and that there are no soldiers or arms there. So the admiral ordered me to go directly, taking men with me and the purser of the flag-ship, on a foraging expedition, and the men recommended one of the large islands outside Degero The admiral was very urgent that I should not go near any armed people or risk being fired on, and I assured him I was quite as anxious on that head, but that there was little fear of our not keeping out of the way, unless in a new place we got on shore and the gun-boats came out; so he has sent *Gorgon* with me, and we are only waiting till the weather moderates There were poor Russian prisoners on board, taken in one of the merchant-ships, and the deserter Finn interpreted for them. They thought they were going to be shot, and the terror of a poor fellow in a sheep-skin coat was almost amusing: he said he had a mother, and he hoped we would let him go back to her. The poor fellow shook with terror, and pressed his hands to his chest as if in pain, and it was some time before we could convince him he was not to be shot, particularly as a party of marines were exercising on the deck above, and he could see them up the hatchway They seemed to see that the officers with most stripes on their sleeves were the great men, and, directly one came near, down they went on their knees and put their heads on the deck; and when at last they were ordered into the

* What about the small craft of the present day in this respect?—Ed

chief's cabin, they went down with such a flop that I thought they had broken their knees and heads. They looked much less terrified when they came out, and had been assured that when we went higher up they should be landed near where they had been taken.

"To return. We went up the channel to Elgo Island, and I soon found these men knew nothing about the place, and that on the island where they wanted me to go there were two Russian telegraph stations. So at last I sent them to see what they could get in their own punt, telling them to tell the people they should be paid for everything they liked to sell. I then went in the gig with six men and Evans (all of course well armed), to see what I could pick up myself, and we soon came to an island, where in a little cove I saw several cows I thought I saw some one; so I landed and went in alone, thinking that would show they need not fear; but I could find nothing but cows, and no sign of dwellings. Feeling sure the people would not have left their cows behind if they had fled, we pulled round the island till we came to some sheep and lambs on a point, and shortly after to a pretty cove among islands, where were several boats and nets and four or five cottages. As we pulled in I waved a white handkerchief, and soon we saw some heads peeping through a window, and as I landed one young woman walked down and met me, evidently in great alarm, and she looked dreadfully frightened as I shook hands with her; then two more came out, equally frightened. (I had a good interpreter with me.) On going into the house, it was a most painful scene! One poor old woman got up in a corner, put up her hands in an agony of terror, and cried bitterly. On a bed in a corner, huddled up, were three young women, also crying, and in all there were about eight or nine, including one girl of about twelve. It took some time quite to reassure them They said they had been told we should murder them all if we came, and destroy all their property. The men had all been taken to work at new batteries where *Arrogant* and *Hecla* had been; and, when the women saw me pulling in on the opposite side, they ran away, and all from the four houses collected in this one room for safety. They were in the act of heating a large brick oven to bake a batch of rye bread, enough to last a fortnight. The loaves are flat, about a foot in diameter, and have a hole in the middle, through which they are strung on a stick. The women soon went on raking out the fire and putting the loaves in, and I got some potatoes to roast in the ashes. They had a bullock and some sheep they would sell ; so I sent off for the purser of the flag-ship, and a boat and the butcher from *Basilisk*. The women were all clean, modest-looking people, though very poor, and they were comfortably dressed, some in English materials, and some in home-made. They could read, but had only a Prayer Book and an English Psalter. Freshwater, my coxswain, just reminded me of the Swedish tracts, and that made me ask if they had a Bible, but they had only the Psalter, so while they were killing the bullock I went off and got a large Swedish Bible and some tracts. We gave them £3 10s. for their little bullock, but the sheep were too poor. We also bought some fresh and salt fish from them, and I bought one of their little wooden spoons, to their great amusement. I brought them also some tea, sugar, and biscuit ; and when we left it was under very different circumstances than when we came. When I gave the old woman the Bible, she got hold of my hand and kissed it, and then all the others did the same. I thought they were going to give me other kisses, they got round me so. When I went off, I sent back some coffee in the punt, and they sent back some delicious cream, and we enjoyed a first-rate cup of tea with it. Egerton of *Basilisk*, the purser, Cudlip, and Evans dined with me, and then at 8 p.m. we weighed and ran out, getting here at 10 30 p.m. The chief was very civil, and I have been with him again to-day, and he now begins to treat me with some confidence I heard that at his dinner-table a few days since the chief said to Admiral Chads that I was 'the most active man in the fleet.' So I hope I may be working myself into a position that may be useful to him. I believe he has quite given up all idea of attacking this place. I am glad to find that after all the Russian ships were not outside Helsingfors in the winter ; they are frozen in, in their own basin between the forts."

CHAPTER VIII.

RECONNOITRING BOMARSUND.

THESE letters, from two distinguished officers who accompanied Captain Sulivan on the expedition about to be recorded, may be inserted here. The following extracts of a letter from Admiral the Hon. Sir A. A. Cochrane refer to this expedition :—

> "UNITED SERVICE CLUB, LONDON,
> "*March 24th,* 1894.

"DEAR MR. SULIVAN,—It has afforded me much gratification to learn that you are about to publish the biography of your father."

After giving a short account of the survey of Bomarsund, he adds :—

"Throughout the whole affair, the *élan,* coolness, and courage of Captain Sulivan, bravely and skilfully seconded by the officers of Engineers, will always be remembered by me with admiration and respect. Captain Sulivan's able reports upon the batteries and the approaches to them enabled the Baltic fleets, English and French, under the pilotage or instructions of Captain Sulivan, to anchor in Bomarsund Bay. . . .

"I entertained the very highest opinion—as did, I believe, all my brother-officers—of Captain Sulivan's ability and devotion to the service, and of his sound judgment and for his *coup-d'œil* in naval and military matters. He was a truly pious and good man, and was alike courteous, cool, and brave.

"His death caused me sincere regret ; and when the hour arrives that England is involved in war and requires brilliant services, our navy will be fortunate if it possesses a few officers as resourceful and as modest as your late distinguished father, who served his country well, and who has now, alas! passed from us.

> " I am yours,
> "ARTHUR A. COCHRANE."

From the late General Sir John Cowell, K.C.B., Master of Her Majesty's Household :—

> "WINDSOR, *March* 10*th*, 1890.

"DEAR MR. SULIVAN,—It is probable that no one but those who have served with the late Admiral Sir B. J. Sulivan could form a correct conception of his character and ability, for he was of a most retiring disposition, and was seldom heard of, except in times of action. Yet there must be many living who have had opportunities of observing his qualities for command, either in the difficulties met with in the navigation of unknown or indifferently surveyed waters, or those incidental to every seaman or in the operations of maritime warfare.

"Sir James's services were of a various character, and in each of these his abilities were conspicuous and universally acknowledged. . . . His ardent temperament was combined with a judgment which inspired confidence, and there was nothing more remarkable in the career of this truly good man than his utter forgetfulness of self and his desire to reward merit wherever he met with it.

"Having been with him on many occasions during the Russian war in '54, when he was what may be termed ' pilot ' to the Baltic fleet, as his father had been to that of Nelson, I had opportunities of learning what he was, and I was often surprised at the accuracy of his forecasts as to what the soundings and lay of the land would be from a few casts of the lead. This intuitive power was remarkable, but he never presumed upon it beyond what he considered justifiable. . . .

"That England may never be without such men is the fervent hope and belief of,

> " Yours very truly,
> "J. C. COWELL.

"H. N. SULIVAN, ESQ."

Sir John Cowell, alas! has not lived to see this letter of his in print. Nor have several other friends who have sent me letters about their old comrade-in-arms. Unavoidable delay in publishing this memoir has lost me the pleasure of being able to send them copies. It may be interesting here to add an extract from a letter written by Captain Sulivan from Led Sound on September 5th, 1854. Cowell had accidentally shot himself in the thigh with a revolver my father had lent to him

"I have been spending two hours with Cowell in the hospital-ship. He is the most intelligent of all the engineers, and I like talking over the professional questions with him better than with any one."

"Near Bomarsund, Aland Islands, *June* 4th.

"I have been so hard at work that I have been unable to write, and yet it has been the most interesting cruise I have yet had. On Sunday last (28th) the chief told me he wanted me to go to the Aland Islands at once; but as he could hardly spare me two steamers, I asked for *Driver*, just come in. She draws only fourteen feet six inches He gave me her, and I made a good selection, for she is far handier than any large steamer I have seen, is well handled, and her commander, Cochrane, a son of Lord Dundonald, is a most zealous, pleasant assistant, and I could not have hit on a better. Knowing that the admiral ought to have sent the senior engineer officer with me, as we were going to reconnoitre forts, I asked him to come with me, and the captain of the fleet got permission for him. Strange to say, the chief never seems to think of them, and at Hango even he never sent one till I asked for Nugent to go with me, and they say they never get out of the flag-ship except when I ask for them I find Nugent a most pleasant mess-mate, and I hope he is seriously inclined There is never a day passes without his Bible being on the table among his plans, etc. I received orders to examine the channels to Bomarsund, to examine the forts, *and to sound alongside them*. Rather an amusing order, considering it is daylight all night, and it is an instance of the way the chief gives orders, for he never meant it, as he cautioned me against going too near, particularly to avoid the gun-boats, thirty of which were said to be here, and said he would 'have no fighting for fighting sake.' I assured him I was not so fond of it as that, and that he might rely upon my taking every care. A thick fog prevented our starting, so I had to run in the fog from ship to ship carrying messages. However, in the evening we were at anchor, and at six I had service on the lower deck. When it was over the fog had gone, so we had to start. It was a beautiful evening, and nearly calm. In the night we met three large boats running to the eastward for Hango, with six or seven men in each, and provisions. I thought they were men sent from the island to work at Hango or Eckness, and perhaps I ought to have stopped them ; but I could not find the heart to interfere with them, their boats being perhaps their all ; so I let them go. In the chart you will see ' Led Sound ' on the south side of the Aland Islands : to the eastward of that there is another passage into the same channel. We entered through that, as there is a track marked in the large chart, but found very bad rocks : once, with a boat near us, we saw the rocks under just in time to go astern, *Driver* being always close astern of us. At last we got in and found the sound, besides a fine clear anchorage for some miles. Just near an east point of Lemland Island we saw a boat going in ; and wanting information about which islands had soldiers on them, and where their gun-boats were, we went in three boats after her ; but we only found the deserted boat and their provisions. There was a pretty farm, fine pasture, and cows, and we walked some way in, but only found barns. I left a shilling in the boat's head-sheets, to prove to them we did not want to injure them, and we then weighed and threaded our way through very intricate places, till we got in the evening off a village on the east side of the sound. The Swedish lieutenant was with us as interpreter in *Driver*. I pulled in in the gig with six hands and Nugent after several boats we saw pulling away from the village. I wanted as soon as possible to show them we were not their enemies, and they need not fear us ; but we found the village deserted, and the boats gone out of sight among the islands. After pulling some way, we saw two men in a large boat with wood. I waved a white handkerchief to them, but they left their boat, jumped into a skiff, and pulled for their lives, as they thought. Just as we got near them, they got through an intricate passage where we could not follow, and, as we pulled round, we had just time to see them land on the large island and run into the wood.

"On pulling round the next point, we came on a fine large village (Degerby), where in a moment there were men, women, and children running in every direction.   Several apparently respectable men halted at some nice houses a quarter of a mile off; and as we pulled in, waving my white handkerchief, one old man, much too feeble to run, came to the jetty.   Seeing no soldiers among the twenty or twenty-five men in the distance, we landed; and after I had made friends with the 'old man' a few others joined us, and those in the distance, seeing we did not murder these, mustered courage to come near.   Among the first were two ladies, very nice looking and well dressed   There was a second large house, and the young ladies told me with great glee that the lady it belonged to was putting up some things to run away as fast as she could   At first we could only understand them through one gentleman, who spoke a little bad English, but soon I sent for Theorell, the Swedish lieutenant, who was with Cochrane in his gig. They had gone to the first village I had passed, and found every house deserted but one, and in that there was a crippled man, and he had made two women of his family remain with him: these promised to have milk ready as we returned.   When Theorell came, I found that one of the large buildings was a Russian custom-house; and one of my friends was the collector, and in fact a government officer, and it became a question whether I ought not to seize him and the custom-house, but after the way I had made friends with him, I could not think of it without giving him reason to consider I had broken faith, so I would not molest him.   Some of the women brought out baskets of eggs, of which I bought about two hundred at one halfpenny each, dividing them afterwards with *Driver* and our officers   After staying about two hours, we parted the best of friends, they promising to let the other islanders know we should not injure them or their property.   We got some milk from women at the other village on our return, and promised to send back their nice white pails, which we did, and I put a little coffee and sugar in them.   The next morning we worked our way through most intricate passages (but I think I can get a line-of-battle ship through them), till we passed the narrow passage leading to Bomarsund, which is in the north-east corner of Lumpar Bay, the passage being round the north end of the island.   But as that passage is so near the forts, where they have a regiment of Rifles of the Guard, and is only three hundred yards wide, with high wooded rocks on each side, I thought I would try to get in by one of the channels among the islands farther north. We got *Lightning* through a very narrow one, with, I thought, three and a half fathoms water; but the *Driver* following, touched in fourteen feet on a little point, and hung a few minutes. I then took her back outside, and went on with *Lightning*. We anchored a little inside, with one of the high tower forts about two miles from us over an island. I then ran in with my gig and three boats of *Driver* to the south-ward of Kalfholm Island, keeping a sharp look-out on all the wooded points, and as we went passing not very flattering remarks on the talents or folly of the governor for letting us pass in this way, when a few rifles would have stopped us. We passed a nice village on Michelso Island, and then seeing no one, and there being a fine rocky cliff

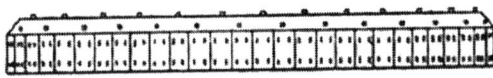

TOWERS

THE LARGE FORT AT BOMARSUND.

accessible on the west side of Michelso, we landed there to get a good look at and sketch of the forts. The large one, mounting ninety-two guns in casemates, exactly resembles a new terrace in a fashionable watering-place, the top having no guns, but a wooden roof to protect it from the weather. The long windows on the west side are all dwellings, I think. The dots show the casemates for guns, like square windows. The towers are just like two or three squares of the fort: there are three of them, each capable of mounting twenty-four guns, but having, I believe, only from ten to sixteen. I anchored a cutter off to look out and cover our retreat if necessary, sent another sounding, and we landed in the two gigs. I then planted four men as sentries a little inland among the trees, and Nugent, Cochrane, and I were lying down with glasses watching the forts and sketching. We were two thousand five hundred yards off, so I wonder they did not disturb us with a gun. We had nearly got all we wanted, when the cutter gave the alarm that a large party of men had landed on the island in our rear, where I have marked the

A [see p. 222], and had boats there. I thought this the very thing they ought to do, as it must oblige us to fight our way back. Cochrane and Nugent hurried to the boats, and I went to bring in my sentries, expecting to see the heads of these men appear every moment. We then hurried to the boats in anything but a dignified way, recalled the other cutter, and pulled back, but to my surprise saw no men on the shore, till I saw about five on the small island, so that instead of being cut off ourselves, we had a chance of cutting them off. We gave way in the gig, and soon left the other boats, and saw three men start in a little skiff and land opposite, and the skiff go back with one man, and, just before we reached the island, pushed off again with two others, one a person of some position by his dress; but he appeared in a frantic state. I thought we had him, for we turned him from the first point, and I, only wishing to speak to him, waved a white handkerchief; he waved another, but pulled the harder for another point. We gained every moment, and, when not thirty yards off, he was foolish enough to level a pistol at us. I had a rifle in my hand, thinking whether I should fire ahead of him to bring him to, but did not show it to him, and feared I should make him think I intended treating him as an enemy; but had he fired the pistol I must certainly have shot him. However, I saw the boat was getting among stones, and I could catch him without firing, which I did not like to do, so I stopped and hailed him, showing him the white handkerchief; but it was no use—he reached the shore, and after laughing at us a minute took to his heels with his two men. That was close to the village; so thinking he lived there, we pulled to it, leaving the large boats outside, and I landed and walked up with Theorell. We saw a number of men and women leaving; but on getting near, could only see one man, who came to us on Theorell's hailing him, in great fear and trembling; soon a second came, and the wife of the first, who was watching behind a house, was induced by his hailing her to come also, but crying and in a great fright. They told us these people we had chased were from the fort and not belonging to the village: had I known that, I would certainly have been less delicate as to bringing them to at all hazards. We then returned on board, and moved the vessel out alongside our *big brother*, that we might be under his protection.

"The next morning we ran back to the entrance of the Ango Passage, as I felt confident they had taken no steps to oppose us there; in fact, the governor seemed entirely to neglect his means to annoy us; but as he had no gun-boats, he had no power afloat. The steamers under Buckle and Admiral Plumridge had been seen round the islands, and they had burnt some vessels, which, I suppose, prevented the gun-boats crossing from Abo. I forgot to say that just as we left our position on the rocks, and had started back in the boats, the fort fired a gun at us, but the shot did not come near us. At the entrance of the Ango Passage we had great difficulty in finding a channel between two islands, a rock with six feet of water on it nearly blocking it up. At last, by shaving very close, we led the *Driver* through; but it was anxious work. We then ran up in a fine clear channel to Lumpar Bay, and anchored about three thousand yards from the forts. We then had a capital view of them, both from the *Driver's* mast-head and from the rocks on the cliff, our old position, and we got some soundings in the bay. I ran a line in the gig across at two thousand yards from the fort, and yet they did not fire at me, which I cannot account for; and then, wishing to cut off a small vessel, I stopped her at two thousand yards from the fort, and turned her head towards the ship, to the great consternation of the six men and two women in her; yet the fort never fired a shot to protect her. After getting all the information we could, we let her go, to their surprise, and we ran out again before dark, in case the governor should recover his senses and send some rifle-men to the shores of the channel in the night.

"The next day we made our way to the northward, past our old anchorage. On our way to try and get down from the northward to the back of Bomarsund, and so see the forts and towers both sides, I wanted to get near behind the two towers. When near the large island to the north-east of Lumpar Bay, we found very shallow water, and had to anchor. There was a large village close by, so I went up to it; and after getting one or two men not to run away, and Theorell talking to them, all soon came back, about twenty men, with plenty of women and children. We found that two steamers, probably Buckle and Glasse's, had been there, and burnt two vessels. The ships had anchored outside in the open, but sent their boats in. We found several coasting-vessels sunk in a cove to save them from the English, and one nice schooner afloat, but empty. I found that the chief wealth of the poor people consists of these little vessels, and I assured them I would not injure or take one of them; even the vessel afloat would not be worth the sending away men in her, and it would be, I think, cruel to burn her, particularly as all these islanders are much attached to Sweden and hate the Russians. I wanted a man to show us the best channel, but all were afraid; so at last Theorell told me one seemed to know more than the others. I determined to take him; so I put my hand on his arm and told him he must go with me, but that when I had done with him he should be landed and paid. He seemed terribly alarmed, but did not attempt to get away, and his young wife was in a sad fuss. His mother was the best: she advised him not to be afraid, and went for his jacket, but he said another man—pointing to him—knew best, so I took him also, but would not excuse the first. When we got them in the boat, they seemed quite satisfied. We found a good but very narrow channel for the ships for some miles, so we returned on board and started, but first landed the men. [The *Lightning* then ran on a rock.] She came off quite easily. We then went on to a good sheltered anchorage near the K in the word 'Kumblinge' in the chart, and I tried hard to find a passage through the numerous islands to the westward, but found so many lumps of rock sticking up one and two fathoms that I could not attempt it; so we remained there for the night.

"The next morning (Friday, June 2nd) we ran out to clear water in the north-east, or what appears on the chart clear water, but is really dotted with islands and rocks. The glass being very low, and the beautiful weather we had before evidently changing, I got into a good anchorage to the northward of two larger islands, where there seemed a narrow but deep passage to the westward. It freshened to a sharp breeze, so I did not like to leave our snug berth, as in a sea-way it is impossible to see the rocks under water in time to avoid them. As it seemed a nice island near us, and there were plenty of ducks about, we determined to have a half-holiday for the forenoon; so Nugent and I, in my gig, and Cochrane and Theorell in his, started. We explored one island, saw cattle, horses, and fences, but could not find a house; we then went back (I having shot

two ducks, our only game bagged), intending to try the
passage to the westward, but it blew so hard that we gave
it up, and crossed to a low rocky island with little wood.
In the afternoon it moderated, and we proceeded through
the passage, which we found very good. After running over
one rock without touching, with only twelve feet over it,
and just having time to save *Driver* going on it, and two
more failures to find water enough where we wanted to go,
we got quite round to the shore of the main island, on
which 'Bomar Sound' is written in the chart, but the
channel we must pass through again to go out is commanded by a fine rocky and wooded point, a thousand
yards off, and as it is only eight miles from the forts, and
the governor has twelve horse-artillery guns, if he does not
try to annoy us from there going back I shall have a
worse opinion of him. The wind was freshening into a
gale, and I was glad to get a nice safe anchorage under the
south side of the same two islands we had before anchored
the north side of, and about six miles from the forts.

"Yesterday was a very dirty day, and blowing a gale at
north, but in the evening it moderated a little, and we
landed at a village, where no one ran away or seemed
afraid ; but a nice family, father, mother, and daughter,
received us with smiles, and we found that the news had
come of our having treated the people well at the other
islands. This family had a nice new log-house, very clean,
like all the others, and with bed-places one above the other,
built to one wall like berths in a ship, in the same room
where they live and cook. This is the general plan with
these little farmers, who have a few cattle and sheep, and
a few acres of land in rye and potatoes, with plenty of
good log barns, cow-sheds, etc., for their stock. A print
of Queen Victoria and Prince Albert preparing for a ball,
she putting her gloves on, hung alongside the King of
Prussia and the Prince and Princess of Sweden. We
bought a few sheep at four shillings and sixpence each. I
got a very decent one. They have plenty of young lambs.
You recollect Moresby, whom we saw at Falklands—
Prevost's brother-in-law : he is first lieutenant of *Driver*,
and a very nice fellow. I see much of him. He was with
us on shore ; and he and I, being, I suppose, west-country
men, hunted out a pan of the most delicious cream. I
am sure you will allow this is much the nicest way to be

making war! The most singular thing is, we got the best information about the forts from the eldest girl: she had been pressed with the rest of the population to work there, carrying up sand on to the top of the fort,—they have sand laid to the depth of three feet. The people were forced to work, but were all paid. We left in the evening, all well pleased.

"This morning was very fine—the gale over. I had decided not to take the ships any farther, as the channels are intricate, but to sound them in the boats, and go as near as we could to the forts in the boats also, as we might have to put the ships near the main island within reach of their field-guns The more I see of them, the more I am interested in the people. It is a pleasure to be able to establish such a feeling with them when they were taught to look upon us as enemies, who would treat them ill and plunder them I hope to induce the admiral to order that no more of their vessels shall be burnt or their property injured. I much fear the French coming, as they will take all their stock at least, if they do no worse. I shall try to get the French admiral to give an order on the subject. To-morrow morning we start at 5 a m. with four boats, and I trust we shall be protected and spared all bloodshed, as we have hitherto been; but they are building a very large new fort nearer the deep water than the others, and I must ask the admiral to let me have two steamers, and prevent it by knocking their new work to pieces, which we can easily do at long range, as at two thousand yards from it the nearest guns they have will be two thousand five hundred yards off.

"I have been so hard at work, also having much 'remark' writing to do at night. I have therefore been obliged to write this on Sunday. The inconsistency of the chief is clearly shown by his refusing to allow me to go with Buckle and two steamers who were sent to do this very work a month since, 'because my vessel was unfit.' Now he sends me with one steamer, and we do all required; while the others, we find, had never got into the inside channels, which I do not wonder at, for they are enough to deter any one not used to such work. . . .

"The gale lasted till Wednesday (7th), when, being moderate in the morning, we started with four boats, and

got down to a good position two miles from the forts, but
we were prevented sounding nearer by the gale freshening
again ; and as it blew right towards the forts with a bad
sea I did not like to risk it, and we had to pull back six
miles against it, dodging among the islands for shelter, our
friend the governor again being very civil, for he did not
even send a rifle near to the point of the main island which
we had to pass.   On our way back we stopped to rest on
a small island.   I let the men have a run.

" In the evening it moderated, so we started and retraced
our steps back to Ango Passage, going through the channels
that had taken us so long to find in a few hours at full
speed.   We anchored off Ango Passage for the night,
wishing to look for deeper water into it.   This we found
the next morning, and then we ran down the sound to the
southward, sounding the parts we did not pass coming up,
but the track through the clusters of islands marked on the
chart as the usual route was more intricate and had less
water than the one we had found on our way up.   We saw
a new vessel building on Huland, and two others lying
near the southern channel you will see into Lumpar Bay.
I landed at one building with Cochrane, and was received
by about twenty men, who made a temporary jetty of logs
for our boats to come alongside : she was a nice vessel of
about a hundred and fifty tons.   The others were island
vessels of about the same size ; so I did not like to take
them.   I then crossed over towards Degerby, thinking I
might get some stock there to take back to the fleet with
us.   I wished to take both our vessels up to the village, but
the channel we first tried had only twelve feet between rocks
a few yards apart ; so I anchored *Driver* and went on in
Lightning, and anchored close off the custom-house, which
was also the dwelling of our fat friend the collector, his
wife being the lady who was packing up to start on our
former visit.   We told him that we must have stock, and
would take them, paying the people for them.   He said of
course we could take what we liked, and even told us the
parties he thought would be best to apply to.   I could not
resist the fun of frightening him a little, and told him that,
the house being a public building, we must seize it, and he,
being a government officer, we must take him prisoner.
He seemed to allow that it would not be surprising if I did ;
but he was evidently terribly alarmed, so I asked him if
he thought we could carry the house with us ; and as he

allowed we could not, he also allowed it would be our easiest way to burn it. But he said, though it was government property, it was also his residence, and a good deal inside was his, and that there were no goods belonging to the government, so he hoped we would not After getting up rather a laugh against him among his friends present, I satisfied him that he and his house were quite safe A party of us from both ships then started with a guide for a village inland, wheie they thought we could get stock ; but when we got there we found only a few lean sheep, except the ewes with lambs. Some of the lambs were just the size for eating and in nice order, but we could not persuade the people to sell them They had killed off so many last winter from the want of fodder that they were now anxious to save all they could to get up their stocks again. About five, having got all we could, we wished them good-bye, and ran out to join *Driver* again. They told us before leaving that they wished we could have taken the government policeman away with us, but that he was away that day ; that he was a regular spy on them, and that he was one they could well spare ; and that if he had been there they would have pointed him out to us, that we might relieve them of him. This I have promised to do if I ever go there again.

"The next day (Friday, 9th), after completing some soundings and finding a good channel out for large ships, we returned to Hango, our little *Lightning* doing pretty well, as she averaged eight and a half knots back, and obliged *Driver* to light all her fires to keep up with us We found the fleet had left Hango ; but *Penelope* and *Alban* were there, so I spent a couple of hours with Caffin and Otter, and then came on to this place—Baro Sound—the barometer being lower than ever we have had it. I was surprised to find the admiral outside at anchor off the Benskar Lighthouse : he received me very kindly, and seemed much pleased with all I had done, and after reading my report he said that it was a very good and complete one, and he was only sorry it did not give him better hopes of destroying Bomarsund with ships alone. I told him that as the bay in front was so narrow only three large ships could get within six hundred yards, and they would be exposed to the fire of all the towers at about fourteen hundred yards, in addition to the direct fire of the

large fort. I thought the ships would not succeed, and the
guns being all in casemates, and the tops bomb-proof,
shelling at long range was useless ; but I asked him to
send three or four steamers to knock down the new work
they are at, which is intended for a very large fort to
command the anchorage. We could knock it down at
two thousand yards with solid shot, as it is new brick-
work, and we see all the arches and the interior, and the
other guns would be two thousand five hundred yards off,
and could not hurt the steamers. They might bring their
field-guns down on the point, but they would be easily
silenced If that fort is completed, the place will be doubly
strong next year. The admiral asked me if I thought the
bad weather over. I told him no, because the barometer was
so very low, and we must have a breeze from the southward before it cleared off. He said that they thought it
was all over, but I stuck to the barometer. Certainly it
was a most injudicious thing to come out of a good port—
Baro Sound—and anchor in the open gulf with a hospital-
ship in company, with the glass lower than it has ever
been since we entered the Baltic."

Captain Sulivan's official report of his examination of
the Aland Island passages and the fortress of Bomarsund
is given almost in full in "Napier," p. 333, so it is needless
to repeat it here. The conclusion is as follows :—

· "I trust, sir, that you will approve of my having refrained
from destroying any of the coasting-vessels, the property
of these islanders, and of my having assured them that
they need not look upon us as enemies so long as they do
not take up arms against us.

"I cannot conclude this report without adding that I am
much indebted to the assistance that I have received from
Commander Cochrane and the boats of the *Driver* in
getting the vessel through such very intricate passages,
and the way in which that ship has been handled in
this very difficult navigation reflects great credit on her
commander."

The opinion he formed was that "an attack by ships

would be attended by a loss and risk too great to warrant the attempt, unless aided by a sufficient land-force to assist, first carrying the tower by assault or by regular approaches." This was the scheme ultimately adopted.

"BARO SOUND, *Monday, June 12th*

"Yesterday about 4 a m. our signal was made *wait*, as I thought proper. It was blowing strong from south-west, and I gladly availed myself of it by running in here for shelter. We were in before eight, three steamers being anchored on the shoals to point out the entrance. We had a quiet Sunday until the evening, when all Admiral Corry's squadron came in, led by *Alban*. All the fleet are now here or outside, except *Majestic* and *Boscawen*. The French admiral is in sight, about twenty miles off, with seven sail of the line, etc."

"BARO SOUND, *June 18th, sent June 20th*

"Since my last we have had little occurring worth mentioning. The fleet weighed from off Helsingfors (the chief's squadron) when I took the news up of the French fleet being near. We joined off this anchorage, and with French flags at our main and English ones at theirs we went into the sound where Corry's division was at anchor. I had the captain of fleet on board, and we went to pay our respects to the French chief, having two other steamers with us to tow, as the French vessels were all sailing line-of-battle ships and frigates, and they only had five steamers of their own ; so when our screw fleet had passed, our steamers helped to tow the French ships, and *Lightning* led them in The same day *Magicienne* arrived from Dantzig without a mail, but with plenty of bullocks ; and the next morning, our steam being up, but there being also a thick fog, I was told to take beef to the ships off Helsingfors, a note from the captain of the fleet saying the admiral wished him to say how sorry he was he was obliged to send me on such a duty ! ! On our return we felt our way in, and got alongside the flag-ship, the fog as dense as ever. When I went on board her, the chief was sitting in the stern gallery with the admiral and captains that had been dining there standing round him , he drew a chair alongside him, made me sit down on it, and immediately apologised for having had to send me on such a duty. I told him that I was very glad he had, for a larger steamer would not have been safe running in such a fog. Hardly a day passes now that he does not send for me, and we have a *tête-a-tête* discussion on different points, and I begin sometimes to get rather fearful that I shall be getting too much his adviser on some points for a junior officer. However, it is very pleasant, after being treated as I was, to find him treating me so differently. It has merely been from his liking my report of the Aland Islands, and of the opinions I have given him on points he has asked me about. And yet I never consider for a moment what I know he wishes, but give him my candid opinion, however differing from his. At present I think I may say I possess his entire confidence. A few evenings ago a small sloop was stealing along the channels. . . . We found her full of hay, and the crew consisted of husband, wife, and son, a boy about ten. We soon quieted the poor woman's fears by releasing the vessel. I was surprised to see in such a little vessel such a nice clean cabin, and a woman doing such work, yet neatly dressed, with a regular fashionable lady's monkey-jacket over-all, and very clean. She was very fair and clear-skinned, with auburn hair like many English women. She had in the cabin a small Testament and Psalter in one case. It is certainly not creditable to us as a nation that we should be so behind in education those we have previously considered half-barbarous Finns. They can hardly believe that numbers of people in England cannot read.*

"A few days since the fleet was rather startled by three cases of cholera occurring in *Duke of Wellington*, and one man being dead and buried in six hours ; but no case has occurred since, several cases of diarrhœa having been checked at once. The fleet is really more healthy than at any previous time. *Neptune's* small-pox and scarlet fever have ceased, and all the ships' sick-lists are reduced. That the hot weather will bring more or less cholera in such a fleet I have little doubt, as it seems hanging about all the northern nations. The only wonder is that men whose skins rarely make acquaintance with cold water are as well as they are. If we could force every man to have a bucket of cold water poured over him daily, we should have much less sickness. We had one man in the sick-list for some days from no other cause than his neglect of cleanliness :

* We have improved in this respect since this was written —ED.

they think when they have washed head, neck, and feet
they are clean   The weather is now getting very warm
and mosquitoes are coming   A few days since the thermometer was 40°, and I warmed my feet over a fire; now
I have got rid of the stove and got my carpet down, and
with the skylight open the thermometer is 72°.

"The *Vulture* arrived yesterday, bringing the sad account
of her boats and those of *Odin* being beaten off with a loss
of forty-six killed, wounded, and missing.   Plumridge, with
the four steamers, had taken possession of several places in
the Gulf of Bothnia, and destroyed a good deal of property,
in one place twenty thousand barrels of tar, and met no
resistance till the two steamers sent by him reached that
place.   I think it is called Great Carleby.   The steamers
could not get within five miles of it, and the boats, with a
hundred and eighty men under Lieutenant Wise of *Vulture*,
pulled up.   The accounts are very conflicting, and in the
papers you may perhaps see the best news; but from all
I can gather he pulled in with a flag-of-truce first, and
summoned them to surrender public property, and asked
them to point out which was public and which private (they
had concealed their force); but they refused to surrender
or show him anything, and said they could defend the place,
and would do so   Yet with this warning he returned to
the boats, and pulled in for the large store-house without
throwing a single shell from his howitzers to clear the way.
The *Odin's* cutter was within twenty yards of the large
wooden store, several hundred feet long, when a plank the
whole length was let fall or removed, and out came a long
tier of muskets or rifles   Ten men fell in the cutter the
first volley; but it appears *Odin's* other cutter dashed in and
towed her out, their boats losing six killed and sixteen
wounded—Lieutenant Carrington, Mr Montague, a mate,
and a mid killed.   The *Vulture's* paddle-box boat was
seen after the first fire with about eight oars pulling; the
other boats were pulling in to bring her out, when, on the
smoke clearing a second time, they saw her drifting on
shore without a man standing.   It is feared they are all
(twenty-two) killed or wounded.   A mate named Murphy
commanded her.   Nothing has been heard of her since; but
of course her gun and flag were taken with her.   The boats
then did all the damage they could with their guns.   Had
they done it first, they might have saved such a disaster.
It will be a good lesson against rashness and holding

the enemy cheap. Perhaps the ease with which they had destroyed other places made them too confident. At some former place some men—and, it is said, a mid—got drunk, and they set fire, among other things, to a house in which one of their own party lay drunk, and the next day they could only find a few of his bones and his knife.

"*Tuesday*, 20*th*.—Otter came in—or rather out—in *Alban* to-day : he has been up among the bays at the head of the anchorage. Last night he landed with thirty men on the mainland, marched three miles to the telegraph, caught the three men stationed there, blew up the house, and brought back all the books and registers. It was rather a hazardous thing to do, as there was a party of Cossacks near, and they (Albans) came on the spot where they had been bivouacking.

"We landed yesterday on an island 3,200 marines, besides artillery and seamen, with field-guns, of which we had about twenty : quite a little army. We can land nearly 4,000 seamen besides, and the French 3,000 troops and 2,000 seamen, making an army of 12,000 men, with guns, sappers, and all complete. I wish they were better trained. We have not landed the seamen at all yet, though my plan is adopted for the organisation, and all is arranged.

"A few days since I dined with Glanville. There were four captains present, all complaining of the disregard of the Sabbath, and three out of the four had tracts for distribution to the Finns and Russians. The chaplain of *Boscawen* completed our party—a good man. They have daily prayers and two Sunday services. It is a pleasure to meet so many in the fleet attending to these things."

On June 11th Captain Sulivan returned from his reconnaissance of Bomarsund, and made his report to the admiral. On the 20th Sir Charles Napier wrote to the Admiralty (see "Napier," p. 186) on the subject of future operations. He says, referring to Bomarsund : "To attempt this, as we have no troops, it would be necessary for the whole fleet to proceed to the anchorage pointed out in Captain Sulivan's chart, leaving vessels in the entrance of the gulf only, to watch the Helsingfors squadron, land all the marines and the French troops, which would amount to

five thousand men, land a great number of heavy guns, and
lay siege to Bomarsund, attacking at the same time in front,
if found practicable, if not, land five thousand seamen and
make soldiers of them. I lean to this, and shall propose it
to the French admiral . . . Since writing thus far, I have
been on board the French admiral. He has some doubts
about the policy of attacking Bomarsund, as well as the
propriety of doing it without troops."

My father's note to this says: "This plan was the
admiral's own I told him it was quite practicable, and
drew up a plan for the whole proceedings, in which Lieutenant Nugent, R.E, agreed. The admiral talked of
carrying it by storm, but I persuaded him that we must
land guns and knock the hill forts down, when the large
fort could not hold out. Admirals Chads and Seymour
quite approved, and urged the admiral to do it; he had
quite decided on it till he went to the French admiral,
when, on account of orders to maintain a force in the Gulf
of Finland, they decided on writing home and asking
for permission to take the fleet to Aland" On p 188
is recorded the approval of the Admiralty to Napier's
waiting for authority. Sulivan remarks: "The Admiralty
having approved of our not attacking it with the fleet
alone, and their agreeing to send out troops, ought to have
prevented the Government blaming the admiral for not
taking the responsibility of going there with all his fleet
without leave! When the French admiral declined to
attack Bomarsund without leave, he agreed that they
should send home directly for permission to do it with the
fleet, and he applied direct to his government. But the
Emperor saw the chance of gaining military success by sending a division of troops, and our Government yielded and
supplied ships to take the French soldiers out The French
general tried to prevent the navy taking any share in it, and,

being supreme over both French services, he would not allow
a French sailor or ship's gun to be landed ; but Napier
insisted on landing his men and guns to share in the work.
The French navy were bitter about it, and they felt they
owed it to their admiral, who would not agree to Napier's
plan in the first instance."

The following notes are from a letter to a friend, written
by Sulivan in 1856 :—

"The only thing that prevented the attempt was, I believe,
that both French and English admirals were ordered to
keep up a strict blockade of the Russian fleet, and
particularly to prevent the Sweaborg division getting to
Cronstadt, which must have been risked if the fleet went
to Bomarsund.

"The admirals therefore wrote home, offering to do it
with the fleet, if allowed to withdraw it from the gulf. As
their governments would not give their consent to this,
but preferred sending out a land-force to do it, they must
have considered the admirals did right in not withdrawing
the fleet on their own responsibility ; and the two governments are therefore solely answerable for having sent an
additional force out.

"It must not be forgotten that the opinion of the
governments on the importance of preventing the Sweaborg
division getting to Cronstadt was strongly supported by
the English engineers (?). It cannot therefore be wondered
at that the two admirals hesitated to withdraw the fleet
without obtaining the sanction of their governments.

"Without taking the whole of the large ships to the
Aland Islands, we could not have landed men enough to
carry on the siege. The screw-ships were all required, as
the channels were so intricate ; and to have taken the
marines from twelve or fourteen sailing-ships of the line,
not very well manned, and to have left them to blockade
twenty-six Russian ships of equal force, would have been
running a risk that no admiral dare venture on.

"It is therefore evident that the whole fleet must have
gone to Led Sound, leaving a frigate squadron to watch
the Gulf of Finland ; the screw-ships and steamers with
the marines and some seamen from all the ships must have

gone up to Bomarsund and commenced the siege, all being ready to embark at a moment's notice, leaving the heavy guns on land, in case the Russian fleet came far enough down the gulf to give a chance of catching them with the screw-ships ; after which the siege could have been proceeded with, and our guns of course recovered. This was the plan approved of by Sir C. Napier, and it only required the sanction of the Home Government to have been carried out successfully."

While awaiting the answer of the two governments to their proposal, the two admirals resolved to have a look at Cronstadt. As will be seen, the secret of a pending attack on Bomarsund was well kept.

CHAPTER IX.

RECONNOITRING CRONSTADT.

"AT ANCHOR THE EAST SIDE OF SESKAR,
"Saturday, June 24th, 1854

"ON Wednesday Admiral Plumridge returned from his long trip. We were all surprised to find the fleet was to sail immediately. It soon became known that it was to look at Cronstadt. The twelve screw-ships of our fleet were to go, leaving *Ajax*, as too slow, with the sailing squadron. On Thursday afternoon we sailed, having six French line-of-battle ships (four towed by their own steamers and two by ours). Soon after we got outside, we went with the captain of the fleet to the French admiral, and then were sent back about twelve miles with a letter-bag for the sailing-ships. I went in a narrow direct passage that saved us a long round, and we soon got out again, and about 10 p.m. overtook the fleet again. The admiral seemed doubtful if we could have been there and back, and asked me from the stern-walk, and, when he found we had, he called out, ' Well done !' We then went off directly to *Euryalus* inshore off Helsingfors, to recall *Arrogant* and *Bulldog* to the admiral, and by the time I reached the *Duke* again it was three o'clock in the morning, and I was quite ready to lie down. Yesterday at eight we were ordered to take *Porcupine* with us, and go ahead to examine Hogland Anchorage (on the east side), and we soon left the fleet behind and led the way up the gulf, no ship having been so high before. The *Porcupine* is a very nice steamer, a little larger than *Lightning*, but with much more power : she was built for a surveying-vessel, and the Hydrographer asked for her for me instead of *Lightning*, but as she was in commission they could not change her commander.

"We ran close round the south end of Hogland, watching each wooded headland to see if there was any battery or any troops to oppose us ; but we saw nothing till we came to rather a large village, where there were a number of women and children and a few men There were two or three small schooners, and a number of boats of all kinds hauled up on the shore. Towards the north point is another and larger village, and the people stood in clusters watching us, and did not even drive away a herd of about twenty cows lying on the beach in front of the houses : it is evident they do not fear us. The women were all dressed exactly alike—a sort of loose white bodice and dark-coloured skirt. We completed all just as the fleet hove in sight. The anchorage is a bank near the shore, like Madeira, going off suddenly to thirty-five fathoms. Instead of anchoring, I found the admirals had determined to go on to Seskar Island, about twenty-five miles below Cronstadt The chief asked me to remain to dinner.

" About nine, when I left, the admiral sent me again ahead with *Porcupine*, to place her on the north point of the Seskar Banks to guide the fleet, and then I was to return to him. We reached the place about midnight, but it was so thick we could see nothing, and had to be guided entirely by the course and patent log. We hit the bank in four fathoms exactly, and again went back to the admiral. We found him anchored on account of the thick weather, and I was able to get to bed again at 3 a.m, not having been able to lie down all day. I slept till six, when I found we were under way, and I should have remained quiet had not our signal been made to chase a small craft between the banks to the southward ; so I had to remain on deck. We caught her at 7.30, and found her a little country schooner going over to the south shore, with nothing but stones in her : there were five men—Finns. I let her go, not thinking it right to detain her, but she has been brought in as a prize by another vessel that fell in with her afterwards ! I hope the chief will release her.

" We anchored off this island about 11 a m. We have lovely weather, but too warm I fancy the smaller vessels will have a peep at Cronstadt, and that we shall take the lead in bearding the bear in his den. I suppose we are come up to try and tempt him out. We have only eighteen sail of the line. They have, I believe, twenty-four in Cronstadt, and eight the other side of us at Helsingfors

" The governor of Bomarsund has been dismissed, and a new one appointed, because he did not prevent our sounding the channels round it, nor attempt to oppose us at all.

" I am almost too sleepy to write, having only had six hours' sleep in the last forty-eight, and the weather so hot and close."

"RUNNING FOR CRONSTADT,
"*Monday,* 11 *a m., June* 26*th,* 1854

" Yesterday we had a quiet Sabbath, though a beautiful day. This morning at four the whole fleet weighed The chief has issued an order that, in consequence of the Russian flag being liable to be mistaken for ours, every ship in action is to hoist the yellow-blue-yellow pendant over the ensign at the peak and the jack at the main. I do not like it : our ensign ought to float at the peak below nothing. He might have made all hoist the white or red ensign instead of the blue, but nothing else We are now running up in three lines,—*Duke* and her division the centre ; Admiral Chads the port ; and French ships in tow the starboard ; *Impérieuse, Arrogant,* and *Desperate* ahead three miles. The chief is very full of the infernal machines, for he has made several signals about looking out for them—as if the Russians would let us see where they are. They are all submerged, we know ; but to ensure the large ships against them, we in poor *Lightning,* instead of going ahead of all, are kept a quarter of a mile right ahead of *Duke of Wellington,* that we may explode any machine in her path. I have just seen the Russian fleet from the mast-head, and instead of being anchored high up the passage in line up and down the channel, I think they are in two lines across the channel ; if so, they cannot be high up, but near the lower batteries, and then we might reach them with our heavy guns. In the sketch the border-line shows the limits of the channel for large ships.

" 4 *p.m.*—The fleet has anchored about eight miles from the lighthouse, and I have just been given the command of the inshore squadron, *Lightning, Magicienne,* and *Bulldog,* to go in and reconnoitre the fleet and batteries—Watson, with *Impérieuse, Arrogant,* and *Desperate,* to keep near outside and support us if necessary. We are going to anchor for the night to the southward of the lighthouse, about five miles from the fort, and to-morrow early a French steamer is to join us and we go closer in. They have several steamers with steam up, but I do not think they will attack us.

"11 *p.m.*—We have just returned from the lighthouse, where we had a fine view of Cronstadt and the fleet, but six miles off. I think there are not more than seventeen or eighteen sail of the line, and they are all moored above their batteries. My division is at anchor about a mile inside Watson's. A schooner came towards us as we approached, but is merely acting as guard-boat, for she turned back, and is now hovering outside the batteries.

"*Tuesday, 9 p.m.*—This morning at 4 a.m. the French new steamer *Phlegethon* joined me; the captain came on board, and said he was directed to place himself under

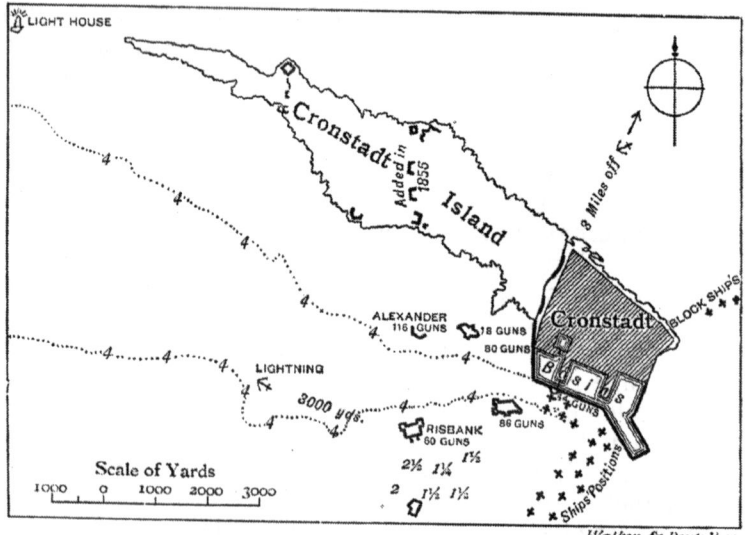

Walker & Boutall sc.

my orders. We then weighed with the four vessels and stood in, *Lightning* leading. The enemy's look-out steamer ran in as we got within shot. We stood on till we were within two miles, when I made the signal to the others to stop, and we went on to about two thousand five hundred yards from the grand fort (Risbank); but seeing them loading two very large guns on the flank nearest to us, and training them on us, I sheered out again to three thousand yards and then anchored, and had a most leisurely look at everything, getting a good sketch of port and ships and doing all we required. They had a large frigate-steamer and four others with steam up, but they did not move out. Their guard-steamer was evidently without guns, merely

a fast little vessel, and she got bolder and came nearer and
nearer every time. She took a look at us; but she being
unarmed, I would not fire on her. One of my captains
asked my signal for permission to fire, but I said '*No.*' We
were doing all we wished quietly, and it might have forced
their other steamers out, while we could have done no good
if they had come, as they could have kept under their powerful batteries   The two lines of ships I have marked are the
positions we thought their ships were in from information,
but we find them all above the batteries where I have
marked the crosses, with their broadsides to the channels
There are only sixteen sail of the line, and a heavy frigate
ready outside and one in the basin   There are three more
as block-ships to the north-east, not rigged, and beyond
them, to the north-east, three frigates ready for sea, and two
frigates and one corvette block-ship. There is also one
two-decker in dock. Having completed all, we ran out,
joined Watson's squadron, and we all went on while I
breakfasted with him, and then we led them all round to
the north side, Watson's ships anchoring when pretty near.
We ran on with the others, and I intended anchoring my
squadron in five fathoms, and then going on to three in
Lightning; but by this time it was blowing hard from the
westward, and, not liking to anchor them in shallow water
with a gale coming on, I hauled off a little to six fathoms,
and we all anchored about three miles north of Cronstadt,
and in front of their line of ships to the north-east, where
they have also in line this evening thirteen heavy gun-
boats, probably to annoy us at night; but it blows too hard
now. I have had three hours' sleep this afternoon, to be
ready for anything to-night   It seems strange that we
should be quietly lying at anchor within three miles of
such an enemy's fleet; but it is all-important steam that
enables us to do so.   In the dusk they might push gun-boats
within range unless a good look-out were kept, so I do not
like to go to bed, particularly as we are the inshore vessel.
A steamer has just been running rather far out on the other
side, where we were this morning, but *Desperate* (which we
left on that side to look out) has weighed and stood in,
and the steamer ran back. I do not think they will
attempt to molest. Their ships look rather slummy
in their appearance; and as they cannot evidently make
up more than seventeen or eighteen sail of the line, it is
impossible for them to come out : our English screw-ships

alone could destroy them. They are all placed to resist
an attack, and evidently think of nothing else. The
channel is certainly formidable and quite impregnable, as
the following sketch of it will show. After passing all

the heavy forts below, if not destroyed by them, our
leading ship would have all these hundred and twenty-
four guns and two three-deckers' broadsides raking her,
besides those of all the ships at longer distances on her
starboard bow. If she could possibly survive all this and
pass between the three-deckers, carrying away their bowsprits, she would find the broadsides of three two-deckers
close above pouring it into both bows. All their ships
are moored head and stern, which, if you do not quite
understand, I can thus explain. When Jim and Tom, at
the Falklands, had the cat with one lasso on her head and
another on her hind-leg, pulling in opposite directions, the
poor thing was moored 'head and stern.'

"When we landed at the lighthouse last night, we found
the doors of the tower well locked; but after some time
I found a shed and stack of wood enabling me to reach
a window in the upstairs passage from the house to the
tower, and with a chisel we got in without breaking
the window, forced open the tower door at the end of
the passage, and then found all the stairs in perfect order:
glass above only whitewashed to prevent our seeing through
it, and the revolving-frame left—merely the lamps removed.

"*Wednesday, 21st.*—*Hecla*, with *Odin* and *Valorous*, have
been shelling Bomarsund large fort, and burning part of
the wooden roof; but I think it is not worth the shot and
shell expended, for *Hecla* has fired away all hers, and the
other ships must have wasted a good deal; and the wooden
roof was only to keep off snow: under it the roof is bomb-
proof, and probably is not hurt the least. If so, it is a
victory for the Russians, as the ships left off for want of
shell, and had five men wounded. I could have burnt the
roof more easily with a few rockets, but it was not worth
trying. A mate of *Hecla* named Lucas threw overboard
before it exploded a burning shell that came on board:

every man had lain down to avoid the explosion. The admiral has applied for his promotion

" *Thursday*, 22*nd.*—I breakfasted with the chief this morning ; and after a long discussion with him on charts, crews, gun-boats, bombarding batteries, etc , he took me with him to the French admiral, from whom I have just returned. The admiral will not go up to see Cronstadt till to-morrow afternoon The old chief is frequently asking me whether I am sure he could go into the lighthouse safely, and seems half afraid of being caught The cholera is increasing in some of the large ships, and they have lost several men within a few days : we have hitherto been most mercifully preserved from it, the one man ill from diarrhœa being now nearly well. But I hope the chief will move the fleet into the open water, north of Gothland, as it would be a much more healthy part, and we could blockade quite as well as here."

" [*Private.*]

" '*Lightning,' July* 1*st*, 1854.

" The admiral went in in *Driver* yesterday afternoon : he would not go with us—I really believe because he wanted us to go ahead to explode any infernal machines before he came to them. His head is full of these things, though we have now run over all the ground outside the forts and actually are not blown up yet. I led him in the north side first, till he turned and then sent for me, and made me point out everything to him ; then we ran round to the grand position We ran on some way ahead, and I hoped he would go where I had anchored before, three thousand yards off ; but before I reached that I saw they had placed a target with a flag exactly where we had anchored, and we heard single guns all day, probably practising at their longest range. We also fancied we saw several guns all pointed for one spot, so we stopped a little outside the flag, the admiral having previously stopped half a mile outside, and was hoisting our recall as we rounded to I asked several officers to go who had had no chance before— Hewlett, captain of flag-ship, both the engineers, the master of flag-ship (a very nice fellow), the chaplain, lieutenant, and a volunteer. The admiral would not go to the lighthouse, so I got leave to go there, and we anchored ; and after all had dined with me, we spent some time in the beautiful evening on the top, returning to the fleet before dark."

"*July 3rd,* 1854.

"Yesterday morning we moved from off Cronstadt down to Seskar. The afternoon before, after closing the mail, the chief told me to take all the captains and commanders in the fleet to see Cronstadt, and a signal was made that all who wished could go in *Lightning*. I had nearly all, besides a few junior officers; but the chief would only allow me to take them to the lighthouse—not inside. We had a fine view of the fleet; and I took a Russian prize—the first I have taken—mounting ten guns; but they are wooden ones, and the vessel is so small that I am going to send it home as a present to the boys. We would not allow anything left in the lighthouse to be touched, but I thought as I saw this little ugly model of a brig about a foot long, I might fairly take it.*

"Yesterday we were moving about all day, so that I could not have service: the whole fleet was kept so long for the French sailing-ships to be towed. They are a sad drag on us, and yet they will not let us move alone We anchored about 6 p.m.; my signal was made directly, and I found the chief wanted me to run through Biorko Sound, to see if there was a passage for the fleet right through and out to the northward. He gave me *Magicienne, Bulldog,* and *Desperate,* under my orders, and he told me to tell Watson to take *Arrogant* and *Impérieuse,* anchor the latter part of the way, and *Arrogant* near the sound, to enable us to communicate by signal. About 10 p.m. we anchored in the mouth of the sound, and thinking that the narrow part at Koivasto would be fortified, and wanting daylight to look at it, we remained for the night. The admiral had given me positive injunctions to have no fighting, saying he trusted entirely to my judgment to prevent it, and that if I got the ships into any scrape *it would kill him.* I promised faithfully I would do all I could to be peaceable; but we saw before dark that there were a number of men on the point with the trees cleared away and a telegraph station, while the thick trees close behind would shelter riflemen. I was therefore in a puzzle. If we went on and they fired at us, we could not help having a fight, as we could not then go back, and yet it would be the thing I was positively ordered to avoid, and also there might be a sore feeling

* The only Russian man-of-war taken during the war !—Ed.

about no French ships being with us if we had a brush,
for the French admiral says that if our fleet had an action,
and he and his ships were out of the way, all the paving-
stones in Paris would not be enough to throw at his head!
So after consulting with Watson, we agreed that if we saw
any guns or preparations to resist our passing we would
wait while I returned and got the admiral's leave to attack,
and then I would take one of my ships and a French
ship round by the north entrance, and so place them
between two fires ; but that if we saw nothing to warrant
our waiting we would go past, and, if they fired, then we
would anchor round the point and destroy everything.
As we could cross our fire over the narrow point everywhere, we could bring off any guns there were. I would
haul *Lightning* close in, bend a strong hawser to a gun, and
steam off till we dragged it into deep water : in this way
we could get them all off. This morning it was foggy,
and we could see nothing for some time ; and fearing that
if the other ships came close, and we found there were guns
and the ships retired, it would look like a victory to them,
I left the other ships below and ran up in *Lightning*
cautiously, watching the point from the mast-head. I
soon distinctly saw a long parapet among the trees, though
masked with small trees, and I saw about a hundred and
fifty soldiers in blue marching among the trees, and also a
number of soldiers in grey about the parapet, whom I took
for artillery. I afterwards went through another channel
to get another view, and I stood up to within twelve
hundred yards, in hopes of inducing them, if they had
guns, to unmask them by firing on us ; but they never fired.
I then agreed with Watson that we would go on, and if
they attacked us the chief could not find fault with our
returning their fire. We arranged that I should lead up,
followed by *Magicienne* and *Bulldog* ; that *Impérieuse* should
accompany us and lay right abreast of the point, and
Desperate should be below it, to cut off the low neck ;
while we, with the two other steamers, should cross the
whole from above, so that not a man could leave the point
over the low part across our fire or a gun be removed.
We already speculated on how many guns we should get!
Now I think it would have been a very good plan, only it
wanted one thing to complete it, and that was an enemy.
As we ran up, expecting every moment to see them open,
and got pretty close, I found that I was quite right as to

the battery ; there was the parapet, evidently just finished, the whole point covered in front by the trees felled to form an abattis, and plenty of men, whom we saw concealing themselves behind rocks, trees, etc. ; but there were no guns, and they had the prudence not to fire musketry ; so we did not fire at them, though we could have destroyed them, or perhaps even cut them off. The battery had been just prepared for guns, perhaps within a week or two. The parapet was of loose stones with clay, something like a Cornish fence or hedge, and covered neatly on its top and front with sods, and hidden by young trees planted before it ; so that I was quite right in my idea. And as under such circumstances there would be guns in nineteen cases out of twenty, I was right in taking precautions, as it would have ensured success with the least possible amount of loss, and nothing is so foolish as holding an enemy cheap. Perhaps I ought strictly to have fired at the soldiers ; but it would have been almost a barbarous cruelty to have poured in all kinds of destructive missiles amongst men only, who had no means of retaliating. We might perhaps have killed or mangled a hundred poor wretches or more, as I could see them crouching thickly among the trees, but it would have done no good.

"So now you have full particulars of our peaceable fight, which we all laugh at now after the preparations we made. But, seriously, I do indeed feel deeply thankful that we were spared the necessity of forcing a passage, and that there was no bloodshed. We are too apt to think of the glory, honour, etc., of a successful despatch, and too many, I fear, would try to write one without thinking of the cost at which it was purchased. I do trust I may be able to set such ideas on one side, and to feel that the satisfaction of preventing unnecessary bloodshed is far more desirable I am afraid some of my colleagues deem me much too merciful. I think this battery has been prepared for their field artillery, several batteries of which (twelve-pounders) are distributed along the coast ; and in case of wanting to place any to defend this passage, they have raised this parapet, fearing to put permanent guns, as we should have been sure to take them ; but if they had their field-guns there, it would have been just the same, for I do not think, gallant as they are, their artillery would have limbered up and carried guns off that point under such a cross-fire as we should have poured on them : they would, I think, have been limbered up by hawsers to the *Lightning's* stern, and danced down the beach to the full power of her engines.

"We ran up the channel afterwards, several little coasting-vessels being deserted by their crews, who dropped the anchors and then got into their boats before we could catch them : at last, by pretending to pass some way from one and suddenly going full speed to her, and firing a rifle-ball over their heads, we caught her with the men. I have two Finns (deserters) on board, one speaking English, which is a great convenience. He hailed them—told them to drop their anchors and come in their boat ; they were terribly frightened—the master, a fine young man, and two others. After getting all the information I could, to their perfect astonishment I gave them a bottle of rum and a good lot of biscuit—two things they are fond of, though they do not drink to excess—and sent them back : they then said they had no idea we should let them go. They made sure they would be sent to England and put in prison. We ran back through the channel without anything occurring, and at 4 p.m reached the fleet again. I trust there is a favourable turn in the sickness, particularly in the *Duke* : no new cases, and those there are not bad ones. We all continue quite well. Johnson (the doctor) says he has found small doses of castor oil and turpentine check all cases of diarrhœa—castor oil almost in homœopathic quantity, and not acting as a dose.

"Cowell, the junior engineer officer, has just sent me a little coloured sketch of the lighthouse to which we have paid so many visits.

"The chief was much pleased with what I did, and he asked my opinion about his movements and what could be done. He wants a good position on the north of the gulf, and asked me about one   I pointed out another I thought better for various reasons, and he seemed pleased with it. He wants to anchor the fleet in a good position, and then examine the shores, etc., with the steamers, to see if there is any place where we can do anything, and I fancy from what he said I shall have the detached squadron. What a change from the time I was doing a lieutenant's duty as admiral's tender, now entrusted with everything worth being sent about! I really think *Lightning* herself feels proud of heading her squadron, for she steps out better than ever, and the large powerful steamers have to work pretty good power to keep their stations. I feel

the want of an armament for this work : we have now had
to cut away our forecastle-rail and bulwark altogether, to
enable us to put our two guns forward, as it is on the
bows we want them going through these narrow channels."

"[Private.]

"Sunday, July 2nd, 1854.

" We weighed this morning from off Cronstadt, and are
now standing down towards Seskar, but I hope going
much farther down. I think it is almost the first time I
was glad to move on a Sunday, for every day seemed
adding to the victims of cholera, particularly in *Duke of
Wellington* Yesterday they had fifty cases of diarrhœa,
eight of cholera, and two died in the previous night. I
was on board her some time, and I urged the admiral to
go right out of the gulf to Gottska-Sando, as the idea to
the men would be everything. I believe even this change
to a fresh air and a broader part of the gulf will do much
good. We have only one case of diarrhœa, and that is
getting well. What a mercy it is! The last few days
the cases have been milder and more like diarrhœa, and
except the *Duke's* the cases have rarely terminated fatally.
The change from the hot, sultry weather and the cooler
water alongside is probably the cause, and now we have
a nice fresh westerly wind, and we are all comfortably
wearing blue trousers again.

"I must not report about our movement in this, or it
will be repeating what I must put in the journal ; but I
must tell you what I do not like to put in the journal, as
so many see it, and that is how I am getting credit for the
work I do. When dining with Commodore Martin yesterday, after returning with my boat of captains from the
lighthouse, I heard him in the evening talking in another
part of his cabin (and I do not think he fancied I was
within hearing, as I was with another group discussing a
question) After some compliments to me, he said that it
was a pity for many to go in ships looking at different parts
of the enemy's position, as it showed them the point
we were thinking of, but that Sulivan alone ought to go
and examine it all, and report what could be done, as he
had such good eyes for it. Yelverton told me that a
French captain asked him what position I held, and if I
belonged to the Hydrographic Office, and whether I got
better paid than any one else—*for I did all the work of*

the fleet. I trust that all this being so flattering, and my position with the admiral now so satisfactory and comfortable also, will not make me think too much of these things, and forget to whom I owe the power and the health to do the work. One ought to live if possible regardless of all these things, when so many poor fellows are being taken in this sudden way.

"If, as I trust, the war ends this year, and I am spared, I think I shall be sure of being able to get something worth having through the Hydrographic Department, but I feel now as if I would prefer being home to anything As to going to sea again, if we have peace, for any advantage of serving time, I trust that will never be the path ordered for me by Providence But how little one ought to care for all this, for how has everything been ordered better than we could arrange it ourselves! More than ever must we endeavour to say and feel from our hearts that whilst we praise Him for the past we will trust the future entirely to Him—only I do desire that, whatever that future is to be, we may be together to share either the joys or the trials, so that we can either rejoice together or else comfort each other in times of trial. This is my greatest earthly desire, and there is no other that I ever think of in comparison with it

"*July 5th.*—We started to-day towards Baro Sound. I hear Admiral Corry's squadron there is so sickly (chiefly small-pox) that he has gone outside, fearing the place is not healthy: perhaps that has brought the chief down. Some of my brother-officers, and the chief also, seem to think it would have been right to fire on those defenceless soldiers at Koivasto, but I am sure I did right. What good would it have done to our cause, or what credit to our navy, for five ships to pour their broadsides on two hundred defenceless men? I could not do it.

"*Baro Sound, July 7th.*—Yesterday morning, on entering this sound, I was sent to place a steamer on one entrance shoal, and afterwards to go myself to the opposite side, where I found the buoy had been removed, probably cut off at night by the enemy, the place being left one night without a vessel. I found the rock, put down another buoy on it, and was waiting while *Duke* and French ships passed, the latter towed by steamers They were half a mile nearly outside us, when one of the ninety-gun ships ran right on a rock we did not know of before, with

only three fathoms on it. She got off this morning, and
I have been out to-day examining the place. We have
had a very hot day. I am thankful to say the cholera
is better, except in *Majestic.* She buried four men yesterday. The *Duke's* last cases were less severe, and she
had only one to-day, not fatal. We are still preserved
from it, and have only one case of diarrhœa, the same
we have had for some days, and that improves slowly.
To-night our men went to an island to bathe, and brought
off a few most delicious Alpine strawberries

"*Sunday, July 9th.*—The fleet has been coaling for the
last few days and preparing to start somewhere. The
Duke buried two men yesterday, and there have been three
funerals to-day. The *Princess Royal* has a hundred and
eighty men in the sick-list, and the *Royal George* a
hundred and fifty, chiefly diarrhœa; but the cases are
milder, and to-day *Duke* has none. We had to coal after
Alban, and she did not finish till eight last night. Had
it been any other day, I should have put it off till this
morning; but knowing we should be made to coal all
to-day if not complete, I worked all night, watch and
watch, having hot tea brewed for the men, thinking that
for health the night would be better for working in than
the hot day. It was our only chance of having anything like a Sabbath. We finished early this morning,
and have had our usual service. I used the prayers 'for
the time of pestilence' for those in the fleet who were
suffering, and returned thanks for the mercy of being preserved in perfect health in this vessel Our only sick man
was sent to duty to-day. I read a very nice sermon on
'a more convenient season,' as there was much in it
applicable to the present time. Just after service my signal
was made: it was to consult me about a report sent from
a ship that had touched on a rock at the Åland Islands.
I had afterwards a talk with the chaplain about the sickness on board, and asked him if there had been a general
use of the prayer 'for the time of pestilence.' I found he
had never used it, though he much wanted to, because the
admiral would not have an allusion made to it in the
service, saying it would depress the men At first, when
he touched in a sermon on the deaths that had taken place,
he was told it would have a bad effect, and he must not
allude to it again. Is not this sad?

"*July 10th.*—We have a nice cool day, and the ther-

mometer only 62°—the ships all healthier. The fact is,
it is the large screw-ships that have been unhealthy.
The sailing-ships have not had a case of cholera. The
heat of the engines confined under the deck seems to
cause it. In *Edinburgh* they have their boilers confined
under the after-part of the ship, and the cockpit, where the
officers sleep, is terribly hot when steam is up. She has
not had a case among the men, but three among the
officers, though all have recovered."

"ADMIRALTY, July 4th, 1854.

"MY DEAR SULIVAN,—All your letters charm me, but
especially your last from Seskar, for it gave me the very
agreeable intelligence that you had at last found your due
level, and were employed in your pioneering, or rather
leading, capacity. Your Bomarsund adventures also much
gratified me, and your soundings were quickly inserted
in the Aland chart In the meantime I send you my
heartiest wishes for the sustainment of your health, and the
credit due to all your exertions in the *chose publique.*

" Always yours,
" F. BEAUFORT."

"BARO SOUND, Monday, July 17th, 1854.

"The only thing worth mentioning since my last is
our trip to Sweaborg (Helsingfors) on Tuesday last. The
admiral sent me with a flag-of-truce to take a letter to the
Russian admiral on the subject of the prisoners taken at
Gamla Carleby. We started from this at 5 p.m. and at 7
were steaming up the channel to Sweaborg. The Russians
have removed a fine beacon on a small island, which
used to form the leading-mark, and have re-erected it
on another islet, thinking to deceive us and run us on a
dangerous reef; but it was too palpable to deceive us
a moment. They have actually put it in a position where,
on with a very fine church, it clears us of the very reef
they thought to run us on, while we ran up the channel
full speed without ever checking the engines, so good are
their charts and so easy to make out the proper marks even
without the beacon, though both sides of the passage are
for six miles bounded by rocks. When near the small
island, and about two miles off the entrance, across which
the admiral's three-decker is moored, she fired two blank
guns, evidently as a signal that we were near enough. We

had hoisted a white flag eight miles outside : at first it was a
sheet, but it was not large enough, so I hoisted a fine large
table-cloth, and took half a sheet for the boat-flag.   I went
to about a mile and a half off, just out of gun-shot, when
they fired another gun, and we anchored.   I then pulled in
as fast as I could in my boat, and saw a boat with a white
flag coming out ; but as we pulled much the faster, we got
within less than half a mile when we met, just as another
gun was fired, as a hint we were too close.   The lieutenant
in the boat said he was ordered by the admiral to say the
steamer was too close, and that if she did not move out he
would be compelled to fire on her.   I told him to give my
compliments to the admiral, and I should be happy to
move out a little if he wished it, but it would be useless his
firing, as the vessel was out of shot.   The officer seemed
very nervous about his orders (I had a Russian interpreter
with me, who also spoke French well) : he would not speak
Russian, only French, apparently that his boat's crew might
not hear.   I had difficulty in persuading him to take
the letter : when he did, I arranged that, if there was no
answer forthcoming, the ship should hoist a flag at her fore ;
if there was an answer, it should be sent out.   I said I
would meet the boat half-way, but he said I must not come
in the boat again, as I had come too close now, but the
letter should be sent to the ship.   I then returned about
9 p m., and shifted the vessel out about a quarter of a
mile, and we lay all night waiting till 1 a.m., when, as what
little dark there was was just closing, we saw a small
steamer coming out · she brought two lieutenants in a boat
with a letter.   With difficulty could I get them to come up
the ladder : when I did, they would only come to the top,
and all my attempts at politeness would not get them
inside.   I asked them how the wounded men were.   The
answer was, 'We know nothing about anything : anything
to be said is in the letter.'   They were evidently afraid of
compromising themselves, and had been told not to hold
any communication verbally with us.   As soon as they left
we started, and, though too dark to see the marks clearly,
we steamed out again at full speed.   I dare say they were
vexed at finding that, in spite of buoys and beacons being
removed, and the tower shifted to another island, we could
run in and out of their passage at full speed, as if we had
known it before.   I would not have any angles taken or
drawings made, as we were under a flag-of-truce ; neither

did I have a leadsman in the chains while near, that they might not say we sounded under cover of the white flag. We got back to the admiral at 5 a.m. The answer was that nothing could be said of exchanging prisoners till they heard from the Emperor, and that the officer and seven men were killed, twelve wounded, and eight unhurt.

"Last packet brought us the news that French troops were coming out, and set all the fleet wondering what is to be done. All sorts of reports are in vogue; and being aware Admiral Chads and myself have been much with the chief, sometimes for hours at a time, and Nugent, the senior engineer, also, officers know that, whatever the plans are, we alone are in the secret, and that makes every one more curious. Till the news of the French troops coming reached us, no one had an idea that anything was in agitation, so well has the secret been kept for nearly a month I only wonder it did not get out through the French, as the French admiral was consulted, and that was my chief fear about it. The fact is, that so many letters of officers get published that it is not safe to let anything be known; and some of them contain most *arrant nonsense*, that must make the writers ashamed when they see it in print. If I ever thought there was a possibility of a line I wrote being known beyond our own circle, I should never write a word on the subject of our movements again. I am glad to see that none of the papers know the real object of the troops coming out: even now it may be kept secret, or attention directed to other places than the true one. If so, you will probably be the only person outside the Government offices who will know all about it, and you certainly have been the only one during the last month who knew that there was something in preparation. You see the advantage of your large organ of secretiveness! Had you not proved so often how close you could keep a thing, I could not have ventured to write privately to you on the subject. The mail to-day brought, among other reports, one that Riga is our object. A brother-captain has been here this minute trying to find out from me if it is true. 'Where are we going?' is the common question I try to look very ignorant and innocent, and say, 'Have you not heard it is so and so?' (the last place reported).

"18th.—We sail to-day. I am now going to take buoys up, so evidently all the fleet are going. I go on ahead with some steamers to place them as marks for the big ships. It is not certain yet whether I shall find a passage for the *Duke*. I have three feet of water more to find. If I succeed in getting her up, it will be a great thing."

It will be well, I think, to give the following letter here; it was written to his old *Beagle* messmate, Captain Hamond, of Fakenham, Norfolk :—

"GUILDFORD, 1856.

"MY DEAR HAMOND,—I see that your neighbour the Marquis Townshend has defended Sir C. Napier against the attack of Sir R Peel I am glad he has done so; for whatever may be said against Sir Charles on other points, it is most unjust to accuse him of want of courage in not attacking with a fleet a place against which it is *impossible* to place ships, so as fairly to try whether their broadsides or the batteries are the strongest. No one but a madman would have run his ships into a long, narrow channel, with at most a foot of water to spare, out of which they could not pass; where there was hardly room for two ships abreast; where the slightest yaw in the smoke must have put them on shore; and where they would have been under the raking and cross fire of hundreds of heavy guns, against which they would have been able only to bring a few bow-guns to bear. The attempt could only have ended in the total destruction of every ship that went in.

"On our way up the gulf I boarded an American from Cronstadt. The captain and supercargo were both intelligent men. They said they had spoken to many Russian officers, who all allowed it was useless to bring their fleet out, as they could not contend with us at sea; but said that their plan was to have their ships quite ready, to let Napier get his ships knocked to pieces against their batteries, and then to come out and finish the work. I took these persons to the admiral, to whom they repeated this statement Common sense must show that this was the Russians' only safe plan; and had Napier played their game for them, and the result had been their destroying our fleet and getting command of the Baltic and North Seas, those who have abused both him and the Government would have been the first to cry out against the *madman* who lost the fleet and the Admiralty that appointed him.

"Those who contend that a fleet can destroy the strongest fortress should confine themselves to places where there is space and depth enough to admit of ships being fairly placed against the batteries, such as Sevastopol and Sweaborg. In both these places, if ships were not disabled on their approach by the raking and cross fire of shells from nearly two hundred heavy guns, they could get within short range of the nearest batteries ; but they would still be exposed to the fire of other batteries, especially earth-works placed higher and at longer ranges : these, aided by the broadsides of ships inside, would probably destroy the attacking ships, even if they succeeded in silencing the batteries they were abreast of. The success of two small batteries, so placed, at Sevastopol, on October 17th, against several of our large ships, shows what the result would have been if an attempt had been made against either Sevastopol or Sweaborg with the fleet alone. No one who knows anything on the question can doubt that it would have resulted in the destruction or disabling of the whole attacking force, and in giving the command of the Baltic or Black Sea to Russia during the summer of 1854.

" It is extraordinary that the public expected only Napier and the Baltic fleet to perform such wonders. Why have the Black Sea admirals not been equally blamed because they did not take Sevastopol with the fleet alone ?

" It is rather amusing to find ignorant persons talking and writing of what Nelson would have done, and to hear a line of block-ships and rafts at Copenhagen which he attacked compared to Cronstadt. If the Russian ships had anchored in line *outside* their batteries, can any one believe that Napier and Parseval would not have given as good an account of them as Nelson did of the Danish ships at Copenhagen in his almost drawn battle? For the batteries, though some distance from the attacking force, were so entirely uninjured, and, after beating off the frigates that attacked them, so annoyed the nearest ships, that Nelson was glad to avail himself of the first break in the action, caused by his flag-of-truce, to get his ships out of the channel.

" If Sir Robert Peel had studied the naval history of the French war, he would have learnt that Nelson never attacked a battery with ships, except very slightly the first day at Teneriffe, when, thinking it impossible to succeed that way, he gave it up and tried to carry the place by storm.

"At either Bastia or Calvi—I forget which—he opposed a proposal of the general's to bring the fleet in against the place, after a principal sea battery had been taken, on the ground that '*it had been proved ships could not stand the fire of batteries, now red-hot shot were used.*' A frigate had been burnt a short time before by red-hot shot from a small battery; and the martello-tower, with one gun, had beaten off a line-of-battle ship and a frigate with great loss, setting them on fire in several places.

"What would he have said if he had seen large ships so beaten by the fire of shell from a few guns as *Alban* and others were at Sevastopol? I should like to hear the opinions of such men as Sir Howard Douglas and Sir Harry Jones on the chance a fleet would have in the narrow channel at Cronstadt, *even if the enemy were to let them get in as far as they could before they fired a shot.*

"These are no new opinions of mine, as I expressed the same strongly after witnessing the effect of firing against earthen batteries in the Parana. Before the failure at Sevastopol, I expressed my conviction that three guns in a well-constructed battery, properly placed, would beat off or destroy any ship in the world. This view I pressed strongly on the Government, when I tried to stop the erection of badly constructed stone batteries at Plymouth in 1846

"I saw more of the defences of Cronstadt than any other person in the fleet, having been entrusted with the close examination of them both years, and I spent many anxious days and nights trying to find an opening for doing something against them. The decision of the admirals both years was in accordance with the reports I gave them; and as that is well known to those who served in the Baltic, I feel personally anxious that injustice should not be done to our services, which hitherto I feel has been the case.

"To those who know the truth about Cronstadt, the opinion now expressed, that it could have been taken the first year, but has since been made impregnable, is really amusing.

"As to attacking it with the large ships by the main channel, that was just as impossible the first season as the last. No additional defences were made on that side the first two seasons, and I believe none have been added since; therefore, if it is unattackable now, it must have been so then.   We had no kind of force for any other mode of attack ; but no one was to blame for that, as gun- and mortar-boats had not been thought of then ; and even if we had been provided with a large force of gun-boats, we could not have succeeded.

"The second year we were more ready, being in a position to attack it in the only way that gave a chance of success ; but we were prevented by circumstances that I cannot more particularly explain, but for which it is quite certain neither Admiralty nor admirals can be justly blamed.

"This last summer, when the place has been pronounced impregnable, we should have been for the first time in a position to make the attempt.   That it would have been made is certain, had the war gone on.   That it would at least have been successful, so far as destroying the town and arsenal by a bombardment, I have no doubt whatever, for we know that the defences necessary to make it secure were only commenced last summer.   That it would have further resulted in our destroying their fleet, and even occupying the place, is, I think, possible.   But of course the struggle would have been a severe one, and the whole mode of operations would have been so perfectly new in naval warfare that no one could be very confident as to the result, particularly as the natural obstacles were so very much in favour of the defenders.

"I am sure that I could convince any practical man of the correctness of these views, by explaining them in detail on the plan of Cronstadt ; and, however the Grand Duke may now try to depreciate our services—or, more probably, to deceive his wondering and ignorant hearers— I am quite sure, by the nature of the exertions made during the war to increase the defences, that he knew well that it was impregnable against a direct attack by large ships from the first, and therefore he wisely directed all his efforts to the really weak points in the defence, which he knew quite as well as we did.

"I do not for a moment wish to defend Sir Charles on every point, as there is no doubt that, if he had closely reconnoitred Sweaborg earlier in the season, it would have been seen how open it was to a bombardment with mortars, and that there were rocky islets at the right distance on which to place the mortars.   Had that been seen by the beginning of June, mortars might have been sent out and the place destroyed that season—that is, if there were thirteen-inch mortars and shell to send. But this I am not sure of, as their value seems to have been quite overlooked early in the war; and out of fifteen we had at Sweaborg the following year, fourteen were new ones

" Sir Charles said, in his speech in the House, that it was not closely reconnoitred because those he sent could not find channels in on that side. If so, it was a great blunder on their parts; for when I first went there on July 13th with a flag-of-truce, I went in at full speed by the Russian charts and leading-marks, without having a man in the chains. It was then too late to send mortars out that season, and the bombardment was managed more easily the next season by the placing mortars in vessels, instead of having the heavy job of landing them; so that no public injury was caused,—only Admiral Dundas had the credit of doing it instead of Sir Charles Napier.

" The only other thing that could have been done by the fleet was to have taken Bomarsund by landing seamen and marines.*

" I wish those who are so ready to accuse our admirals of wanting the courage of Nelson and his followers would really study the career of Nelson, and also of Sir James Saumarez, one of Nelson's most distinguished seconds. He attacked *three* French ships at anchor, aided by two batteries, with six ships of the same class, and was beaten off, losing one ship. A few days after, with his damaged ships, he followed and defeated his late opponents, though, with the Spanish squadron that had joined them, they were double his force. No one who reads that account can doubt his firm determination to bring an enemy to action where he had the slightest chance of success, and it was certainly one of the most gallant actions of the war. But a few years after we find him opposed to a Russian force so inferior that two of his ships with the Swedish squadron had driven them into Port Baltic before he joined with the English fleet. The Russians had landed some guns and thrown up batteries to assist in the defence, and Sir James, thinking they were in too good a position to be attacked, contented himself with blockading them.

" If Sir Charles Napier and Admiral Parseval are to be so severely censured for not getting at the Russian fleet inside the strongest fortress in the world (against an attack by

* See page 182 for the reasons why this was not done.

ships), what would have been said of them if they had
found an inferior force of the enemy in such a place as
Port Baltic and had declined attacking it? Yet Sir
James Saumarez is one of our brightest examples. This
will, I think, show how very unjust it is to compare the
conduct of the Baltic admirals, who never found an enemy's
ship outside their batteries, with that of Nelson and others,
who never attempted to attack fortified places, however
inferior to those in the Baltic, but persisted in long
blockades, till they forced the enemy's fleet out to meet
them, or caught them at anchor unprotected by batteries,
as at the Nile.

"Yours, etc.,
"B. J. SULIVAN."

CHAPTER X.

THE FALL OF BOMARSUND.

"ALAND ISLANDS, LED SOUND,
"*July 25th,* 1854.

"ON the 19th I left the fleet at anchor thirty miles outside, and came on with three vessels, besides *Lightning*, to
examine the passage in, before taking the fleet in. I had
been unwell for two days, which made me rather unfit for
the hard work that was to follow."

Much difficulty was experienced in navigating the four
vessels in a thick fog, and in seeking a way in amongst
the rocks. It was evident there was no passage for a
fleet.

"All that day we were hard at work looking for a
better passage in to the westward, through Led Sound. We
found a safe but very narrow one, with five and a half
fathoms, which we buoyed for nearly a mile; and having
placed buoys and two ships on outer shoals, and left *Alban*
to examine farther, I got back to the fleet at 9 p.m., passing through the islands close to Vitko Island. On the
21st, having left a squadron with Commodore Martin to
return to the Gulf of Finland, and despatched *Dauntless*
home, the fleet proceeded for this place, and we led them
in about 9 p.m.

"I had little doubt of finding a good passage for the
large ships to Bomarsund; but the admiral said I should
take up the *Edinburgh, Hogue, Blenheim,* and *Ajax* first, with
Amphion (my old friend and comrade Key), *Alban,* and
Lightning, all under Admiral Chads. I went in *Edinburgh*,
and we had an easy run for six miles, then anchored
to find a better channel than my former one of four
fathoms. I went in *Lightning*, soon found a narrow one,

but with five and a half fathoms, bounded by rocks with
only four, three, and two fathoms on them. We put some
buoys down, and then I returned to *Edinburgh*, and we went
on swimmingly through channels so narrow that the line-
of-battle ships seemed like giants looking down on the
small islands, and so right into Lumpar Bay in front
of Bomarsund   But we passed very close to a rock I knew
nothing of, nearly in the middle of the narrowest channel.
Fortunately all the leading ships cleared it without knowing it, but the last one, *Ajax*, ran on it : however, she came
off directly with her engines, and followed us ; so that I
may almost say I got them up without a mishap Admiral
Chads was greatly delighted ; and as Mr. Brierley, who sends
sketches to the *Illustrated*, was, with a host of amateurs,
in *Lightning*, I dare say you will see a sketch of it.   It
was the prettiest sight by far yet seen in the Baltic.   To
complete it, the enemy had built a new battery on a point
with five heavy guns, and I saw it just in time to anchor
half a mile farther out than I intended ; and I thought I
had brought up *Edinburgh* at two thousand five hundred
yards, but it was only about two thousand two hundred,
and the guns opened on her and on *Amphion*, and threw
the shot so unpleasantly close that Admiral Chads moved
both ships farther out.   All this made the scene more
interesting.

   "I returned the same evening, but found the admiral
would not let me take the large ships up : he had doubts
whether he would take them up at all.   So next day I was
asked by the French admiral to take one of his ships with
a number of officers and pilots to show them the channel,
Evans at the same time having all the masters of our fleet
in *Lightning* to go with me.   We had a nice trip, and
I proved the safety of the channel by running the French
screw-steamers back in an hour and fifty-five minutes the
distance of eighteen miles   Yesterday I had to start at
3 a.m. to pilot *Gorgon* into an intricate channel, where
poor Buckle had *Valorous* aground, and so injured that,
though off, she is leaking terribly.   This was close to my
old friends in the village of Degerby, where you will remember the custom-house and collector and the nice ladies
were.   You may also recollect that the people complained of
a Russian police officer being 'the very devil,' and wished
I would take him away ; but he was not there then, and
I said jokingly, ' If I ever come back, I will take him away

for you.' I waited up there a short time to go on shore
and see my friends (some of those in the other ships had
landed there) On the way to shore with Evans in the
gig, I told the ship's crew that if they saw me pat a man
very affectionately on the back to seize his arms behind
and take him to the boat. On landing, all the people
were indoors but the collector, who came gravely forward,
bowing, till he came close and recognised me, when his
countenance changed most wonderfully. He began shaking hands very energetically. I saw a lot of faces peeping
out of one room. Soon all my lady friends rushed out
of the door. They had not recognised me through the
window till they saw the collector shake hands with
me. Even the collector's old wife, whom you remember
had been 'packing up to run away' when I first landed,
ran out and shook my hand with both hers, as if she
recollected my not burning the custom-house down ; and
the nicest-looking young lady, the married one with the
baby, ran in and brought out a most beautiful nosegay
of roses of all kinds, which she gave me. I then complained to them all that the villagers were acting as our
enemies, in spite of all I said when last here, as they were
cutting away the buoys we put on rocks ; and I said that if
they did not prevent it, I should have to burn all the boats
of the nearest village, and, if that did not stop it, the
village itself. They said it was the police officer made the
people do it, threatening if they refused to send them off
to the fort. Shortly after a gentleman in a green uniform
came, and told me he had charge of the place, and I saw he
must be the very man. He certainly was a bold one. I
soon after said I must have some sheep, etc, and as the
people could not sell them I would take them and give the
money. The gentleman in green said he would not allow
it, and they should not take our money. I went up close
to him and said, 'Then you mean to act as our enemy.'
(I had an interpreter.) 'I cannot allow them to take the
money. I have charge here, and it is my duty to prevent it.' 'Then,' I said, 'I must treat you as an enemy,'
tapping him on the back at the same time In an instant
his arms were pinned, and he found himself in the embraces
of three men, who walked him off to the boat The ladies
screamed ; the old Mrs. Collector got hold of my hand,
went down on her knees, and cried terribly, saying he had
a wife and seven children, the youngest only a year old.

[To face p. 210.

"Ajax."   "Blenheim."   "Amphion."   "Alban."   "Hogue."   "Edinburgh."
"Lightning."

THE ALAND ISLANDS.

(Rear-Admiral Chads' squadron proceeding through the Ango Channel to Bomarsund, led by "Lightning," July 28th, 1854.)

I told her I had just the same, but it would not prevent a Russian officer taking me prisoner ; and as this man avowed himself a Russian officer and acted against us, though he did his duty only, I was obliged to do mine and take him prisoner. Some of the younger ones screamed, one tall fine young woman went off nearly faint, and there was such a scene, but more with fright at the thing than care for him. I believe they thought they were all to be carried off. Soon his poor wife came down in terrible distress, and his eldest daughter begged me very hard to let him go, and almost tried my feelings too much ; but all I could promise was, I would take him to the admiral, and I would ask for him to be allowed to go to Bomarsund, where his family might join him, provided he promised not to return here, but that would rest entirely with the admiral. His wife went off with him ; and I, with two men, walked to our old village a mile inland, where the people had said they could not sell us lambs ; but, now they heard the police officer was gone, they were ready to sell anything. Evans and more men soon joined, and we took back several sheep and nice lambs at three shillings and sixpence each, milk, and cream ; and as we could not carry all, I took off my coat and backed a fine lamb. When I came back I invited the ladies off, and all but the old one accepted, and brought off the poor man's eldest daughter. The poor people on shore had been crowding round me, begging me not to let him come back again. The ladies certainly did not seem to think I had done very wrong, or they would not have so readily come off. The husband of the nice-looking one stood on the jetty. I begged him to come, but he said he could not. I said I would keep all the ladies prisoners, and his wife too. He said he was quite willing to trust her with me. They remained an hour, had some wine, biscuits, figs, etc., admired your likeness, took a number of tracts, were rather surprised that the figure of England in *Punch* praying for the success of the war should be kneeling before a cross, and asked if the figure were not that of a Catholic. I assured them we were Protestants, and I gave the young mother a Swedish Testament for her little daughter when she could read, and then we parted the best of friends, though it was sad to see the poor wife and children taking leave. I think no one ever before captured a prisoner in an enemy's country, and at the same time had a party of six ladies on board to lunch."

"Napier," p. 315, records the progress of Admiral Chads' fleet to Bomarsund. This, then, was the first attempt to take large ships up to the place. After an hour's examination of the most difficult part, Captain Sulivan found sufficient water, and *without any buoys or marks* took the ships up through the passages. This exploit was never noticed by Napier in any way, nor in any despatch, but the return of the ships was signalled by a notice, after Captain Sulivan had taught the masters the pilotage and *buoyed the whole passage!*

"Sunday, July 30th, 1854.

"I do not like writing on Sunday, except my private letter, but I could not possibly write to you at all if I did not. The whole week has been spent in one continual work of piloting ships either to Bomarsund or through the channels to the north-east, in buoying and marking the main channels to Bomarsund, reconnoitring the shores near Bomarsund to find the best landing-place, piloting the admiral up in *Driver* to see the place, and finding a new channel round from north to south of the fort without passing within range of the batteries. We have been working from 4 a.m. to late in the evening, and yet expected to be back alongside the flag-ship every night, which we have only failed to do once, when I was too tired to return, and getting alongside *Arrogant, Amphion,* and *Alban,* my old shipmates Yelverton (Henry), Key, Otter, and I had a most pleasant evening together. One day Caffin, Scott, and Henry were sent with me with the masters of their ships to see the channels, and they said they had the most pleasant day they had spent in the Baltic. I had a letter to deliver at Degerby to his wife from the prisoner I took, and had orders to bring his clothes down, he being kept in *Duke of Wellington*; so we all landed, had a walk to the village out in the country, got some cream and milk, called on all our lady friends, got lots of roses from the gardens, had a very kind reception even from the prisoner's wife, and, knowing that from the blockade they were deprived of all their common necessaries, I was in the act of sending on shore some coffee, sugar, and a few bottles of wine, when a boat came alongside, put a large

basket of green peas and a wooden milk-bucket of rasp-
berries in the cutter, said they were for the captain, and
pulled away before an answer could be given. Thinking
we were about to start, they could have expected no
return. It was a very nice way of showing a civility. I
also had the luck to collect three hundred nice fresh eggs
at a cost of five shillings per hundred—of course some are
for my friends.

"Yesterday I got to bed at 12.30 and slept till seven this
morning, and was just congratulating myself on a quiet
Sunday, when my signal was made, ' Get up steam and weigh
instantly,' and a boat from *Duke* brought Moriarty the master
—a very nice, excellent fellow, whom I like to have with
me—to say that the squadron with troops was in sight,
and I was to go out to pilot them in, Moriarty coming if
I wanted more help. We met the four line-of-battle ships
outside about twelve miles ; and sending Moriarty to *St.
Vincent* and Evans to *Royal William*, so that we need not
wait for them, I went to *Hannibal*, the commodore's ship,
and we pushed on, followed by *Algiers*. On our way in
we met the master of the fleet with a message to me
that the admiral wished the two screw-ships inside him, and
the two sailing three-deckers outside. It was a lovely morning—a light breeze, not hot—and the ships crowded with
troops in all colours. The fleet inside was anchored pretty
thickly ; but I found no difficulty in helping the effect of
the saluting, cheering, flags displayed, etc., by running first
past a French liner, then between the two French admirals,
cheered French fashion by each (hardly able to make
the helmsmen hear me for the row); then close under
Duke's stern, where cheering began English fashion ; and
then brought up between *Cumberland* and *James Watt*.
But to the surprise of every one the *Algiers*, instead of
following, anchored outside with the sailing-ships ; and
when Talbot came on board, he said that the master of the
fleet had come on board and taken charge, saying he was
to take her inside ; but that when he came near his heart
failed him—he said he could not get her through the ships,
that there was not room, and he anchored her outside ; so
half the effect was lost.

"You will recollect in my last my describing taking up a
French steamer with the officers and pilots of the fleet to
teach them the channels. The commander seemed intelligent, and took notes and sketches innumerable, marking

everything I told him on the chart, and I thought he seemed quite up to it. I told the admiral he seemed thoroughly to understand it. A few days after he went up again in his little vessel, and in coming down actually mistook the channel where it was most plain, and ran her into one where there was only one and a half fathoms water Of course she was soon hard and fast, and the master of *Edinburgh* had to go to her assistance, and after getting her off pilot her down. So much for their attempting to pilot their own ships. I suppose it is no harm my telling my own friends that I met with plenty of compliments. One brother-officer asks, ' Do you ever sleep ? ' another, ' When are they going to give you a little rest ? ' ' How do you stand it ? ' etc., etc. The French admiral told me a few days since that he ' thought I must be made of iron,' and that he had felt it his duty to specially report to the Minister of Marine how much I had assisted them by my exertions. Another French officer asked Yelverton, ' What will they do for Captain Sulivan when he goes home ? What will they make him ? ' Hall is really a very fine fellow, but after his coming into Cronstadt with the signal flying ' Have successfully bombarded Bomarsund,' every one who looks at the fort and sees only a few external marks of shot on the granite wall naturally laughs at the idea of their having at all injured the fort, or done more than burn a few wooden houses.* Buckle, who was there, laughs at it himself; yet the papers at home speak of it as if the fort had been silenced by three steamers, when now a whole fleet and ten thousand troops are going to attack it It is too bad the way the papers publish directly false articles. A few days since we read, under the head of ' Surveying Work in the Baltic,' an account of the arduous duties in finding channels for the ships, etc., and that among other ships that had taken a prominent part in it was the —— and three others, not one of which had ever taken the slightest share in it Yet neither *Lightning's* nor *Alban's* name was mentioned in the article. This is a specimen of

---

* *Hecla's bombardment.*—" So useless was this waste of shot and shell that the granite was scarcely marked, and the Russians, in derision, *painted black marks near each hit to mark the spots* The forts, being casemated, the guns could not be elevated at long range, so that it could be shelled out of range of its guns One might as well have thrown peas at the fort, as the bomb-proof roof had four feet of sand on it The real force opposed to the steamers was the masked battery of field artillery, which came down to the point of the bay "

the truth of such puffs. In fact, there are a set of people who try through their friends or by more direct means to puff themselves off, and make the public believe they do everything, while here they are laughed at.

"We expect the French ships with the remaining troops on Tuesday, and I suppose by this day week they will be hard at it. I hardly expect the governor will surrender when summoned, as some think ; but I fancy, when the west hill fort is taken, he will see how useless it is to continue the defence, so that there will be very little to do I think we have selected a nice landing-place—a smooth, grassy flat at the head of a cove, on which guns, etc., could be landed, and where I could run *Lightning* within a few yards, and close to it a nice steep rocky point, rising to a little hill, no trees to cover riflemen, and yet a strong position for the leading troops to hold and protect the others landing ; while at the entrance of the cove the *Edinburgh* may lay within a hundred yards of both shores and sweep them, so that nothing can oppose us ; besides which, we may tow all the boats four or five miles above, as if going to land at Castellholm, then turn and go fast back to the cove, before any soldiers could return there. They have only five hundred riflemen that they can venture to detach from the forts, and they will, I suppose, do all they can to check the advance ; but a regiment of the French chasseurs will be landed first, and they will soon deal with the riflemen if they make a stand. Our share of the whole thing will be trifling, as no seamen will, I believe, be landed, except a few with guns. The French commander-in-chief has gone to Stockholm, and will not be here for two or three days.

"We continue to be quite free from sickness, and the fleet is generally healthy, though a case of cholera occurs now and then in a screw-ship.

"It was a curious sight seeing a thousand French soldiers paraded on the deck of an English ninety-gun ship. They have got on capitally, all pleasant and mutually pleased.

"*Monday*, 31*st.*—We have been all day with General Jones, Commodore Grey, Captain Mundy, and all the engineer officers, showing them the forts north and south. On the north side the two round forts tried to reach us with shot, both by ricochet and direct fire ; but I kept just out of range, so they failed to hit us. I had eight to dinner with

me after leaving.   I have since been with the general and
commander-in-chief till late in the evening."

"Yesterday the two commanders-in-chief—Napier and
Duchesne—the French general-in-chief, four other French
generals, General Jones, and all their staffs, went in the
Emperor's yacht to examine the place, *Lightning* going
with them and leading through the channels   When we
reached Bomarsund I went on board, as did Admiral
Chads.   It was evident they did not like taking the
yacht close along the shore, as she drew more water than
we did ; so they all, great and small, went on board
Lightning, and what with colonels, naval captains,
captains and lieutenants on the staff, etc, they crowded
our deck under the awning from the main-mast to the
wheel.   I gave them a good look at everything, got in on
the flank of the battery on the point recently constructed
where no gun could bear on us, and then went to the
landing-place in the bay Admiral Chads and I had looked
at before, and of which the French general highly approved.
After seeing everything, and shooting the poor forts
tremendously with spy-glasses, and carrying off every bit of
them on paper, they wanted to go round to the northward.
I told them I could not take the yacht in that way, as it
was too intricate ; so they all agreed to stay in *Lightning*,
and meet the yacht on our return.   On our way round
I got lunch, in the shape of cheese, sardines, biscuit,
wine, etc., on the table, and in turn had the whole party in
the cabin, beginning with the 'great guns.'   They seemed
particularly well pleased with a very good cheese, and still
more so with ale, which the Frenchmen pitched into
uncommonly, and said was far better than wine.   As we
entered the northern harbour near the forts, I said to Evans
I would go closer to-day, as we saw they could not reach
us by three or four hundred yards yesterday, adding
jokingly it would not be fair to the Russians not to
give them a chance at such a party   Evans said, 'Take
care, sir, they don't get a bag of extra strong powder to-
day.'   I then went aft and stopped her abreast of the forts,
and, as I thought, two hundred yards out of their range.
I was talking to the general-in-chief and the admiral
just abaft the main-mast, where all the six generals, three
admirals, and the colonels were congregated, when one

fort, the low one, fired a ricochet shot, which, after making fifteen ducks and drakes, ended a hundred and fifty yards short of us. The general asked me which fort was nearest. I said the high one by a hundred yards. As I spoke a gun flashed from it, and I was watching to see the shot coming, and how short it would fall, when to my surprise it rushed close over our heads abaft the main-mast, and fell about fifty yards beyond us. It was evident that they had an unusually large gun there, for it made a great noise. I did not wait for a second, but went on full speed, and kept her right off for two or three hundred yards more; but no shot reached us again, and we went on examining the shore. It was a most providential thing its passing just over us. Had it been a little lower, or we fifty yards farther off, it would have come in among all the great men, who were so crowded that it must have made fearful havoc among them, and it would have been entirely my fault for going so close when there was no necessity for it; but they certainly had never before thrown a shot so far by two hundred yards. On our way back I had to pass rather close, and the old admiral was at me about it, saying I ought to go farther off; but I pointed out to him some nasty rocks near, and said I did not like going too close to them, as it was better to risk a shot than risk running her on shore in such a position, which he allowed. I assured him we would not pass within shot again; and as they fired at us again in passing, the nearest shot did not come within a hundred yards, and most of them shorter by far. One shell burst nicely in exact direction, and high; so that, had they cut their fuse better, it would have nearly reached us; but it burst four hundred yards short of us. We then returned to-wards this place, met the yacht, put all the Frenchmen in her, and got back to the fleet at about 7 p.m.

"If I was not pretty well proof against flattery, I should have had my head turned yesterday. The channels to the northward are particularly intricate, but we went on full speed in *Lightning* all the way, and astonished the big-wigs not a little, particularly the French general and admiral, as well as our chief and Chads, and I had many compli-ments paid me by all. Napier said, 'How did you ever find it all out? It seems to me wonderful how the ships were ever got up here at all.' And he repeatedly inter-preted for me sundry speeches of the French chief. One person likened me to the dogs that dig for truffles in France. I suppose he meant that they find them by smell, and he thought I found the rocks the same way. When I showed them a rock under water a few feet from our side, with not more than four feet of water on it, they seemed greatly puzzled to know how I found them all The chief told me that the French admiral had been writing most strongly about me to the Minister of Marine, and they would be sending me the Legion of Honour. At present I have really done nothing to deserve anything of the kind: the distinction would only have value if given for some real service, such as at Obligado. I have been up to-day with some captains and masters to show them the channel. The French captain, who commands a steamer, and was yesterday in the yacht, came to-day, before I was dressed, to ask me to give him some instruction about the channel I kept him to breakfast, and before it was over my signal was made, and I found it was to ask me about some arrangements and to go with him to the French admiral; but just as we were going in the barge these captains and masters came, and I was sent off with them instead. One was Clifford, who was a youngster in *Undaunted*; another Broke.

"On my return this evening I had another chat with the chief and General Jones about the plans, and to-morrow I am to be there at breakfast, that we may settle everything. The general is to land to the northward with seven hundred marines and his hundred sappers, to make a diversion in favour of the grand landing to the southward, where all the French will land I shall have to arrange about the steamers that can get through the channel into the northward, as no one else knows the channel. I want to get Otter to have the leading of the vessels and boats of the other landing; he is up to the northward with Plumridge, and I am doubtful if he can be back in time. We are only now waiting for the two French line-of-battle ships that ought to have been here also. I do not think there will be much, if any, resistance to the landing, as they will not know in time where we intend doing it."

"LED SOUND, *Friday, August* 4*th*

"We are still waiting for two French ships that have the artillery and sappers on board, and the general will not move till they come through, though our admiral and

General Jones want to commence with the force in hand.
Yesterday I took General Jones and Buckle up, the general
wishing to have another look, and Buckle going merely
to look at it and learn the channel. We found the enemy
had burnt down all the houses outside the fort, so as to
deprive us of any cover near it. I went to *Edinburgh's*
mast-head to get a good look at the inland portion of the
ground our northern party have to go over after landing,
and saw it was very favourable to us,—sloping gradually
over clear land, with corn-fields, etc., and a village at the
bottom, so that there is little or no cover for their riflemen
for a mile beyond where we land and crown the ridge
near the coast. This will be done, if opposed, under the
fire of the vessels. I also saw that the besieging force must
occupy a new work or entrenchment of some kind being
thrown up on a hill, which was not known before   I believe
eight hundred marines and marine artillery, with four field-
pieces with seamen, will constitute our force, and the French
add two thousand to it. I had this morning to settle the
steamers, etc, with the French captain of the fleet. I am
to have *Driver* and *Pigmy*, besides *Lightning*, and I have
tried hard for *Alban*, but cannot get it settled yet. The
French send four steamers that I have selected from their
draught of water for the shallow passages; and I was
nearly having the old *Fulton* also, that suffered so at
Obligado. To-day I went up with some masters who had
not seen the channel, and with Stewart, captain of *Ter-
magant*, whom you will recollect in *Rattlesnake* at Falklands.
On our arrival there we found the village on Presto Island
opposite the large fort in flames. It had the best houses
in the islands; but they feared, I suppose, our advancing
under their cover. This seems the first step in the horrors
of war. It looks as if they intend to defend it to the last.

"A deserter soldier and two convicts took a boat and
escaped to our ships last night from the fort.

"*Saturday*, 5*th*.—The French ships have just arrived,
Vulture also.

"It is now settled that I take *Driver* (our old friend
and companion Cochrane, whom I have manœuvred to get
with us from the first, and prevented his being left up the
gulf) and *Pigmy* with *Lightning*, and seven hundred marines
and a hundred sappers, General Jones and his staff,
four field-pieces from the block-ships manned by seamen,
and our rocket-tube, which the general wants; and I

claimed the privilege of landing our own men with it, so the gunner and ten men from us, with ten from some other ship, take it, and Cudlip (lieutenant of *Lightning*) will command. As he is the senior lieutenant in the fleet, it will ensure his promotion if he lands, so as to get his name mentioned. I take five French steamers under my orders, and old *Fulton*, that I so often piloted in Parana, with them. I understood at first I was to command afloat in the northern division; but now Admiral Plumridge is to meet us there, which will cut me out. I have just left the French admiral, who waited to see me, and who was most anxious to know how I would get the French ships through the difficult channel. I told him I proposed putting an officer (Evans) in one in the middle of our line to keep it straight, and when we got to the difficult pass I would take them all through one at a time, and then we would go on in line again. He seemed quite delighted at my making sure of taking all through, and shook hands with both of his. In fact, I am a much greater man with the French than I shall ever be with our own service. Their captains come to me and consult me and ask my advice as if they were youngsters and I was their admiral. Mind, this is private, and must not be mentioned out of our own circle. If it were not for my feeling certain these things will never be mentioned out of it, I might be accused of egotism in writing them, but I know you expect to hear all particulars.

"*Sunday, August 6th.*—This day has been like anything but Sunday. The admiral came on board *Lightning* this morning at nine, to go to both Admirals Plumridge and Chads and arrange all about the disembarkation of the troops to-morrow. The general and Admiral Seymour were with us, and we were busy all day, not getting back till near 7 p.m., when we found the mail arrived. I find General Jones is an old friend of Tucker's, and has often enjoyed the hospitality of Trematon : he is a very fine fellow. I wish we had other such clear heads; but the difficulty of planning and arranging everything with the French chiefs is very great. The want of *one head* is very evident, and we have not very good managers to assist our chief, so that there is a sad want of method. Then there is too much desire on the part of certain persons in power to have all to do and to share out all the ships lying here, so that the captains of the senior ships have to lie doing

nothing ; and, even now that guns are sent from all the
ships to put into batteries, they are not allowed to send
men, but all is to be done by Admiral Chads' block-ships
and the smaller steamers.   I cannot help exerting the
influence I have with the admiral to endeavour to get
things managed justly to all ; and where that clashes with
the wishes of some above me, they show that they think
I have too much power—at least in one instance it has
been so ; but I do not care, as I feel I have had no
motive but the good of the service and the success of our
attack with as little bloodshed as possible, which to me is
of more importance than that certain parties should keep
all to themselves.   I have succeeded in getting two or
three included in the business that would have been left
out, but entirely from a desire to do them justice and from
no other feeling.   However, I think there are very few who
do not believe I take a right view of these things, and I
am very pleased to find that my views on most points
have been confirmed by the great soldiers who now
manage affairs.

"We move the troops into the smaller steamers at 1 p.m.
to-morrow and start directly, getting to our positions
before evening, ready to land at daylight next morning.
I take *Driver, Pigmy*, and three French vessels under my
orders, and land eighteen hundred French and eight
hundred English marines and sappers, four guns, and
two rocket-tubes.   Admiral Plumridge meets me at the
landing-place and takes the command, bringing some
steamers with him, and their paddle-boats for landing the
troops.   While at anchor to-day at Bomarsund three
Russian deserters came down to the shore, and we brought
them off.   They are Polish Jews, and have been seven
years here as soldiers.   They gave us much information
about the place.   The houses outside and villages have
been all burning the last two days, and they seem determined to make a strong resistance.   I do not expect to
find the landing opposed on our side at least ; and as the
general-in-chief leads with three thousand men in the first
boat-loads, they cannot well be opposed either.

"To have seen the old admiral with me to-day, no one
would have supposed he could have let out at me as he
did for a fancied error two days since.   When several
were discussing to-day the position some would hold,
others being shared out, one of our leading men said that,

no matter what difference of opinion there might be about these points, there was none as to my position, for all felt that our great success lay in having brought such large ships where they thought it impossible, and that all the information they collect up there confirms this;

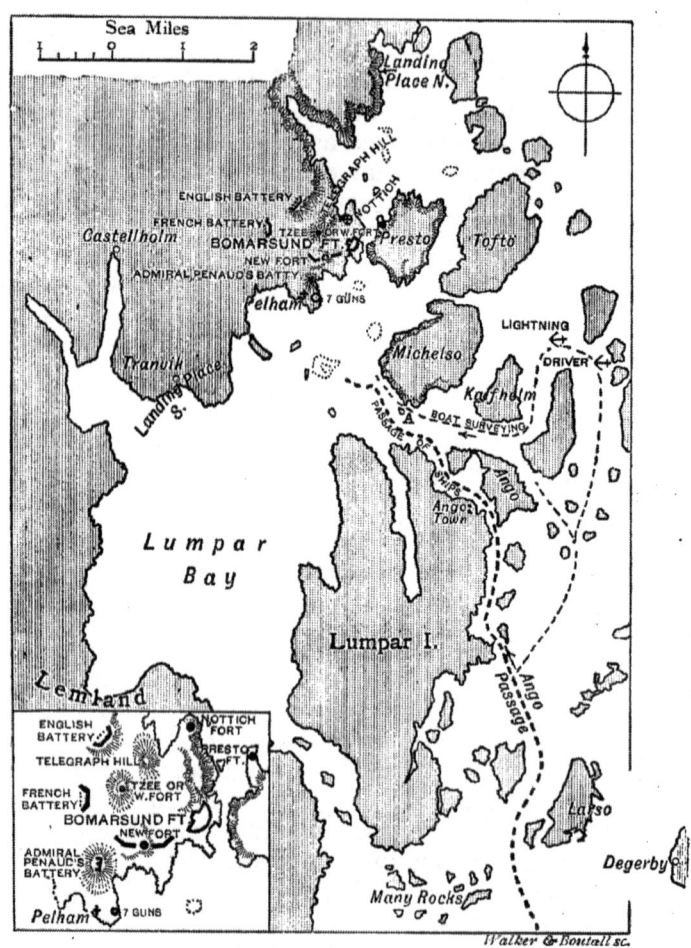

in fact, if all said was to be believed, I am to be made a ' bishop ' at least !

"*Monday, 7th.*—We are off with the troops, and we land at daylight to-morrow."

A short outline of the operations will enable the journals

to be followed more readily.   It will be seen by the accom-
panying plan that the large fort of Bomarsund was supported
by the round towers of Tzee, Nottich, and Presto, and by
the seven-gun battery at Tranvik Point.   The latter was
attacked'and destroyed on August 8th by Captains Key and
Desbois.   On the same day the British force, of about seven
hundred sailors and marines and seventy sappers, together
with a covering force of two thousand French marines,
were sent in vessels conducted by Captain Sulivan through
an intricate channel to the landing-place chosen by him
to the north of Bomarsund.   Thence the guns (three short
thirty-two-pounders, four field-guns, and the rocket-tube)
were dragged over steep and rocky ground four and
a half miles to the spot chosen for the battery, seven
hundred:and fifty yards north of Fort Tzee   The officers
in command were Captain Ramsay, R.N., and Commander
Preedy, R.N.   On the same day the French force, conducted
by Commander Otter, R.N., and numbering about ten
thousand men, was landed to the west of Tranvik Point.
They had fifty horses to help drag their guns (four long
sixteen-pounders, and four thirteen-inch mortars) to the
station fixed upon, four hundred and fifty yards west of
Fort Tzee.   The French battery, being ready early on
the 13th, commenced firing without waiting for the British,
and Fort Tzee surrendered the same evening.   When
ready, on the 15th, Captain Ramsay turned his guns—
not now needed for Fort Tzee—against Fort Nottich, at
a distance of nine hundred and fifty yards, and breached
it in eight hours.   Meanwhile Captain Pelham, R.N., had
landed his ten-inch pivot-gun at Tranvik Point, and used
it against Bomarsund.   The combined fleet kept up a
harmless fire against the fort, and the French general
prepared his breaching battery north of Tranvik Point.
The Russian general, seeing he was done for, surrendered,

and the commander of Fort Presto did likewise. Three of our ships to the north of Presto Island had joined in the bombardment.

"BOMARSUND, *Tuesday, August 8th,* 1854

"We got up all right yesterday. I got *Driver* through the difficult passage, and took all the troops up to the landing-place, meeting there Admiral Plumridge and his steamers. Otter had been there early, and had gone a mile inland to a village on the road the troops advance by, and saw no enemy; so he goes now with the general as guide."

Here follow regrets at his not receiving any position in connection with the action, and even not being allowed to remain to look on after the landing.

"We heard firing, which was Key in *Amphion,* who went in six hundred yards on the flank of a mud battery, which did not return a shot. He quickly sent the people out of it, landed, and spiked six guns. When we came the chief was in *Bulldog,* with *Stromboli,* firing long-range shot at the west tower, the French all landing, and the chasseurs on a hill about half a mile inland. The chief then came to *Lightning* and hoisted his flag, and we are now waiting for him while he has gone to see Admiral Chads. The forts are firing shell occasionally at the nearest ships: none came within four hundred yards of *Bulldog,* but they burst near enough *Amphion* to send a few bits beyond her. There will be little for the navy to do, except the men landed now from the block-ships with four field-guns— Cudlip with the gunner and ten men from here, and Wells and ten men from *Driver* with the rocket-tube, and the men who get the battering-guns up. I had General Jones and staff, Captain Mundy, and the chaplain of *Duke* with me. Dinner for six at 8 p.m.; beds in cabin for four; went to bed at 11.30; got up at 2 to breakfast; landed at 3."

"BOMARSUND, *August* 14th

"On Tuesday (8th) the troops all landed early. The chief hoisted his flag in *Lightning,* and, after taking him to one or two points, we took him round to the north to Admiral Plumridge, and then returned. All the troops advanced without firing a shot, and closed the enemy up in their forts. Wednesday and Thursday (9th and 10th) we were landing guns, stores, etc., the forts sending only an occasional shot or shell inland. The marines and seamen were rather exposed about fifteen hundred yards from the fort on the hill. The marines had bought a potato-field for £3 from the owners, and a number were digging potatoes, when a shell burst in the valley, scattering balls six ounces in weight. One hit the pillow of a lieutenant who was lying down, one went into our men's hut, and others in different directions, but hurt no one. I walked out to see the camps that evening. It was a curious scene,—the French advanced chasseurs, with their little tents, hidden under rocks or rise of ground; the park of artillery behind some rocks ready for placing in battery; thousands of men in red inexpressibles in every direction; and the round fort on the hill looking down on all within good range, but only firing an occasional shot or shell. At the village headquarters there was a beautiful band playing while the general was at dinner. Several native women mixed with the soldiers listening, which I was glad to see, as it showed they were not ill-treated. People were at work getting in their hay and corn in one field, while in the corner of another several French soldiers had just dug a grave for a comrade alongside two others: all three died of cholera; but they brought it from the ships, where it began to be very bad,—they are now very healthy.

"We had an unfortunate occurrence on Friday (11th), by which some lives were lost. Admiral Chads has been anxious from the first to send ships through the channel round Presto Island near the fort, and to send two block-ships through, as it is difficult for them to get through the channels round outside. The admiral always seemed to object; and when he asked me I told him that if there was any object worth risking lives for they might go through, but I thought not otherwise, as they must pass under the fire of the large fort. The day the troops landed (the 8th), when the chief and Admiral Chads were on board *Lightning*, the latter again spoke on the subject. The chief told me to bring him the chart. Admiral Chads said that a ship would not pass nearer the battery than two thousand five hundred yards. The admiral asked me, and I said two thousand one hundred, or at most two thousand two hundred. Admiral Chads said it was no such thing I could not get him to examine the charts for himself, so I let it alone, and pointed it out afterwards quietly to his son. The next day the admiral let a steamer go through, and no shot reached her. The morning after at breakfast he said to me, 'You see Admiral Chads was right and I was wrong.' I said, 'I suppose, sir, I was wrong also.' However, that morning we were coaling in the ship, and therefore, not having men to spare, Evans and I took the dinghy with only two men to get angles on a point of Michelso Island. Just afterwards we saw *Penelope* passing under the pilotage of the master of the fleet ; and just as she reached the nearest point to the fort, and the shot were reaching her, she ran on a rock, and could not back off again. We went to her directly, and were the first that reached her. Just as we got alongside we saw the splinters flying from her, showing that they were hitting her. While I was on board speaking to Caffin two more shot struck her, and others were passing over her We got a lead-line, and Evans taking an oar, we sounded near her, to find the deep water. She was on the edge of a rock with five fathoms on the side farthest off the fort, and deep water ahead and astern. Even with only two or three boats sounding, the shot pitching round us came unpleasantly close. At one time two fell close on each side of our dinghy, the one on the off side passing the stern very close behind me. Seeing the *Gladiator* coming through the channel to assist, I pulled to meet her, and told her the deep side and where to go *Hecla* at the same time having just arrived, came down the other way, and both got hold of *Penelope*. The fort soon struck them also. As we passed *Hecla* we saw the splinters fly from her quarter. As the boats began to assemble I feared they must be hit, but providentially only one was struck—a French boat, and one man killed. Seeing I could do no more good, and also seeing that the block-ships were getting up steam, and thinking they were going in to cover her, and I should be wanted to pilot them, I went back to *Bulldog* (the flag-ship) just as Buckle was ordered to take *Valorous* into long-shell range and shell the fort. I went to place her at two thousand five hundred yards, but was too close at first, so that the shot came over us, till we moved out a little and anchored just at the enemy's extreme range, only a shot or two going over and none striking *Valorous*, while she threw her shell well. Out of a few she fired there were four struck the roof of the fort. Just as the chief sent a boat for me to pilot them in *Bulldog*, the *Penelope* got off and the recall was made. She had two men killed and three wounded, and *Hecla* three wounded—a loss quite useless, and which might have been saved. Had I been piloting her, I have no doubt many would have cried out against the surveyors. However, I believe no one was to blame, as the rock was not known before. The fault was sending her at all that way."

In spite of Captain Sulivan telling him he was waiting till the bright moon was obscured, or rose later, to sound the bay closer to the fort, and that to go in on light nights would be useless and draw the attention of the enemy, the master of the fleet, with three large black boats, went in on a bright moonlight night, and was fired on at a thousand yards from the fort, outside the small bay. Two nights after, when cloudy, Captain Sulivan went in in a small boat painted light blue, the crew dressed in the same colour, and he was enabled to go closer in and examine the bay thoroughly five hundred yards from the fort. The buoys dropped at night and fixed by day showed the exact position the boats had been in. On page 360 of " Napier " the master's exploit is mentioned, with the name of every master who went near Bomarsund, but none of the work of the surveyors is referred to. Captain Sulivan again went close in another night. Commander Otter and Lieutenant Ward of *Alban* had landed and examined the line of advance for the troops for some distance the day before the attack, and guided the force on the advance, but no notice of this appeared in the despatches.

" [*Private*]

" *Sunday, August 13th*, 1854

" I succeeded in doing all I wanted that night, and was close in without being discovered, though the moon shone out brightly. To-day the fire from the French battery opened on the west tower, and with some effect.

Before breakfast we had to tow a collier, and then had a quiet day and our regular service. After dinner I went ashore with Key, and soon after we saw a white flag from the tower I hoped it had surrendered, but it proved a false idea, for they have been firing as hard as ever since. I saw the general and returned with Key. He wanted me much to dine with him, as Hope was with him (three old Paranas); but I told him I preferred a quiet evening on board, and would not go. I had our evening service : one or two extra men and two engineers attended. I hoped to have written more to you to-night, but the admiral has ordered me to complete the soundings inshore to-night, and it is now past nine o'clock, so I shall not have a Sabbath to the end. There is one thing that would remove all hesitation on my part in doing it to-night, and that is that it is dark and gloomy—a fresh breeze, and by far the best night we have had for such work, and therefore the risk of men's lives is less, which makes it a work of necessity. I was in hopes to-day it was really all over with trifling bloodshed, but I fear it is to go on longer.

"On Sunday (the 13th) the French got some sixteen-pounders in battery, and worked them all day against the west fort on the hill, while a cloud of chasseurs fired rifles at the casemates to prevent the enemy loading In the night all was quiet ; but the tower was so shaken by the shot, that is the outer stones, and the swarms of rifle-shot had killed and wounded so many through the casemates, that this morning they did not fire a shot in return, and some chasseurs, running up, found the soldiers would not stand any longer, but gave up their arms The commandant refused to surrender, and made a pass with his sword at a chasseur, who bayoneted him : he is only wounded, and is in the French hospital-ship with his wife, who was sent off to him. [This gallant Russian officer afterwards died of his wounds.*—Later note written by Sir B. J. S.]

* "Napier," p. 369, gives an account of the firing of the land batteries Sulivan remarks in marginal notes: "The French general ordered our battery not to be prepared, saying theirs would not be ready, and then pushed on his own battery, and opened fire the morning of the 13th, hoping to prevent our having any share in the success. They had heavy siege-guns, sixteen-pounders, or about seventeen and a half English, and nearly the same charge of powder as our thirty-twos. If they had fired as well as our men, they ought to have

" *Tuesday*, 15*th*.—Only time to give a short outline of an
eventful day.   I had to go at daybreak to put buoys down,
and on returning at eight I found that the English battery
had opened against the north tower, and a French mortar
battery at the big fort, and a ten-inch gun, under Captain
Pelham, mounted on shore in the old mud battery also.
I forgot to say that the night before last I was sounding
in before the battery when a panic seemed to seize them,
and all the forts fired guns and muskets in all directions.
It was a beautiful sight! I knew they did not see us, and
it was safer for us.   The burning fuses of the shells showed
the red tracks passing high and beyond us, and a good
many were fired at the battery which Pelham was preparing for the ten-inch gun.   I went to it on my way
back, and saw them hard at work at a new parapet, all
done by sailors, but beautiful work.   I returned on board
at two, and was up again at six.   To-day I got leave from
the admiral to go on shore on my return ; and with Evans,
the chaplain of flag-ship, two marine officers, and my
coxswain, we went to the scene of action.   I wanted particularly to see the rear of the large fort, and what effect
our ships' fire—for several were shelling with heavy guns
at long range—had on the fort.   The west tower had
been set on fire by the French, and the flames were
coming through every casemate ; but I did not know
there was powder in it.   After trying with Freshwater (my
coxswain), the others having left us, to look over Telegraph
Hill (the rifle-balls were sounding over our heads too
much to go there), I found a fine stone about twenty
yards from the burning tower, over which I could look
and see everything, with my cloak rolled up to put before
my head to peep over.   I had just seen several French
officers and men near the tower, which made me think
it safe, when in a moment there was a loud rumbling shock,

breached Fort Tzee (the western fort).   But the effect on the front of
the fort was that it was only slightly honeycombed ; no stone was
displaced, as they had not put their shot into one place, but spread
them over nearly the face of the tower.   The fort was really taken
by their riflemen, who killed so many of the enemy through the
embrasures.   From the delay caused by the French general's strategy,
Captain Ramsay's battery was not built in time to join in the attack on
Fort Tzee ; so later (15th) he turned his guns (only forty-two cwts.)
against Fort Nottich, nine hundred and fifteen yards, *at double the
distance the French had fired at*, and so good was the practice made
that the fort was breached."

and I saw the tower in the air in a dark mass, that looked as if it would overwhelm us It was an awful moment! But I was given presence of mind to see that it was useless to run, as the masses of stone were flying beyond our position: they were then in the air, and as I looked up I saw them coming down in every direction. My eye caught one large one falling near me, and then a rather clear space with only splinters, two or three yards wide apparently. I had no cap on. I saw the thing was to avoid the big pieces, and try to keep on this open space, not minding the little stones. I moved one step on one side clear of the largest stone, and in another moment found myself unhurt, and saw Freshwater rolling down the rocks. I thought he was killed, but he got up almost unhurt: he had a slight blow on the shoulder. Now the special providence that preserved us was in this way: On all sides but one the fort went outwards, as well as into the air, and the mass was carried farther than our distance, enough to bury any number of men. On our side alone the outer wall stood for about one-sixth the circumference of the tower, and that saved us from instant death ; while the stones were prevented on that side flying out, and went right up into the air. Directly the stones had fallen I ran, fearing another explosion, and about fifty yards farther off met a French midshipman leaning against a rock, looking up as pale as death. I found he had been struck in the leg, and his trousers were torn ; but it was not much, and he soon walked pretty well. Evans and the others were about four hundred yards off, and the French soldiers were asking where the English captain was, as they had seen us go up. I then found a snug nook between two rocks, occupied by a chasseur, who had two sand-bags placed, and who fired at the casemates in the rear of the fort, where guns were firing in different directions, one right over our spot ; but it was as safe as possible, as we had only to sit down when the gun flashed, and everything, either shot or grape, whistled over us. I had a capital view of the rear and interior of the fort, and of the destruction going on from the shells of those fired from the ships : one-third only went in, the others falling short ; but the destruction was very great. I then went to the English breaching battery firing at the north tower to see the effect of the fire. There were two guns firing at the battery from that

FORT IZZE AT BOMARSUND, WHICH BLEW UP WHILE CAPTAIN SULIVAN WAS BEHIND THE STONE IN THE FOREGROUND.

(*After a Sketch by* BRIERLEY.)

[*To face p.* 230.

tower and two from Presto Fort, so I watched the effect
from a position a hundred yards from the fort, so that
all the shot went well clear of me, and, watching when
all had fired, I ran up under the safe sand-bag battery
of the fort, where directly the enemy's guns flashed every
one ran behind the parapet   I found Creyke in the battery :
all the three guns had been struck, but all the day only
one man was killed, one severely wounded, and several
slightly touched.   Old Ramsay, captain of *Hogue*, was
commanding, and in great glee at seeing the wall go
down by wholesale under his guns ; but for want of
rifles like the chasseurs to fire at the casemates, the enemy
were loading and firing their guns through their ruined
masonry.   The one unfortunately killed is an engineer
officer—the Hon. Mr. Wrottesley—who lost a brother
last year in the Kaffir war.   Having seen all I wanted
there, I returned to my safe position near, and there
watched while Ramsay's shot broke through the wall and
opened the interior of the fort.   The battery was entirely
worked by seamen.   Cudlip and our party had their turn
at it to-day.

"On my way back I paid another visit to my friend
the chasseur, and had a good look at the big fort and the
firing.   The gun sent several shots over us, and I watched
with my glass when the men showed to load it for the
chasseur to fire.   You may fancy what my feelings were
and are at looking at the ruins of the fort that blew up.
I shall not easily forget that moment.

"I came off afterwards, giving the chief the first report
of the tower being opened by our shot.   I had to dine
with the French admiral—the admirals, flag-captain, and
myself being invited for Napoleon's fête day.   I am now
writing in a great hurry at 10 p.m, Admiral Seymour
lying asleep alongside me, ready to go with me at 2.30 a.m.
to tow the boats through Presto Channel, to pass over
eleven hundred English and French marines to occupy
Presto Island.   I believe all the ships are to assist in firing
at the fort to-morrow morning.   I am happy to say
the north tower has shown a white flag to-night, and
our marines are in it ; so Ramsay has done his work well.

"[*Private.*] *August* 15*th*.—I am sure you will agree with
me that my preservation to-day, amid the falling ruins of
the exploding fort, calls for special remembrance from us
How true 'God protects where thickest dangers come'!

One piece of wall standing was the means of saving us I will try to get a sketch of it, to keep in remembrance of such a mercy. I hardly knew how to feel to-day at the compliments paid me at dinner with the French admiral Many were in French from one to the other. I find the French admiral has specially requested that the Legion of Honour may be sent to me. Do not mention this The chief says it is no use any' one else going to the French admiral or officers about moving the ships, etc., *but Captain Sulivan*, but they will do anything he wishes. The old man seems rather proud of it, and not at all to think it strange He said to-day he believed they were jealous of everything English, *except Captain Sulivan*, and that they seemed not to have the slightest jealousy of him. It would give you pleasure to hear the way all brother-officers speak of the credit due to me. There seems no jealousy of my position, but real friendly desire on all sides to see me rewarded

" *Wednesday*, 16*th*, 6 *a.m.*—We went through the Presto Channel at 3 a.m. with boats in tow : they never fired at us We then passed over eleven hundred men and four guns, and anchored with two small vessels to cover the landing, if opposed. On our way back the fort fired several shots at us, but none struck us Some of our steamers are in position for shelling at two thousand four hundred yards, but no move is made French mortar battery and our ten-inch gun battery are throwing shell steadily into the fort. I think to-day may decide it; but if they hold out to the very last, as some forts have done in olden times, they may stand two or three days' shelling yet."

" *Saturday, August* 19*th*, 1854

" The telegraph will, ere this, have told you of Bomarsund having fallen Shortly after I had closed my last letters on Wednesday morning, I went on board the flag-ship and asked Admiral Chads if he did not think that our breaching battery might be turned on Presto Tower, as it was only fourteen hundred yards off, and at that distance, and from our being high above it, I thought we might do it much injury, if not silence it. He agreed with me, and spoke to the chief about it, and gave me a note to take to General Jones, asking him to try it. He also gave me a note to the French general-in-chief All this time a steady fire of shell was kept up both ashore and afloat, and apparently with some effect, as the roof was fast being destroyed. When I reached the French general, I found I had to settle with him the signals for the next day, as it was determined to send in ships to batter the front, while the French breaching battery made a breach in the rear, and when that was done another signal was to be made for our ships to cease firing, and then our storming parties were to advance and carry it by assault. Having settled the signals and left the general, I had a walk of nearly a mile to General Jones' camp. On my way you may suppose I thought much of the horrors of the following day, and most earnestly did I pray that the Almighty would so guide those on whom it depended as to prevent the necessity of its taking place. I had been about half an hour with General Jones, and we were just discussing our right to have a portion of the storming column formed from our marines, when a lieutenant galloped in saying the fort had surrendered unconditionally. We hurried off for it as fast as we could, but before we reached it I met Ramsay, who said, 'The admiral wants you.' And on my joining him outside the fort, I found it was to order me instantly to Led Sound, to direct Commander Grey to prepare his ships to take home two thousand Russian prisoners, so I lost the sight of the surrender and the troops laying down their arms. I think he might have thought of that, after my having so much to do with it! However, all other feelings are sunk in those of gratitude that with so slight a loss the place has fallen in the very way I said from the first it should be attacked, though I little thought it would fall so easily. The fact is, the towers falling made the fort untenable, and knowing the breaching battery would be ready that night, and that there are weak walls in the rear of the fort that would not stand an hour, the governor very properly surrendered before extreme measures were used. My report that the fort was protected against shelling by its bomb-proof roof, on which four feet of sand had been added, has been proved correct to the very letter. Not one shell out of the immense number thrown has gone through, so that the interior, both in casemates and officers' quarters, is *perfectly uninjured*. The best way was to take the towers, and then the fort must fall. The whole loss in the fort does not exceed seven killed and about twenty wounded. Nearly the same number were killed and wounded in the

north fort that our batteries breached. It is an extraordinary sight to see the interior of that fort in the
casemates immediately exposed to our shot—guns dismounted or disabled, and the whole wall for about twenty
feet beaten in. It is extraordinary that three guns should
have done so much work so well. The Russian commandant of that fort, when taken through our battery,
asked where the other guns were, as he would not believe
it had all been done by three guns, and latterly by two,
as one was disabled. I fear people at home are too apt
to measure the credit due by the number of killed and
wounded, and so will think lightly of our work. They
may well be astonished at the providence which preserved
all but one through the dangers of a whole day ; and if
they will consider that the men in that battery did their
work coolly and quickly, under a fire in return which
struck every gun and disabled one, and which, besides all
the shot and shell that came in through the embrasures or
passed through parts of the parapet, *lodged thirty-eight
large shot in the parapet* among the sand-bags, where they
have been found in taking the bags away, I think they
will be satisfied that our men deserve double credit for
doing it all so carefully and with so slight a loss

"I have carefully examined the scene of my wonderful
preservation from death by the fort blowing up I was
farther off than I thought, being forty-seven yards off,
but *in every other direction* the ground is covered with the
ruins above a hundred and fifty yards from it, and the
heavy stones in the face of the building have been driven
above two hundred yards, tearing up the ground like shot
At forty-seven yards the ruins are from ten to twenty feet
deep, so that, had I been on any other spot, or had the wall
on my side been blown out like the rest, we should have
been buried deeply under the ruins. The shower of falling
materials on my side was composed principally of bricks
from the interior. They fell chiefly about twenty yards
outside me, so that, had I run, I could hardly have escaped.
Mr. Brierley, the artist, has made a sketch for me of the
ruins, showing the standing wall, and the stones where I
stood, with the masses of ruins right and left to treble the
distance It will remind me, should I ever for a moment
forget it, of the merciful Providence that watched over me
at that moment and throughout my life. Whilst watching
the falling fragments, rifle-balls were singing past me.

While behind my stone, with my cloak rolled up on it, I
was well protected; but as I got up and ran a yard or two
till I stood still, they saw me to my feet from the fort, and
of course popped away at me.   You may perhaps think I
had no business there at all, and certainly I was not sent on
duty, but there were reasons why I ought to look at what
was going on, and particularly to get a good sight of the
rear of the fort, and watch the effect of our shelling, otherwise I could not give the admiral advice on many questions
he was likely to put to me, so that it was my duty to
obtain all the information and knowledge I could of the
place.   I was to the admiral in the position of an engineer
officer, and might at any moment have had to give an
opinion on the use of shelling, battering, or assaulting   I
have received many congratulations from brother-officers
on the share I have had in the success.   There has been
much ill-feeling and jealousy about the way it has been
managed—some ships excluded from all share, etc., etc.;
but several in speaking of that have said, 'There is no doubt
about your share in it, and the position you ought to hold,
whatever credit others may get.'   Admiral Chads told me
yesterday that every one had felt how well my share of the
work had been done, and that the chief felt it strongly,
and had given me credit for it in his letters.   I do not
anticipate more than very faint expressions on the subject
from him, as he is, I think, one who will write short
despatches, with no more mention of individuals than he
can help.   The French will, I think, make a much grander
story of the whole affair

"I do not think anything more will be attempted this
year.   It is too late for Sweaborg, even if we had force
enough to attack, which we have not.   I believe I am
going there shortly with all the head men to reconnoitre it.
Some are beginning to talk already of our moving down
the Baltic; but I do not see how we could leave the gulf
till the beginning of October, and be out of the Baltic about
the end of that month.   The weather is very warm yet; in
fact, it is the middle of summer, so that I cannot fancy the
winter drawing near.   The cholera still lingers in some
ships.   It commenced severely in *Hannibal* directly she
arrived, and with nearly two thousand men on board it
was no wonder.   She has now a hundred and fifty sick
out of six hundred, and has, I think, lost about twelve; and
now that Russian prisoners are going home in her, I fear

she will not get better, especially as the cholera is in
England also. I am most thankful to say that we have
not had a sick man for some time. Cudlip will, I suppose,
be promoted for this, as he is the senior lieutenant either
afloat or on shore. Our gunner was the only one in the
land party, and worked the powder of the battery all
the time. He was close to the poor young engineer
officer when he was killed. They had been on guard
together the night before, and he told the gunner of
his brother having been killed in the Kaffir war last
year. One marine lost his leg from a shell bursting
when in the act of putting a sand-bag on his back, which
our gunner had lifted up for him. No one else was
struck by the fragments of the shell. Captain Ramsay
spoke very highly to me of the conduct of our ten men,
as many from other ships behaved so ill they had to be
sent off after giving much trouble. There was much
corn brandy to be got from the cottages, and that caused
it all.

"Since then I have been rather completing my former
survey. I have been lying close under the walls in the
channel, which I find more dangerous and intricate than I
supposed, and it quite settles the question as to whether
we were right in not taking the ships in. I thought so
when I supposed three might go in, but now I find there
is only space for one, and then the channel is so narrow
that *Lightning* could not swing in it with only twelve
fathoms of cable out, and I had to move her out. What
chance would there have been of bringing up a large ship
in such a place under a heavy raking fire? Yet I expect
still to hear that there are men who pretend to think ships
could have gone in. They are parties interested in getting
up a feeling against the old admiral. A man yesterday
introduced himself to me as a brother of —— (using two
officers' names). I thought him only a travelling gentleman, but he put such questions to me that I declined
answering him. In fact, he tried to pump out of me
opinions (which I do not hold) that would convey a
censure on the chief, whom he evidently wanted to find
complaints against. I was obliged to be rude to him to
get rid of him, but before he went over the side he avowed
himself the correspondent of the *Morning Herald*. Then
I gave him my opinion on the subject of newspapers and
their correspondents, and the falsehoods they publish, and

the system of puffing some parties that was springing up, in a way that will get me anything but favourably mentioned, particularly as I bowed him over the side in anything but a civil way afterwards. There are parties in the fleet in league with these reporters for the sake of getting themselves puffed. We are all amused at seeing that even here, according to the newspapers, we had nothing to do with getting the ships up, the only mention of *Lightning's* name being that 'the masters of the fleet had surveyed the channel in *Lightning*, and found it fit for the largest ships.' They forgot that a preceding paragraph mentioned the large ships as having gone up, though it did not mention who took them up—the truth being that, after I had found the channels and taken up the large ships, the admiral directed me to take the master of the fleet and all the masters in *Lightning* to show them the channels, that they might be able to help taking other ships up ; and this is called their 'surveying the channel in *Lightning*.' "

I remember my father saying that the French general was anxious to lay regular siege to the big fort with trench work, after the destruction of the two towers, etc. ; but my father pointed out it could be taken by simply placing two guns on Telegraph Hill to the rear of the fort, looking down into the interior and the rear windows of the casemates, with only a brick wall to resist the shot. This would gain our end with little loss on our side, perhaps with not enough to gain a marshal's baton! Napier was much perplexed, hesitating between the two ideas, when my father said to him, "If you adopt the plan entailing greater loss, when you can effect your object with hardly any, on you will rest the responsibility of the death of every man that falls unnecessarily." By the time the French general had laid his breaching batteries against the great fort, the governor, seeing he was checkmated, surrendered.

After the peace, when my father was talking with

General Count Ignatieff in London, the former said that, although the Russians blamed the governor for surrendering so soon, he himself thought the governor had shown great moral courage. He risked his own reputation to save the lives of his defenceless soldiers. A weaker man would have held out until many had been killed, for the sake of his own credit. The only point on which he might be censured was in not doing more to hinder our going up the narrow channels

As to the new batteries which "Napier" (p. 395) says would have rendered Bomarsund unassailable, if completed, my father's note says :—

"It would have fallen just as easily by a land attack, as only one more tower was to have been added on the high ground, and the same battery that breached Fort Nottich would also have breached that The new forts would then have been useless. If they had held much larger bodies of troops, a larger attacking force would have been necessary, but success would have been as certain. The forts at Bomarsund would have been trebled in strength by the new works, but they would have added very little to the land defences"

Referring to Napier's proposal (p. 404) to attack Abo, after the fall of Bomarsund, with the French troops, and the objection of General D'Hilliers to do so, a note says :—

"The French general was quite right There was no object worth the risk. The French troops had lost one-eighth of their strength by cholera, and the men were affected by it in health and spirits. At Abo they must have landed in a wooded country and in the face of a force of at least equal strength, and our vessels could not have covered the landing on the mainland. I believe they would have failed. General Jones quite agreed with the French general."

The military chest taken at Bomarsund contained only paper roubles. Sulivan suggested to the admiral that our

Government might utilise them by handing them to Russia as part of our payment *for the Dutch loan*, and so save the value of them.   As it was decided that we had to pay on that loan, though at war, it would, he thought, have been fair to pay them with their own paper!

I extract the following from Captain Sulivan's evidence before the Royal Commission on Naval Promotions, 1863 :—

"There was a case in which a commander (Preedy) and gunnery lieutenant (Somerset), who fought a breaching battery in a very gallant affair, as far as a few were concerned, and who were specially recommended by the admiral in the body of his despatch, were passed over in the selection for promotion, and other officers, who only dragged the guns on shore, and handed them over to these to fight, were promoted, although I do not think that those officers were selected by interest.   Yet it is true that the two officers, the commander and lieutenant, who fought the guns and astonished the French by the accuracy of their fire, breaching a large granite fort in eight hours—those two officers, in spite of the recommendations of the admiral, having been passed over in the Board promotions, never got a step for their gallant conduct until they got it by another action in the next year ; and if they had not then got it, they might have been left unpromoted for years.   The commander, although a young commander, was known to be one of the best officers in the service. That was such a striking case, that, when speaking upon the subject to the First Lord of the Admiralty, I could not help pointing out the case to him, and his answer to me was that this officer was a young commander.   But he was about forty years of age ; he had been serving long as first lieutenant and mate ; and there were much younger men in point of age promoted, who had not played such a distinguished part as he had   Had those two officers, with two others who were promoted, been alone promoted for that service, although the officers of the fleet would have said it was rather scanty promotion, no one man could have complained."

The following despatch from Napier, showing how well

the officers of both surveying-ships worked, makes some amends for former omissions :—

"'Duke of Wellington,' Led Sound,
"<i>August 27th</i>, 1854.

" Having received information that Russian troops and gun-boats were among the islands, I sent Captain Scott with a small squadron to find them out. . . . Captain Scott threaded his way through the islands in a most persevering manner, as their lordships will see by the chart I send. His ships were repeatedly on shore, and the *Odin* no less than nine times, before they discovered the enemy's gun-boats and steamers lying behind a floating boom, supported on each side by batteries and a number of troops covering the town of Abo, where they have collected a large force.

" I take this opportunity of bringing under their lordships' notice the very great exertions of the surveying officers, Captain Sulivan, assisted by Mr. Evans, master of the *Lightning*, and Commander Otter of the *Alban*, and I have no hesitation in saying that it is owing to their exertions this fleet have found their way, with comparative little damage, into creeks and corners never intended for ships of the line ; day and night have they worked, and worked successfully Commander Otter is an old officer and well worthy of promotion, and Captain Sulivan and his assistant surveyor deserve the protection of their lordships "

The ships sent to Abo were the *Odin, Alban, Gorgon*, and *Driver*. The object was a reconnaissance only After going in as far as possible in the *Alban*, Commander Otter pulled in with his gig, sounding just within range of the batteries, which were all the time keeping up a constant fire. Captain Scott's despatch spoke in high terms of Otter.

The following is the copy of part of a letter written to some newspaper by Admiral Sulivan in recent years It may not be out of place here :—

" I believe I first started the idea of plating [our ?] ships with thick iron, and even in 1855 floating batteries had been built, protected by armour. If our Government had persuaded the French Government to send them to the Baltic instead of the Black Sea, it would almost certainly have resulted in the destruction of Cronstadt By the year 1859 the French were iron-plating some of their ships. We had several two-decked ships building about the year 1860 that would have been useless if opposed to iron-clads, even of inferior force , and feeling anxious on this point— I was then naval officer of the Board of Trade—I wrote either to the Secretary of the Admiralty officially, or to the First Lord's private secretary—I forget which—suggesting that these ships building should be cut down to frigates and iron-plated ; and I knew that Admiral Sir R. S. Dundas, then Senior Lord, strongly approved of this being done.

" The wooden iron-clads have one great advantage over those built of iron, in case of war, though not perhaps sufficient to compensate for the extra durability of iron ships. I allude to the additional safety in case of getting on shore

" No officer who had the experience of the inshore squadron in the Baltic, if he had to command a squadron on similar service, would, I think, hesitate for a moment in preferring ships with wooden bottoms. Most of the ships and smaller vessels employed inshore among the rocks of Finland were so often on shore that their bottoms were terribly damaged, and in my own small surveying-steamer the bottom was torn in places deep into the timber. In a large paddle-steamer—the *Leopard*—the flag-ship of an inshore squadron, the whole bottom was so torn to pieces that in dock at Woolwich she was visited as a curiosity. Captain Cooper Key, in a large frigate, saved her on one occasion by forcing her in a gale by a press of sail over an extensive reef, when every blow in the hollow of each sea jerked up the boats on the upper deck. Yet these and other ships much damaged remained out and did their work to the end of the season : had they been iron ships, they would have left their bones on Finnish rocks. If such work was required again as was done by Plumridge, Yelverton, Watson, Buckle, Hall, Key, and others in the Baltic, without losing a ship, it could not be done by iron bottoms without losing many of them. We had only one iron ship there, a transport, bringing out stores, etc., and taking home invalids. . . ." * (Continuation missing.)

* She, I believe, was the only vessel lost.—ED.

CHAPTER XI.

THE LAST OF BOMARSUND.

"ADMIRALTY, *August 22nd*, 1854.

THE good work done by the surveying officers was much appreciated in the Hydrographic Office. On the retirement of Sir Francis Beaufort, his assistant, Captain Washington, succeeded him as chief of the department.

"DEAR SULIVAN,—Accept my hearty congratulations on the success which has attended your indefatigable labours, which I trust will meet with their due reward. All admit that without your pioneering they would not have gained their object as they have done, and happily with little loss of life. I trust the admiral will have given you full credit in his despatches. Your account is very interesting ; but ought you to expose yourself to unnecessary risks ?

"I have been three weeks in Paris, when I had the gratification of seeing the *Lightning's* name repeatedly mentioned in the French newspapers. I feel so thankful there has been no loss of life except the poor *Penelope*.

"I consider that *Lightning* has conferred great credit on the Hydrographical Department, and heartily thank you all for it.

"With best wishes,
"Ever faithfully yours,
"JOHN WASHINGTON."

"'LIGHTNING,' RUNNING FOR LED SOUND,
"*Monday, August 28th*, 1854.

"On Wednesday morning we sailed with the French steamer, the French admiral and all the generals, General Jones, with Captain Chads of the army, and young Cochrane (the general's naval *aide-de-camp*) coming with me. I was ordered in writing to take her to Sweaborg, and then deliver a flag-of-truce about an exchange of wounded prisoners. The admiral, as usual, left half my orders to be given verbally, and he told me they would all want to see Revel also, and I must settle with the French admiral which to go to first. He arranged with me that we should go first to Revel, then Sweaborg, and take Hango on our return, and that he would wait for me whilst I settled the flag-of-truce business. I mentioned to our chief that it might lead to something being said by the Russians if *Lightning* first went in with the generals reconnoitring the place and then went with the flag-of-truce, and I suggested that I had better leave her outside and take another vessel with the flag-of-truce. He said, 'Arrange it as you like with the officer there, Captain Watson, and do whatever you think best '"

On arriving at Revel Thursday morning, they found Admiral Plumridge with the squadron at anchor under Nargen. Some little difficulty arose when Captain Sulivan, having explained the purport of the expedition to Admiral Plumridge, received written orders from the latter which conflicted with the spirit of the verbal instructions from Sir Charles Napier ; but the French admiral explained that Captain Sulivan had been placed at his disposal. Again some slight friction occurred, when, the glass commencing to fall, and the wind to blow from the southward, Captain Sulivan desired to wait before proceeding to Sweaborg, knowing *Lightning* could not ride out a storm on a lee shore. But the admiral, nevertheless, ordered him to proceed. However, the French admiral preferred to wait, so the matter was settled.

" On Thursday evening we steamed into Revel just in the middle of the bay, three thousand yards from the batteries all round, so that it was useless their firing ; but we had a capital view of everything, and saw five new batteries round the beach to the eastward of the moles. A large number of artillery batteries were going out to exercise, and we had a capital view of them. A number of captains were with us, and they said that they owed to me the pleasantest afternoon they had had. Directly General Jones expressed a wish to go in, I had let as many as I could know of it, that they might come also. Whilst inside, a boat with six women came across the bay under sail, so we cut them off, and, I fear, frightened them terribly. But finding they could not escape, they were at last induced to come alongside, several crying bitterly. An old woman was coxswain   I gave them some sugar, tea and biscuit, and a bundle of tracts, and you may fancy their astonishment and altered countenances, and they went away delighted   The old woman took my hand and kissed it very hard, and quite cried again, but a very different cry from the first.   On Friday it blew a heavy southerly gale, and I told the French chief I did not think it safe to start, the glass being very low.   On Saturday it still blew strong, the glass scarcely rising, so I feared still taking *Lightning* on a dead lee shore "

This again led to some discussion, the French admiral ultimately declining to start in such weather.

" The wind moderating rapidly about eleven o'clock, and the glass rising steadily, I went to the French chief and said we had better start. He declared he was under my orders, and he would go if I thought it best. We started directly, and by the time we got across it was a beautiful evening   Watson joined us with *Impérieuse*, *Rosamond*, and *Magicienne*, and sent the latter with me, as a large Russian steam-frigate had come out once or twice after a smaller steamer of ours, and Watson thought, as there were two frigates, they would come out when we went much closer in than usual. We led in, followed by the French steamer and *Magicienne*, Watson waiting about five miles outside where the shoals became thicker. When we drew near the island that I anchored inside of with the former flag-of-truce, the French steamer and *Magicienne* rounded to half a mile outside us. We ran inside the island. The fort fired two blank guns and then a shot, which fell four hundred yards short of us.   I knew we were three thousand yards off. The steamers inside were getting up steam and making a great smoke. We stopped

inside the island whilst General Jones had a good look, and
then steamed slowly along to get as much view farther
west as possible; but before we could get as far as we
intended, the French admiral made the signal, 'I shall
return,' and he and *Magicienne* began steaming out, so we
had only to follow them, as the steamers inside had their
steam up.

"We then anchored together for the night.   Watson,
Woodhouse, Yelverton, and I passed the evening on board
Arrogant, all of us old college-mates or shipmates.   They
all said it was fortunate we had not come over the day
before, for it was a tremendous gale.   *Euryalus* tried to
ride it out and parted her cable, and they all had to get
off under steam and storm-sails.   They said we could not
have got off, and, had we tried to ride it out, we must have
parted cable or been swamped.   We should probably have
had to run in under an island to save ourselves, and the
Russian steamers would have come out and gobbled us up!

"Yesterday morning I was obliged to go in under a
flag-of-truce, as the French admiral was to wait for us
at Hango, if we could get there in time.   I went in at five
with *Rosamond*, and anchored near where I did before.
A boat soon came out with a white flag, and the same
lieutenant I saw before took the letter.   I explained it had
reference to wounded Russian prisoners in our hospital-ship.
Shortly after one of their steam-frigates came out with a
white flag and anchored near us.   I had no idea they had
such a beautiful vessel.   She is about our *Leopard* or *Retribution* class: seven guns of a side on the main-deck, two heavy
shell-guns aft, one forward, and two smaller guns like the
main-deck ones (about thirty-two-pounders) on the forecastle—in all nineteen guns.   She seemed in beautiful order.
Though carrying her guns higher than our vessels, she
seemed a much lighter and prettier vessel, and was perfectly
upright even when turning short round.   Our steamers
like *Leopard* or *Magicienne* are put on one side by the
most trifling thing, so that they could not always fight
their guns.   We saw another steam-frigate exactly like this
one inside, towing ships from one position to another.   With
two such ships they ought long since to have cut off one
of ours.   At one time *Rosamond* alone—six guns—was off
the port watching, no other ship was within reach, and I
am sure they must be faster than she.   The one that
came out seemed very fast.   She had a number of

officers on board, and a very large crew, dressed in white frocks, except a small number in red blouses, apparently the marines. I felt strongly inclined to go to her and call on the captain, but feared they might not like it or might misconstrue my motives. We laid all day till 2 p.m., when a fast little steamer came out, and a very fine, handsome, gentlemanly young lieutenant brought a letter for Sir Charles Napier. He was not reserved and frightened as the other had been at the idea of speaking to us or of disobeying orders We asked him below. He smiled and seemed to hesitate, and then said in French, 'Thank you, but I cannot, because—because—because——' and then, after hesitating and smiling, said, 'You understand,' and he went down the ladder. Just as he shoved off he asked the name of the vessel. We then steamed out, and I immediately started in *Lightning*, but too late to see Hango or catch the French chief, so we pushed on for Led Sound all night, and are now, 11 a.m., getting in sight and all longing for our letters.

"It was most gratifying and flattering to me to receive from all my brother-captains up there such real warm congratulations on what they thought I am sure to get for my share in the work. My kind friend Yelverton had, I think, rather overrated my work in telling them all about it. Still it was gratifying to see all absence of jealousy from those who had been out of the way, and such a desire that I should be rewarded. One was quite sure they could not give me anything less than the K.C B. I pointed out to them that I had done nothing to come within its reach, even if the rules allowed it in my case, which they do not.

"*August 29th*—On our way here we heard that the French admiral on his way back found the Russians themselves destroying Hango and blowing up the forts I am very thankful for it, as it saves us many lives. We must have destroyed it before we went home. I had just suggested to General Jones a plan for landing a large force by daybreak above on the neck of land, and so cutting off all the force on the point (from two to three thousand men) besides . . ." (Continuation missing.)

"'LIGHTNING,' BOMARSUND, *September 1st*, 1854

"On Wednesday the chief came up here to see the last of the place, the blowing up of the forts, etc., and to see

Admiral Chads try his guns at the masonry. He said I could lie down at Led Sound to do my work completing charts. I told him I should like to see the last of the forts, as I had seen the first, and I could lie here and get up the work, besides being on the spot to get any more work for the chart, if necessary. So he let me come up. Admiral Seymour came up with him in *Odin*, but preferred a bed in my cabin ; so he has been with me at night. He is such a good, estimable man that it is a pleasure having him with me. Yesterday morning he asked me to walk over the different points with him before breakfast. The night before Admiral Chads sent for me to the chief's ship. He was in great anxiety lest he should not be able to fire at the big fort, as the French general did not wish it, but said he might have Presto Fort. Now to get at that we have to pass the very narrow channel near the large fort, and he was very anxious to know if I could take *Edinburgh* in through. I said I thought I could, as there is seven fathoms water ; but the doubt was if there is breadth enough. I took the master of *Edinburgh* with me, as he knew best what space the ship would turn and steer in. The channel proved even narrower than I thought, but we found about ten feet more breadth than the breadth of the ship, and decided to take her through ; but before anything could be done the fort to be fired at was blown up, so there was an end to that, and I lost the chance of taking a line-of-battle ship through a narrower channel than, I think, was ever attempted before, unless it was through a dock-gate ! The general then agreed that Chads should fire at the large fort, and a piece is to be reserved for that purpose. The French are burning everything they can that has to be destroyed, and are anxious to embark the men as quickly as possible, for the cholera has been making sad havoc among them. They have already buried about seven hundred out of ten thousand men, and, though it is better, twenty-four died yesterday. I went to one or two more points to complete my work, and particularly to make a plan of all the new batteries building, etc., and in passing through one small encampment we saw two poor fellows just laid out on stretchers, dead. A few natives have also died, but it is the first time they have ever had cholera in the islands. The poor people will be helped through the winter by the supply of meal in the fort. It is given to all who come, and hundreds of carts and carriages of all descriptions and boats of every kind are loading all day.

"To-day I had to go up to the north fort to complete some work at that point. It was blown up by the French yesterday. One part, that where our breach was made, did not fall, and it was singular that the only gun not buried under the ruins was the same one the enemy had fought so long and so gallantly against our breaching battery. It was still pointing exactly at our battery, as if it would stand to the last. The front wall was all down, leaving the arches of the upper tier of three casemates standing, so that you could see the interior, and on the right-hand one lay the gun alongside its carriage. The new batteries building would have made it a tremendously strong place. There were two of seventy guns each, and two large towers, or rather circular forts, capable of mounting forty guns each. The Emperor must have put a very great value on the place to add so enormously to the fortifications. The work is beautiful : the face of all would be cut granite, fitted in blocks, and the embrasures, etc., were as beautifully worked as in the finest London buildings. General Jones says the work is very superior Thousands of beautifully cut granite stones, all fitted for their places, are lying in every direction One fort was half built; the others had only the foundations laid. To-night the massive scaffolding and platforms round the building are all in a blaze, and all the work will be blown up. The only reason I can see for such an outlay is that the Emperor intended making it his chief naval port, in which he would have his fleet almost always free from ice, and at the same time advanced towards Sweden and the Atlantic. He would then have had his fleet in by far the finest port in the Baltic, with anchorages for the largest ships.

"This evening when dining with Admiral Chads, the chief, Admiral Martin, and others also, a small Russian steamer hove in sight with a flag-of-truce. Her boat brought two officers, one a lieutenant, the other a nondescript, wearing a sort of uniform coat and cap, dirk, and a collar and cross round his neck. He, it appears, is the owner of the Russian steamer, and belongs to the yacht club of St Petersburg ; she is now hired by the government. They came to the place Otter was to take the women to, to receive them ; and not finding them there, they came on, I

FORT NOTTICH, BOMARSUND.

FORT PRESTO
(or Fort on Presto Island).

[To face p. 248.

suppose glad of an excuse to see what had been done here. The vessel has been allowed to come in, and is at anchor near us.

"The weather is getting colder. The chief fully expects the fleet will be home by the end of October. I think some ships will be left out longer for blockade. I wish I could hope that the war would be at an end by next spring, and that I should be quietly settled at home again. One thing I must really try hard to accomplish this winter— that is, to gain some knowledge of French—for I find the want of it a terrible drawback, thrown as I now am with the French so much. We must try to get a governess who cannot speak a word of English, and I must go to school like the children!

"*Sunday, September* 3rd—Yesterday, at seven in the evening, the large fort was blown up. Many of the casemates and all the barracks in the rear of the court had been filled with fire-wood, and were fired at the same time, so we had a grand display. The sight as the successive mines exploded was very fine; some shot in the air, others burst out in front: all did not explode at first, so as the fire spread we had the repeated explosions of shells as the fire reached them—there were many thousands—and occasionally another mine. The fire was splendid as it grew dark, and at the same time large wooden buildings and scaffolding round the new forts were all in a blaze, so that one could hardly keep one's eyes from the sight. I was working at the chart till midnight, but running up repeatedly to see some outburst. This morning all that is left entire is a piece of the fort about seven casemates wide, for Admiral Chads to fire at for experiment. The ships, all close in, had every spot aloft and on deck alive with people, and the troops on shore crowded on every bit of rising ground around; and when the splendid column of smoke burst up after the first grand explosions, a cheer burst out on all sides and rolled round the hills. It was a fine but melancholy sight. To think that, had it not been for this war, all would have been peaceful and quiet, as I first saw it, pretty houses in every direction, a fine hospital on Presto surrounded by fine buildings, but all now smoking ruins! Besides, many men have fallen in action, numbers suffering from wounds, and the bodies of nearly eight hundred French soldiers left on the ground, and all because a man, possessing the largest territory in the world, with absolute power over it, wanted to seize on still more. I am sure he looked on this place as a step towards seizing on Sweden and perhaps Denmark at a future time, and he is justly punished in having all he possessed in it, and all his ambitious plans for the future, founded on the enormous outlay he was making here, end in a heap of ruins. I only wish I could see Sweaborg and Cronstadt in the same state; and if he does not come to his senses, and make peace on just terms this year, I hope we may see them in the same state as Bomarsund next summer.

"I forgot to say that Admiral Seymour had expressed great surprise that the chief had omitted my name and that of the surveyors in thanking the officers and men of the fleet. He said he was sure, from the way the admiral always speaks of our work, that it was quite an oversight, and he offered to speak to the chief about it and have it corrected, but I did not like him to do so. I thought it best to let it rest, and trust to his having done us justice in his despatches.

"*Led Sound, Tuesday, 5th.*—We came down last evening with the admiral on board and his flag flying. We have been flag-ship pretty often now. It is blowing the hardest gale from the north-west we have ever had, and, though in this fine anchorage, we have had to let go two anchors. Several ships were driving in the night. I am glad we are not in the gulf. It will try Nargen anchorage well. The French army all sailed on their way home yesterday. I trust the cholera has not gone to sea with them. It is wonderful how they could have suffered so much and the ships escape. I think the damp ground at night, or their eating every green thing they could lay hold of, must have something to do with it We were lying in the *Lightning* between Presto Island and the fort, not a hundred ards from either shore; yet they were dying on each side, whilst we had not a man sick. In Presto there is a very pretty cemetery attached to the hospital, now burnt down. In it all those who died on Presto are buried. I did not see it, but I hear that the French soldiers have decorated their cemetery graves very prettily, and have written nice mottoes on the head-stones, or in some cases pasted paper on the head of each. There were only about six hundred soldiers there of the colonial or marine battalion, yet it is said about a hundred graves are to be seen. The poor fellows who died round the main camp the other side are buried in every direction in fields and gardens, and the little crosses will mark for some time the last resting-places of hundreds of fine young men cut off in a few days by one of the most extraordinary visitations of this extraordinary epidemic. We have had no fresh cases even in our ships lying up there, while they have been suffering so on shore."

The following is a draft of a letter to some newspaper :—

"August 2nd, 1884.

" SIR,—I am sure that many will read with pleasure your advocacy of baths for Whitechapel and other of the poorer parts of London, and they would be of the greatest value should London be visited by cholera, as the following facts will prove.

" When our fleet went to the Baltic in 1854, the weather was cold till June, when it suddenly changed to very warm and calm weather. There was cholera at the time in St. Petersburg, and, a few days after the hot weather set in, some cases occurred in the fleet, then at anchor in Baro Sound.

" I then commanded the surveying-steamer *Lightning,* and directly the first cases occurred in the fleet my surgeon, Dr. Johnson, told me that he thought one cause was that the men, large numbers of whom were not men-of-war's men, had been so wrapped up in warm and thick clothing till the hot weather commenced, that their bodies were not very clean, nor the pores of their skin in a healthy state, and he asked me to let him examine our crew on this point, and also to ascertain if any had premonitory symptoms. He reported to me that out of our small crew there were several with the first symptoms of cholera and one rather bad case, and he requested me to send the whole ship's company on shore in the evening on a small island near us, with order to the petty officers that while bathing the men should all be thoroughly well washed, the nearly fresh water allowing the use of soap. For some time they were all hard at work in the slightly warm water, and the result was that in three or four days all the slight cases were well, and the worst recovered in a week.

" During the summer a number of men died in both English and French ships, and after Bomarsund was captured about eight hundred out of nine thousand French soldiers died in two or three weeks.

"The *Lightning* during that time had to remain in the narrow channel separating the French camps, where she had hardly space to swing. Yet during this time our men were perfectly healthy. This great mortality was, perhaps, caused by the French soldiers clearing every field and garden of cabbages, turnip-tops, mangels, beet, etc., and eating large quantities of green vegetables of every kind uncooked, but made into salads, after having lived in the English ships that took them out chiefly on salt beef and pork, which they were not accustomed to

"I feel convinced that providing means for frequent bathing in fresh water, with the free use of soap, for those classes who cannot well have them in their own dwellings, especially in towns, would do more than anything to protect them from cholera or any other epidemics."

Another reason for the immunity of the *Lightning* from cholera was, doubtless, the use of distilled water for drinking. The exhaust steam-pipe led against the inside of the paddle-box, a copper-plate, kept cool by the splashing of the water on the outer surface. The steam water thus condensed was caught in grooves and led into buckets. Captain Sulivan noticed the engineers using this soft water for washing, so ordered it to be placed in tanks on deck to be aerated, and this was afterwards the chief drinking water for the crew, and, I believe, the first of its kind used in ships (?). Afterwards other ships adopted the system.

"Admiralty, *August 29th,* 1854.

"So, my dear Sulivan, you have at last accomplished the Aland job, and in a very satisfactory and workmanlike manner. The above word *you* was meant, while running from my pen, in a plural sense—you collectively. *You,* fleet, etc., which was rather unjust of my said pen, being firmly convinced that but for *you, singular,* it would not have been done at all—at all events not this year. And yet the lame un-English despatch of your admiral does not even mention your name. Not so the just and honest Sir W. Parker—not so the generous and noble-minded Nelson ; and I have taken the opportunity of saying all this, and spitefully too, to the former. But do not you feel spiteful; your day will come, and all the sooner and all the more gratifyingly by your dignified bearing on this occasion. We shall have, of course, a good sketch of Bomarsund and its channels, in expectation of which I have made no use of your last hints and tracings. Your letters to me and to Washington have been very delightfully clear and explanatory, and the last touches upon some abstract points about guns and walls which we may discuss *viva voce*, and endeavour to apply to places yet to be smashed.

"In the meantime I am always yours,

"F. BEAUFORT."

"LED SOUND, *Saturday, September 9th*, 1854

"We have been kept here since Wednesday by the worst weather we have ever had in the Baltic, heavy gales from N.W. to N.N.E. every day, and here in a snug harbour we had French ships driving, and all the fleet with two anchors down and topmasts struck. I have been very anxious for our fleet at Nargen, as it has been the worst wind for that anchorage; and if a ship parted or drove, she had the enemy's coast to leeward. What made me more anxious was, that I have always advised the chief to use that anchorage in preference to any other in the gulf. I was therefore greatly relieved to-day by the arrival of *Rosamond* with the news that they all rode it out well with only one anchor and without striking topmasts. They appear to have had it less violent than we had. Evidently the draught of the Gulf of Bothnia made it heavier here. To-day I had a long interview with the chief, and a long talk about the movements of the fleet. He has given up going up the gulf, and I was glad to find had decided to send the sailing-ships home directly: his only doubt seemed whether we had force enough without them, in case the Russians ventured out. He forgot one of our screw-ships, and only counted twelve; and as the Russians have about twenty-four or twenty-five fit for sea, he seemed to have some doubt about it. I counted over thirteen screws to him, and the French one, besides our three heavy frigates, equal at least to seventeen sail of the line, and quite a match for all theirs; so that if by sending the ships away there was a chance of drawing the Russian fleet out, it was the best thing we could do.

He thought of going southward shortly with all the ships; but I pointed out to him that the anchorage here was the best in the Baltic, while it had the appearance of shutting up the Russians better than the anchorage in Kiel or the belts; and while we must have a frigate force blockading the gulf, this was much the best anchorage for the screw fleet to support them and to remain in till we were actually going home I think he will adopt this plan, but we shall evidently be home sooner than I thought. The sailing-ships and hospital-ships and small steamers will go at once, and I expect to find us all at home by the middle of October. *Lightning* will, I think, be home much before, but I shall of course offer to remain out with the chief, to assist him in getting the fleet safely through the belts and Kattegat. We are all looking anxiously out for the next mail, which we expect will bring the promotions Whether any of the surveyors are included will depend entirely on whether the Government published all the chief's despatches.

"The *Rosamond* has brought down a letter for the admiral from Helsingfors, sent out with a flag-of-truce. I cannot help thinking every time I am with the chief now, when he tells me all his plans, shows me his letters, and asks my advice on nearly everything, how very different it was during the first two months I heard at first that he was too obstinate to take advice, and that there was no turning him from his opinion, and that it was no use suggesting anything unless you made it appear that it came from himself. Now I never met any senior officer who was more open to reason, and I have even given him my real opinion without caring whether it agreed with his own or not, and never found him mind my doing so, however much he differed; on the contrary, I believe he sees opinions are better worth having when they do not merely echo his own, and I am sure now by explaining to him why I thought a thing necessary I could almost make him adopt any opinion I give him. Every one who reads this must of course be doubly careful not to let a hint of what I write on these subjects ever slip out in talking to any one about the fleet or the admiral.

"I forget whether I ever told you that the forts at Bomarsund were offered to Sweden, but were ordered to be destroyed if the king refused them. He did refuse them, but at the same time wanted them to be preserved.

I suppose he could not make up his mind to join in the war; and he is quite right, as his interest, I think, lies in neutrality, and it would only make peace more difficult for us if we had to insist on any part of Finland being made over to Sweden; but at the same time it would have been folly for us to have preserved the forts and had to garrison them, unless for Sweden. They are much better destroyed, and may save us trouble hereafter."

"September 11th, 1854.

"The *Daily News* has by far the most truthful accounts of the proceedings of our fleet, without exaggeration or puffing, and the correspondent, whoever he is, evidently has means of knowing what goes on, and writes impartially and fairly. But what they say in leading articles about batteries, gun-boats, etc., is great nonsense (as it is in all the other papers), and only misleads people. If our fleet had madly tried to attack Cronstadt, and been beaten and partly destroyed, as it must have been, the papers would have been the first to cry out about knocking our ships to pieces against stone walls. Taking Bomarsund has nothing to do with it, as the large forts in other places, and particularly Cronstadt, are so situated that ships going alongside them would be raked by a number of other forts, and would be destroyed before they could silence the forts they were alongside. If it were merely a question of one of these large forts like Risbank or Alexander at Cronstadt being attacked by ships, there is no doubt that four ships could get alongside either, and, if there were no other forts, would very soon silence them; but as the ships would have at the same time above a hundred heavy guns pouring hot shot and shell into their bows from batteries that ships could not go alongside of, nothing could justify such a mad attempt. I fear the papers writing so much on these points may do much harm by raising a feeling in the public mind that enough is not done with our means, forgetting that these opinions are from people sitting down at a desk, perhaps at home, and not quite as well able to give a correct opinion as those who have seen the forts and anxiously looked for any opening that would justify an attempt being made. Now at Bomarsund the position of the hill forts, and the shape of the ground, etc., on the land side, gave such an opening, and I reported on the practicability of it, which the result has proved. When openings offer themselves in other places, they will of course be laid hold of; but the opinions given publicly in newspapers of the weak points in different places, where they happen to be right, will do great injury, as they make public to the enemy what perhaps at the very time is being planned by those who have seen the place, and so may assist greatly to make that very plan more difficult to carry out by drawing the enemy's attention to their weak points   I think the Government would be quite justified in saying to the Press, 'You shall not publish opinions of that kind, or any statements of what are supposed to be our future plans.'   Let them give full particulars of our proceedings and criticise them as much as they like, but not publish anything that could give an enemy a useful hint.   If we have any important attacks going on next year—which we certainly shall—this may be of the utmost importance to our success   If there had been any idea publicly about our attacking Bomarsund by land, when we had just planned it all, and the papers had dwelt on it and on the weak points, we should certainly have had much more opposition.   They had thrown up a new battery some way out on the road we advanced by, and marked it well, but had not got it quite ready for the guns —a few days more would have lost us many men there ; and had they known of our plans about two months before, they would have had a strong position fortified, that would have had to be carried by assault with much loss

"*Tuesday*, 12*th*.—Sent early this morning to Bomarsund to catch *Alban* going with the recovered Russian wounded officers and men to Abo ; met her coming out.   She had been on shore for two and a half hours (report said four days) in the gale, but got off all right.   She went on, and we waited for letters from Admiral Martin about an hour, then started on our return to Led Sound, and directly we got out of Bomarsund Bay poor *Alban* got hard and fast— ran right up, and heeled over very much.   We have been three hours trying to get her off, tugging at her and heaving till we carried away everything we had, so now I am running down to save the mail and to get more assistance. Otter was trusting to a native pilot, who had gone that way once before with him, and they were going full speed with sail, and he ran them right on the point of an island. I never have trusted, or will trust, one of them."

"*September* 14*th*, 1854.

" I have heard of some promotions being out, and was indeed astonished at the injustice of them. Nothing can explain the rule they have followed   Admiral Chads' three block-ships have each their first lieutenant promoted, who were never under fire, and only dragged the guns four miles over a road to the camp   A lieutenant of *Blenheim* in the battery with Pelham, two years standing, I believe, is also promoted. But the commander and gunnery lieutenant of the commander-in-chief's ship, who had all the dangerous work of getting the guns into battery and working them so well under a heavy fire, are not included, and Cudlip (my first lieutenant), the senior in the fleet, on shore all the time, and at the battery all day, not noticed Otter, though senior commander employed, not noticed ; but I think that will be remedied, as Washington writes me that a despatch of the admiral's, speaking very highly of the surveyors, and particularly of myself, Otter, and Evans, would be immediately published.

" Cholera seems steadily increasing in London, and will, I fear, get up to its former number of two thousand weekly I am thankful to say we have nothing of the kind here now. It is astonishing the way it fell on the French troops. It seemed to be caused by sleeping in tents on the ground, as those in the fort escaped ; but officers and men are away from some of our ships on shooting excursions for days in a tent, and no one ill. They kill numbers of black-cock on the outlying uninhabited rocky islets with very little cover—not in the woods. I am too busy to have a chance at them.

" I went back on Tuesday night with *Bulldog*, got her just astern of *Alban*, got *Lightning* alongside of her and took out some coal, and then, with a good pull with steam and cables, got her off about midnight. The Russian officers (doctors and other non-combatants) going back with the wounded were enjoying themselves, and singing a number of things, some in parts, very well indeed. They said they did not care for the getting on shore, and only hoped it would last a day or two longer, they were in such good quarters. They were all at breakfast in the gun-room when she struck, and it knocked them all down and smashed all the mess-traps on the table.

" When I returned to the fleet with *Bulldog* yesterday

17

morning, I asked the chief to let me get on with the survey, and I am now alone among the islands, doing all the work I can I was at Degerby yesterday. The policeman is sent home as a prisoner. The admiral would not let him return to his family, because others of his position had been giving much trouble and threatening the poor people with the vengeance of Russia There is some fellow acting the spy still at Degerby, and I may have to walk him off

"We have no difficulty now about provisions; boats bring plenty of things to sell alongside. I bought a lamb from a servant, which she said was part of her wages, so I asked how they were paid I was told they get about eighteen shillings a year and two lambs to keep as their own, so they get up a little flock All clothing is also found them.

"The wife of the farmer was away in their vessel, of which he is half owner, going to Stockholm with two cows to sell, to get money to buy what they required. The women here are quite as good sailors as their husbands and brothers. We find little boats carrying a press of sail, and in a nasty sea, with perhaps only two or three women in them, and always part of the crews women: they seem born to it. In the summer they are fishing, milking, shearing sheep, or perhaps going in a boat to the cows morning and evening, as they put them on all the smaller islands to eat up the pasture. Sometimes we meet a small boat with two or three people in it, and a cow standing as quietly as possible, though looking too large for the boat to hold in safety.

"*Friday*, 15*th*.—To-day the weather prevented our working all the morning; it was foggy with rain, and the barometer lower than we have ever had it in the Baltic, so that we must be going to have regular equinoctial gales.

"I heard that Captain Mansell of the *St. Vincent* had died after leaving this, and that Captain Clifford of *Sphinx* had both legs broken by a hawser being carried away when towing the *St. Vincent*"

> "'Duke of Wellington,' off Revel,
> "*September 25th*, 1854

"I have rather a larger ship than *Lightning* now. The chief wanted me with him to visit Revel and Sweaborg;

and as *Lightning* is small for any heavy weather in this gulf, and might be a tax on the other ships, I asked him to let me leave her about the survey, and come in some other ship. He said I should come here, so here I am very comfortable, forming part of the admiral's staff, having one side of the fore-cabin (General Jones having the other), and nothing to do but answer the chief's questions when required, occasionally go over plans and letters with him, and a walk on the island (Nargen) when he goes. He is most kind and flattering in his manner and treatment of me.

"We came here on Thursday, and on Friday I took the general and others in off Revel in *Locust*, attended by *Wrangler*, a new screw despatch-boat   In the afternoon I took all the admirals in *Wrangler*. We were just out of range of all the batteries, so they did not fire ; but all were manned and troops drawn up   It is a very strong place, and it would be folly to attack it with ships. A large fleet would, I have no doubt, destroy all the forts, but would be pretty well destroyed also, and be as unfit for anything afterwards, till refitted, as some of our ships at Algiers were, while all we should gain would be destroying some stones and guns and killing some men, and our fleet might be no match afterwards for the Russian ships. I wish some of those fighting newspaper men were put into a ship by themselves, and anchored off one of these batteries to have their fill of it ; they would then know a little more on the subject (those that were left) than they do now, and would not write such utter folly and nonsense   Unfortunately some in authority, sitting in their offices, who ought to know better, write almost as great nonsense. With all the old chief's failings, it is lucky we had a man with moral courage enough to stand firm against the whines of the Press, as well as against the wishes of some men out here, who, caring only for a chance of personal distinction, would have wanted him to run their heads against any stone wall that offered.

"On Saturday we went to Sweaborg in *Driver*. The chief the night before and this morning at breakfast had repeatedly said to me, 'Now you are sure you will not run us on a rock : if you do, I shall be taken prisoner.' I always said I could not feel sure, as there are so many rocks ; but I saw little chance of it, as I had been in and out safely three times, and once with three ships, but that I would never speak too confidently, or I should expect to meet with an accident. We took *Basilisk* with us, and outside made Watson's signal to join in *Impérieuse*, to have a good defence if necessary against the two large Russian steamers coming out. When near the narrow parts of the channel, knowing there was less risk with one vessel, we made the others' signal to wait, as being within five miles of where we were going they could be ready. The admiral often repeated his warning not to put him on a rock, as he had no wish to visit St Petersburg, and he did not want to go so close as we had done before; so I said I would turn round outside an island that I had always gone round inside of before. I knew by the Russian charts there was a rock outside, but these being on such a very small scale I could not exactly know its position. I wanted to go as far to the west as possible, also to get General Jones as good a view that way as I could (besides the chief and the general, Admirals Chads and Seymour were on board) It was very different turning a steamer of a thousand and fifty tons and *Lightning*, and I took every care, scarcely moving now and then to keep her way; but the engine stopped as we turned, when, instead of being outside this rock, as I thought, we were between it and the island, and some other rocks near above water. Though going so slowly, we shoaled rapidly from eleven to seven fathoms, and, by the time I had checked her way, to five and four and a half, which must have been very close to the shallow part. We were in such a position that I dare not go astern for fear of going on other rocks, and there was no chance but turning her on a pivot in the spot she was, and going out the way we came in It was an anxious few minutes, everybody watching eagerly, but not saying a word. The captain suggested something I saw would not do, so I did not hesitate for a moment about the best way, knowing at the time that if we struck they would have their steamers out as soon as ours could get in, as they were not half the distance, and if they towed out two line-of-battle ships (which they would have done if they had been worth anything as officers) they would certainly take us before ships could get from Nargen to help us. Having four big officers under my charge of course did not lessen the anxiety. However, in a few minutes (during which you might have heard a pin drop almost when the engines were stopped, and during which we several times deepened and shoaled our water)

she turned right round and came out as we went in all
right. The old chief, though generally so nervous, behaved
very well—quietly walked the deck, only once or twice
asking me a question   Directly she was in the channel all
safe I went to him, expecting to see him rather angry with
me; but instead of that he seemed pleased, and said,
'Upon my word, you did it uncommonly well: if you had
not, I should dine in Helsingfors to-day.'   I told him that
the admirals, in the event of our grounding, ought to have
gone off in a boat—I thought that their duty in such
a case, rather than stay to be captured; but he would not
allow it, and said he would never have left her. (' Na, na ·
do ye think I would have left ye?') He allows that his not
wishing to go so close as I wished caused me to turn
round in ground new to me; whereas, had he gone inside
the island, it would have been in *Lightning's* tracks.   In
one of our walks on the island we went to the village, and
saw an old woman of seventy-one, active and intelligent,
speaking a few words of English, who washed for Lord
Nelson's officers in 1802.   The admiral asked her if she
recollected Admiral Saumarez in 1809   She said, ' Yes—
Admiral Pickmore too.'

"In his letters the chief does not hesitate to mention me
several times as authority for certain statements bearing
out his views, and it is very flattering to me altogether, and
shows he does not try to deprive a junior of any credit due.

"I think I could leave for home any day I like, as the
chief is rather anxious to get all the small steamers away;
but I do not like to leave him so long as I can be of any
use to him, and without being an egotist I may say that
I think I can save him much anxiety if I remain.   He
must not leave too soon, or the Russians will come out
in the Baltic and crow.   He does not like being so far
north as Led Sound, and I do not like his being so far
south as Kiel Bay, too far from our frigate squadron; so
I mean to try and compromise a little, and get him to
Elgsnabben instead, which Gordon also recommends, and
as he wants to visit Stockholm again I think he will go
there: if so, I shall try to keep him there all October, even
if I send *Lightning* home without me

"My anxiety lest the admiral should leave this too
soon, and so cause rejoicing to the enemy, overcomes the
desire to get home. . . . I am quite satisfied with the
credit every one gives me, and the way the admiral treats

me is sufficient reward for all I have done, besides the consciousness of having done one's duty, and last, though not least, the satisfaction of having slightly altered the admiral's declared opinion that 'a surveying-ship would be of no use except to make a fire-vessel of!'"

"'DUKE OF WELLINGTON,' OFF REVEL,
"*October 1st,* 1854

"We have had uninterrupted bad weather, and the poor admiral getting as anxious as possible, particularly as Admiral Plumridge, with the sailing-ships, started on Wednesday for Kiel, and there has been no good weather since, but no gale till yesterday, when it blew hard from south-west and drew round in the night to N.N.W., and blows strong. However, it has proved the correctness of my view of the anchorage, for even now, with the gale right in, there is no sea, and all the vessels lying with slack cables

"To-day at breakfast the admiral said there was still his first despatch unpublished, and it was a great shame; he had sent it home again, requesting it might be published. He said my name was mentioned in it, and he handed a copy to Admiral Seymour and me to read; we were both mentioned in it, so that I have been right after all that he wrote, but the Admiralty did not publish The chief is very civil, and rather too prone to speak favourably of me to my face, whoever happens to be dining here. He now declares that if I do not see the rocks under water I must smell them I have asked him, if I can be of any assistance to him, to keep me out and send *Lightning* home; but he thinks it unnecessary now, and so it really is, for he has excellent assistants for the simple navigation of the fleet homewards, and I could do no more than others, but I think he will from habit feel the want of having me close at hand to answer questions on all sorts of subjects—forts, guns, shelling, plans of attack, pilotage, charts, and plans of all the fortresses to look over and explain; in fact, he makes me engineer, artilleryman, pilot, etc., in turn; and though I am very careful how I say anything, so as not to let him think I am presuming too much on his confidence, yet I speak my mind most freely and without the slightest attempt to humour his views, and I am sure he likes it. General Jones said to me one day before he left, 'You always give the admiral plain home-truths; he hears nothing else from you.'"

"Just after I closed my last letter the mail arrived, and letters received led the chief to give up going to Kiel for the present, and to determine to remain in the gulf You know by my former letters how necessary I thought it to remain here, so as not to give the Russians a chance of raising the blockade. The poor chief is sadly nervous about remaining here, in spite of all that Admiral Seymour, Gordon, and myself say to keep up his spirits ; but the fact is, he is ill both in mind and body, and quite unfit for the hard work a man's mind must stand who has such a charge. What adds to his illness is the attacks on him in the papers, which he cannot stand or treat with contempt as he ought. He did not mind the *Herald* much, as every one knows that it only published malicious attacks, or the letters of some discontented parties in the fleet, which contain scarcely a word of truth and many falsehoods But the *Times* having lately commenced attacking him for not having taken Helsingfors or Cronstadt with the fleet, he cannot treat it as he did the *Herald's* attacks, and is feeling it much, though he ought to know that every man in our service, both here and at home, not influenced by spite or prejudice, must know that, so far from blaming him, he would have been unfit for his command had he for a moment thought of placing his ships against either of those fortresses. What is more unfair still is expecting us to do with ships alone what seventy thousand troops are sent to do with a fleet larger than ours at Sevastopol. Yet no man who understands anything on the subject can take the plans of Sevastopol and Cronstadt, and carefully examine the depths of water, etc., and not allow that it would have been much easier to attack Sevastopol with a fleet than Cronstadt. At the former there is a clear harbour and plenty of water alongside all the batteries and the enemy's ships, and it would only be a question of ships against batteries ; but at Cronstadt ships cannot get alongside any but the two outer forts, and then the ships would be raked by two hundred guns from other forts and the broadsides of two three-decked ships, and if any ships attempted to get at these other forts and the ships, they would have to pass up a narrow channel where only one ship could go abreast under all that fire, and then that one ship only could get her broadside to bear, and would be surrounded by hundreds of guns, while all ships astern of her in the passage would be raked by *a heavy fire without being able to return it.* Now, is it not too bad that the chief of a fleet should be attacked for not committing an *act of madness?* Then, again, at Helsingfors, the probability of a successful attack being made on it by ships may be judged of by the following particulars No ship can approach it except through a nest of rocks, the widest passage being two cables' lengths; they would have to advance under the raking fire of a hundred and sixty guns, and when they passed that, and got alongside the fortress, they would find space to place only eight ships against all the batteries Now, at a low estimate, these ships with three hundred and fifty guns would be opposed to about two hundred and fifty heavy guns in batteries, and the broadsides of at least two or three line-of-battle ships raking them. It would take several more of our ships to keep the enemy's ships in check, as well as the other batteries on Helsingfors, which would otherwise rake our eight ships also, so that at least fifteen of our ships must be taken in, and would be in no condition for any other service for some time, even granting them perfect success. They must then pass inside to get at the enemy's ships (which would of course move up the harbour inside), and they would be opposed to fresh tiers of batteries as strong as those outside Now, can any man say such a thing should be attempted, when we have to keep in reserve in good order enough ships to meet the eighteen sail of the line from Cronstadt if they came out? But now as to the chance of eight ships with three hundred and fifty guns in broadside against a number of batteries with two hundred and fifty guns If they were large casemated batteries like Bomarsund, and the ships once got fairly alongside, the latter might succeed; but they are nearly all single-tier batteries with earth parapets, which are the very best for contending against ships. Some of them are near the water, and would be only five hundred yards from the ships; others in the rear, and higher; and others again nearly a thousand yards off, and still higher. I have not the slightest doubt that eight ships would be either beaten off or destroyed, and probably most of them set on fire by red-hot shot and shell To give ships a chance of success, they must be able to bring

four or five guns against one in a fort.* We know that
two guns have beaten off two large ships with great loss.
Had Nelson been here with thirty English ships (we have
had, English and French, twenty-seven), he would have
blockaded the gulf for years, without thinking of attacking
such fortresses to get at ships inside. Brest, Toulon, and
Cadiz were probably much weaker than these places.
Mind, I do not say that these fortresses are safe against
all attack, but they are quite so against direct attacks of
heavy ships, or with any means we possess this season.
Cronstadt is, I think, most difficult to attack in any way :
there is only one way that we could even do much damage,
and that plan I proposed directly I reconnoitred it, but
we had not the means here. Sweaborg can also, I believe,
be attacked, and at least greatly injured, and most probably destroyed by a naval force alone, when properly
prepared and provided. With a large land force also it
must fall.

"Disappointed as I am at not coming home soon, great
is the satisfaction I feel at the fleet remaining to the last,
so as to ensure that the enemy's ships do not come out
and drive off our blockading squadron of smaller ships.
For the last four days we have had the most lovely
weather you can imagine, nearly calm, bright sunshine,
and more like summer, except that in the shade it is
chilly.

"Yesterday I had a long walk through the island for
many miles with Admiral Seymour, Gordon, and Pelham.
The woods are very pretty in some places, particularly
where the fir-trees have been cleared, and some open
grass-land is surrounded by weeping-birch and other trees ;
but they are now putting on their winter dress.

"I suppose there will be an outcry at home about doing
nothing here, but we might as well try to reach the moon,
and I think when people consider that even Anapa, a small
place with only fifty-eight guns on the sea defences, was
not attacked by the Black Sea fleet till an army was ready
to go with it, they ought not to be surprised at our doing

---

* " Un canon à terre vaut un vaisseau à la mer " (French proverb),
" Une batterie de quatre pièces de gros calibre . . . doit avoir raison
d'un vaisseau de 120 canons " (" L'Aide-mémoire d'artillerie français "),
" Four guns . . . are equal to a line-of-battle ship " (" Treatise on
Naval Gunnery," W. Jeffers, U.S.N.) —Ed.

nothing. Why, one single fort at either of the places here is stronger than all Anapa, and I wonder now that our fleet did not take the latter long since, as it could not have stood even a bombardment from steamers. It shows how unjust it is for people to blame one fleet for not taking places stronger than Sevastopol, and yet never to remark on trifling places not having been attacked by the Black Sea fleet. I have no doubt they were right out there, knowing all the circumstances."

Here end the journals for 1854. The *Duke* arrived in England before Christmas, and I presume it was in her that Captain Sulivan returned.

Before closing the account of the work done in 1854, it will be interesting to consider the various plans then proposed for attacking Sweaborg, and to show clearly the part Captain Sulivan had in planning the measures which were carried out the following year.

It will be remembered the Admiralty had given orders that Sweaborg was to be examined as early as possible. In "Napier," p 154, May 25th, we read : "The *Dauntless* was sent to look at Sweaborg, and saw thirteen men-of-war there." But this was from a distance of ten miles, and cannot be called a reconnaissance.

On June 5th the admiral wrote home he had "reconnoitred Sweaborg" This, again, was no proper view, the steamer having gone in by the eastern passage to Miolo roads, whence only the tops of the buildings could be seen over some islands The only guns seen were six on an island. The admiral wrote, "It is impossible to touch them." On June 12th ("Napier," p 175) the squadron was again off Sweaborg, but it left again without any one in the fleet having seen the fortress *nearer than twelve miles.* On page 176 the report of the master of the fleet is given, but it shows that the channel to Sweaborg was not looked at. It was reported that the Miolo channel was useless for

the fleet without buoys, yet the marks were so good the
Lightning afterwards went up it full speed. The Grohara
Beacon, reported to be "wrongly placed," was actually
removed purposely by the Russians to mislead us over the
outer rocks. Captain Sulivan, afterwards going in closer,
found the old foundations of the beacon. On page 180 it
is distinctly pointed out the master went no farther than
Miolo roads, yet no other person was sent. Therefore, so
far, no report on Sweaborg could have been sent to the
Admiralty.

Old plans had been provided by the Admiralty; and
though there were competent engineer officers sent out to
assist the admiral, no attempt was made to ascertain the
correctness of the old plans.

On June 20th the admiral writes home, mentioning
Admiral Chads' report and plan for taking Sweaborg by
means of a large military force of six thousand troops,
besides four thousand seamen and marines, occupying the
islands, and throwing shells into it ("Napier," p. 186).
This shows that no one had thought of bombarding it
from the scattered islets in front, until Captain Sulivan
went in with the flag-of-truce in July. Admiral Chads'
scheme was based on the old plans, as he had not seen
Sweaborg. This would have been the proper mode of
attack with a land force.

Without then knowing of Admiral Chads' idea, Captain
Sulivan had drawn up a similar plan, but one requiring
thirty thousand troops. A force of ten thousand men
must have been driven off, killed, or taken, as an army
of perhaps fifty thousand Russians would have been
thrown in our rear at the north channel by another island
or peninsula. There were fifty thousand Russian troops
in the neighbourhood, and twenty thousand more could
have come from Viborg We should have required a force

in Sandham, strong enough to hold its rear against this
army, whilst another force carried on the siege of
Sweaborg by Bakholmen. In this way the place could
have been taken.

The shelling Admiral Chads proposed was to be with
heavy guns. Mortars had not been thought of before
Sulivan's proposal. Had he been sent to reconnoitre early
in June, mortars, if there had been any in store, could have

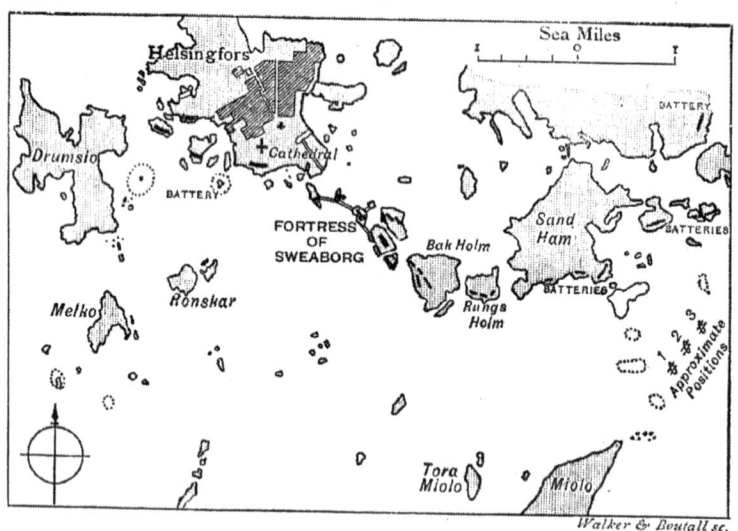

been sent out in July, and the bombardment have taken
place before the close of the first year. There was no
occasion for the mortar-vessels. It is possible, if this had
been successfully executed the first year, it might have had
some effect in hastening the settlement of peace.

In "Napier," p. 194, is given the long report on
Sweaborg procured from a Swedish source. This report
Captain Sulivan never saw at the time; but as it talked of
shelling from the rocky islands, it ought to have drawn
attention to bombarding it from them. All the barbette
guns mentioned had been covered by earthen parapets

with embrasures. All this information was obtained from
the report, yet Napier never sent in any one to look at the
fortress.

Before leaving England, Captain Sulivan had studied
the chart of Sweaborg, noticed the rocky islets, calculated
the ranges from the forts, and marked them down. But
not having been consulted by the admiral at first, he could
not suggest anything, neither did he like to offer an opinion
without seeing the place. He had, however, talked the
matter over with Admiral Seymour, and suggested shelling
at long range. This made Seymour, when the Odessa
news arrived, say, "This proves your idea is a good one."
Sulivan never thought of mortars until he had, by accident, seen the place and noticed the fine mass of buildings
within range of the islets.

Captain Sulivan returned from Sweaborg, where he had
been with the flag-of-truce, on July 15th. He reported
that the place *was made for shelling*, and islands and
rocks were provided by nature *at the right range for
mortars*. This was the first time mortars were ever
thought of; or why had they not been mentioned when
Admiral Chads' plan was sent home? A month had
elapsed ; no one had seen the place until Captain Sulivan
went ; and on the 20th, five days after his return, the
admiral ("Napier," p. 305) writes home suggesting mortars.
This proves beyond a doubt that Captain Sulivan was the
originator of the idea which next year was put into execution.

Thirteen-inch mortars, protected and assisted by the
heavy guns of the paddle and smaller steamers, would have
been quite sufficient. The real work was to be done with
mortars, the ships merely protecting them and drawing off
the enemy's fire from them. Captain Sulivan suggested
placing two Lancaster guns on Langhara Island to fire at
the three-decker between Bakholmen and Sweaborg.

On page 410 Napier admits it was "Captain Sulivan who went in twice with a flag-of-truce, and reported to the Government how it might be taken when means were provided the next year" The French generals did not go close in, and only had a hurried view going in and out.

On page 411 General Jones, after his inspection in *Lightning*, on 'August 27th suggests a bombardment from the land with a large land force, and proposes to do *from the land* exactly what was done next year *in two days* from the mortar-boats. At Bakholmen there was nothing to prevent the enemy throwing on shore from ten to fifteen thousand men inside the island, so that General Jones' five thousand men were insufficient

The plan was for a bombardment, not for an occupation ; therefore why land a force to erect batteries when the mortars could be so easily placed on the rocky islands ? All overlooked this but Sulivan

General Niel's scheme is given on page 417. He recognises the danger of Bakholmen, but proposes to carry it, a work sure to entail heavy loss. He suggests the fleets should anchor under Sweaborg. Sulivan's note says :—

"His final remarks are very good, but the ships must have advanced under the raking fire of a hundred and six guns, and the three-decker's broadside of sixty more, and must then have gone alongside the chief front of the work, *which General Niel never saw* They would have been raked by other batteries at ranges of about twelve to fifteen hundred yards, and with the greatest care not more than five or six ships would have space to get alongside the fortress."

As to the belief "the *stone* splinters would soon have rendered defence impossible," Sulivan says :—

"Out of a hundred and six Russian guns commanding the approach, only three were in casemates, the others behind earthen parapets, which everywhere capped the stonework. On the chief front it would have been just the same, so that General Niel's *stone* splinters would have proved as incorrect as the *wooden* splinters in the ships would have proved a certainty. His opinion as to Bakholmen is very similar to that which I gave the admiral at the time. I was satisfied that if ships were placed very carefully and no space lost, they would only be able to oppose two guns to each one in the batteries abreast of them, while they would be raked by numerous batteries, to which they could only reply by a few bow-guns at ranges that made ships' guns useless, and all this after having passed through a raking fire."

" All these plans proposed to risk hazardous attacks for the purpose of establishing batteries to bombard the place, when so many islets offered equal facilities and no danger."

CHAPTER XII.

1855.

ON Captain Sulivan's return to England in 1854, the First Lord (Sir James Graham) and Admiral Sir M. Berkeley asked his opinion as to what could be done in the Baltic the next season. After verbally explaining his views of attacking Cronstadt and Sweaborg, he was requested by the First Lord to draw up a report on the subject, dividing it into three heads: (1) What would be possible with a naval force alone? (2) What if a combined naval and military force were to be employed? (3) And what force of ships would be required for the Baltic, if it were decided to confine the work there to a simple blockade? Sir M. Berkeley asked him to bring his portions of the report as it was written; and when the last sheets were finished and Sulivan was to have gone with the admiral to read it to the First Lord, he found that Sir James Graham had resigned that morning.

As soon as Sir C Wood commenced his duties as First Lord, he went into the subject, and had the report printed in the Secret Department. A proof was given to Sulivan to correct, but he could not obtain a copy for himself, as he was told that only six were to be printed, one to be given to each of the following: the Queen, the First Lord, the Minister of War, the English admiral, the Emperor, and the French admiral.

The plan afterwards carried out for bombarding Sweaborg formed one portion of the report, but it was recommended that this should be quite secondary to an attack on Cronstadt, which should first be attempted. This could be done only with the floating batteries then building, while Sweaborg could be attacked without them.

His plan for attacking Cronstadt was the following : He saw at once that the Russians, whilst making Cronstadt almost impregnable by way of the main channel, had totally neglected to protect it from attack on the north side, trusting only to the shoalness of the water and the barrier they had made across the only channel that existed. Sulivan saw the only chance lay in this direction, and proposed that a bombardment should be attempted from mortar-vessels and floating batteries of light draught, protected from the attack of the large Russian flotilla of gun-vessels by a force of light-draught gun-boats, etc. He saw the possibility of destroying the dockyard, the fleet, and possibly the fortifications themselves. The only things wanting for the carrying out of the plan were floating batteries and gun-boats.*

When Captain Sulivan left England in 1855, he understood that his proposals had been approved of by both the British and French Governments, and that the necessary

---

* Preparations were being made in the winter of 1855 for an attack, which would have been carried out the following season, had not peace intervened. The Admiralty had sanctioned Sulivan's scheme of attack. As it would have been necessary to survey the channel nearly up to the walls of Cronstadt, with the object of moving the attacking vessels nearer, after the first bombardment, Sulivan had proposed a plan, and, I believe, prepared the material for carrying this out in a novel way. He and his brother were to survey the channel in a small double canoe. (His brother, now Admiral George L. Sulivan, a noted swimmer, had distinguished himself by receiving three medals and parchments from the Royal Humane Society. When the *Jasper* was wrecked in the Sea of Azoff, he had dived down to place charges under her to blow her up, remaining sometimes two minutes under water. It was thought he might in a similar way undermine the barrier) As it was necessary

means would be provided. Whilst waiting for these off Cronstadt, he was chiefly employed in sounding its approaches. As a barrier was known to exist on the north side, and a successful attack could only be made by getting gun-boats, mortar-boats, and floating batteries through it, it became necessary to find out the depth of water at and inside it, especially as the depths on the banks were invariably found to be less than those shown in the Russian charts.

As later it became doubtful whether the French Government would send any of their floating batteries, and therefore whether the whole of the ten calculated on might be available, Sulivan gave it as his opinion that if only six could be sent the attack might be tried with fair prospects of success, as the depth of water at the barrier had been found sufficient ; but as it was finally decided to *send the floating batteries to the Black Sea*, the idea of attacking Cronstadt had to be abandoned, and the gun-boats and mortar-vessels that were coming out could then be used only against Sweaborg *

Admiral Dundas, though very anxious to do all that was possible, felt much doubt about succeeding in this latter plan, and much influence was used in an important quarter in the fleet to convince him that it could not succeed, and that the small mortar-vessels could not safely lay at

to go so close that even the canoe would have attracted observation, they were later to trust to their swimming powers, clad in oilskin dresses, lined with wool to resist the cold, with pockets for holding small sounding-lines and lead   The Russians must at this time have noticed the defencelessness of this side of Cronstadt, for they began erecting forts to protect the north side, which, however, would not have been ready in time. (See p. 367.)

* There were—

	Planned for	Forthcoming.
Floating batteries . .	8 .	. 2
Mortar-boats . .	. 30 .	. 15
Gun-boats . .	. 30 .	. 15
Steam-frigates .	4 .	. 1

anchor under the fire of such a strong place. Captain Sulivan had great difficulty in successfully opposing this view. He compared the difficulty of hitting such small vessels at such a range to that of hitting a sparrow at a distance with a pistol-bullet. Whilst waiting at Nargen for the arrival of the mortar-vessels, it seemed probable that the attempt would be given up, and some minor points on the coast attacked instead. On one visit to the flag-ship, Sulivan was told by the admiral that he had decided not to attempt it; and it was only after using every argument to combat the adverse view, and pressing his opinion also on the French admiral, who generally supported him, that Sulivan got Admiral Dundas to alter his decision and make up his mind to carry out the plan; but he made this condition—that Sulivan should agree to place the mortar-vessels three thousand three hundred yards from the fortress, instead of three thousand, as proposed by him. It was only after the mortar-vessels had arrived, and he had consulted Captain Wemyss, of the Marine Artillery, who thought that even at that distance the mortars would be able to cover all the fortress, that Sulivan yielded the point, pointing out, however, that it would make a serious difference in their range for reaching the farther portions of the fortress, which extended nine hundred yards in the rear of the batteries.

When about to go to Sweaborg, Admiral Dundas said to an officer, who repeated the remark to Captain Sulivan, "I am going to court defeat by attempting what I have not the means of succeeding in"—or words to this effect.

It will thus be seen that this, the only important event of the year in the Baltic, and the only important purely naval success of the war (i.e. one in which the military were not also concerned), was entirely owing to the plan and to the determined stand made by Captain Sulivan.

With this introduction, I go on with the ordinary account and journals.

Sulivan had been given a larger and more powerful vessel than the *Lightning*—namely, the paddle-steamer *Merlin* (six guns instead of three ; three hundred and twelve horse-power instead of only a hundred).

His officers were as follows: Richard B. Creyke, commander (assistant surveyor), who, besides having been at the bombardment of Acre, had done good survey-ing service and boat action against pirates on the west coast of Africa ; lieutenants—William Hewett, Charles J. Bullock ; staff-commander—Richard C. Dyer ; surgeon—J F. Johnson ; paymaster—R. W. Warrick.

"'Merlin,' *April* 12th, 1855.

"Running down the Kattegat, Thursday, April 12th, 4 p m. Fine weather. How I shall ever write, except at anchor, I do not know ; for the vessel shakes so much, even in dead smooth water, from the engines alone, that plates, glasses, etc., dance on the table, and the chair and table are now dancing to the tune of the paddle-wheel. We left Sheerness at 1 p.m. on Monday, April 9th."

They had heavy weather from the south-west, and the powerful engines in the weak vessel, combined with the heavy head-sea, caused so much vibration and motion that almost all on board were ill.

" The weather moderated in the evening of the 11th, and we had made the worst of our passage, having entered the mouth of the Baltic, after a run of four hundred and thirty miles, in about two days and seven hours. The day it blew so hard against us part of the time, we made a hundred and seventy miles, so that we ought to be very well satisfied with *Merlin's* performance.

"We reached Wingo Sound at twelve to-day, under three days from Sheerness. I found no colliers in the sound, but saw some vessels inside a channel blocked up by ice. As, if they were colliers, we should lose time by going

round to look for another passage, I determined to push on
to Elsinore for coal, having only twenty-four hours' supply
left. Her consumption of coal is tremendous, and yet we
cannot keep up steam enough for the engines at full
power : the boilers hardly seem large enough. We have
been steaming to-day about nine knots against a moderate
breeze."

"ELSINORE, *Friday*, 13*th*.

"Arrived this morning, having got into a bight at anchor
(in the thick, dark weather at midnight) about ten miles
from this. And fortunate it was for our paddles we did so,
for this morning we saw fields of ice passing down the
channel outside, and several vessels in it On reaching
this through several fields of ice, we found nearly every
vessel had gone adrift in them last night. To-day
Yelverton, with seven vessels, got clear of ice that had shut
them up for a week in Landschrona in the heart of the
town, where the Swedes gave them a grand ball last night.
Several ships have lost anchors, and the three frigates
Impérieuse, *Arrogant*, and *Amphion* have been aground
since they came out."

"RUNNING FOR KIEL, *April* 19*th*, 1855.

"We left Nyborg on Sunday at 5 p m. with only one
pilot, leaving *Firefly* (Captain Otter) to bring others, if she
could get them. We pushed on all night, and Monday
morning the weather was so thick that we had to feel our
way from rock to rock on the Swedish coast till we got to
Wingo. There we met two steamers, and heard the fleet
was at anchor near the Scaw, having arrived the evening
before. We reached it at 5 p.m., blowing hard from the
north-west, but then clear. I proposed starting at once,
running down by the light-vessels, and the chief wished
it also ; but the pilots, some of whom came from near the
Scaw to the fleet, preferred waiting till next morning.

"We started early on Tuesday, 17th, with a rattling north-
west wind—fleet under sail. fires banked up ; and we led
them all day. After passing Anholt, the wind very scant,
we got up steam, furled sails, and at 9 p m. anchored near
Foreness. At daylight yesterday I went on with *Vulture*
and *Bulldog* to place them as guides for the two narrowest
passages, at Nyborg and the Veryeam shoal, and I then
returned a few miles, met the fleet steaming, and led again

till we cleared all the Belt shoals by 5 p m., and at 7 p.m.
anchored half-way down Langeland Island. The day was
lovely, nearly calm, and too warm for a great-coat. Otter
joined us last evening from Nyborg, having been unable
to get any pilots

"This morning we started an hour before daylight to get
pilots off ready to meet the fleet off Kiel. We are now
near there. A lovely day, but we have just passed through
much drift-ice, and the thermometer at 6 a.m. was only 36°.

"3 *p.m.*—Sent off pilots, went in for letters, went out
to the fleet, led them into Kiel, just anchored, and have to
dine with the commander-in-chief. Lovely weather. Face
and lips all sore and burnt with sun for want of beard."

"Kiel, *April* 20th, 1855.

"Yesterday I was at a court-martial all day, and dined
with Robb in *Cæsar.* The general feeling and attention
shown me are most gratifying; and Robinson, my old
shipmate in *Undaunted,* told me how pleased he was to
hear from all quarters such things said of me.

"We hear nothing either way about peace. I fear there
is little hope of it now, but I will not give up the hope
that God will yet overrule the congress, and put it into
their hearts to agree to terms"

"At Sea, *Saturday, May* 5th, 1855.

"We sailed, or rather steamed, with the fleet from Kiel
on the morning of the 3rd, and we have been under steam
nearly ever since, the wind either foul or a calm ; but there
is nothing to interest except the comparative merits of the
different ships, which are chiefly shown by the daily consumption of fuel. The old *Royal George* does wonders—
never drops—always close to *Duke* ; while the block-ships
half her size, but same power, cannot keep up, and her
consumption of coal is less than many of the others.
Among similar ships, the *James Watt,* built especially for
screw, has expended forty-five tons to keep her station
during the last twenty-four hours ; whereas the old lump of
a three-decker has only expended thirty-three tons, though
under sail a slower ship We have done much the best of
the paddles, having, with three hundred and twelve horse-
power, only used twelve tons ; *Firefly,* of two hundred and
forty horse-power, sixteen tons ; and *Locust,* of a hundred
horse-power, ten tons ; little *Lightning,* a hundred horse-

power, five tons. So we shall evidently have a much smaller consumption than is usual (when working at slow speed) for our power."

"FARO SOUND, *Tuesday, May 8th.*

" We are off in a hurry, as the wind is coming in strong, and the large ships are at anchor outside. We came here on Sunday, and I am glad to say all the coaling was postponed till Monday morning, a new thing in the Baltic fleet. The ice is gone from the gulf, and all is open. We are all well and going on comfortably."

"OFF SWEABORG, *Thursday, May 10th.*

" We sailed from Faro Sound, Tuesday, 8th ; had a strong gale all day, which nearly shook *Merlin* loose, and made me very ill. Yesterday it was finer, and we entered the gulf, seeing neither ice nor snow on the land, and, strange to say, not one ship of our blockading squadron ; so that we have broken the blockade with nine sail of the line, which will raise a laugh at Watson's party. To-day, at 5 a m, the fleet anchored at Nargen, and I started to look into Faro Sound, to see if any of Watson's ships were there, and what the state of the ice was To my surprise, not a vestige of ice was to be seen, nor any ships either ; so, before returning, I ran up to my old haunt off Sweaborg, to see if the Russian ships were still there. I did not go very close in, having no vessel to back me if I got on shore. I could only see three ships, all dismantled and laid up in creeks ; so I suppose it is true the others went to Cronstadt last autumn. The day is beautiful, quite like summer."

" [*Private.*]

" ' MERLIN,' NARGEN, *May 13th,* 1855.

" With regard to our proceedings, I think all seems to indicate a decided opinion in favour of my plans. I do trust the simple thing yet wanted, and without which nothing can be done, will not any longer be neglected. I had the admiral alone in my cabin yesterday for some time, urging it all on him ; he is very kind, and seems to rely greatly on my views, etc., which is very gratifying ; but of course I am obliged to be careful not to appear to take too much on myself, being a junior. I fear we have not a sufficient force of vessels of good armament under

a certain draught of water.   More exertions ought to have
been made to have every such vessel within reach recalled
in time to send here ; but even one at home, particularly
pointed out by me as of the greatest value to us, has been
sent to the coast of Africa.   I am satisfied that all will
be done that ought to be attempted with our present
means, but I regret that more exertions were not made
to provide every possible means to ensure success after
such an enormous outlay in different classes of vessels.   We
have only three screw-vessels of any armament drawing the
water required, and unfortunately one of those has just
been cut down and her main-mast carried away by *Impérieuse* running into her.   Both are going to Sheerness to
repair.   Of course you know how secret all this must be
kept.   I believe few men have such perfect confidence in the
secrecy and *judgment* of their wives as I can show to my
darling wife on these points.   I fear sometimes that our
chief is likely to speak to too many about his plans, instead
of keeping everything quite close   There is great curiosity
of course, and my brother-captains are constantly trying to
get things out of me, as if they considered I had all to do
with it.   Sometimes a more prudent one says, ' Now of
course I do not expect you to tell me what you are going
to do, as your tongue must be, to a certain extent, tied ; but
now can you tell this much ? ' etc., etc.   Then others say
very quietly, some even seriously, ' Do think of me and
get me a share in what is to be done.'   Then another very
confidentially says, ' Do recollect that my vessel or ship
only draws so much water when light, and that she mounts
heavy guns ; do put in a word for her.'   The fact is, if I
were at all inclined to be conceited, I have enough to
make me so ; but I can assure you the effect is to make
me feel more the anxiety and the responsibility of my
duties, and, I trust, lead me to pray for more grace and
strength to enable me to go through with it all, if the
Almighty does not think fit to put an end to the war
before the time comes for active operations.   I believe
there is no idea in any quarter of there being any possible way of acting with a chance of success except by
my plan.   My chief anxiety is lest I may not have the
power to carry it all out as I wish, or lest I may not
have all the means to ensure success I asked for, and yet
get the blame of any failure.   I like all I see of our chief—
cautious and careful, but with much judgment, and, I should

think, firmness; but I wish I could instil a little more activity into his disposition—I mean activity of mind. Oh, how thankful should I be to have all my plans frustrated at the eleventh hour by peace! I know it is, apparently, impossible now; but I recollect how impossible it seemed that the scene of slaughter arranged for the next day at Bomarsund could be avoided, and yet in half an hour it was prevented by the surrender. If war is still to go on, then we must endeavour to feel that God has some wise purpose in permitting it, and that all is for the best."

Here follow minute directions for his wife to come out to him, should he be wounded, knowing she would, in that case, be less anxious with him than at a distance.

"NARGEN, *Tuesday, May 15th, 1855.*

" Since we arrived here, our missing vessels and Watson's squadron have been dropping in; but for some days we gave the Russians a chance of coming down if they wanted to try their chance, as we had at one time only nine sail of the line and *Merlin.* They have about twenty-two good ships of the line at Cronstadt and one screw 'eighty' ready, with a screw-frigate, and, they say, twenty-four steamers of all sizes, but only sixteen, I think, really war-steamers, four very heavy ones.

"On Friday the admirals and staffs went in with us to have a look at Revel—the weather beautiful. We saw three new earthen batteries, with about thirty guns, in addition to the three hundred and thirty-eight guns on the sea defences seen last year. There are also posts along the hill, evidently for an electric telegraph, which we hear they have got the wires for. In the evening I dined with the chief, and arranged for leaving at 5 a.m. on Saturday with the same party for Sweaborg, taking *Euryalus* and *Cossack* as body-guard. We had a beautiful day; ran up the passage among the rocks close to the spot where I so nearly ran the *Driver* on shore with all the admirals and generals last year. There I anchored the two frigates, and, leaving *Merlin* under way, I took the admirals, etc., in two boats to a rocky islet, just out of gunshot, that I thought would give us a very good view of everything. We remained there a long time, evidently affording amusement to thousands of both sexes at

Helsingfors, and the soldiers in the fortresses,—every hill and rise were crowded with people. We saw about seven new batteries in different parts, in addition to those of last year, mounting between them about sixty guns. They are all in the very best positions, and are entirely of earth, with apparently heavy guns. Only four line-of-battle ships are left there, three dismantled ; the fourth has her masts out, and is housed over in dock ; also one frigate and two small steamers. After getting a good look at everything, we returned, and, when half-way back to *Merlin*, saw a small steamer towing out a gun-boat towards the islet we had left, evidently intending to drive us off Having gone up to another position in *Merlin* to get a further look at the east side, we joined our ships and returned to Nargen."

"*Friday, May 18th,* 1855.

"On Wednesday the admiral left in the *Duke* for Faro Sound to land the sick, in consequence of the rapid spread of small-pox (fifteen cases in three days). So, I suppose to guard against any dash of the Russian fleet on the ten sail left at Nargen, Ramsay was ordered with *Euryalus, Merlin,* and *Magicienne* to cruise to the eastward till Saturday, going beyond Hogland. We were also to put a buoy on the Kalbaden Rock, about half-way between Helsingfors and Hogland We sailed on Wednesday afternoon, and just as we were leading the others round the Nargen shoals, going out on the east side of the bay, a hail-storm came on with a squall from the southward that beat all I ever saw. The stones were as large as marbles It did not last long, and was fine afterwards ; but soon after we got outside the first of the May fogs came on, and we could only keep near each other all night by the aid of muskets, bells, etc. We lay till the afternoon by our kedges, when it cleared a little, till we could see the Kokskar lighthouse, and then ran across for the Kalbaden. It soon became very thick again, so that we lost sight of ships and everything, but hit the rock exactly, just stopping as we shoaled to five fathoms. Just after it cleared on the north side we saw a lighthouse, which ensured our being on the right rock We put down a large Trinity buoy left in one of the ships from last year, and, rejoining our friends, stood up the gulf ; but the fog was so thick that we only showed them our positions ahead by muskets, and occasionally by mast-head light showing over the fog. At midnight it became so dense that Ramsay made the signal to anchor, and we remained quietly anchored with the kedge till six this morning, when a breeze sprang up too strong for the light anchors, but it blew off the fog a little. Ramsay thought it too thick to attempt going higher up, as we were ordered to be back to-morrow, and I agreed with him; but having steamed back about twenty miles, the fog gradually lifted, and we had a beautiful clear day; so I hailed Ramsay, and said I thought we might rely on having it clear now, and there would be time to go round Hogland after all and return in time. I was anxious to find out if the people were left on the island. So we turned round again, and steamed full speed up the gulf."

They saw a number of women and children at the southern village, and a boat—"manned, as Paddy would say, by women "—came off to *Merlin*.

"We then ran up to the northern village, and stood into the cove, *Euryalus* coming close alongside us. Again there were plenty of women, boys, and children looking at us (the old women told us that every man had been taken away from the island); and on the opposite side of the cove to the village, where there is a pretty country house in the trees close to the point, and within about three hundred yards of *Merlin*, a young lady, nicely dressed in a pink skirt and black jacket, with a shawl over her head, came out close to the shore, and watched us till we were going out, when she tripped away towards the house. Fancy the ladies of any of the villages on the eastward of England or Scotland coming down to watch three Russian frigates standing into the cove! I wish we had had time to land there, where also I am anxious to establish friendly intercourse with the poor people, because I think it may be very desirable to have our hospitals in that island, if we have any wounded at Cronstadt. It would be a very healthy island—high hills—different from every other land here, and in the middle of the gulf, free from all the marshes of Finland.

"We are now (10 p.m.) steaming back to Nargen, where we shall be to-morrow morning. The Grand Duke Constantine might have had a chance of saying he had driven off the English ships, if he had been looking out below Cronstadt with his steam force, which would have obliged us to retire. I do not think he will have a chance again, as when we next go up it will be with a much larger force."

"Yesterday I landed for the first time here to pay a visit to some of my friends of last year. I found the mother of the little child I saw dead, and to whom I gave the Bible, looking very much better, and her three little girls grown much and seeming in better health She seemed very glad to see me. The children, though the youngest could not be more than six, could all read. Only a few of the families read and speak Swedish ; the others are Esthonian, which is nearer German than Swedish or Russian. If you get 'Letters from the Baltic, by a Lady,'* from the library, it will give you an entertaining account of Esthonia, Revel, etc Yesterday was lovely—the woods so quiet and still. On the village green a cricket match was going on between the officers of the *Cressy* and the *Royal George*, nearly all in red, pink, or blue flannel shirts, which have generally superseded white ones in the fleet At other parts there were games of quoits going on. All looked so cheerful and pretty, with the fine buildings and towers of Revel in front of us, that I could not help thinking, 'Can this be war-time?' The weather and the whole scene were much too lovely to be broken in on by the horrors of war. What a mercy it will be if yet at the eleventh hour we have peace !

"I found that scarcely one of the Swedish families, or rather those speaking Swedish, had Bibles ; and when they heard that I could give them some, I had several applications. The old woman (mother of my friend) who recollects the fleets here in 1802 and 1809 is as well as last year.

"*Monday*, 21*st*.—The *Duke of Wellington* and the *Orion* came in last evening

"I have had a long confab with the chief this morning about our future movements. We shall probably be off in a day or two with the fleet to look at Cronstadt. If they have their twenty-two sail ready for sea, with their steamers to tow many of them, they ought to come out and try their chance with us We have twelve screw-ships and one frigate, and not nearly so strong a paddle force as

* By the late Lady Eastlake, then Miss Rigby.

they have ; but I do not expect to find many of their
ships fitted out, and they will, I think, merely moor them
as block-ships. The *Duke* landed no less than thirty-eight
men with small-pox at Faro Sound, but no dangerous
cases. *Arrogant* still has cases occurring ; so with *Impérieuse* gone home, we lose our two fine frigates."

"' Merlin,' Monday, May 28th, 1855

"We left Nargen on Saturday with the fleet, and
yesterday at 8 a.m., off Sommars Island, we were sent
with *Magicienne* under my orders to the north-west
entrance of Biorko Sound, to see if there were any gun-
boats or defences in the place. On entering Viborg Bay,
we saw a schooner going into the sound, and, on rounding
the north point of Biskops Island, came suddenly on
several small vessels working up the channel. You may
fancy their consternation. Some anchored, and their crews
pulled on shore ; the largest pushed back before a fresh
breeze towards the narrow part of the sound at Koivasto,
where the troops are stationed ; but only a few light ones
escaped us. We secured seven. Three small ones, empty
or with a little wood in, and evidently belonging to poor
people, I would not touch ; but the four largest proved to
be all loaded with flour, provisions, etc.; and as they have
about four hundred and fifty tons of cargo among them,
it becomes one of the best takes made yet ; and, what is
more pleasant, is, that nearly all, if not quite all, is Russian
Government property, probably provisions for the troops
at the out-stations. Three or four little light coasters got
into the cove, where in all there were six or seven little
craft ; but we heard from the men in one vessel we took
that there are fifteen hundred troops there with a battery
of six field-guns, and I saw breast-works thrown up in
more places than last year. To get the vessels out we
must expose the men in boats close to thick woods, where
we could not protect them from musket fire. I would not
risk a single man's life for the sake of a few empty small
craft, such as those I would not take before.

"Having secured the four vessels, I towed them out to
Magicienne, and then left them with her, while I returned
to the admiral to know what should be done with them. . . .
I went back to the chief at midnight, breakfasted with him
this morning, and then started to bring *Magicienne* and
prizes round to the south end of Biörkö Sound, to be near

the fleet in case of being wanted. I then returned to the
fleet, to go with the chief to-morrow to reconnoitre Cronstadt. Erskine went up in *Orion* yesterday, and anchored
near the lighthouse. He reports six sail of the line fitted
out, and about eight steamers lying near the outer forts.
It does not say much for them that their eight steamers
like *Orion*—four very heavy ones—lay there all night
without attacking her. All firing from different points
with heavy guns ought to tease a line-of-battle ship very
much.

"On reaching *Magicienne* to-day, I found she had taken
and burnt two fine galliots They proved full of fine
squared blocks of granite, of great size, for Cronstadt.

[*Merlin* had caught another vessel.] "She turns out
a Russian Finnish vessel, but unfortunately in ballast,
belonging to an old lady, but the master is in great
distress at having to go to England. She is a snug
little craft, and looks just fit for what we wanted—one
that is to take the cargo of our smallest craft that is not
seaworthy. He says his wife will die if she hears he is
sent to England. I have tried to comfort him, and have
just had him down to tea with me. There are four
Russians on board, taken in a wood vessel by Otter last
night, and I am going to land them They really seem to
appreciate kindness, and it is some comfort to be able to
brighten their trouble. The vessel went to pieces in tow
of *Firefly*, or else she would have been returned to them
after taking the wood out.

"If I get £150 prize-money I shall be lucky, but they
may give us something for the two government vessels full
of granite This was in blocks six feet cube, numbered
ready for placing, evidently for forts at Cronstadt, and we
ought to be paid as for government property destroyed."

On the way to Viborg Bay *Merlin* captured three vessels
laden with wood for the Russian troops. One vessel, containing birch, was kept, the others, with fir, burning too
quickly for the stoves, were burnt. Another prize was
taken laden with rye-flour.

"OFF CRONSTADT, *Friday, June 1st,* 1855
"Not having had more than two hours' sleep Monday
night, and having been up all this night till 5 a m., I went

to bed and slept till nine, when our signal was made to join the admiral.

"On Thursday morning we all got under way for Cronstadt, *Merlin*, *Amphion*, and *Euryalus* looking out ahead of the fleet. On getting near, I saw some people at the lighthouse, and a boat ; so we pushed on, and by sending the whale-boat after her when we got in two and a half fathoms water we caught her, but she proved to be the private boat of a poor man with his son, and a boy and girl about fourteen, going from Cronstadt across to the north shore, with a bag of sugar and a bag of salt, which they had purchased with milk and butter brought from home, and they had been two days wind-bound at the lighthouse. They seemed terribly frightened ; but after I gave them some biscuits and tobacco and a Finnish Bible, they became quite reassured, and I sent them away quite happy The fleet anchored in line across the gulf about three miles below the lighthouse ; and in the afternoon, when the sun, being to the westward, threw a nice light on everything at Cronstadt, the admiral and staff with Admiral Seymour came with us. Attended by *Euryalus*, *Amphion*, *Dragon*, and *Magicienne*, we went in to the lighthouse, and anchored close to it in *Merlin*. We then landed and got to our old station on the balcony round the top. We found it in beautiful order, very clean, and all the rooms in nicer order than last year.

"We saw that only five sail of the line are fitted out and have sails bent ; of these three only are moored in the passage as last year. These, with a screw-frigate and nine steamers of good size (four of which are heavy ones), were outside the basins ; all the rest, including the two fitted, and thirteen or fourteen with lower masts only, are moored along the basin walls inside. On Cronstadt Island, two miles from the town, a series of large earthen batteries have been built, extending right across the island, and adding greatly to the strength of the place, as no ships can get near them, and no army could get within range of Cronstadt till these works were taken. It was a beautiful evening, and the sun lit up the gilded steeples of Cronstadt, St. Petersburg (very distant, just seen), and the palace at Peterhoff most beautifully. After finishing our view from the lighthouse, we sent back all ships but *Amphion*, and then ran up towards the forts till we were three thousand one hundred yards off, when

we rounded to and had another good look. The steamer
that watched us so close in *Lightning* was again just
outside the forts as a guard-boat; there were two others
inside with their steam up, but they did not attempt to
drive us off. We had heard so much of additional
machines put farther out, that we were speculating on
the chance of finding one; but as they have to blow you

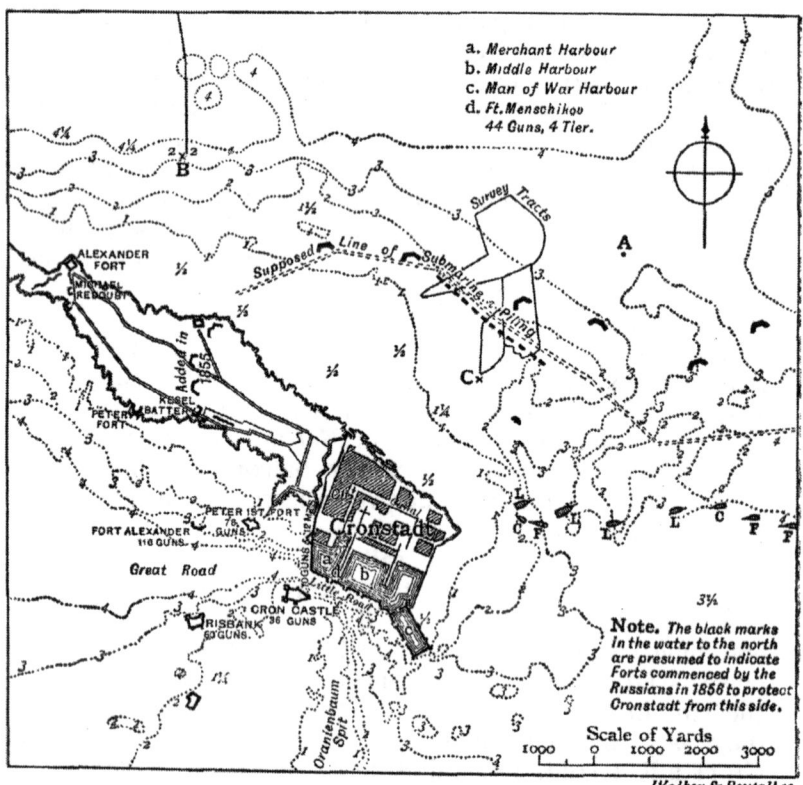

a. *Merchant Harbour*
b. *Middle Harbour*
c. *Man of War Harbour*
d. *Ft. Menschikoo*
   44 Guns, 4 Tier.

Note. *The black marks
in the water to the north
are presumed to indicate
Forts commenced by the
Russians in 1856 to protect
Cronstadt from this side.*

Scale of Yards

Walker & Boutall sc.

up by connecting the galvanic wires on shore as you
pass over the machine, by going full speed there would
be little chance of their catching you at the moment, even
if you did pass one near enough. So we got back without
being blown up. But, joking apart, I am confident there
are none outside the forts; they would only be in the narrow
channel inside.

"This morning we again started with the admirals,
Dragon in attendance, and we went around the north

side of the island till we got well round the north-east side, where we found four sail of the line, six frigates, and two corvettes moored as block-ships inside the barrier, which extends from the island to the mainland. My prisoner says it is so shallow there that no coaster has passed that way for five years, and they have been throwing more stones down since last summer. We stood in towards the block-ships, leaving *Dragon* outside, till we shoaled to less than three fathoms, then anchored above four thousand yards from the nearest block-ships. There were twenty-four gun-boats just inside the point of the town, and they ought to have come out near the barrier and driven us off, which they could easily have done, but though we lay there an hour, they took no notice of us, and we had a capital look at everything **(A)** The northern end of the new lines across the island is very strong—two immense earth-works, the outer one finished, the inner one worked at by thousands of men, like ants on an ant-hill. On our way out we went closer in to have a good look at these lines, and we stopped as close as I dared go to the edge of the bank, just three thousand yards from the forts, not having less than three and a half fathoms ; but just as we were going on again we suddenly shoaled to two fathoms (six inches more than we drew), and for some minutes we could not get any more water either ahead or astern **(B)**, and I certainly expected every moment to get fast; but turning her gently round with the jib, we at length began to deepen, and went right off shore till we were quite safe again. I wonder that they did not fire at us, as they had nearly twenty guns bearing our way ; and though it would be difficult to strike a vessel at that distance, yet they might have dropped shot round us. I cannot understand how it is that we have never found them in the Baltic fire a very long-range shot : the longest I saw was the one over *Lightning* at Bomarsund, at about two thousand seven hundred yards ; yet at Sevastopol they threw shot over our steamers up to four thousand yards, when the steamers' longest guns, ranging three thousand six hundred yards, could not reach the shore.

"We got back to the fleet at five, just as the French squadron of three liners and one frigate, all screws, joined us, with the usual saluting, hoisting French colours, etc., and after that I dined with the admiral."

19

"I must write a little to-day, though Sunday   I have to be all to-morrow preparing a chart for the admiral to send home with the positions of the forts, dam, etc. Yesterday at noon we went in again, with *Dragon* to back us, as close as we could to the north-east corner, and anchored in eighteen feet water—quite close enough ; for we afterwards found six feet outside us in one place, and three feet a cable from us inside.   It was rather unfavourable for us, as a fresh wind made a bubble of a sea for the boats ; but no steamers or gun-boats inside were moving, and we shoved off, the admiral going with me in the gig, Admiral Seymour with Creyke in the whale-boat, and we pulled direct for the town.   We carried in very regular soundings, shoaling gradually from eighteen up to nine feet near the bank of stones, on which once stood a fort.   We ought to have passed the dam outside this, but never shoaled to less than eleven feet ; and as we pulled a little farther in, to two thousand eight hundred yards from the town, a good bombarding distance, and had no less than eleven feet there, I thought it was all right, and that we had no dam to contend with, and I congratulated the admiral on the certainty of being able to get in any distance he liked with small craft.   We then pulled out, and, when outside the patch of stones came on the dam nearly up to the surface.   It being made in detached blocks, we had passed between two of them without seeing them or shoaling the water.   Each block is about twenty feet long by eight feet wide, and is made by piles forming a kind of box, braced together with pieces of wood and filled with stones, the intervals between each box being about fifteen feet ; and on going in we had passed through one of these intervals.

"We then pulled in and out and along the dam for above a mile, going within two thousand five hundred yards of the town (C), and about the same from the nearest block-ship, a two-decker ; but they did not molest us for some time   A small steamer with two boats in tow lay between us and the block-ship, and nearer than *Merlin* was. We saw her getting under way, and we turned out all ready to pull for it , but to our surprise, instead of coming out, she turned the other way and ran in ; but soon after *Merlin* hoisted the signal arranged for ' boats coming out,'

and we saw two large boats coming out fast under sail ;
so we gave it up and pulled out, having done much more
than we expected.

"Having put the chiefs on board their ships, I returned
to get some more angles from the lighthouse to fix our
work well. Mundy of *Nile*, Nugent, the engineer officer,
and the master of the fleet remained with us, and had a
hurried dinner with me going in   After finishing at the
lighthouse, we ran in to look at the north end of the new
works, our little Russian steamer friend of last year
watching us at a respectful distance. The admiral sent
Dragon in to join us. We got back to the fleet about
nine, and I felt thoroughly tired with standing on the
paddle-box so many days running, and quite glad to think
this was to be a day of rest, which, I am happy to
say, our Sundays now are. Both admirals and Pelham,
captain of fleet, wish to make them so : no coaling or
other work goes on. My whole afternoon has been broken
in upon by callers. I had put off calling on the French
admiral and captains till to-morrow, so as not to have
to go to-day ; but three of the French captains came here,
two new ones, introduced by Laurenston of *Austerlitz*, and
they paid me many compliments on the way my name
is known in the French navy. Then Key came, with whom
I was enjoying a quiet talk, when we had an addition of
Erskine, Caldwell, and captain of fleet ; and in this way
the whole afternoon has been spun out, so that I have not had
the boys in as usual. However, they are all gone now, and
I shall have my tea in time for the evening service at seven.

"The weather set in so hot to-day—the water like glass,
not a breath of wind "

"CRONSTADT, *June* 10th, 1855.

"Through the kind providence of God we have been
preserved from what might have been a great danger.
Yesterday we went to show the defences, etc., to the French
admiral and captains, and about ten English captains,
besides many junior officers. We went as close up to the
north-east side as we could, till we got in three fathoms
water, higher up than we went before, but not so near the
town. Inside the dam, where we before sounded in the
boats, were two of their new steam gun-boats. We went
to another place purposely to draw their attention from
the point we examined before. Just as we were turning

round, one of the gun-boats fired a gun at us, so far off
that the shot did not come within half a mile. As they do
not generally fire in that random way, I am now sure they
wanted to provoke us to go in towards them, where they
had laid another trap for us. We have heard much of the
'infernal machines' that were to blow us all up, and last
year much speculation and some amusement were caused
by the *Driver* fishing up a beacon-moorings for one. This
year we hear of one blowing a wood vessel to pieces
accidentally, and of their having been laying down many
off Sweaborg since we went in there the other day with
the admiral, and that for an experiment they blew a small
vessel there into pieces ; but we have hitherto rather joked
about them.

"We had left that part and were steaming about two
and a quarter miles outside the island along the shore to
show our party the new batteries. *Firefly* was following
us, and *Dragon* and the French *Dapas* keeping farther off,
when suddenly the vessel received a heavy shock, which
shook her more than any running on shore, and in a different manner. I thought some large part of the engine or
the boilers had broken, and ran to the engine-room. Seeing
them working well, I stopped her ; and as we were still
going fast, and still had five fathoms water, I knew she
could not have struck the ground. Some said that it was
an explosion, and that we had hit an infernal machine.
When stopped and going astern very slightly, Erskine
called to me from the port paddle-box that he could see
a stone I crossed over, and saw just under the paddle-
beam what appeared to be the head of a large pile three
feet under water We were just watching for it to come
under the leadsman, who had still five fathoms water, when
a second and much sharper explosion took place, just
before the starboard paddle-box, where the artist of the
Illustrated London News was sitting sketching, having
just before expressed his fears that it was a shot that had
struck us. The second threw a mass of water three feet
above our hammock-netting, and gave us a terrible shake ;
the vessel seemed jerked on one side, and heeled over a
little, the masts shaking so that some ran from under them.
A strong smell of sulphur left no doubt that it was a
veritable infernal machine. We had warned Otter off, and
he had stopped and hauled inside us a cable-length, when
a third exploded under their bow, but with much slighter

effect than ours. The thing we saw under the port
paddle-box must have been another one, as it answered
the description exactly, but not being in near contact we
were saved from it. Had two burst at the same moment,
one on each side, as the ship could not have given to it,
it would have been very serious.

" I went down to see if she made water, and was told it
was coming in fast, but we soon found it was only the pipe
of the engineers' bath broken, through which a stream
poured. When plugged up, she was quite tight. But the
blow had driven her side in for the moment, over an extent
of many feet each way, and everything inside in contact
with the side suffered. The engineers' mess-place and store-
room under it got the full benefit. Their mess-place was
a wreck ; their lockers with their private stores, and their
sideboard, etc., with all their mess-traps, being next the
side, *everything* was smashed and scattered over the place—
lockers, plates, cups, glasses, sauces, pickles, and the bottles
containing them, all smashed up, not a thing left. Below
in the engine store-room, where the full blow had struck
four feet below water, a heavy tank of tallow, fixed and
cleated to the side, weighing twelve hundredweight, together
with all the paint-tanks, casks, etc, were torn from the
side and thrown about three feet against the opposite
bulkhead. A large wooden diagonal girder and a diagonal
iron one crossed each other there : the wooden one was
broken and the iron one bent in. The shelf-piece under
the deck was split and broken, and the bulkheads drawn
away from the side, copper linings, etc., torn off, but the
vessel's side had resumed its proper position, and seemed
uninjured, showing that the blow had driven it in for
a moment, and afterwards it sprang back as before. The
iron girder crossing just there, and the resistance afforded
by the heavy tank against it, I have no doubt greatly
deadened the blow and prevented the side giving in.
The bulkheads across the ship, including the one where
you sat at church, are broken or crushed a little by the
lateral pressure, and the pitch in the beams in the lower
deck is crushed up, showing how great the pressure must
have been for the moment. The first explosion on the
port side did nothing but break some men's mess-traps
and knock down their tables. The second one smashed
all the things in the after-mess—the marines'. It is evident
that the first machine was not so close to the side as the

second, as the copper is not injured. Now we do not
know how close either was, and the second may have
been far enough off for the water to deaden the blow ;
whilst, had it been in contact, it might have blown the
side in. We cannot decide how far they are dangerous,
from not knowing how close they were. Otter had the
sail-binns next the side on the orlop-deck driven quite
away ; but his copper, like our port side, is uninjured

"And now I have a much more serious thing to
mention, that will cause great excitement in England.
The two masters of the prizes we took, who were so
anxious to be landed, and the two men with them, as
well as two other prisoners taken in merchant-vessels,
were sent in *Cossack* to be landed The man who,
you will recollect, told me it would kill his wife if he
were sent to England, Fanshaw had previously landed at
Hango Point, and said there were no batteries or troops
there I said at the time it would not do to depend on
it and land on the mainland, or we should be played a
trick. He went off Hango, but not close enough even
to see the boat land, and she pulled in with a *flag-of-truce*,
taking the six prisoners, the third lieutenant, surgeon,
assistant master, and mid, the captain's and the gun-
room stewards with their baskets, in all seventeen besides
the six prisoners. On pulling in to a pier—so says the
only survivor—they saw several hundred men, dressed
as riflemen, close down. They went alongside the pier,
and the officers and two Russian masters went up on
the pier with the flag-of-truce. The poor little man who
so feared his wife dying if he went to England hailed
them, and pointed to the flag-of-truce An officer who
spoke English well answered, 'We don't care for your
flag-of-truce ; we will teach you to fight against Russians';
and instantly a volley was fired, which killed all who had
landed, friends as well as enemies, and then everybody
in the boat was shot down When every one had fallen,
they rushed into the boat and began to search her for the
arms, throwing overboard all the dead and dying in their
way. Having found the arms under the thwarts, they
left the boat with five still laying in her, four dead, the
only survivor having three bad wounds The next morning the ship stood in to look for her boat, and saw her
with one man sculling off. This poor wounded fellow had
actually got her away, and was trying to scull her back

to the ship. Even if they could not acknowledge the flag-of-truce, they had our men in their power, and could have made them prisoners if they had chosen. A nice return for liberating their poor countrymen, all Finns ; while these were, I expect to find, the new Finnish militia rifles raised this winter. We have heard the Finns are terribly exasperated against us, through the destruction of their private property by Admiral Plumridge last year in so wanton a manner. The Gamla Carleby slaughter of last year was the first effect of that un-English and un-Christian proceeding, and I have no doubt this may be traced to the same feeling. So terribly do unjust acts lead to retribution I think Admiral Dundas is going to send me to Sweaborg with a flag-of-truce about it. I do not think any of their regular troops would have been allowed by their officers to act so How little my poor prisoner could have thought that his safety would have been in going to England ! I trust there may be a chance of some few that fell on shore having been only wounded.*

"5 *p.m.*—Just as my boys were coming down for our afternoon school and singing, there came a succession of visitors to see the wonderful effects of the explosion—Admiral Dundas and Pelham, two French captains, and Admiral Seymour (who apologised for coming on Sunday) and his flag-captain. . . .

"I have been disturbed by three more curious friends wishing to see the whole after we had cleared everything away, they having been with us at the time. Erskine is one of them. The more I see of him, the more I am convinced that he is one of our very best officers You will be surprised at my having had the artist of the *Illustrated London News* on board. But just as we were leaving, a lieutenant of the flag-ship brought him with the captain of the fleet's compliments to me, and asked if I would take him in with us ; so as I did not ask him to come, I was not sorry to have him ! He first sketched the quarter-deck with all the big men grouped on it, and I had then recommended him to sit on the steps of the fore-side of the paddle-box, where he could rest his book on his knees and have a good clear look. After the gunboat fired, he was rather anxious that 'the captain should not go too close.' When the first shock struck us, Mundy

* The explanation given by the Russian general showed that it was a real mistake, the flag-of-truce not being observed.—ED.

was talking to him, and he exclaimed, 'There! a shot
has struck us,' and looked very pale   As he was getting
over it, the second explosion took place, close under his
nose, driving up the water just before him, so that he had
the nearest and clearest view of it; but I think he was not
quite able to sketch it!   His great delight seemed to be
in the engineers' mess-place, with all the smashed crockery
and mess-things; and I expect you will see a sketch of it
in all its glory.   He is going to show me the drawings
I want to prevent any exaggeration.   The smash in the
store-room, where the real damage was done, and the heavy
tank thrown away, he could not, he said, *make a point of—*
that is, I suppose, it was not *picturesque* enough; but the
smashed crockery seemed to have a great charm for him.
He kept some fragments of cups and glasses as relics of
it, and I think you may see a wonderful sketch of broken
tea-cups.

"We find that our timber on the side, just under where
the iron rider was bent in, is broken, but the diver has
been down outside, and reports the planking quite perfect,
though for twelve feet long and eight feet deep the copper
is all torn off and twisted up"

"'Merlin,' *Sunday, June 10th*

"Though it will by-and-by disappoint the public at
home, you will not be unhappy at knowing now that the
more we see of this place, the less likely it is that we can
do or even attempt anything.   Had they sent out here
everything first intended, and concentrated all their efforts
on Cronstadt, it must, I think, have been destroyed; but a
portion of the force will not do   The enemy have not
been idle, and out of the thirty-four steam screw gun-boats
we heard they were preparing, fifteen showed yesterday,
all ready and manned, and they have a much heavier
flotilla than we can bring against them.   Besides, all their
steamers are able to act inside, whilst ours cannot get near
to help our gun-boats   I can see the admiral is very doubtful, and I dare not urge him on to try it, unless with a force
sufficient to give every probability of success.   We may
perhaps have a chance of a distant bombardment of Sweaborg; and if managed well with the necessary means sent
out, we may do great injury to the enemy without the
loss of a man to us: that we can do even with the smaller
force said to be coming out.

"You will see in the journal the particulars of the wonderful escape we had yesterday from a very great danger: it is the nine days' wonder of the fleet, and the numbers coming to-day to see the sight below where the damage was done have quite broken in on our Sunday. But we have not lost our service, and I have had two good half-hours morning and evening with the boys singing. It was warm, and all the skylights open; so I think, as we are close to the English and French admirals, and the transport under our stern, our singing must have been heard by many. I tried to point out to the boys that it was not merely singing, but every verse was either prayer or praise, and they must be thinking of that when singing.

"We had a grand dinner in the French flag-ship—the admirals, two of our senior captains, and myself. The French officers are very complimentary, particularly the French admiral; it seems as if they could not make too much of me.

"I begin to think and almost to hope that we shall have a bloodless campaign. We may perhaps bombard Sweaborg.

"I see that a French paper mentions the plan for the future conduct of the war as positively agreed on between the Emperor and our Government. It is that, after some decided success in the Crimea to enable us to do so with credit, the armies will be withdrawn entirely, and the future operations be confined to a close blockade of all the Russian coasts till they choose to ask for peace. We might do that with very reduced forces and little expense, and I wish we had done it and nothing more from the first. It is our truest policy. It would never have raised in Russia the national feeling for the war caused by their good defence of Sevastopol, and it would only have made the war felt by all classes by stopping all trade and ruining their merchants and rich families. We should in future want only about four combined line-of-battle ships and some small craft in the Black Sea, and ten screw-liners and a lot of small craft in the Baltic. Both nations might reduce their line-of-battle ships more than one-half, and all transport expense would be saved. The expenses might be nearly reduced to our peace establishment."

CHAPTER XIII.

INFERNAL MACHINES—A RUSSIAN COUNTRY HOUSE.

IN this chapter will be found further particulars of the "infernal machines." I have thought it well to enter into these details, seeing that the "infernals" were the fore-runners of the submarine mines of the present day.

"'MERLIN,' RUNNING FROM SWEABORG TO CRONSTADT,
"*Monday, June 18th,* 1855.

"On Thursday we left Cronstadt in the fleet, and moved down to Seskar   From Seskar I started on Friday for Sweaborg, with a letter to the general commanding respecting the murder of the *Cossack's* men   We reached there Saturday at noon.   I went in by a new passage through many rocks, trusting to the admirable Russian charts, and knowing they had been putting down infernal machines in the usual channel, which would not at all respect a flag-of-truce, *if we ran foul of them.*   I anchored just out of gun-shot, and a boat came off to us.   We had one of Her Majesty's *table-cloths* flying, and a table-napkin for the boat if wanted.   The Russian boat would not, as before, come alongside, but laid on her oars a short distance off, so I went to her in the gig with Crowe, the interpreter   The officer was very grumpy   I told him I should have gone in the boat at first had not his admiral last year requested no boat should leave, but that they would send one alongside.   He said he had nothing to do with that, but had only to obey his orders.   I gave him the letter, and he returned.

"We remained at anchor twenty-eight hours, till 2 p m. yesterday, when my friend came out as before, and I went to him.   He brought a letter nearly a foot square, with a very grand black seal the size of a watch.   He was much more gracious, actually smiled, so I shook hands with him on parting, and we came out; but he hung to and fro in the boat near us, till we were fairly going out the way we came in, when he pulled back. I thought he might be watching to see if we went out by the old passage, to warn us if there were really 'infernals' there; but perhaps I gave him credit for too much honesty. We joined the fleet here soon after midnight. It was so light that some of our men were reading on deck at midnight

"You will be glad to hear that the Russian general's answer tells me that none of *Cossack's* officers were killed, only the five men in the boat and my poor Finnish captain —several others wounded. I hope it was a mistake. They did not observe the flag-of-truce; and he says, with some reason, that a flag-of-truce should only go to a large place like Helsingfors, or that prisoners we want to send back should be landed on an island. In this he is right, for I had landed some last week, and would not put them on the main, but sent them to an island. We are all delighted at the news from the Black Sea I am glad George is in the Sea of Azoff They have done their work well."

" OFF CRONSTADT, Thursday, June 21st

"We have again moved up to Cronstadt, but only for observations. The chief will not, I think, attempt anything without a proper force. My plans were drawn up for eight floating batteries, thirty gun-boats, thirty mortar-boats, with four large frigate-steamers. We have one such steamer and two batteries coming, and about half the gun-boats and mortar-boats. We might try a good deal if we had the floating batteries, even with the small number of other kinds; but I am sure we could not have a chance of success without six at least: it is a pity they send any, if only two. The chief has written very decidedly and firmly about it, and I could not but feel pleased at his mentioning my name in the way he did: he only quotes the opinions of Admiral Seymour and myself, and he says I am the most anxious and sanguine about doing what we could at Cronstadt. I do not think we can try anything here with the force coming, and we shall merely watch, and perhaps try mortar-vessels, etc, elsewhere, where we can do so without risk and without the need of floating batteries I am sorry we came up here, as, if we can attempt nothing, it would be better to keep out of the way, only preventing any coasting trade. Though I am

sorry on public grounds that all the force was not sent
out, yet it is a consolation that much bloodshed will be
spared ; and I could not look at the quiet-looking, pretty
buildings, churches, etc, which the sun shone on beautifully
this evening, without feelings of regret that war should make
it a duty to carry on such a fearful work against them as a
bombardment would be It is lovely weather, cooler than
last year, and I trust will continue much healthier than then.

"Sabine tells me she saw in some paper *Merlin* is
called ' Dry nurse to the *Duke.*' I am sorry for such expressions, as it may annoy the chiefs and make them more
shy of consulting me, but I find the officers of *Duke* gave
us the name, and mentioned it before Creyke and others
here I have not seen the chief for two days now, and I
have heard nothing more about what I told you I thought
would be done soon ; but I think with all the mortar-boats
out here something must be tried. I do not think anything
very decisive could be done, and I doubt if it is not better
to stick to the shutting up of the coasts; but as a good deal
of damage may, I think, be done with very little risk to us,
it ought to be tried perhaps The admiral has a difficult
game to play and a very heavy responsibility, and the
difficulty is increased by the divided authority with the
French admiral I am very sorry now that I led
the Admiralty to think so much might be done. Had
I known that we should have had no floating batteries
ready, and so many fewer gun- and mortar-boats than
was intended, I would at once have advised that nothing
but a very close blockade should be attempted, and the
destruction of all their coasting trade "

"NARGEN, *Sunday, July* 15*th*

" We sailed from Cronstadt yesterday at 8 a.m. with all
the fleet, but *Duke, Exmouth, Euryalus, Vulture, Princess
Alice,* with four mortar-boats and one gun-boat (*sic*). These
came on here, and we arrived this morning at 7 a.m., so
that we have again a quiet Sunday.

"You recollect my mentioning about two months since
going near the village at Hogland, and a young lady in
pink coming down close to us and tripping back to the
house. Yelverton has been there several times, and the
house is the residence of the head man, a sort of magistrate
or governor of the island Yelverton asked him with his
wife and daughter off to dinner, but he was afraid to accept,

saying he dared not go on board, and could not unless forced to go ; so, when dinner was ready, Yelverton landed the jolly-boat boys, armed with drawn cutlasses, and then marched the father, mother, and daughter down to the boat, and they apparently enjoyed their dinner very well. They enjoyed the joke more, probably.

" I fear the poor people on the coasts are suffering fearfully. Occasionally a boat is stopped trying to get into Cronstadt. One poor man said his wife had urged him to risk it, as they were actually starving, and that it was better to do anything than starve. It is very sad, but it is the only way we can make them feel the war, and I fear we must even destroy all their coasting-vessels without mercy, or we cannot shut up the trade at the end of the season, when our vessels dare not risk being caught in the ice."

" Cronstadt, *Saturday, June 23rd.*

" We came up here again from Seskar on Wednesday, and are anchored on the north side of the island, except five cargo-ships off the south entrance by the lighthouse. On Thursday afternoon I saw that boats were creeping in different places, and one of the officers said he thought they were looking for infernal machines, and they had had some explosion at *Exmouth* ; but I thought nothing of it till yesterday morning. To my astonishment I found that *Vulture* had exploded an infernal machine in the middle of the fleet, though we had led the fleet up through the very place and were anchored inside all. This made them hunt for them, and several ships soon crept up some. I have tried to describe them in the sketch. They are made cone-shaped of strong zinc, about two feet deep, and fifteen inches wide at top. The bottom holds the powder, about eight pounds ; the top is full of air, to keep it up ; a strong tube (B B B) goes through the top, and reaches the powder ; a small tube about the size of a lead pencil is hung in the centre of the large one (D D)—it pivots on its centre ; and fixed in the bottom of the large tube, in the little chamber of priming-powder (C), is a small glass tube (+), sticking up into the bottom of the small tube. You will see that if anything pushes the upper end of the small tube on one side, as I have tried to show in figure 2, as it is pivoted in the centre, it must break off the glass tube, which is filled with some ignitible stuff, which fires the priming-powder (C), and of course explodes the machine. Now the two thin tubes of iron on the top (A A) slide to and fro, but are kept away from the tubes by slight springs. On being touched by a ship's side, or even pressed with a finger, they shove the small tube

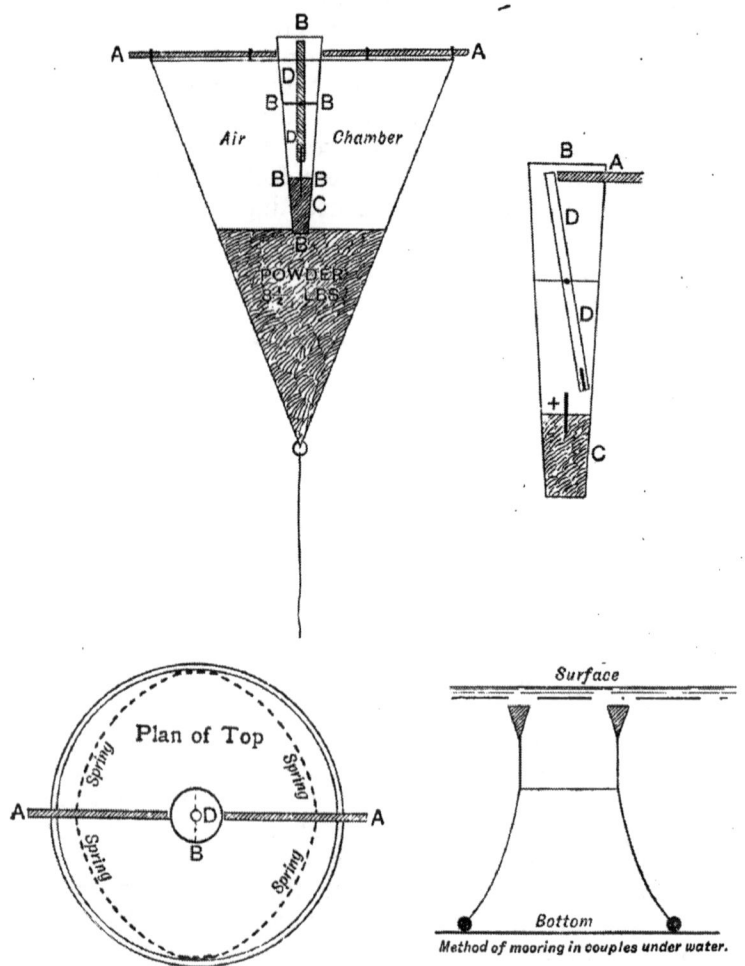

Method of mooring in couples under water.

aside, as in figure 2, and explode the machine. How any were hauled into boats without exploding seems marvellous; but some lost their tubes when canted up to be hauled in; others had been put down with caps on the tops, which prevent their going off. These ought to have been removed ; but the parties putting them down had been so afraid of them, they had preferred leaving them safe for us to risking removing the caps themselves.   I don't know what the Grand Duke will say if he knows this ! Admiral Seymour and Hall got one up, and hauled it over the bows of the gig.   How the little slides were not touched is wonderful.   It was then passed aft; and the master of the fleet joining them, they, thinking it was damaged with wet, got discussing the way to set it off   Stokes touched the slide, shoved the tube a little on one side, but evidently not enough to break the glass tube.   They then took it to Admiral Dundas, and again they all played with it ; and Admiral Seymour took it to his ship, and on the poop had the officers round it examining it.   Hall, being in the act of hoisting a second one, was on the quarter-deck.   Some of the officers remarked on the danger of its going off, and Admiral Seymour said, ' Oh no ; this is the way it would go off,' and shoved the slide in with his finger, as he had seen Stokes do it.   It instantly exploded, knocking down every one round it   As Hall looked round he saw the captain of marines, a son of Sir John Louis, carried down the ladder, with every bit of clothes burnt off him and covered with blood.   He then heard, ' The admiral is killed.'   The latter was lying insensible, his face covered with blood ; but he soon recovered, though very seriously injured in one eye and the head.   The poor captain of marines had pieces of the machine in his legs, besides the burns.   Pierce, the flag-lieutenant, much hurt, a piece of iron going through the peak of his cap, and knocking it into the mizzen-top, but not touching his head ; a young volunteer also.   The signal-man holding it up at the time not very much hurt, though burnt; and one lieutenant and the chaplain, though next to Admiral Seymour and close to it, only had their hair singed, and were not hurt at all.   Two or three men also slightly wounded.   It is a wonderful escape, for pieces of it flew down the main hatchway ; and we know that the Russians getting one into a boat exploded it, and killed seventeen men.   Admiral Seymour is much less hurt than was first supposed, as he is able to sit up to-day ; but concussion of the brain is what they fear.   He can see a glimmer of light with the eye, so it is hoped he will recover the sight. The marine officer's is the most dangerous case, but it is hoped he is doing well also.

   " The extraordinary thing is that the same evening

Admiral Dundas and Pelham were examining a tube ;
so Caldwell went and got an empty machine (that had been
cut open) to put the tube in, to examine how it explodes.
While they were close round it, the admiral shoved the
slide, and the tube exploded, shooting up in the middle of
them, and hurting the admiral's eyes so much that they
were looking inflamed and bloodshot yesterday morning
when he was explaining all this to me.   I am very glad I
did not know what they were about all day, or I should
have been about it also, perhaps ; and several had been
wondering ' why Sulivan was not there, as they seemed
his special friends !'   The fleet had anchored just where
a lot of them had been put down.   They are numbered as
high as ninety-nine.   About twenty-four have been fished
up altogether, and now they are more careful about them.*

"Yesterday Creyke and I went with two boats to buoy
and examine the shoal off the new batteries, where in *Merlin*
we shoaled to twelve feet the first day, and put a buoy on
it ; and it is very fortunate we did not ground, as there is
ten feet only in one part, and it is only two thousand nine
hundred yards from the guns, and they have since put
a target on the spot and have been practising at it   I then
in the evening asked the admiral for a gun-boat to go
down to the lighthouse to get some more angles, and took
the *Magpie*, commanded by an old surveyor, Lieutenant
Pym (the officer who first discovered Captain Maclure and
the *Investigator*).

"This morning the admiral sent a boat to ask me to come
to breakfast, and then take him in to have another look
at the north side   We started at 1 p m., *Dragon* with us.
Just as we were starting, Ramsay of *Euryalus* came, and
the admiral asked him to come, ' if he did not mind risking
being blown up'   I thought we must have come across
some of the ' infernals,' as we were going into the most likely
ground ; but we did not touch one.   There was a line of
steam gun-boats inside the dam ; and not having any idea
their guns had such long range, I should have anchored
where we did once before , but having got shoal water farther
out in another position, and there being no boats about, we

---

* A small "infernal" Captain Sulivan brought home he gave to his
brother George, who presented it to the museum of H M.S. *Excellent*,
together with a gutta-percha trough of a battery which was found connected with an "infernal" off Yenikale, in the Sea of Azoff, by the
boats of H M S *Vesuvius*, when attacking that place —Ed.

determined to anchor there and push in in the gig. The admiral came with me, and we pulled in towards three new corvette block-ships, placed since we were last in ; and keeping, as I thought, a respectable distance from the steam gun-boats, we pulled on till we shoaled to ten feet. We saw a gun-boat fire occasionally ; we could not see any shot fall near us, though the *Merlin* hoisted the danger-signal to us. . . . We went on sounding. . . . The firing had been at *Merlin* ; one shot had dropped just under her stern, though she was three thousand seven hundred yards from the gun-boats inside the dam. We had been only two thousand three hundred yards from the gun-boats, yet, strange to say, they never fired at us in the boat, though so much nearer than the ship.

" The Russians certainly deserve credit for their work here. They have ready twenty-three fine screw gun-boats, larger, I think, than ours ; some with three heavy guns each, with a range equal to that of the heaviest gun we have, and yet they have only had machinery of railway engines to fit in them. They had to-day inside the dam and the shallow banks moored in line as block-ships seven two-deckers, seven large frigates, and five corvettes, and with them, ready to move anywhere along the dam, twenty-three screw gun-boats, beside many row gun-boats and thirteen small steamers from *Merlin's* size downward ; while inside, ready to act also where required, are a screw-frigate and four paddle-frigates with main-deck guns, beside two or three sloop-steamers. The whole of this force is guarding the passage of the dam and shallow water. To force this and make a gap in the dam, etc., we have at most fifteen gun-boats and one or two small steamers ; all others draw too much water to go near enough to help. Even if the two floating batteries come, they would never stand such a tremendous force. But without beating off their entire force and removing a part of the dam we cannot get a mortar-boat . . . within range of the place. Yet there are wiseacres who abuse us for not taking Cronstadt, as if we could prevent shallow banks, and a dam twenty years old on these banks, keeping us at a distance, or could by any means carry our large ships (drawing twenty-five to twenty-seven feet) over ten feet water which separates us from their heavy force. It would be exactly the same as if in the Sea of Azoff the Russians had a lot of line-of-battle ships, frigates, steamers, and gun-boats, where the water is deeper, and we could only get in the small steamers and gun-boats drawing under fourteen feet water, which depth must be passed at the entrance. Were that the case, could we possibly have sent a small force into it?

"*Sunday, 24th.*—A nice quiet day, as all our Sundays now are. Admiral Seymour and Captain Louis are going on favourably, and are, I hope, out of danger.

"*Monday, 25th.*—Last night we had a heavy thunderstorm. The fleet remains very healthy; no symptom of cholera, as last year at this time."

"*July 9th,* 1855.

"On Friday I went with Boyd of *Royal George,* who had slung a thirty-two-pounder in a coaster, to try its range against the new earth fort on the north side. At four thousand four hundred yards the shot went on shore ; but, to our surprise, the battery fired in return, and actually threw the shot out close to us, full four thousand four hundred yards ; so they have as heavy guns and longer range than anything we have, as these guns were fired from carriages. On Saturday we went in *Merlin* with the French and English admirals to look at the south side again, and to get as close as we could towards the south shore; but the hint the guns had given us the previous day made me keep four thousand two hundred yards from Risbank, instead of three thousand five hundred yards, as we did the last time we went. We found the banks, as usual, with less water than we expected, three fathoms only, just outside the four fathoms line of the chart. We then steamed across, keeping four thousand two hundred yards from the fort, and stopped in the middle, having a very good look, it being a very clear, beautiful evening. Risbank fired a shot at us in a perfect line, but three or four hundred yards short. We steamed ahead a little, saw them give the gun more elevation, and the next shot dropped a little astern, but exactly in our wake. Alexander fired also, but did not reach us by two hundred yards. They seem to have these long-range guns everywhere. We had heard that there were many much larger 'infernals' on that side; some with thirty-five pounds of powder, which would certainly blow *Merlin's* bottom in ; but we had three gun-boats to pick us up, if necessary. There were many speculations on the probability of her not coming out again, or having to run on a bank before sinking. The French admiral congratulated himself on being able in that event to reach the main-mast head, which would be well out of water. They are probably inside, more where ships would go if attacking the forts. Admiral Seymour was pulling about in his gig last evening ; he seems not to have suffered in health, but fears the sight of the eye is gone; he can only see a glimmer of light."

"'MERLIN,' INSIDE DAGO, *Sunday, July 22nd*, 1855.

" . . . I have always been particularly anxious, as you know, to make Cronstadt our point ; but that being out of the question, I have urged Sweaborg as the next important point, and have never varied. There have been other points talked of, and some doubt in the admiral's mind whether we can do anything of importance or worth the expenditure of shell, etc. The French chief has wished to bombard Helsingfors, the town at Sweaborg, and not the fortress. This, I think, would be almost a cruelty, to destroy private houses, churches, observatory, etc., particularly with a large fortress, full of docks, buildings, barracks, etc., close at hand—a legitimate object of attack."

"NARGEN, *Thursday night, July 26th*, 1855.

" I have busy times, all to prepare for leaving this to commence buoying Sweaborg on Monday. It is an anxious time for me, having urged the attack so much, and the chief saying he is very doubtful of success, and allowing his judgment to be against trying it ; so that if we do no damage of consequence, I may have been the cause of a failure. But I am convinced it is the only thing we can try, and it ought to be tried, or the mortars, etc., will go home, having been useless.

"*Sunday, 29th.*—The French chief has been with me some time to-day. I fear he is bent on burning the town (Helsingfors) if he can, as well as the fortress. I suppose, as it is covered by the batteries, it is a legitimate object of attack ; but I would rather show a more Christian spirit and spare it."

"NARGEN, *July 29th*, 1855.

" Last Thursday week I went with the French and our admiral to Sweaborg, Key in *Amphion* and *Dragon* going

near to look out for us, and a gun-boat and a French small
screw with us. We had a good look at every part ; went
to *Amphion's* mast-head, anchored nearer Helsingfors, and
had a good look from there, then to an island closer in.
The enemy were in the act of sinking a two-decker to
block the western passage, one having been sunk within a
few days in the same passage. In turning to come out in
one place, the French screw astern of us exploded two
'infernals,' but nearly twenty yards from her. Probably
they were exploded by wires from the shore. They threw
the water to a great height. The next day we went into
Revel, and had a close look at all the batteries, several new
ones of turf thrown a little back from the shore, so that we
could not get within one thousand five hundred or two
thousand yards with large ships, while the stone one
advanced in the water had all the guns removed. They
know well what they are about. The same evening I was
off with two gun-boats to examine all the shores inside the
large island of Dago and Ozel at the south entrance of
the gulf, a large trade in boats and small craft having
been going on from those parts to Sweden for salt.

  " The next day (Saturday) we reached the sound inside
Wormso Island, and I tried to go to Hapsal, a town you
will see on the chart on the main, inside Wormso. It was
too shallow about five miles off for *Merlin* to pass, having
only eight feet, with large stones three and four feet high
on that. But by looking over the bows for the stones, and
steering between them, I got both gun-boats (drawing
seven feet) through, and had then a good channel up to
the town, within gun-shot, and we could have gone very
much closer   There were no vessels and no defences, but
crowds of people, with large parties of ladies with parasols
of all colours. I should have gone in with a flag-of-truce
to tell them not to be alarmed, had it not been for so much
dispute about flags-of-truce lately. After a good look, and
after catching a boat with a man and boy, and sending him
away astonished (with some tobacco, coffee, and biscuit),
we went out, little thinking what consternation we had
caused. Hapsal is the ' Brighton ' of Russia, and the chief
bathing-place of the ' big wigs,' who come from the capital,
Revel, etc., for the bathing in salter water. It is a pretty
place, houses being mingled with trees, and a fine old ruin
of a bishop's palace towering in the centre.

  " On proceeding towards Dago, after lying quiet all

Sunday, we followed a small cutter, about thirty tons, into a cove on the south-east point, finding a passage for the gun-boats and *Merlin* six miles outside. I had been ordered to burn everything we found moving about, but not any vessels dismantled or hauled up. We set fire to the little cutter, which seemed more of a pleasure-boat than a coasting-vessel, and just after we saw a flag-of-truce on the shore. I landed and met a gentleman driving down in a handsome carriage and pair, a young man about thirty or thirty-five, who told me the vessel was his; that he was the Baron Sternberg, proprietor of nearly all Dago; that the island was defenceless, all troops having been withdrawn at the outbreak of the war; that there were fifteen thousand inhabitants, five thousand able-bodied men. He had been asked by the general commanding to organise them as a militia, but he declined, knowing it would only tempt attack, which must end in destruction of all property, and that he preferred trusting to our forbearance. He hoped we should not injure any private property on shore. I assured him we should not, and explained why I burnt the vessel, but left a larger one near her, dismantled, uninjured. He allowed that losing the vessel, which was his, was merely the fortune of war, and I told him I was glad she belonged to him and not to a poor man. He said that his castle was only three miles off, and he hoped we would visit it (he spoke English pretty well). I could not then, as I wanted to push on.

"The next day we went in the gun-boat round the shores of Ozel and Dago. We landed at one nice-looking farm-house in Ozel; found only a very old woman with white hair, a cripple, and a man and woman servant, sheep, cattle, and horses. We saw a man drive off in a carriage—I suppose the proprietor. The man came down with us, and we gave him some coffee and sugar for the old woman, and some tobacco for himself. There was a fine flock of geese, which he was willing to sell; so we drove them to the shore, and made a circle round them with Creyke, Hewett, Lord D. Cecil (commanding a gun-boat), and the boat's crew. There was one fine brood of young ones, nearly full-grown, which I picked out, and then we rushed in on them, and geese, officers, and men were sprawling together. I got my pair of the fine young ones, and all got a good handful but Hewett, whom, after the chase, we found holding between his legs a gosling about the size of a young chicken, which was all he had succeeded in catching. We gave the man a shilling each for them, with which he seemed well pleased.

"After coming round to the cove where we burnt the cutter (about 2 p.m.), we saw the baron's carriage down again, and on landing he introduced me to the baroness, a young, nice-looking, delicate lady of about twenty-two years of age, who spoke very good English. They repeated the invitation to go out to their castle; so I got in alongside the lady, the baron mounted the box alongside a great Russian coachman in a long blue robe, a funny hat, and a splendid beard, and with two very fine horses we started, going first to the farm near, to provide a conveyance for Creyke, Hewett, and Cecil. They got a little hay-waggon with one pony, in which, after two breaks-down, they reached the castle about twenty minutes after we did. It is a splendid house, shaded over the entrance by fine horse-chestnuts, beautiful grounds round, and inside like a handsome English country house, but that there are polished oak floors, except in the drawing-room, which is thoroughly English, and inside it a perfect bijou of a boudoir, which the lady took me into through the drawing-room; and I almost thought myself in fairy-land, so beautifully was it fitted up with green velvet, etc., but nothing gaudy. Inside this was the lady's dressing-room, which I cannot report so particularly on, except that the glimpse I got of it showed it to be in keeping with the boudoir. It was a very hot day, but a nice little breeze, though the thermometer was higher than they have ever had it before. Outside that front was the garden; the flowers, just the same kind as in our gardens, were rather poor, but the roses numerous and beautiful, and we got fine bunches of them. The stables were very good, and full of fine horses and stout island ponies about thirteen hands high. Her favourite English mare, which she showed me, was a great beauty, and I should think thorough-bred; she had also a very nice island pony for rough work and for hunting. There was a very fine English riding-horse of the baron's, a pair of English carriage-horses, and the handsome Russian ones we drove out with. It really all seemed like a dream: three miles inland in an enemy's country, and going over all these quite English-like scenes, with a nice young lady speaking as good English as I did, except the slightly foreign accent.

She was born at St. Petersburg, and only spoke Russian as a child, but had been entirely educated by an English lady, a Miss Meara, who seems to have remained with her till her own marriage about two years since. The family consists of one pretty little girl about fourteen months old, who was at first rather frightened at me. The lady, though nice-looking and very intelligent and sharp, is too delicate to be very pretty, and is very thin for so young a person; but she said she was very well able to walk and ride, and the people in the island are generally very healthy, there being only one medical man to the fifteen thousand two hundred inhabitants, and she thought they might do better without him.

"She expressed surprise at our not having burnt Hapsal. I asked her if she thought us savages, to destroy defenceless towns. She thought we would do so, and instanced Nystad and Lovisa this year, besides all the wanton destruction of property last year. The latter I could not defend; but I told her that Nystad was perfectly uninjured, that Lovisa had been so protected by Yelverton that at the request of the people he would not even burn the government stores, but destroyed them as much as possible, fearing, if fired, it might spread to the town, but that the same night a house in the opposite direction caught fire and burnt down all the town except the government stores, the burgomaster explaining that the fire was caused by a woman throwing out hot ashes or some such accident. I also pointed out to her that Yelverton at Ekness last year would not allow a shot to be fired at the town, though the batteries near it were firing at him, and Port Baltic and Fredricksham were quite at our mercy also. She said that Hapsal was full of the principal families from St. Petersburg and elsewhere last year, and also this, they thinking the shallow water would prevent our going up to the town. This year, fearing Revel being bombarded, many ladies from there went to Hapsal, including the wife and daughters of the general commanding, and she thought our going so close must have frightened them sadly. She had a sister there, and as the post would be over in two days (if we did not take it, which I promised not to do), she would hear everything.

"We had a splendid dinner, but more plain meats, game, etc., than I expected. Coffee and tea were carried out under a tree, and we left about ten, just at dusk, the baron driving me at a rattling pace in a light phaeton with the English horses and a thorough English-dressed groom, leather belt, boots, and all. The others came in a Russian carriage with the big coachman driving four large ponies abreast, with three reins in each hand. I asked them to come on board *Merlin* if she came close in, and I promised to come near the east shore on our way back, where the water is deeper and a road from the castle runs to a jetty where the boats from Hapsal land.

"When we reached the gun-boats, we found the crews arming to come out to the castle, thinking we were made prisoners, from being so long away. I hope I may never have *a worse prison or a more unpleasant jailoress !*

"The baron told me that the salt trade in the boats was carried on by the poor fishermen of the islands, who were dependent, as are many of the inhabitants, on the salt fish for winter food, and who suffered much last winter from want of it, or from eating fish bad through being too little salted; so they risked anything to prevent suffering so again; but several boats having been lost with all hands, and numbers taken by *Porcupine* outside, they dare not continue it. He assured me that no salt went to the mainland, as it was too necessary to the poor people, and he urged me to ask the admiral to let them have salt for their fish, and he would pledge his word none should be sold or taken to the mainland. I pointed out to him the difficulties in the way of making such an exception to the blockade. He said the rich did not feel the blockade, as all necessaries, such as coffee, sugar, tea, etc., and particularly all luxuries, were only increased a small percentage in cost by the land carriage from Memel and Austria, but that salt could not be brought that way, the carriage being so large a proportion to the price, and therefore the poor on the coasts were the sufferers

"The next day I went to the southward, round the southeast side of Ozel, to Arensburg, the capital Knowing there were no troops, I meant to have landed there ; but it being dusk when I got off, and not liking to remain all night, I did not land, but returned to *Merlin* at 5 a.m. the next morning. We only saw one little vessel afloat and fitted out, and I was going to burn her, but reflected on the poor man seeming so distressed, and made them promise to haul her up. We weighed in *Merlin* at nine, after I had had three hours' sleep, and I went towards the part of Dago on our way

out that the baron told me was nearer their landing-place
and deeper water. We anchored some way off, but could
have gone close in with a foot of water to spare : the gun-
boat could lie alongside the jetty. We found the baron
down in his carriage, but no baroness ; he came off to lunch,
and when I took him back I found he expected me to go out
to dinner, and had brought a large carriage to take us.
I told him I could not wait ; but he seemed to expect it so
much that at last I agreed to go out for a short time and
to say 'good-bye' to his lady ; so Cecil and I started with
him. The first road for a mile and a half was good, and
led through an avenue of weeping-birch, and the four ponies
abreast went away at a tearing gallop, which was very well
till the road got uneven and stony, little sharp pitches up
and down hill ; and then, when they still tore on at the same
pace, I wished myself out of it once or twice, particularly
when dashing round corners and into the park through
gates at the same pace, and with a double turn round the
terrace up to the door I never saw such fearful driving.
The new leader, that is the outside of the four, was a beauty.
They are very hardy, and rarely get tired, so he said.

"I found a nicely-dressed, lady-like woman and her
husband (who is only a better-class farmer) there to meet
us, and we so far dined with them that we sat at table , but
having all the officers and the lieutenants of the gun-boats
to dine with me on board at six, I having just made a good
lunch on board, I could not of course have anything to
do with dinner. The baroness told me that she had not
come on board, fearing to compromise her husband, who
would have sufficient reasons to justify his going, it being
necessary to establish friendly relations with the ships, as
the islands were unprotected, but her going would be quite
a private act, so she thought it better not to.

"She had heard the day before from her sister at
Hapsal. When they saw us pass the shallow water, they
thought it was all over with them. Several ladies started
off immediately ; others began preparing and packing up.
And when they found we were within gun-shot and went
away, they could only believe it was to bring up the larger
steamer, as they thought it impossible we should spare
the town when we got close to it ; so they went on packing
up, preparing carriages, etc., and stationed men on the
church-tower to report when we were returning. Their
grand ball was that evening, and some did not return for it.

When on Sunday morning they found we were farther off, they thought they were safe; so they had a thanksgiving service and a grand Te Deum in the church for our having spared the town.   I sent a message to the ladies, which she promised to write to her sister—that they ought to have sent off and invited us to the ball and also to the Te Deum, and that I hoped to pay them a visit again, when I expected an invitation to land.

" She tried hard to get out of me whether Revel would be bombarded, so I let her rather fancy it would.   She said she hoped their house in the Domberg would escape ; and I told her I knew the Domberg was the west end of Revel (she knows London), and therefore it ought to have an extra share of shells, because the owners could afford the loss   A house her father had given her on her marriage outside the lines had been pulled down last year with a suburb of the best houses, and that is where they are now constructing so many earthen batteries.   She hoped I might be able to visit them when at peace, and bring you with me.   She was writing to Miss Meara an account of our visit, so I offered to send the letter in our mail-bag.   She at first thought it would not do, but the baron said it would be a good joke, and she gave it to me to send.   I told him I thought a ship would be stationed there later on in the season to blockade inside. They hoped it would be ours, as a stranger might not treat them so civilly, and they promised me plenty of shooting and fox-hunting, the latter consisting of foxes being carried to an island where they cannot escape and only run a mile in any direction, and sending their horses and hounds over there for the month of September.   If we had been two or three days sooner, we might have made their acquaintance under different circumstances, for they had crossed from Hapsal in their sailing-boat, and were becalmed eight hours on the way.   What a chance to have made prisoners of a real live baroness and baron ! It would have been a great catch.   I have promised her a passage across to Hapsal if we return, providing she takes me on shore with her to see her friends.

" You will recollect our catching a boat full of women off Revel last year, and sending them away quite delighted with a Bible, tracts, tea, sugar, etc.   The baroness was at Revel at the time ; many were watching our proceedings and among them the Grand Dukes, who sent for the women afterwards, and they showed some of the 'little books' I had given them. The women got plenty of presents from different people, so it was not a bad day's work for them.

"On my way back here I called at Odensholm, where you will recollect the men lived to whom I gave a Bible as a sort of pass to protect them from capture with their salt from Faro in April. They were very glad to see me. We got some milk and eggs, but the man whose boat it was would not let me pay for the milk we had.

"I trust with God's protection my next may report our successful bombardment of Sweaborg, for which I believe I start to-morrow or the next day to buoy and prepare for the force following the day after, but we can only do much damage to fortress, buildings, stores, barracks, etc. The admiral is most kind, and treats me with very flattering confidence, approves of nearly everything I suggest, and yesterday, when asking me how I was, as I have been a little unwell for some time, he said very kindly, 'You must not be ill just now. What should we do?' I may mention this, as it is only for those to read who will, I know, see how strictly private any remark of this kind must be kept. But I am sometimes rather puzzled by it, for all my brother-officers seem to think I can arrange everything, so they come to me. 'What are we going to do? Do get me there'; 'Do put in a word for me'; 'Don't forget I have two sixty-eight-pounders'; 'Don't forget I have two ten-inch'; 'I draw only sixteen feet water'; 'Don't leave me out, there's a good fellow.' All quite as if I could arrange things even on points that I am careful not to interfere in, and I am always afraid of giving offence to some, though I try not to say a word on these subjects except on purely public grounds, and where I think it best for our success. . . . I honestly try to suggest the best ships for the service, without caring for my friends. I do believe I can keep clear of all bias.

"*Monday*, 30*th*.—We start to-morrow morning. My poor friend Key, who has been stationed off Sweaborg all the summer, and was to have been with us, has come in with main-shaft broken : the ship will not be ready for a week. I have asked the admiral to let him go with us without his ship in some capacity. I am now waiting for the French admiral, who is coming here when he leaves our flag-ship."

His old friend Admiral W. A. B. Hamilton writes thus on his retirement from the Secretaryship of the Admiralty :—

"TYRINGHAME, PRESTONKIRK, N B , *July 2nd,* 1855

"MY DEAR SULIVAN,—I am sorry to miss to-morrow's post in thanking you for your most kind and welcome letter. There is no mistaking the sincerity of your congratulations, or the cordiality and warmth of your expressions, to what relates to your own good wishes for myself, and your grateful feeling for anything I may have been able to do in advancing your strong claims.

" My service at the Admiralty, as you well say, has been long and hard. I can scarcely yet believe in my liberty, nor is it yet altogether complete. Of course the incessant toil of the post I held has told upon me, and some repose is required. I hope it may set me up. Such genuine wishes as yours greatly aid in the operation, and they have been far more abundantly and warmly bestowed upon me than I could have expected. It is a very generous payment and acknowledgment of a very poor attempt, during a long spell of office, to do as I would be done by.

"Your letter was begun just before starting for Sweaborg with a flag-of-truce, and it contained the first intelligence I had of the officers of the *Cossack* being safe. Your account of the infernal machines, too, was very interesting , and notwithstanding your wily way of saying nothing about Cronstadt, concluding that we should hear everything, the little you did say, and the observations you make, comprise more real information about the place than anything I have yet seen. I do pity you, if, from want of proper means and appliances, the services you and others might render should fail of being turned to their proper account.

"I only wish that your admirable commander-in-chief will *forget Whitehall*, if circumstances should ever *seem to* offer of *possessing himself* of appliances that he has failed to receive from England, and that no consideration of *cost* or fear of rebuke would for a moment deter him from making himself master of them.

" With every good wish for yourself in return for all your kind wishes for me,

" Believe me to remain,

" Yours most faithfully,

"W. A. B. HAMILTON."

"ADMIRALTY, *July* 10*th*, 1855.

"DEAR SULIVAN,—It is very gratifying to find the *Merlin* at every advanced post, and that our surveying-ships lead the way and are sent on missions of confidence on every occasion.   The prominent position you occupy, and the kind terms in which the admiral speaks of your services, are very encouraging, and cannot fail, I should hope, in bringing their just and well-earned reward.   I trust the means sent out will enable you to bombard, otherwise there seems to be no chance of anything of importance to be done in the Baltic, beyond the blockade and the distracting the attention of the authorities and the troops from the south.   The Russians have shown much energy in building thirty screw gun-boats during the last year; the engines have been chiefly made by the American locomotive company who work the railway to Moscow, and not by Baird— at least, so our last information from St. Petersburg says. Baird has long been a Russian subject, but I rather think he refused to make them.

"With best wishes,
"Ever faithfully yours,
"JOHN WASHINGTON."

At this time a number of honours were distributed, Captain Sulivan being made a "Companion of the Bath."

CHAPTER XIV.

BOMBARDMENT OF SWEABORG.

REFERENCE has been made to the French chief's desire to destroy Helsingfors. The saving of this town afforded Captain Sulivan moie gratification than the destruction of Sweaborg, in both of which he was mainly instrumental.

"'MERLIN,' SWEABORG, August 2nd, 1855

"They have thrown up batteries all round the town on all sides, and so it becomes a fortified town, as some of these batteries have already fired on our gun-boats. The people have long expected an attack, and have been moving out with their property My own view would be to send in a flag-of-truce and promise not to injure the city, provided the city batteries did not fire at us.

"*Friday, 3rd,* 10 *p.m.*—We have been sounding and laying down buoys all day, and have had a strong blow, which it is fortunate occurred before the fleet came, or it must have delayed all proceedings. The Russians are working away tremendously at new batteries, but all in places where they cannot interfere with our plans, except a new one commenced to-day, which will be four hundred yards nearer than any other guns to the stations intended for the mortar-boats I wish some of the steamers were here, as we might try throwing shell to stop the working by day. I hope we shall have finished before they are ready. This weather must delay us some days

"They must know we are going to attack here, for I see by the *Standard* that one of the royal dukes is here. When I think of the prolonged horrors at Sevastopol, and the destruction and loss that may be caused here even in a city, I cannot but wish that our Government had agreed to Lord John's views and accepted the terms proposed. We may go on for years, and after all get no better terms ;

we should have gained all the objects we went to war for, as Sevastopol and the fleet had nothing to do with the origin of the war. Now the door of peace seems closed, for if we destroy Sevastopol and every ship, it will only make the Russians more determined to hold out. While all produce can be exported and all goods imported through Prussia, we cannot make the people feel the effects of war by a blockade."

"'MERLIN,' SWEABORG, August 2nd, 1855.

" I am going to try to-night to find out whether they have any 'infernals' in the place where I want to place the mortar-boats. I do not mean to risk getting them up to a boat, as in the night one could not see how to handle them ; but I mean to creep about four fathoms under the surface, and, if we catch anything, run a long line to an island and haul whatever it is on shore, keeping well out of the way. If any should be hooked, by dragging them on shore among the stones they will soon explode when they touch the bottom. I also mean to creep inside where I think they may be with a light creeper along the bottom, and try to hook up any of the electric wires that we hear they have connecting them with the shore. It would be great fun to hook them up and cut them, and then trace the 'infernals' outward by the cut wires ; they could not then explode ; and fancy their astonishment on shore afterwards when they tried to explode them, and wondered why their electric battery would not act !

" Oh, how I wish all this horrid work had been stopped by peace ! To see this beautiful place, fine buildings, churches, etc.; to see us to-day with our church flags up, and the enemy's also, both professing to serve the same Master—a Master of peace ; and to see them toiling all day raising works to defend these buildings, and we striving to reduce them to a heap of ruins ! It is very sad ; and though never had a nation greater cause for war, a fearful responsibility will rest on any who prolong that war a moment longer than is necessary to accomplish the objects for which we entered into it. Had we never sent that expedition to Sevastopol, we should have had peace now ; and had we confined ourselves to removing the enemy from Turkish ground, and then merely blockading closely, we should have saved nearly all the

blood and sickness and half the expense, while there would
have been no point of honour or heroic defence to raise
the national spirit of the Russian people.   The war would
have been more unpopular with them, and peace would
not leave the feelings of hostility against us now implanted
in the minds of the Russian people.   And oh, what
misery would have been saved to thousands of families.
in all four countries!   I cannot but feel we are all now
going on with the war because we do not know how
to give it up, with our armies unsuccessful at Sevastopol,
and that for all other purposes we could gain the objects
for which we went to war.   The fact of Russia consenting to place Turkey under the united guarantee of *all*
the European powers for her integrity, in addition to
yielding the other three points, should, I think, have
sufficed, and *would* have sufficed, had we known how to
get over the Sevastopol difficulty, while the hopes of
saving Sevastopol perhaps induced Russia to yield what
she did."

The following is an outline of the plan of attack on
Sweaborg :—

Sixteen British mortar-boats (with sixteen 12-inch
    mortars) ;
Five French mortar-boats (with ten 13-inch mortars) ;
Four French mortars (10 inch) on islets,—

to open fire at 2.30 a.m. at a range of three thousand three
hundred yards from the forts.   The mortar-boats (anchored
in a segment of a circle) to be supported by four covering
frigates anchored outside them.   British and French gun-
boats to circle inside the mortar-boats, using their guns
against the forts, and drawing the Russian fire away
from the mortar-boats.   Three ships were ordered by the
admiral to attack the Russian fort to the eastward.

Before the fleet crossed over to Sweaborg, Captain
Sulivan and his officers were engaged for three days
and nights finding places for the vessels clear of the
numerous rocks, making an accurate plan of the position,

ranges, etc., and at night creeping with grapnels as close
as possible in front of the fortress for the reported electric
wires of the infernal machines, but without finding any.

On the fourth day the fleet came over, and, after piloting
the ships in, Sulivan gave a copy of the plan to the British
and French admirals.   Under the circumstances, he of
course supposed that he would be allowed to carry out
his own plans, under the admiral's command, as any failure
would have been attributed to him ; but, to his surprise, the
admiral told him that two officers would have the command, both senior to him—he himself was to have no
command at all.   He was so astonished at this that he
had not the firmness to say, as any officer in his position
ought to say, " If I am not allowed to carry out my plan,
I cannot be responsible for its success," especially as the
very person who had argued that the scheme could not
succeed was now to have the control of the operations.
But Sulivan was so hurt and surprised that he made no
reply, and immediately left the flag-ship and returned to
the *Merlin*.   He had intended, directly the plan was
approved of by the two admirals, to prick it through a
number of sheets, as he had done at Obligado, and so
provide a copy of the plan and programme to every officer
in command of a ship.   But he was now unable to interfere with the directions to be given to the junior officers.

He had not long returned to his ship, when he saw the
gun-boats bringing in the mortar-vessels, and he was hailed
by Captain Seymour, " Sulivan, the captain in command
told me to bring you the mortar-boats, and that you would
place them."   Now Sulivan's plan was to anchor the
mortar-vessels exactly six hundred yards outside their
right positions of three thousand three hundred yards from
the forts, so that they might be out of reach of the enemy's
shot until the action was to commence.   After dusk,

kedge-anchors were to be laid out in the direction of the fortresses, with four hawsers of two hundred yards each, in all eight hundred yards. Then, just before opening fire from the mortars, the crews were to haul in three hawser-lengths, or six hundred yards, the vessels thus lying with one hawser out at exactly the proper range of three thousand three hundred yards. This was all explained on the plan which the admiral had given to the officer in command. The exact positions and the hawsers were marked in red, and the distance " six hundred " yards between the outer and the inner positions.

After anchoring all the mortar-vessels himself in a curved line three thousand nine hundred yards from the batteries, and the four covering frigates three hundred yards farther, Sulivan returned to his vessel, and found the admiral and captain in command awaiting him on board her. It was a beautiful, calm, clear day, and the batteries therefore looked closer than they really were. The captain declared that the mortar-vessels had been anchored closer than he had agreed to, that they were now within range of the enemy, and that even the frigates were. He urged the admiral to move them all farther out. Sulivan assured him that, if his scale was correct, which he did not doubt, the mortar-vessels were three hundred and the frigates six hundred yards out of range of the batteries, and that if the frigates were moved farther out they would not be so well able to protect the mortar-vessels at night or supply them with fresh ammunition, etc Notwithstanding his remonstrances, the admiral ordered him to move all the frigates farther out. Sulivan thereupon ventured to do what was akin to the action of Nelson when he put his blind eye to the telescope. He took three of his own officers with him, put one on board each frigate, instructing them to weigh anchor, turn the ship's head off a little, and drop anchor again *without moving the ship her own length!* He himself went on board *Euryalus*, and went through the same farce with her, knowing how important it was to keep the frigates close.

No doubt this manœuvre will be recorded in the logs of those ships, but it will not be explained therein why ships, just before anchored among sunken rocks, where safe places were not easily found, weighed and anchored again in the same place.

On Sulivan's return to the *Merlin*, the officer in command said to the admiral, " Now, sir, make him move out the mortar-vessels." This Sulivan could not stand ; so he said, " Admiral Dundas, they are now at the distance you decided on, and three hundred yards farther out than I think right ; and if you make me move them any farther, I cannot be answerable for the success of the plan." The admiral replied, " They shall stay where they are."

Late at night, when he was again with the admiral, the latter urged Sulivan, as he had not been in bed for three nights, to go to his ship and get a little sleep before daylight—about 2 a.m —when all would be ready for opening fire. He went to *Merlin* about midnight and lay down, but was too anxious to sleep, fearing things might not go right, so about half-past one he went in his boat to take a look round. He found boats laying out the hawsers, some having been already laid out ; but seeing one boat going to drop the kedge much too close to the vessels, he asked how many lengths of hawser were out— they told him *two*. This was half the proper number, or four hundred instead of eight hundred yards, as shown in the plans, by which means the mortar-vessels would be hauled in two hundred yards only instead of six hundred, thus leaving them four hundred yards farther off than was intended. At such a distance the attack could not possibly succeed, *as the mortars would be out of range of the arsenal and all the most important objects of attack.* What a painful position for a junior officer to be placed in! Neither of the senior officers' in command were on the spot If he allowed the action to go on, it would be sure to fail most ridiculously when daylight came, and there was not sufficient time to procure the double quantity of hawsers and get them laid out by daylight If the action were postponed a day, the beautiful calm weather might be lost ; and if it came on to blow, which was a likely event after two or three calm days, the only opportunity for the season might be lost, and in that case he would have all the blame thrown on him if he interfered without authority. Further, he would be running the serious risk of opposing the orders of his superiors. I have often heard my father lay down the maxim that no man is worth his salt who is not prepared to take great responsibility upon himself if the occasion require it. Here was such an one, and he hesitated but for a moment in taking a responsibility which probably no junior officer has ever before done—that of his own accord postponing a general engagement He felt that anything would be better than a ridiculous failure, through keeping our vessels *out of range of their objects*, in order that the vessels themselves might *be out of range of the enemy's guns.* So he ordered all the officers employed under the seniors—who were quite willing to act as he directed—to weigh the anchors laid out and leave the mortar-vessels in their old safe positions, and go back themselves to their ships, giving up the work for that day How such a mistake occurred it is difficult to say. Sulivan then went to the flag-ship, awakened the admiral, told him what he had done, and received his entire approval.

The next day the right number of hawsers were seen coiled ready in every vessel. Sulivan remained until nearly midnight with Admiral Dundas, who then urged him to get a little sleep, saying, " You may be quite satisfied *now* that everything is rightly arranged, and will be ready by daylight." Sulivan went to his ship, and, lying down outside his bed, fell fast asleep, till he was awakened by some one shaking him, and he found the officer in command with a light, who said, "Can you tell us what we are to do about hauling in." Sulivan said, "What time is it?" " Past one." By the time he had got into his boat and to the nearest mortar-vessel it was half-past one, and day was breaking. Every vessel should have been hauled in by that time, as the hawsers were all properly laid out ; but Sulivan found some hauling in, others waiting for boats to help them, and the crews of eight out of the fifteen mortar-vessels *asleep and doing nothing*, because they had received no orders ! Captain Sulivan thought this showed such a want of common understanding of a simple plan, and such unfitness in the officer commanding, that, hearing some of his officers remarking on it, he begged them all not to mention it to any one. He was more anxious that it should not be mentioned, because the officer alluded to was personally as gallant and good a man as any in the fleet. He had before, as a junior, done work he was ordered to do at Bomarsund well and gallantly ; and during the attack at Sweaborg, wherever vessels were more exposed to fire than others, or in moving closer in brought on themselves the special attention of the enemy's gunners, there he was sure to be seen. His only fault was not understanding the principle on which the attack was founded, and not having the necessary qualifications for more important command.

When the fleet was at Spithead the following year, Captain Sulivan's officers said that it was nonsense keeping them to their promise not to mention what had occurred, because it was openly spoken of in the fleet. He then ascertained that the officer in command had gone to one of the ships under his orders, and asked if they knew what they were to do about hauling in. The answer was, they did not, but perhaps Captain ——, the second in command, knew. The first lieutenant of the ship was sent to Captain —— to ask if he did, and brought back the answer, " I don't know anything about it, and I don't believe any one does but Captain Sulivan ", and then the commanding officer told the lieutenant to take him to *Merlin*. Having been in the cabin when Sulivan was called, the lieutenant knew what had occurred and told it to others. It is necessary to mention these things to show what great difficulties Captain Sulivan had to contend with in getting his plan of attack carried out successfully.

Captain Sulivan left on record the following observations ·—

" The experience gained at Sweaborg should be a lesson to any officer who, having proposed a plan of attack, finds it is to be adopted No delicacy to others, or hesitation in being firm with his superior officer, should prevent his insisting that he should be allowed to conduct the proceedings he was responsible for

" I feel confident that if an attempt on Cronstadt had been made in the same manner, and before an enemy well supplied with an active force afloat, we should have been defeated For there the difficulties and obstacles were so great, and the contest would have been so severe, that nothing but the greatest care in the arrangement for and management in conducting the attack could have given us a hope of success.

" That others were of the same opinion as myself on these points is shown by the following facts :—

" A captain of a ship in the Baltic fleet, much senior to me, during the winter, when preparations for the attack on Cronstadt the following season were being made, urged me strongly to insist on being put in the position of captain of the fleet, if my plan was to be carried out, on the ground that, if I had to contend there with such difficulties as I had at Sweaborg, nothing could save us from defeat, and that I ought not to have anything to do with it unless I were given a position that would ensure my being able to conduct the operations under the admiral only. But though I was very anxious on the subject, I could not bring myself to ask for a higher position at the expense of another, and I explained to my adviser that I was trying to guard against failure by getting certain officers, in whom I had great confidence, both senior and junior to me, placed in positions which would enable them to aid me materially in carrying out the plan, and that with their aid and the admiral's support, which I might now expect, I would trust to all going right."

We must now revert to the journals.

"SWEABORG, *August* 11*th*, 1855.

" Thank God with me for a bloodless victory—on our side at least bloodless, but I fear not so to the enemy. Sweaborg is in ruins after two days' bombardment, and not a scratch on our side. My letters will have told you I thought we might destroy it without losing a life, but it is a special Providence apparently that preserved our people in the little vessels amid showers of shot falling among them, and I have to be thankful that I am again spared through much danger. You can fancy the delight it gave the admiral and all, and not the least me, for my credit and the soundness of my views were at stake. All has far exceeded my expectations, for hardly a building is left except as blackened walls, and such fires are seldom seen. It is almost enough to excite my pride to hear what all are saying about my work ; but I really planned all, placed the vessels, selected the spots to shell, and was allowed really to do anything I wished, and the admiral speaks most feelingly and warmly of what thanks are due to me. He told one captain who congratulated him, ' It is all due to Sulivan.' I cannot describe to you my feelings—not, I assure you, those of pride ; for when all was finished at last, and I went below, having just been told what the admiral said, the conflicting feelings of gratitude and pleasure were such that, when I went on my knees to offer thanks to that God who still so wonderfully aids me above my deserts

and in spite of my neglect of Him, I could only burst
into tears   I never felt so weak or so little inclined to any
feelings of pride.

"I have hardly a moment in which to write, and have
had but seven hours' sleep in the past four days and
nights, and yet I am better in health than before."

"'MERLIN,' OFF SWEABORG IN FLAMES,
"*Friday, August* 10*th*, 1855.

"I must try to write you a hurried account of the last few
days. On Tuesday and Wednesday I was hard at work
night and day, either sounding or creeping for 'infernals'
at night, and making the plan complete, discussing it with
the admiral, and placing vessels by day. In the evening
the captains having the control of each portion of the
gun- and mortar-boats, and all the lieutenants, etc., commanding, were called in in batches by the admiral, who
gave them their orders, which I explained on the plan as
carefully as possible, till they had got their lessons perfect
. . . Being anxious about all going right, I went down
the line at 1.30 a m., and to my horror found only one
or two moving in, and others with their crews all asleep:
they said they had no orders to haul in ; yet the day *was
actually breaking.* By the time I had gone to every one,
roused them into activity, and got the officers who were
sent from the frigates to hurry their parties (I actually
found that no order had been given clearly how far they
were to haul in), and explained to all how much of the
hawsers they must haul in to get to their stations, it was
quite daylight ; but the enemy did not seem to notice our
change of position, and we could not commence firing,
because the French mortar-vessels were not ready ; so in
the meantime I went back and explained all to the
admiral, and he and captain of fleet came in *Merlin*, and
we ran down the whole line. The gun-boats were to
circle round inside the mortar-vessels, always in motion ;
but it was necessary to explain to the lieutenants the
dangers close to them, all under water, but all buoyed.

"You will see the place was pretty thickly strewed with
rocks and islands, but there was a part where I could place
all the mortar-vessels in an arc, equidistant from the
fortresses of Swarto and Vargon Islands, which were the
great object of attack, the shaded parts being thickly
covered with fine buildings, of which I dare say *Illustrated*

will give you an idea—the shores of course lined with
batteries of all kinds, and heavy earth-works in front of
the masonry ones.

" Of course everything depended on our knowing accurately the distance from the mortar-vessels.   If we put
them too close, they would be unable to stand the heavy
fire that would be poured upon them ; if at all too far off,
they would not throw shell into the buildings ; and I fixed
(with the admiral's approval) on three thousand three
hundred yards off the batteries (only exposed to long-
range guns and heavy mortars), which would put them
three thousand nine hundred yards from the buildings in
the centre.   I can hardly describe to you my anxiety lest
I should in any way have mistaken this, because every one
would have thrown the blame on me—very justly.   While
waiting for the French, we ran down all the line in *Merlin*,
the batteries on shore taking no notice of us.   There were
four divisions, each requiring a slight difference in range,
as each had a part of the buildings to direct their fire
to, as a centre.   I carefully fixed the position of each
division in *Merlin* ; and with the captains of marine artillery
on board (my old Parana friend Laurence being one), and
the admiral present, I gave each his range and pointed
out the object.   We then went back near the flag-ship, and
lay waiting till the French were ready at seven o'clock.   I
cannot describe to you my anxiety ; for though I had only
two hours' sleep the two previous nights (last night I had
four, so that I have had six hours in the last seventy-two),
I could not go to sleep, but was fancying how all would
be thrown out if I had made any mistake.   You know
how I can fancy things sometimes !   At last up went the
signal, off went Captain Wemyss's mortar (each division
trying one shell for the range).   After an anxious thirty
seconds, a little cloud of smoke with some fragments of a
roof, *just in the right position*, took a weight off my mind ;
and when two, three, and four *all went in well also*, each
showing its little cloud of smoke over some devoted building in the right spot, I believe I showed my delight in
some rather extravagant and unusual capers on the paddle-
box!   About this I need not say more than that no
change whatever had to be made in the charge or in the
range.

"Well, after a little spell, batteries from all directions
on shore sent shot and shell out in return, but so many

fell short that it was soon reduced to a few guns of long range, and two or three *uncomfortably* heavy long-range

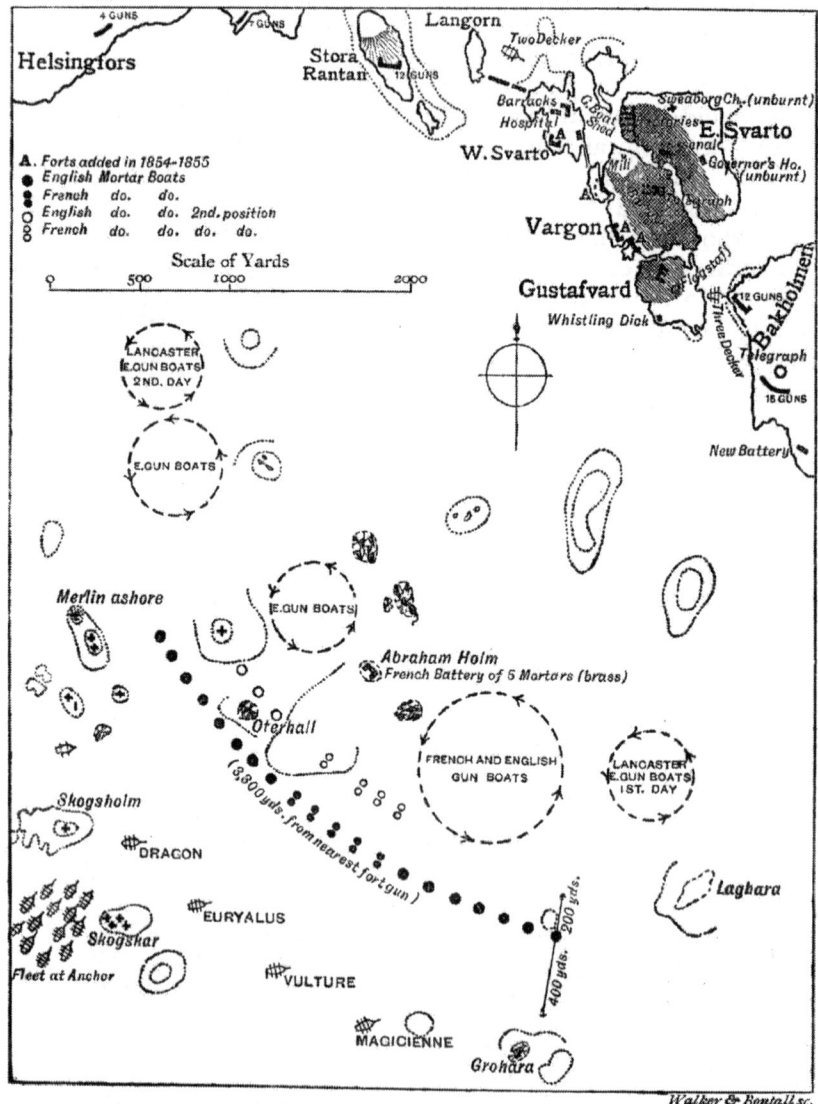

mortars, which sent shot and shell well out to the line if they wished to. But soon our gun-boats went in and began firing at shorter ranges, and this made the fire from the shore little or nothing for the mortar-vessels, and they steadily went on, causing little clouds and occasionally more smoke, which soon began to show itself in good columns of smoke, and fires were established in several places.

"About ten we could see we were evidently successful, and that total destruction was only a question of time. At ten a magazine blew up, bringing rounds of cheers from the crews of the large ships swarming on every top and yard like bees. Still went on smoke and fire, followed by flames through roofs and windows. We were running up and down along the line, with the admiral on board, occasionally being able to swear we were under fire by a stray shot dropping near us, and one shell of the big mortar (named 'Whistling Dick,' after his Sevastopol brother) bursting a little over us, throwing the fragments on both sides of us, but not one touched us anywhere. One of my greatest pleasures, next to the feeling that I had proved to be right in my ideas about the effect of shelling in this way, was to see the changed visage of the admiral : instead of the anxious, thoughtful face of past weeks—anxious to do all he could, doubtful if any success to warrant the risk could be gained—he was looking bright and cheerful, and expressing surprise at the result. At twelve another small magazine exploded, bringing more cheers ; but at 12.15 a tremendous column of smoke, mixed with fragments of all kinds, masses of timber, etc., showed we had found out a large one ; but no sooner was the astonishment over and the cheers roaring in different directions, than up went another column and more fragments, and again another and another, with only intervals of seconds, till at least twenty explosions had followed the first in quick succession. Occasionally towards the end a longer interval would make us think it was over, when again masses of building would fly up in all directions, but all near one spot. At last it reached a larger new earthen battery on the top of Gustaff Island, and away went one side of it, guns and all, leaving, instead of bright-green turf, a heap of stones and rubbish. I think it was all on the inner slope of Gustaff, where I have written m. Now nothing is to be seen about there but bare space ; and even on the next island, Vargon, the buildings on the point nearest to it are a heap of ruins. I think such an extraordinary explosion never occurred before. There might have been greater single ones. The fort I was under at Bomarsund, from the account of those who saw both, was a more tremendous explosion than the first ; but a succession of at least twenty—some say thirty—is the extraordinary part. I think they must have had the magazines formed in cells or compartments of masonry, and that these went in succession, each blowing up its next-door neighbour by smashing the intervening wall, which might have caused the second or two's interval between each.

"The gun-boats gradually worked nearer the shore, and sent plenty of shot and shell in, but, except smashing the batteries and houses, did little damage ; it was the *plumping*, heavy mortar-shell that did the work, and the gun-boats played a good part by taking the attention of the enemy's guns off the mortar-boats Shot dropped round them, shell burst over them, but they escaped wonderfully, being so small and in constant motion. They were handled very well, though two or three times I had some trouble with stupid ones, who would forget all about the shallow ground they were to avoid. The admiral had declared he would not recommend one of them who did not attend strictly to the directions on that head. Once I recalled one and pointed out that he was in dangerous ground, and again showed him the places he must keep in. Not long after one got on shore in the *very place*, and it took three gun-boats a long time to get him off. Fortunately for the lieutenant, I did not see it was the same I had recalled, for the admiral was on board us, and if I had known it I should most certainly have pointed it out to him, for this was my duty. The officers would not tell me, knowing I would do so ; it would have lost him his promotion to a certainty.

" In the evening the fires were very fine ; all the buildings on Vargon were in flames, shooting through roofs and windows in streams The fine centre building, many stories high, with ornamental turret, with the telegraph and flag-staff on it, and the flag flying, escaped for some time, but at last a stream of flame poured up round the posts and trellis-work of the turret, and staff and all soon fell, and soon after the fire poured through the windows, and then ran on through the large range of buildings extending from the central one. But it was evident that the mortar practice was so true that, instead of spreading round the two islands, it was just destroying the ranges of buildings fired at ; so I advised the admiral to move in four of the more distant mortar-vessels four hundred yards nearer during the night, so as to reach Swarto. The mortars were failing, so that they dared not increase the charge This was ordered ; and as the admiral had urged me to get some rest in the night, instead of going myself to place them, we had the lieutenant in charge of all the mortar-vessels on board, and pointed out the spots they were to go to on the chart, and sent him to the captain of that division to explain it. Having had one hour's sleep each of the two previous nights, I went to bed at eleven, and had four hours' sleep, when I was called, as the signal was made to fire. When I got on deck, the mortar-boats were firing and the gun-boats going in, *but not one of my four distant ones were in position.* I found that it had been necessary to fill up their shell in the night, and that they could not be got ready before daylight ; but Vansittart was working very hard to bring them in, and had just got one in when I got there. The enemy had evidently plucked up spirit, for they were firing from every direction, and shot and shell were going farther than the first day. They had evidently been increasing the elevation in the night. Even in the *Merlin*, though I left her a little farther out, while I was placing the mortar-boats, shot went over her ; and as we were doubling our line of mortar-boats in that spot, which was sure to bring more fire, as they would be thicker, I was annoyed to see that several gun-boats had left their proper station at the east end, and had crowded into the space for two, just inside my inner mortar-vessels, so that it brought such a cluster together that nearly all the guns were firing at it. Shots were dropping in all directions, splashing the water against the vessels' sides, and occasionally, though very rarely, one going into a gun-boat. In one of the mortar-boats I was standing talking to the captain of the fleet, my gig close alongside, when one of the large mortar-shells plumped down *close* to us, about two or three feet from the side we were standing against, and close to my gig's stern, and the next moment I saw a large shot strike near one of the outer mortar-boats. As that gun-boat's ground was Stewart's (of *Dragon*), and I found he with me disliked the others coming, these drawing fire on his two, I told him to send all the others away to the eastward, their proper station, where they could draw the fire off the mortar-boats instead of on to them, and immediately the heavy fire on that part stopped and the others got their

share.   Hewlett* had two gun-boats with Lancaster guns,
specially trying all the first day to hit the three-decker;
but though he struck her a few times, she seemed not much
hurt.   It made them remove her in the night, which was
an advantage, for she had one of the longest range, very
heavy guns firing from her gangway port.

"I am sorry to say the admiral let two 'blocks' (*Hastings*
and *Cornwallis*) and *Amphion* engage a small fort to the
eastward, where they happened to be stationed, about six
miles off; and though they did it some damage and upset
a gun, yet it was soon replaced, and one 'block' and
Amphion were struck many times in the hull, and *Amphion's*
main-yard shot in two, so that they hauled out.   Providentially no man was killed, but eleven in the *Cornwallis*
and three in *Amphion* were wounded, and all for nothing.
It could have done no good had they knocked the fort to
pieces   They told me that soon after they went out the
fort was as perfect as ever   It may be of use to show the
folly of putting ships against such batteries.   We destroyed
a large place, without a man being hurt, in spite of the
numerous batteries to protect it.   They met loss and
damage in trying to silence one small battery.   It was the
only part of the play I had nothing to do with, for the
admiral did not tell me they were going to do it till after
the vessels had started, and then I told him it could do no
good, and only risk damage and loss.

" We soon got our four vessels in, and two French mortar-
vessels were also closer, and I hoped we should reach
all Swarto; but the mortars were beginning to show such
signs of danger of bursting from cracks in the chambers :
one had burst in two pieces, one going overboard, the other
in the forecastle, without hurting a man, and the cracks in
others were being filled up by the engineer with tin and
zinc to keep the powder out of them, so that we had to use
smaller charges   Robert's slung mortars were the first to go,
from their slings breaking; but the chambers suffered less,
and the engineers refitted the slings, and they were again
got into play.   The French mortars, of a new construction,
stood well, even with twenty-two pounds of powder, ours
going bad with only eighteen pounds; but theirs did not
range as far as ours—they were twelve inch, ours thirteen.
In consequence of the mortars failing, we did not reach
the northern part of Swarto; so that while we had plenty

* Captain of the *Edinburgh*.

of damage and destruction and roaring fires all day, the
large white house on the east of Swarto, and the large
buildings near the church in the west, seemed to escape us.
In fact, our fire reached up to a certain point, and we could
not get it beyond : had the mortars stood, we could have
ensured every spot going.

" I ought to have stated that in my orginal plan, printed
by the Admiralty, I had proposed placing mortars on all
the rocky islets in addition to those in the vessels ; and
therefore the French sent a land-service mortar-battery of
four mortars, which, though on a rock closer than intended
(as they were only ten-inch mortars), did good service
without the loss of a man.   Our Government did not send
any land-service mortars.

" I have tried to show by the shaded parts the extent of
the destruction by our fire.   The front of Vargon had few
buildings, only lines of forts   Two escaped burning, but
were much hit by the gun-boats.   The very black parts
show the large masses of buildings destroyed.   The mortars
not so close were completing the destruction of the portions
of Vargon, and soon a tremendous fire commenced raging
on the north part of Vargon, where I have marked docks,
etc. (the dense black smoke and flames of which raging up
in the air showed it was caused by tar-pitch or some such
combustible).   It evidently spread rapidly, and soon we
saw it extending to the extreme west point of Vargon,
swallowing up lines of sheds, etc.   Not long after the
large range of sheds on the west point of Swarto, called
gun-boat sheds, caught fire, and the fires were far more
extensive and brilliant than the first day (I forgot to say
that in the night the rocket-boats went in and threw
hundreds of rockets in).   The first day it was chiefly the
grand public buildings and houses, but to-day they were
evidently stores or combustible matter of some sort, with
more wooden buildings.   A very extensive and high building, near the gun-boat sheds, was in flame this evening, and
at last a brilliant fire coming out of the hollow between the
islands, just in the spot of the arsenal, showed that it had
been fired.   The space between the islands was one dense
mass of fire by night-time, showing the lines of the large
buildings on Vargon clearly, as the fire was shining through
their empty window openings.   The dense fire prevented
our seeing what damage was being done to my friends the
white house and the building near the church, which I

had given as special marks to the sergeants of marine artillery, but when I could get a glimpse of them they seemed uninjured. The fact was, we could not range to them, from having to reduce the charge of powder in our mortars ; but the white house as a mark was just the thing to drop the shell on the arsenal.

"During the day I assure you I got plenty of compliments on the result of the attack, from admirals downwards, but I was also to endure a severe trial and mortification when taking the admirals on board to go our evening rounds with them along the line   I had just started, fortunately with a boat in tow, which obliged us to go less than half-speed, as a little breeze made a sea that threw water into her. We were just entering one end of the line, and were close to a mortar-vessel, when, to my astonishment, we ran bang on shore on a rock with only six feet, on which poor *Merlin's* fore-foot and some feet of keel were fixed so firmly that two heavy steamers, with anchors laid out and full speed in addition, could not start us. Fancy my feelings! There was a rock I knew well a little inside, but this one had escaped us in all our soundings and running to and fro, there being seven fathoms close to it. We must have shaved it often before, and often at full speed. Had not the boat prevented our going fast, we should have torn her old weak bows out, and she would have sunk there. As it was, she has torn off nearly three feet in depth of her fore-foot, and pieces of keel are all sticking out several feet long. I had bargained for a few hours' good sleep that night, and yet had to work all through it, trying to get off. I feared when daylight broke they would point all their guns at our group. At 3 a.m. Captain Wemyss came to me to say that two more mortars had burst, but had hurt no one, and that the others were complaining so much that he feared to go on, so I advised him to stop all till he told the admiral. And there really ended our attack, for it was decided not to fire them any more. We ought to have had a duplicate set to replace them. However, there was little left to do. The line on the north side of Swarto being untouched, that would have been a good place to shell ; also the small island of West Swarto, with three good buildings on it, which had only been shelled by gun-boats. A fourth mortar burst immediately after.

"[*Private.*] *Sunday*, 12*th* —I will continue the journal to-morrow. We have had a quiet Sunday, and we go to Nargen to-morrow. Some have tried to induce the chief to make an attempt on Helsingfors; but it is very different. We should have to go half the distance from the batteries we were at Sweaborg, and then, with no good mortars, would have to depend principally on our rockets for burning the town, and the only part that we could reach would be the poorer part of dwelling-houses; so that, for our own sakes, I could not advise it, as a repulse there would undo much of our success here. But on far higher motives I have always opposed it. I think it far more honourable to us as a Christian nation to spare the city of private property, while we destroy the fortress and arsenal. Should we not think so of a French general if he *could* burn the dock-yard, etc., at Portsmouth (and of course there the town would have to take its chance), but who went away without destroying Cowes and Ryde? If cities and towns are to be destroyed when a fleet can reach them, why not every city or town on shore that an invading army marches into? I look upon Cronstadt, Sevastopol, and places like that— Brest and Toulon even—as government arsenals, and the towns as part of them, which must take their chance with the arsenals; but I hope we shall never set an example of destroying coast towns, or war will become more barbarous than it was fifty years since. They fully expect us to bombard Helsingfors, for the inhabitants have fled; only soldiers are to be seen, and ladders are placed against the buildings, as in Sweaborg, for putting fires out. I may be wrong; but if we had new mortars out, and every means at our disposal, I would advise the admiral the same, though I would undertake to destroy it with the means we have here, if I thought it right.

"But I must not run on. We had a nice quiet forenoon, and I think I never saw the crew more impressed with the service. I did not omit adding thanksgiving for the great mercies we have received. I was glad to find that the admiral would not write his despatches to-day, as he could do so to-morrow; but as we were to sail early to-morrow, he wished me before we went to take him to two islands in the extreme east and west positions, where we could see most of the destruction, in order that he might be sure what to state in his despatch. He was obliged to go this afternoon, but he took a little steamer instead of *Merlin*. We had a good view, and he was much surprised at the complete destruction of everything that came within the

22

range of our shells; not a roof of any kind left over the whole space—utter destruction. As I know what I write will not be mentioned beyond those who read this, I will venture to tell you the gratifying way the admiral spoke to me to-day when alone in his cabin I asked him if he had any objection to my writing him a few lines to recommend my officers, and especially the first lieutenant (Hewett), for the assistance they have given me. He said, 'Sulivan, I will do anything I can for the *Merlin's* officers, for I owe you a debt of gratitude that I cannot repay,' and he became quite overcome and went out into the stern gallery. After a little, though he could hardly speak—neither could I—he said, 'You may depend I will specially recommend Mr. Creyke—you need not write about him; but I must tell you that there is not an officer in the fleet but must feel that we owe this success chiefly to you.' I am sure you will all acquit me of egotism because I mention this, but it was the most gratifying moment of my public service. I tried to thank him, but could not say much, and we parted with a warmer pressure of hands than often takes place between a senior and a junior. Is it not very noble of him to show such utter neglect of wanting to take the credit of it, even that justly belongs to him, who had all the anxiety and responsibility of it? One of the most gratifying rewards I receive is the general expression, from Admiral Seymour down to the youngest officers, of congratulations to me on the success, and all captains, senior and junior, showing such feelings of interest in my favour, without the envy or jealousy that some might be expected to feel. It makes me condemn myself, and wonder how I have been spared, protected, and assisted, when I have been so little thankful for previous temporal mercies, and have even been discontented with my lot in some respects. I am very sorry Otter was not here. I asked the admiral at Cronstadt to have *Firefly* here before we began, to help us in the surveying work, wishing Otter and his first lieutenant might not lose the chance. He promised me he would At Nargen I reminded him of it, but he said he had heard from the senior officer of the Bothnia squadron of so many of the ships getting on shore that he could not take *Firefly* from him, as a surveying-vessel was so needed there; and I think he was right, but I am very sorry for them."

" I will try to continue from Friday evening. We were tugging at *Merlin* with *Cossack* and *Geyser* fast to her, but had to lighten her by throwing coals overboard. I thought the three ships would draw all the Russians' fire on us at daylight ; but as our mortars were done up and we were not firing, they seemed unwilling to commence against us, which saved us annoyance from shot and shell, as we were just within the limit of their longest ranges. While clearing, at noon I got a gun-boat from the admiral, and went to the east side of the place as far as I could to look through the islands. The arsenal fire was still raging, and the ruin over the back part of Swarto, as well as Vargon, was complete. The devastation caused by the grand explosion was terrible on Gustafsvard, but my friend the white house had only one shell-mark, and a house beyond it was uninjured ; the long house west of it was burnt out at its south end, showing the extreme limit of destruction in that part. In the evening I went in my boat with Creyke to a nice place for looking between the islands from the westward, an island off Helsingfors, with a high rock, but only two thousand yards from all the Helsingfors batteries. On all the batteries men sat quietly looking at us, officers watching us with spy-glasses, but they did not fire. From there we saw that within the limits I have shown dark the destruction is so complete that not even a portion of a house is left, all a blackened, shattered ruin, but the windmill and two wooden houses on the eastern front, which seem to have been charmed. Between the large black building on the west end of Swarto and the church just outside our range, a little cluster of wooden houses stands quite uninjured, affording a striking contrast to the blackened ruins. The space between that black building and the long storehouses in the middle of Swarto is covered with the ruin of smaller stone houses, apparently dwellings.

" Our mortars having all broken down or become dangerous to fire, the thing was over at 2 p.m. *Merlin* hove off, and I am glad to say only grass and false keel have suffered. The second night the rockets went in beautifully in all directions, the boats going closer in ; these were fired at with shot and shell, but no one hurt, except by two accidents. A stupid lieutenant in *Vulture's* boat had two rockets lying uncovered under the thwart when firing another. He was warned of the danger, but neglected it. The rocket was fired, and the back-fire fired the rocket in the boat, which went through her bows, wounding seven men. In Luckraft's boat a rocket burst in the tube—an accident sometimes occurring—and, breaking the tube, wounded four or five men; but to the last, by the enemy's fire, not a man was hurt, thus bearing out fully the hopes expressed in my last letter to you that we should have success without losing a man's life.

"Yesterday all sailed for this place, *Merlin* remaining with *Locust* to take up all the buoys and say 'good-bye'!

"We have just got the mail. All the papers seem to have articles complaining of our doing nothing. I hope they will be satisfied I wonder if they know that the vessel with the shell only reached us three days before we commenced operations? Surely we did not lose much time, as it has turned out that the delay was to our advantage, the longer nights helping us. The four fine days ended yesterday, and to-day we have dirty weather, the glass falling much, though everything seems to have favoured us, except the rotten mortars. It is a disgrace to our iron-founders that *one old mortar of the last war* stood three hundred and fifty rounds, while all the others, quite new, were unfit for use, or burst after two hundred to two hundred and fifty. I hope the Government will have a good row with the contractors. The iron is said to be bad. There is much in this that I should on no account like to be read, except by the immediate elder members, because children will talk; and on no account must anything relating to personal matters, the admiral or other officers, go beyond those.

"A major of Indian engineers says that eleven days' bombardment at Mooltan did nothing like the damage, and when he left Sevastopol not long since it was not nearly so much damaged."

The following note shows why the fleet could not destroy the forts as well as the arsenal :—

"With all the buildings in flames, the batteries were not at all weakened, and the men were in them, free from all the fire, as there were open parades between the mass of buildings and the fortifications. Besides, the flanking batteries in other parts sufficiently protected the front of the main fortress from any attack."

The following is an extract from the Sweaborg despatch of Admiral Dundas. Seldom, perhaps, has a junior officer been so strongly commended :—

> "'DUKE OF WELLINGTON,' BEFORE SWEABORG,
> "*August* 13*th*, 1855.

"SIR,—The intricate nature of the ground, from rocks a-wash and reefs under water, rendered it difficult to select positions for the mortar-vessels at proper range. In completing the arrangements for this purpose, I have derived the greatest advantage from the abilities of Captain Sulivan, of H.M.S. *Merlin.* . . .

"Late on the evening of the 10th inst., H.M.S. *Merlin*, under the command of Captain Sulivan, struck upon an unknown rock, on ground which he had himself repeatedly examined, while conducting me along the line of the mortar-vessels. No blame whatever can attach to this officer on the occasion, and I gladly avail myself of the opportunity which is thus afforded me of calling the especial attention of their lordships to the unwearied activity of this valuable officer. It is to the singular ability and zeal with which his arduous duties have been performed that much of the success of the operations of the fleet may be attributed; and I trust that I may be permitted on this occasion to recommend to the especial notice of their lordships the services of Commander R. B. Creyke, of that ship, whose conduct has been most favourably reported.

> "I have, etc.,
> "R. S. DUNDAS,
> "*Rear-admiral and Commander-in-chief.*
> "THE SECRETARY OF THE ADMIRALTY."

The importance of the action is well shown in Admiral Penaud's despatch. I have only a translation of it :—

> "'TOURVILLE,' OFF SWEABORG, *August* 11*th*, 1855.

"MONSIEUR LE MINISTRE,—I am happy to announce to you, Monsieur le Ministre, that this operation succeeded perfectly; it was not only a simple cannonade which the squadrons have made against Sweaborg, it was a real bombardment, the important results of which have exceeded my utmost hopes.

"Every one had only one object—to rival each other in zeal, and cause the enemy the greatest possible mischief; and the success of a vessel of one of the two nations was applauded by the other with the same cries of enthusiasm as if it had been gained by its own flag. Doubtless, Monsieur le Ministre, the bombardment of Sweaborg will exercise considerable influence on the Russian people, who have not acquired the conviction that their fortified places and their arsenals are not completely sheltered from the attacks of the allied navies, which may and must hope to be able to deal destruction on the enemy's coast without suffering any very considerable injury themselves.

" I am, etc.,
" PENAUD." *

The following letter to Captain Sulivan from Major Wemyss, the marine artillery officer in charge of the mortars at Sweaborg, may be of interest :—

" PORTSMOUTH, January 7th, 1857.

"I thank you for your hearty congratulations. I had been looking out a long time to see some reward conferred on you for your valuable services, both in suggestion and execution in the Baltic. Well do I recollect your anxiety that an expedition should be sent to bombard Sweaborg, and your great activity and clearness of judgment in making the arrangements and dispositions for carrying out the affair.

" It has escaped the notice of many people that I had in the Baltic not only to organise a new service with a long-forgotten weapon, and answer for its effects in action being destructive at a great distance, but also that I departed from the old custom of slow firing. . . . I had to undergo criticism, until subsequent experiments proved that it was the bad mortars, and not the bad usage of them, that brought us to so crippled a state. But the responsibility of departing from long-established precedent was a heavy one. Vertical fire from the sea has now been greatly developed, and will be made great use of by the power that commands the sea in a future war. May that power still be our own country ! . . .

" I agree with you perfectly that mortars should be

---

* From "History of the War with Russia " (W. Tyrrell).

expended at bombardments like any other stores, but ours were infamously bad. . . .

"If it is unpleasant to stand over a bursting shell, how much more so is it to have to serve a mortar which is likely to burst the next round! I think our men in the Baltic behaved splendidly in making no difficulty when three mortars had burst, and the remainder were so unsound."

NOTE.—A French naval officer has drawn conclusions from the operations in the Baltic and Black Seas which support Captain Sulivan's views as to the value of vertical fire, described in a later chapter: "C'est à des feux courbes, partant d'une flottille de bombardes et combinés avec les puissants feux de brèche des batteries flottantes, que nous semble appartenir l'avenir des attaques maritimes. C'est par l'emploi persévérant du tir vertical . . . que la marine pourra . . . agir . . . contre les places de l'ennemi. . . . Cette nouvelle tactique navale. . . . La déstruction opérée à Sweaborg par une trentaine de mortiers marins . . . à Odessa, Sébastopol . . . confirment ces prévisions sur l'avenir réservé aux feux courbes de la marine. La flottille française lança sur Sweaborg 4,150 projectiles, dont 2,828 bombes. Un auteur anglais évalue à 3,099 bombes la quantité de feux courbes lancés par les 16 bombardes britanniques. . . . Les cinques bombardes françaises, spécialement construites pour cette destination, et plus solidement installées, en armaient chacun deux (mortiers). La flottille anglaise aurait lancé, en outre, 11,200 boulets ou obus" ("Attaques et bombardements maritimes, Obligado, Bomarsund, Sweaborg," etc., Lieut. M. Richild Grivel, 1857).

CHAPTER XV.

AFTER SWEABORG.

No active operations were undertaken by the Baltic fleets after the bombardment of Sweaborg, consequently the journals that follow record no striking events. But the accounts of further intercourse with the islanders, and the opinions given as to the principles of humanity on which a war should be conducted, may be found interesting and instructive.

"[*Private.*]

"NARGEN, *August* 16th, 1855.

"We are lying here quiet, preparing mortar-boats for going home, and I hope all hostilities are over for the season, because there is nothing that could be done with a prospect of success that is worth the risk of loss and failure. There was a comparatively trifling thing for some time on the admiral's mind instead of Sweaborg: the only advantage would be destroying a town, and there was every prospect of defeat in attempting it, and certain considerable loss of life if successful. Yet the chief had feared we could not succeed at Sweaborg, and thought it was better to do a small thing well than fail in a great one ; and my work for two months had been persuading him that the certainty of success was at Sweaborg, and the risk of loss and defeat at the other place. It is because I induced him to give up the other and to determine on Sweaborg that he feels so grateful to me. It shows how much risk of defeat and loss of life may be saved by thoroughly considering and weighing well these subjects. Captain Caffin to-day, whom I had not seen since the action, told me that the chief spoke to him of me in such terms that he could not repeat them.

"*Monday,* 27*th.*—The admiral sent for me to-day, and has had a long talk about the French admiral wishing to try some new rockets against Revel. They have great range,

344

so that they are fired out of reach of the enemy's guns.
He also wants to use his mortar-vessels again, as at Sweaborg. Now he cannot reach the town with them, and so
would only make a half-and-half thing of it. I quite agree
with the admiral [Dundas] that it will be better to try the
rockets only ; but if he [Penaud] is determined to try the
mortar-vessels, it is his own look-out if he fails. I think
he is anxious to do something *alone*, knowing we can have
no share in it now our mortar-vessels are gone. Of course
if he chooses to act he can ; but I hope the admiral will
not have anything to do with it, further than allowing me
to give them the distance and put down some buoys for
them, if they like. Otter has had a brush somewhere in
Finland. They had a concealed battery, and he went up
to try and destroy some timber, etc., thinking he was only
likely to be exposed to musketry ; but being unable to go
where he wished, was trying to get back, when the battery
opened on him, and he had to go out backwards ; but he
only had one man wounded. A deserter, who has been
landed, and been to Helsingfors, says that no one is allowed
to go to Sweaborg, but that the accounts brought over to
Helsingfors are that stores of hemp, pitch, rope, and corn
were burnt, besides houses and eighteen vessels, including
some hulks the sailors lived in, and that two thousand were
killed (quite impossible). But it is certain that the hospitals
in Helsingfors are full of wounded, so that they cannot
hold more. I was afraid there was sad loss among them.

" 28*th*.—I have just heard from those in ships far to
the eastward of Sweaborg, who had a better view of the
north part than we had, the fires were distinctly seen to
spread far northward of the church, and some inflam-
mable material burnt fiercely on the north shore of the
island for three hours, so that it did not escape, as I
thought. Our shells did not reach it, but the fire must
have spread across the middle of the island, where there
were numerous ruined houses, and so reached the large
boat-sheds on the north side ; so the destruction is more
complete than I fancied. I am going to ask the admiral,
after all the other work is over, to let me spend the
remaining time completing surveys of different parts."

"' MERLIN,' NARGEN, *September 1st*, 1855.

" We returned yesterday from a trip to near Cronstadt,
to take lights and buoys to Admiral Seymour, and we

have been away with the admiral all to-day to Baro Sound, looking at the snug places I have picked out for the colliers, etc, to anchor in. I think we have nothing more to do now than to select good anchorages for the rest of the season, for I believe both admirals have deferred trying anything more this year, and I hope the mortars talked of will not be sent. The admiral wants me soon to make a plan of the anchorage between Wormso and Dago, which will, I think, be a good one for the large ships ; and I shall perhaps be there next week, and shall see my friends the baron and baroness again, and have some more ice-creams and roses! You would, I am sure, have been gratified, could you have seen the kind reception I met with at Cronstadt from all my brother-captains, who soon came on board to congratulate me on the success at Sweaborg. It is the more gratifying to see such thorough kindness and absence of jealousy at juniors getting such positions, when we consider that they are all our seniors— leading men, such as Hope, Codrington, Erskine, Elliot, and Watson, who have themselves been shared out of everything through commanding the larger ships, and who have to see their juniors in small ships getting a name in the service. Gardner has been here the last few days. He said a blessing seemed to rest on what I and others did ; for Otter had been surprised in a most dangerous position, and had to escape with thirty-four men in two crowded boats, under a fire of six hundred rifles, and though the boats had twenty-four balls in them, not a man was hurt. Ward had a narrow escape, a ball grazing his head. I am sorry to say they retook Otter's prize from him, in which were all the men's arms, rifles, cutlasses, etc. You may suppose many are very anxious for the mail to-morrow.

"I wish the poor fishermen at Dago and other places could be allowed salt for their own use to cure fish for this winter, or their sufferings will be terrible, and this will have no effect on the war either way. I fear they will all try to cross in the boats before the ice forms, when the severe weather has forced our ships away, and then numbers will be lost, while some will get a little salt over. I hope many escaped this spring when others were taken."

The following is a copy of a letter which appeared at

this time in the *Cornish Gazette* (it is said to have been written by a seaman of the *Duke of Wellington*):—

" At five o'clock the *Merlin* got on a rock, commanded by Captain Sulivan, son to Admiral Sulivan, who resided at Falmouth : the most enterprising officer in the fleet ; for his abilities in surveying, and his qualities in other respects, endear him to the seamen. If they could do it, they would make him chief in command, I think, without opposition. ' Paddy Sulivan ' they call him, not out of disrespect, but for his daring and brave qualities. I must say I am glad he has relatives so close on board the ' one and all boys.' We were sorry to see him on the rock, for he must have been as uneasy in mind to be detained on the rock as a ' cat in pattens ' He is such a funny turn, always on the move."

" ADMIRALTY, *August 21st,* 1855.

" DEAR SULIVAN,—Accept my sincere and cordial congratulations on the success of your attack on Sweaborg, which the admiral justly attributes to your skill in placing the mortar-boats. The admiral's praise is very gratifying ; it does him great credit , and we are all thankful to you for the high character you have obtained for the surveying service. I am glad Creyke has been found so useful ; he will certainly be promoted. Sir C. Wood has promised it to me.

" JOHN WASHINGTON,
" *Hydrographer.*"

" NARGEN, *September 30th, 31st, October 1st, finished 2nd.*

" Yesterday week the admiral sent for me in the evening, and told me he wanted me to start early next morning (Sunday) to the reef where —— had been on shore. So we started at break of day ; and as the wind was southerly, I went along the coast, and, never having seen Port Baltic closely, I went close round the head inside the shoals. On the head (cliff) where the lighthouse stands, there was a party of soldiers occupying the house of the lighthouse. The sentry was pacing up and down with his musket, but others were unarmed, standing or lying down on the edge of the cliff, looking at us passing under them : very wisely, they did not think of firing at us. After giving orders to the *Bulldog*, I went on to the entrance of the Wormso Sound, and anchored under the outer bank about 2 p.m., ready to begin our work the next morning, as I was to remain there to make a survey of the place, to see if I was quite right in thinking it would be a secure anchorage for the large ships. We had our service in the afternoon I felt weak and unwell all day. On Monday I was in a good deal of pain inside, which affected my legs, so that I could not stand for many minutes at a time, but having a beautiful day for our work, by sitting out and sometimes reclining on the paddle-box, I was able to get on till the afternoon, when we went into Wormso Sound; and I lay down for the rest of the day by the doctor's orders. By Tuesday morning I was quite free from pain, but my head felt very uneasy. The day was again lovely, so I could not lose it, and I landed on an island, while Creyke went to another, and got all the observations we wanted. After dinner, feeling pretty well, I tried to work at the chart; but in half an hour, from merely thinking over it, my head got in such a state that I had to give it up, and I think I have not for years suffered so much in that way as I did all the evening till I could get to sleep about eight. It was not like a headache, but pains flying about and quite overpowering me; but a good sleep removed it, and on Wednesday morning, though I felt weak, my head was free from pain, and we started on our work.

" I went on Wednesday to Wormso Island, where I thought a walk would do me good, and where I wanted several stations The French admiral had told me that he had given directions to two small vessels of his down there, that if any of the buoys were removed they should hold the baron responsible, and they were to take fifty of his cattle and cut down a hundred of his trees. I, thinking he alluded to my friend Baron Sternberg, said I was sure no one in Dago would touch the buoys, but it would be done, if at all, by the authorities from the mainland, so that it would be hard to visit it on the islands On landing at Wormso, we saw two men and some women on the point, and about three hundred head of cattle and a flock of sheep, every one of which we could have made a prize of if we chose The first man we got to proved to be the same we caught in the boat off Hapsal two months since. When we went up to two young

women to speak to them, they began to cry, and were so
terrified that we could only pacify them by going away,
though the men seemed to assure them that we should
not hurt them.   We saw some nice-looking buildings about
two miles off among trees ; and after we had finished at the
point and were walking along the shore (Hewett was with
me, with the coxswain and Pierse the Finlander), a respectable man rode up to us, and with many bows told us that
'the baron' was coming down immediately.   I asked
him what baron ; he said 'Baron Stakleberg,' and soon
after he came, a young man about thirty.   He could only
understand a few words of English, but with Pierse we
got on with Swedish.   He begged me to go up to his
house, where I should meet an English lady, and a carriage
would be down directly ; he asked me to take his pony,
and he mounted his head-man's.   We passed the carriage
which went on for Hewett.   I found a very nice house,
though on a smaller scale and less splendidly furnished
than Baron Sternberg's, and breakfast on the table.   He
introduced me to Miss Cooper, who spoke English with
a slightly foreign accent.   She has been twenty years in
Russia, and had not often a chance of practising English.
Shortly after a good-looking young lady entered, with
remarkably sharp, bright eyes, and evidently plenty of
intelligence : this was madame the baroness.   She spoke a
little English, but preferred carrying on the conversation
entirely through Miss Cooper.   After some little talk,
they asked me the name of my ship.   When I told them,
they all exclaimed, 'Then you are Captain Sulivan ?' and
certainly they did not seem less pleased to see me.   She
said, 'Baron Sternberg will be very glad to see you again.'
They had seen him in Revel last week.   They said they
had read Admiral Dundas's despatches.   The lady, like
the other baroness, seemed the politician of the party.   The
fact is, she is Russian—he *Esthonian.*   When I said I
hoped the fall of Sevastopol might lead to peace soon, she
quite fired up, struck her little fist on the table, and the
fire seemed to flash out of her bright eyes, as she said,
'What ! peace now ? *No, never* till we have driven you
out of the Crimea again.'   The *Cossack* had been in a few
days before, and Captain Cochrane had dined with them.
While at breakfast we saw from the window the 'demand'
up in *Merlin.*   I thought it was *Magicienne,* as she was to
be stationed there, so I promised to return to dinner at

five and bring Vansittart with me, and they told me where
we could anchor near the west landing-place with a road
to their house. They then drove us down in two carriages,
Miss Cooper being with me.

"When I got off, I found the vessels were two French
gun-boats. I spent the afternoon sounding outside in
the ship, and then anchored at four just as a carriage
came down, and Hewett and I went out to the house.
I was really better for my day's exercise. We had a
very plain, neat little dinner, all on a much smaller
scale, servants and all, than the Dago baron's We
had a long chat till half-past ten. Miss Cooper has the
Illustrated L N. regularly, but in every paper whole para-
graphs are painted out before they are allowed to be
circulated. I had brought the same numbers from the
ship, and they were all very anxious to know the forbidden
parts. They were entirely remarks on the late emperor
or the Russian objects of the war.

"The baron was very sore on one point, which he
did not hesitate to express when his wife was out of
the room, and only Miss Cooper to interpret; and that
was the injustice of his being compelled to bring up
his son in the Greek Church because his wife is Greek
Church, though he is a Protestant. While, if he had been
Greek and the wife Protestant, the children must be
Greek, and also that a Greek dare not change his religion
for Protestant. On leaving, I promised to stop there on
my way back from Dago if I could.

"On Thursday morning it was blowing hard from the
westward; and as the Dago side was sheltered, I started
early, intending to get as close as I could there, and then
go to see my friend and endeavour to get up in his church
steeple, which would be a capital station for the survey.
I was half-way on shore in my boat, and a carriage had
already reached the shore for us, when we saw a vessel
coming in, and I had to go back to go out in *Merlin*
to meet her. It proved to be *Cossack*, with two gun-
boats, come to be stationed here instead of *Magicienne*.
I returned in *Merlin* to Dago, taking Captain Cochrane
with me and the gun-boats, and we ran in in one to
the baron's pier, where we found him waiting with a
carriage. We got a pony-cart from the house there for
Bullock and Dyer. We had not gone far when we met
the baroness driving a nice pair of horses, so I got out

and joined her, and then we returned to the castle. I
got up in the steeple, and had a beautiful view; and as
there is another church nine miles off overlooking the
sound, which made another excellent station, the baron
arranged we should drive there the next day. You may
suppose we passed a very pleasant afternoon. We dined
at four; and as it was blowing so hard, and Cochrane had
to go back to his ship ten miles from *Merlin*, we could
not remain till after dark, but returned at six. In Cochrane's ship Prince Ernest of Leiningen, the Queen's
nephew, is a lieutenant, and the baron lived near his mother
in Switzerland, and knew them well, so we arranged that
a gun-boat should bring the prince in early next day to go
with me; and the French gun-boats having joined, I asked
the senior officer, Lieutenant Mer, to go also. As he was
going to remain, I wished him to know the baron, thinking
he would be more likely to prevent his crews committing
any depredations on the people, which, *like some of our
own*, the Frenchmen are rather apt to do. The prince
came in early on Friday, and we landed at nine, where the
carriage with the four ponies abreast was waiting for us,
and we rattled out at a famous pace. The strong wind of
the day before had ceased, and we had again a most lovely
day. At ten we started for the other church with six
ponies, two ahead of the other four, and had a beautiful
drive to the distant church. The steeple was not so
nicely fitted as the first one, and up the narrow part there
was nothing but a single piece of wood with some very
doubtful-looking fir pegs sticking out of it to form a ladder,
and to get up this with a sextant was no easy matter.
Up in the top there were merely a few pieces of wood
across and some loose boards, the diameter of the spire
there being about five feet. The boards were the resting-
place of numerous birds, apparently jackdaws, and there
through a hole I got the observations, the prince also
getting up with the spy-glass and book, and writing down
the angles for me. We were pretty figures when we got
down to the others, who reached the top of the tower, but
did not attempt the spire. I think it was a unique surveying cruise,—some miles inland in an enemy's country;
driven in a carriage and six, accompanied by a Russian
baron, a prince, and a French lieutenant; and the prince
acting as assistant surveyor! It did my work beautifully;
and, as I got the exact distance between the two churches

from a map of the island of the baron's, it gave me the
very best base for my work. They are nearly eight and
a half miles apart, and we drove about eleven to reach it.
We returned an hour before our four o'clock dinner, and
discussed the war till dinner-time.

" The baroness wore a very sensible bonnet, coming well
over the head; but she allowed that even in the depth of
winter, in St. Petersburg, they are such slaves to fashion
that they wear the bonnets only on the backs of the heads,
leaving all the top exposed to the intense cold; and she
says she never wears a veil except to keep wind off, yet
the cold does not hurt her. One fancies that in these
countries they sit in the hot stove-heated rooms, and never
change from them; but she says she goes out walking or
driving regularly all through the winter, and in the most
severe weather has every window open while the rooms
are being done and fires lighted. The stoves are stacks of
masonry in the corners of the rooms; they are heated once
by a wood fire every morning, and then no more fires for
twenty-four hours, but the mass retains its heat all the
time.* The heated air certainly keeps all the room at an
even temperature, which no fireplace can. But in all their
rooms they have also English grates, for the sake of the
cheerful look and ventilation; but they are useless for
warming, they say.

" They had been at Revel the week before, the people
all returning there, now they do not any longer fear it is
to be destroyed by us. The Grand Duke Michael had
just been there; and the baron's brother, who lives there,
was one day with him. He asked if some English officers
had not been visiting his brother in Dago; he said 'Yes.'
The Grand Duke asked if we burnt and destroyed his
property; he said, 'No, only a vessel that was sailing,
but that we treated them very well.' The Grand Duke
said, 'So there is at last one honourable act done by an
Englishman.'

" You cannot imagine the impression that is gone abroad
against us: stories have been invented or exaggerated, and I
believe many think us most brutal barbarians, who burn and

* *Russian heating apparatus.*—In the evening, the chimney being
well heated, the fire is left to die out. When all danger of charcoal
fumes is over, the flue is shut by an iron slide, and a hole under this
(near the top of the room) opened. The air, passing up the grate
(which is usually in the hall), is warmed by the heated bricks, and comes

destroy without mercy ; but sometimes they have too much cause for thinking so. They told me that two women were wounded by rockets in a hay-field, one of whom died. This was of course set down as a deliberate act, though it occurred by some Cossacks coming down to the boats and firing at them, and a random rocket, going inland, unfortunately doing the harm. Besides this, a Count Stakleberg, a relation of the Baroness Sternberg, has a pretty villa and bathing-house on the coast, where he had his whole family, wife and daughters, and some visitors. One beautiful evening they were dining in the verandah, and were looking at some of our vessels off there, and were remarking how pretty they looked. The count had his glass looking at one, and, the dinner being over, the ladies were sitting watching the vessels, when one fired a shot at the house. A large shell went just over their heads into the roof of the house, and burst inside. The ladies were of course greatly alarmed ; horses were put to the carriages instantly, and, just as the first carriage was starting with the ladies, another shell burst so close that one piece struck the carriage. Can you wonder at their thinking us brutes? The baron said that they thought the vessel might have fired at a telegraph on the hill above, and that the shot fell too low, and I thought so too ; but to-day Gallagher, who was surgeon of *Arrogant*, came to see me, and on my asking him he confirmed the whole story. Yelverton and Vansittart had anchored their ships, and went inshore in a gun-boat They saw this house, and Gallagher tells me they saw people at it, when to Yelverton's horror the lieutenant left in charge of *Magicienne* fired from her at *the house*, and they saw the shell strike it. He says he never saw Yelverton so excited. He ordered them to hoist a signal immediately to stop it ; but they were not very quick in the gun-boat, and, before the signal was hoisted and answered, the *Magicienne* fired two more shells. They saw the carriage drive away, and they thought two shells struck the house. Now this shows the Russian accounts are pretty correct. The fact is, there is a kind of unfeeling, senseless anxiety

out through the hole into the room. Thus the rooms are kept warm with fresh air for twelve and even twenty-four hours after the fire has gone out. The rooms being kept by this system at an equable temperature, the Russians are enabled to grow plants indoors as high as the ceiling.—ED.

to fire at anything that gives a chance, for the sake of
firing, and some, I fear, for the sake of notoriety, or the
chance of bringing about the pretence of a fight, so that
they may write a letter.

"I hear that one captain has made himself the laughing-
stock of his brother-captains at Seskar by writing such
a long, flaming letter about taking out some dismantled
little coasters from the cove at the village where we took
our prizes this year, and where last year I had that sham
attack, thinking there was a battery; but there were no
guns in it. You will recollect it, as I would not fire on
the soldiers on the point, though at our mercy—though
some thought that I ought to have done so. Well, this
celebrated battle consisted, I hear, of two muskets being
fired by militiamen on shore, for which a fire was opened
on village, houses, church, and all. The magistrates of
the district were assembled in the clergyman's house, when
the shots began to come into it, and they all had to fly;
and for this a despatch longer than would be necessary
for a general action has, I am told, been written and sent
home, and more names mentioned than in many serious
despatches. Is it not enough to lower us in the estimation
of our enemy, when they, knowing the truth, read such
letters? I am told Yelverton is much annoyed, as this
is where he has been stationed. He would not take out
their little vessels, and knows that if he had wished
to take them he had only to send word to the village
that he was going to do so, to ensure their being given
up without resistance. I am afraid there are few of our
men that can really be trusted in command, or are fit
to decide on what should and should not be done. As
to younger officers, I am sorry to say I see little signs
of any prudence or judgment to prevent them doing any
silly or disgraceful thing, if they can only have a shot
at something, or try to get up a fight for the chance of
getting their names mentioned. One captain, who I hear
is not celebrated for brains, the other day got up a fight
with a fort and some gun-boats, quite useless and sure to
be against him, and the ship with him was much damaged
by a shell. For this I hear there has been a flaming despatch.
But the baron tells me that two large ships (which must
be the same) went to Pernau, and the senior officer sent
on shore to say that all the soldiers in the town must be
surrendered as prisoners, all the vessels given up (there

were some small craft moved far up the river), and all
government stores surrendered, and the burgomaster was
to come off to the ship—the penalty of not complying with
these demands being the destruction of the town.   The
burgomaster went off, and replied that there were no troops,
so he could not surrender any, that the vessels he must come
and take, but they would resist, and that there were no
government stores.   Of course this is the Russian version,
which goes on to say that the captain was so pleased at
the burgomaster's bold conduct that instead of destroying
the town he asked him to dinner.   Now I happen to know
that the said captain asked the admiral to send him gun-
boats to destroy that very town (as ships cannot get within
shot).   The admiral asked me about it, and I advised him
not to allow it, as it would be only wanton destruction
of a defenceless town, and could do no good; and so he
refused him the gun-boats.   That looks as if the story
were correct, but that, as his ship could not carry out
his threat, he tried to get gun-boats to do it.   If so, I am
glad I helped to thwart him.   You must be all very careful
not to let a word on these subjects be mentioned as coming
from me.

"We left them at six, the baron going down with us to
the gun-boat in which we went off to *Merlin*.   The night
was getting dark, and I was doubtful if it would do to let
the gun-boat return to the *Cossack*; and when I expressed
this doubt, Prince Leiningen said he hoped I would not, as
he then would get a night's rest, which he would be glad
of, as he had kept middle and first watches alternately
since he had been in *Cossack*, and it was his middle watch.
So I gave him my spare cabin, and we sat till past ten,
during which he gave me a good deal of interesting information about the Queen, the royal children, etc.   It was
amusing to think that one in his position, with his home
at the palace when on leave, should be anxious to get a
night in bed; but he is a thorough lieutenant, sinking the
prince entirely.   He seems a very intelligent, straightforward person, with a regular John Bull face.

"As I had done all I could towards the chart, I determined to come back here on the Saturday, without waiting
to pay my promised visit to the Wormsö baron's party
again.   So I sent a message to them by Cochrane, and a
Swedish Bible (all the Wormso people are Swedes).   I
told them I could give the people some Bibles, and the

baron said he should like to see what General Grable (who commands all this district from Revel, and of whom they seem afraid) would say, as he told him they must take nothing from us. So he said if I would give him a Bible for an old man who once served in an English man-of-war, and would write my name in it, he would write to General Grable asking permission for the man to have it, just to see what answer he would give. I forgot to say that they 'were at Hapsal when I went there in the gun-boats, and they gave a similar description to my last of the consternation there Miss Cooper offered to come off to us in a little boat, but they would not let her. The man in the boat to whom we gave the things was coming to them with a letter. He landed away from the town, for fear of the custom-house officers taking away his things, and he got to the baron's house just as some of them were following him. So he rushed in, to their astonishment, and began throwing tobacco behind one piece of furniture, biscuits here and there in corners out of sight, and sugar and tea in the same, so that he got all out of sight before the custom-house officers got in. The people were expecting us to land, and one carriageful and some horsemen we saw on the point had gone down to speak to us if we landed there.

"I dined with the French chief yesterday. He is very kind always He said that Admiral Dundas told him there was nothing he could possibly do that he would not do for me. Admiral Penaud wants me to come to Paris this winter, but I told him I should not have too much time at home."

"NARGEN, *October 8th*, 1855

"On Friday last I went over to the Finland shore to Sibbo Fiord, a good anchorage, where Key had been stationed, cutting off the coasting trade ; it is only about ten miles from Sweaborg. The admiral wanted me to see the anchorage, and also to send back the gun-boats with Key, as all of them are going home immediately ; at the same time I wanted to take up a large buoy from the Kalbaden shoal to put it off Wormso on the Apollon, where it will be much required when the ships withdraw from this part of the gulf After getting up the buoy, we went into Sibbo Fiord, the Russian charts being admirable, so that there is no difficulty in entering, though by the charts it seems bounded by nests of rocks. We found Key and his two 'children' anchored near a point on the mainland, where nothing could pass him, and in the act of bringing four vessels loaded with wood, taken the previous night. There had been a strong report of six steam-boats having escaped from Cronstadt to go to Sweaborg, though I don't believe it : and they at night put his two gun-boats outside the islands, where they might pass clear of the *Amphion*, and in the night they saw several vessels close to them. They felt confident they were the Russian gun-boats, and they slipped their cables and ran their two small craft in among them ; they proved to be these four vessels full of wood for the government at Sweaborg, where they were hard up for it ; and these men thought they would run it in the dark outside, so they were greatly surprised when pounced on by the two boats. Key had had an anxious time of it for some nights since the moon had gone. We knew some time since that they had organised two hundred row-boats at Sweaborg, manned by three thousand volunteers—the seamen of the fleet chiefly—for the purpose of boarding any one of our vessels in the night, and from the fishermen and others on the island who went about as usual Key heard this confirmed, and that it was likely *Amphion* would be attacked, so every night was passed at quarters and prepared in every way ; and three nights previous a fire of musketry opened suddenly about half a mile from the ship. The next day the fishermen told them that, while fishing just in the channel from Sweaborg, they were suddenly fired on by Russian boats, which took them for English guard-boats. They were then quite surrounded by a large number of boats, but these returned to Sweaborg, apparently thinking they had discovered themselves by firing on the fishermen. Both Key and myself thought it unsafe for *Amphion* to remain there alone, without either her gun-boats or a second vessel, not but what he would in all probability have defeated an attack, but it would not do to risk it, as with such masses of men they ought to succeed. They at first organised the boats to attack *Edinburgh*, and she moved into a clear place to have room to act more freely ; but if they would dream of carrying a two-decked ship, of course there was double the risk for a frigate. The next day I returned with the two gun-boats to Nargen, and told the admiral I did not like Key lying there alone, and

asked him to send another vessel over.   As he had none
ready to send, he sent me back to recall Key and bring
him to Nargen for a day or two, till he could give him
another vessel.   When I got back it was a dense fog, but
I got in and found *Amphion*, though they first knew of our
being there by the noise of our paddles   We got out
before dark.   I pushed back to Nargen that I might not be
out on Sunday if I could help it, and got in at 11 p m.

" Key had many deserters from Sweaborg, and all agreed
as to the immense loss and destruction there   He also
had regular communication through the fishermen on the
islands round him, who went regularly to market ; and an
old woman did their marketing for them, bringing them
things regularly.   They were capitally off—fresh meat and
poultry from Helsingfors, and good fish, cream, milk, and
eggs from the islands; Key having wisely got a supply
of Russian money, so that the people were not afraid to
take it.

" Now as a set-off to the disgraceful acts of some of our
people I mentioned in my last, I must show how different
it is when such men as Key and Yelverton are concerned.
On the point of mainland near Key are a large number of
riflemen, but he never fires at them (being out of their
rifle-range, and they well within that of his guns), knowing
it is useless and almost murder to kill them when no
ulterior object is to be gained   On the islands the people
were as much respected by the men as if they were in
England.   Key allowed them to go about among the little
villages, with a clear understanding that taking the slightest
thing from a house or island would be as much theft as
if taken from one of our own countrymen.   And one day
an officer saw a woman crying, and she said a man was
in her house and had broken open a cupboard.   The officer
found the man inside, and found the cupboard had been
broken open, but he had taken nothing.   They flogged
him severely, and no other case occurred.   When I went
to recall Key he was at the village, and he sent his boat
back to pay some money and bring off his washed clothes ;
and when the coxswain told the people they were going
away and might not come back, some of them began to
cry.   So you see we have not everywhere such a bad name
in Finland as the Russians make out.   Such men as
Yelverton and Key are above making war unnecessarily
distressing.   No wonder we are sometimes the laughing-

stock of the Russians, when a ninety-gun ship and two frigates fire broadsides into a defenceless village because a few militiamen were there, some of whom were foolish enough to fire their muskets. One small steamer, *Bulldog*, had gone into the same place a few days before to take out a vessel she chased in, leaving those that we laid up there all the summer, but could easily have taken all if thought necessary.

" I hear to-day that —— has been writing some long-winded despatch about some chance he has had of firing at something. Yet these trumpery despatches are sometimes published, and lead to men being promoted where real service, if not puffed off by the captain, is neglected. We have a proof of this now. Key, in *Amphion*, has had perhaps more real service than any vessel out here in the two years, except it is *Arrogant*. This year she has had twelve shots through her hull, and is much damaged aloft, and two men killed and about ten wounded on board, which can be said of no other ship in the Baltic except *Arrogant*. But Key has never made much of anything—simply written a few plain lines stating the facts, and recommending his first lieutenant. Because not exaggerated and made a good story of, his letters have not been published, while things not worth mentioning have been. In consequence his first lieutenant is the only one not promoted, although he has served both years in the Baltic, and was present at both Bomarsund and Sweaborg, besides their own minor actions. Key is, justly, much hurt, and I have advised him to write plainly about it, and state that it encourages officers to exaggerate what they do, and that it makes men suffer because they are above such un-English tricks. The promotions for Sweaborg are fair and pretty liberal to the seniors in the larger ships, but they had little to do with it, merely going in the rocket-boats at night. The lieutenants of the gun-boats, who really had the brunt of it, have been treated much less liberally, the two seniors only made, out of about thirteen.

" The weather remains singularly fine. Last year we had one succession of gales from southward and westward. Key goes home to-morrow, lucky fellow! I hope in a month we shall be on our way (D.V.). This evening all the gun-boats started in a flock, in high glee, for home; and just after passing the ships two or three stopped and a boat was lowered—evidently a man had fallen overboard.

At last up went the signal, 'Man is not saved.' Poor fellow! it quite cast a damp on our talking of home and envying the gun-boats. It is doubly distressing at such a time.

"The accounts from Helsingfors all agree in showing the deep gratitude of the people for our not destroying it, and at the same time paint in terrible colours the horrors and misery they went through, expecting hourly to be bombarded. They carried away everything they could inland, the government stores, etc., being all removed. Had we shown intentions of attacking it, they were going to send a deputation off to beg us to spare it, as it was all private property. I would rather have had a share in saving that place, and the ruin and misery its destruction would have caused, than the share of credit I received for Sweaborg. It is a comfort to me that I always tried to prevent it when planning beforehand, as my letters to you will have shown you, and also after Sweaborg I said all I could against trying to burn Helsingfors; and I have the same feeling about Revel. But as the poor Finns have had all the suffering of the war, and Esthonia nothing, if a town must go, I would rather it were Revel; but if it is decided not to spare it, I would much rather defer it for next season, when the means of doing it effectually and without much risk could be prepared; and besides, if we have peace in the meantime, it would save the sad misery.

"I confess, if we are to destroy towns and carry on a war more barbarous than was known in Napoleon's time, I hope I shall get on shore as soon as possible. There is only one more place worthy of our attack, or that we can do any good by destroying, and that is Cronstadt. The destruction of every town on the coasts would not lead a bit more to peace, would multiply the horrors of war, and leave a spirit that may prevent any friendly feelings between us for a generation after peace is made. If I thought the blessing of peace would be brought about by destroying Revel and Helsingfors, I should feel it a duty to destroy them; but as it cannot affect the question of war or peace, but, on the contrary, excite a spirit of war and revenge in Russia, it is not only useless, but un-Christian to do such a barbarous act.

"The new block-ships, not being efficient vessels, and all the small craft will be home in October."

" [*Private.*]

" There is great anxiety about the promotions which are expected to-morrow. I do not expect any honours will be out yet. I look more anxiously every week for some hopes of peace than anything else. Last week the papers had some rumours of it, but Sevastopol is the difficulty. Had it not been for that sad expedition we should have had peace now, every object of the war gained, and, oh ! what blood, misery, and treasure would have been saved ! But we must think it has all been permitted for some wise purpose which we cannot now understand. The alliance between England and France may lead to such national blessings and destruction of old animosity, that it may, by preventing a worse war for us, repay us for all the misery of the present time. I do hope there is a strong feeling leading all Christian Churches at home to pray earnestly for peace, and to check those feelings of *fancied military honour and glory* which lead so many to counsel and wish for war. If they could feel a little only of the horrors suffered by the poor people at Kertch, and the misery and anxiety caused by driving people with their things from their homes in Helsingfors and Revel, they would think very differently about war.

" The accounts (if true) from Helsingfors show a much larger loss at Sweaborg than the Russian despatches allow. One account says that a regiment of a thousand men was nearly destroyed at Gustafsvard—that is where the heavy explosion occurred."

" NARGEN, *Thursday, September 13th.*

" I saw the admiral to-day, and I find he wishes to go up to Admiral Seymour, near Cronstadt, to arrange with him before he goes to Stockholm, so he starts in *Duke* to-morrow very early, and we go with him. The French Government quite decided that nothing more should be attempted, so their small craft are all going home. Ours will go early next month. I wish I were a small craft ! I went on shore for a walk, and saw them playing a cricket match, and then came off in time for the officers' dinner, this being my regular day for dining with them. I have been reading Wellington's despatches, and it is singular how exactly he complains like us of the falsehood and injury of the newspaper articles. They

were abusing him for doing nothing at the very time he
had more difficulties to struggle with than ever, and was,
by his care in avoiding a battle, actually saving Portugal,
and gaining all he wished for. But no paper had the
influence then with the public that the *Times* has now,
and these attacks on us all are, of course, delightful to
the enemy. We hear that the *Times* is received inside
Sevastopol the day it reaches our camp, and eagerly read
for information about our army, etc. Yesterday our gun-
boats were taking some good oak timber off Wolf Island,
when a baron somebody came over in a small boat from
Revel and said it was his ; and as we paid for everything,
—milk, fish, etc—at Nargen, he hoped the admiral would
pay him for his oak timber, which was part of the cargo
of a wreck he had bought. Caldwell explained to him
it was rather different ; but out of sixty fine logs only
took thirteen. The baron said they thought we were
going to destroy Revel after Sweaborg ; but that it would
have done us no good, and could not have any effect on
the war cither way This is, I think, the real truth. He
certainly showed great confidence, for he came over without
a flag-of-truce. He said the war was doing one good in
Russia ; it was making them bring out their internal
resources more than ever, as they were now working salt-
mines, etc., that were not worked before, and opening out
roads for inland conveyance, though their rivers enabled
them to do much by water. There were two small vessels
taken full of wood, and stripped of each rope, etc., as usual,
before being fired at as targets. To-day the crews, including
one woman, said that one belonged to the baron ; but the
other to the men themselves, and her loss would ruin
them So the admiral had her sails and rigging restored,
and had her rigged and fitted out, and gave them all
leave to go in her to Revel. These little merciful acts
will do great good, I am sure

"*Friday night.*—Instead of starting to-day, we have been
detained by a gale from the north-east, blowing right into
this bay. But it has quite confirmed the view I have
always urged, that the banks protected it well, and that
it was a safe anchorage, even with this wind. There has
been little sea, and nothing for large ships. I have always
urged not having colliers here ; and if any of those here
go on shore to-night, it will not be my fault. The same
with the gun-boats Only yesterday I urged the admiral,

if it blew from this quarter, to send them round the other side of the island, which is quite sheltered; but it has not been done, and they have all this gale to stand. However, they looked to be riding very well at dusk. It is odd that the September gales last year were from south to west, and this year the three hard blows lately have all been from the north-eastward. This wind will try the anchorage for the Cronstadt squadron at Seskar; but I do not fear it for large ships. I have urged the colliers going to Biorko; but I fear they have a collier at Seskar, and if so they may lose her. These are points more directly under the captain of fleet, and he is very undecided and nervous about their being anywhere *near* the shore, even if at very long shot, for fear the enemy will bring guns down. At Baro Sound, where I succeeded in getting some colliers sent, the result had proved the advantage; yet we have three or four here now, exposed to this gale, when a land-locked cove is within twenty-five miles, where all ships might go to coal. Now if these colliers were all lost, I know the captain, who has not liked this anchorage for the fleet, would say, ' There, this is your favourite anchorage,' forgetting that I have expressly said only for large ships, and that colliers, etc., *ought not to be here.* But this again shows the unfair position I am in, as I am looked to for advice on these points, but have no power to get my advice carried out, and yet have the responsibility. The admiral is so kind that I cannot show any feeling of this sort. Were it only the captain, I would just give him an opinion in writing about the safety of the ships, and have no more bother about it, leaving the responsibility resting with him, I having proof of what my opinions were in the written document. But I cannot do that now. One comfort is, it is all passing the time away, and that is everything now to me. I do trust before next spring peace may end it, for I feel a longing to be quietly home again, free from the anxiety and excitement which I cannot very well bear, even with everything going most smoothly and favourably for me."

" [*Private.*]

" NARGEN, *September 20th,* 1855.

" All the ships and their masters and captains are going crazy. This morning I had to go to Baro Sound to find out about *H——* having got on shore in there. She

relieved *H——* and *R——*, ordered home immediately.
The first thing the admiral tells me on my return is that
R—— had touched on a rock coming out of Baro
Sound, having actually mistaken the passage I took her
in through, and going the wrong way. Also that *H——*
in the night had run on a dangerous bank, the Nye ground,
which you will see in the chart farther down the gulf.
Two vessels have gone to help her. All this is very bad.
Directly the ships are trusted about singly they get into
these scrapes. Fortunately the weather is beautifully fine

"I believe the poor people, especially the Finns, are
suffering sadly. When I went up to Cronstadt, I took two
boats crossing the gulf, one loaded with corn, the other
with brandy, and five men in each. The poor men in the
corn-boat had been across to buy it, and were going back
to Finland The poor creatures said, when I told them
they must not cross or their boat would be taken, that
they could not starve, and must risk anything rather than
their families should do so I could not take the poor
fellows' all, so I let them go, corn and all, only taking one
bag for our poultry, giving them tobacco for it, to their
great delight. The poor fellows went on their knees and
tried to embrace mine with joy at being released, and
prayed for every blessing for me they could. The brandy-
boat was from the south side, going to cross and try to pass
through the Finnish islands *all the way to Sweden*, to
change their brandy for things they were greatly in want
of. They were in a low, poor boat, with two boards nailed
up its sides, but quite unsafe. I explained to them that
they could not pass our ships at several points before they
got to Sweden, and that they would be taken and lose all,
and I persuaded them to go back, which they did ; I could
not find the heart to add to the misery of these poor
people. Those at home who are so anxious to prolong the
war little understand what they would feel were our country
in the state of this one ; and I fear it is the poor who suffer
most, and the Finns more than all, as they had the most
trade and ships "

Calling to inquire about a sick peasant he had seen the
year before, and finding the daughter in, he adds :—

"When she recognised me she brightened up, and was
sorry she did not recollect the 'good captain,' whom all the

people here liked so. About three weeks since some sailors broke into the house in the night, and stole what little tea, sugar, and coffee they had got from the ships, as well as a few silver spoons—all they had. What is more cruel still, they had just stored their hay—their only food for the cows and stock in the winter—when some of our men set fire to it, and of course destroyed hay-house and all. They will probably lose most of their cattle through it. She said she thought they were French sailors ; but I fear not, for we have had many vessels here, and I do not think the French have. We have also several colliers, and perhaps their crews may have done it. I fear the poor Alanders have suffered much this year ; their vessels have been taken, and all that understanding I established, and Admiral Napier approved of, has been done away with. A new vessel was building when the fleet was lying here last year. The men went on working at her on a promise from Sir Charles that she would not be destroyed. She was launched this summer, and since taken by us. The Russians have ill-treated them for their supposed friendly feelings to us, and now we treat them as regular enemies also."

Soon after the work and anxiety at Sweaborg were over, Captain Sulivan, who had not felt it at the time, became very unwell with pains in the head and severe spasms in the spine. The doctors said it proceeded from the brain having been overstrained, and advised his going home. Through this the *Merlin* returned home some time before the rest of the fleet. On arriving at Woolwich, Captain Sulivan was sent for by the First Lord, Sir C. Wood, who, before Admiral Sir M. Berkeley and Captain Sir Baldwin Walker, asked him what could be done the next year at Cronstadt, telling him how many guns and mortar-vessels could be ready, and wishing to know whether there was sufficient prospect of success to justify further preparations. Captain Sulivan assured him that even with fewer small vessels, if the floating batteries answered, there could be no doubt about burning the town, and after that probably taking the place, or at least destroying the fleet He explained step by step, at subsequent interviews, how it could be done with such probability of success as quite to justify attempting it. The next day he went with the First Lord and Sir B. Walker to try a new class of gun-boat, in order to decide whether more of them should be built, and then, after dining with the First Lord, spent the evening with him and Sir B. Walker in discussing the future plans. He urged that, to be independent of the French floating batteries, in case they were not brought from the Mediterranean, two more should be built, and a few days after Sir B. Walker told him that he would be glad to know they were ordered.* This shows how thoroughly the First Lord knew his services, and put confidence in his opinion.

When Admiral Dundas returned, he said to Captain Sulivan, " So you have been assuring the First Lord that we can burn Cronstadt and perhaps take it ? " " Yes." " Well, I fear you are much too sanguine ; I don't think it is at all certain." " Recollect, sir, you thought the same before Sweaborg." This was the substance of a long conversation on the subject, but the admiral never would express the slightest confidence in the success of the plan.

Early in the spring of 1856, however, peace was made, so that the plan for attacking Cronstadt was, fortunately, not required to be put into execution.

The Baltic fleet was reviewed by Her Majesty the Queen at Spithead on April 23rd, 1856.

Captain Sulivan had previously applied for the two surveying-vessels to be given the honour of leading the two divisions at the review, as they had led the ships in the Baltic against the enemy. Accordingly, the starboard

* See illustration of these vessels in the *Daily Graphic* of November 2nd, 1895.

division was led by him in the *Merlin*, the port by Captain Otter in the *Alban*.

It is probable that the success at Sweaborg had some effect in helping to bring about the peace, for it made the Russians fear for Cronstadt, as they well knew that preparations were being made for attacking it. After the war my father had many conversations on the subject with (then) Colonel Count Ignatieff, who was then a member of the Russian Embassy, and who had during the war been stationed at Cronstadt and at Sweaborg. The count particularly asked Captain Sulivan whether we really intended to attack Cronstadt, and on the latter assuring him that we did, and that it would not only have been burnt like Sweaborg, but would have been closely attacked, and probably taken, or at least the fleet burnt, Ignatieff asked him how he could suppose this, when they were building new batteries on the north side, and floating batteries also. Sulivan replied, " Because we should have attacked it early in June, and you would not have had the new batteries armed or a floating battery ready by that time, and I believe not till August." " How do you know that?" " Never mind how we know it ; but was it not so?" At last he, the count, confessed that they would not have been ready in June. Sulivan said he thought the fear of our succeeding at Cronstadt had much to do with their consenting to make peace, and Ignatieff allowed that it might have influenced their decision to accept the terms.

The Russians having removed their buoys and beacons in the Baltic during the war, Ignatieff was instructed to ask Captain Sulivan's advice as to the best places on which to put them down again, as he knew more about the subject than the Russians themselves!

The honours for Sweaborg did not come out till early in 1856, when there was every prospect of peace. Captain

Sulivan's brother-officers had so frequently assured him that he must get the K.C.B. if any honours were given, that he expected it, more particularly as it was well known to many at the Admiralty that the C.B. had been promised him long before for the Parana campaign. His disappointment was therefore all the greater when he found liberal rewards were given to nearly every one but himself. The admiral was made a K C B. (it ought to have been the G.C.B.); all the captains, except two or three who were C.B.'s before, received the C B ; liberal promotions were given to juniors; and the officer who commanded at Sweaborg, being a C.B. before, was made an A.D C. to the Queen. The senior marine artillery officer, Captain Wemyss, was made a major, and shortly after a C.B. and lieutenant-colonel. This was the first instance in the naval service of the C.B. being given for service as a captain of marines, but in his case most justly given, as he held an important command, and by his throwing aside old ideas and pouring in a more rapid mortar fire the first hour than had ever been thought of before, he greatly contributed to the success, as it got up rapidly such a body of fire that it could not be put out. (Colonel Ignatieff told Captain Sulivan that it upset all their arrangements for putting out fires.) But if the service was of such special merit as to obtain for a captain of marine artillery two steps in rank and the C B , it might have been supposed that a captain in the navy, a C.B. at the time, who was ten years standing in the rank of colonel and lieutenant-colonel, who planned the attack, really conducted it, and placed every mortar-vessel, giving the marine artillery officers the exact ranges, which enabled them to do their work so well, would receive some slight recognition of his services ; and that if the K.C.B. (which was given freely at the time to colonels in the army, his juniors, in addition to special pro-

motion to major-general) was too high an honour for a naval
man of the same rank, the First Lord would at least give
him the slight reward of a good-service pension or A.D.C.
to the Queen. But no, he was considered "too junior" for
any reward. Not too junior to be worked nearly to death,
to be consulted and used when he could be made useful,
and not too junior to win by his exertions and success
honours in plenty for others ; and yet this argument
against his being deserving of any reward whatever was
actually used against him by the very admiral who had
told him, " I owe you a debt of gratitude I can never repay."
That others did not think this was shown by the late
Admiral Sir James Hope (then Captain Hope) refusing the
good-service pension when offered him, and telling the First
Lord he hoped he would give it to Captain Sulivan, as a
reward to him would be received with satisfaction by the
whole Baltic fleet. The answer was, that he knew he must
do something for him, but that he could not get over
difficulties of seniority ; so he gave the G.S.P. to Captain
——, who entered the service four years after Captain
Sulivan, but through interest had got four years' start of
him as a captain, and therefore, without having ever in
any rank been engaged with an enemy, was thought more
deserving of an honorary reward than one who had as
commander and captain shared in three important campaigns, and been specially recommended and gazetted for
each of them. Captain Sulivan allowed this apparent
slight to affect him more than it perhaps should have done,
but he was one who never saw an injustice committed
without strongly protesting against it, without the least
considering how such boldness might affect his own
interest. It was not merely his own part he was taking,
it was that of the service in general. It had seemingly
been laid down by the Lords of the Admiralty that naval

officers of a certain rank were not entitled to certain
honorary rewards, freely given to their juniors in the army,
unless they happened to be serving with a military force.
Again, the maxim was laid down by Admiral Dundas, that
honorary rewards were to be given by seniority, not for
special service !   Sulivan saw in himself the representative
of the navy, and protested against these opinions.   There
was no question of the services he had rendered the
country—these were freely admitted—but "overstrained
ideas of seniority" were allowed to deprive him of honorary
recognition.

In 1857, when further honours for Sweaborg had been
given, he wrote to the Admiralty, asking to be informed
why he had been passed over.   The reply was that he
was "too junior, his turn had not yet come."   He did not
again publicly allude to the matter, until further honours
were contemplated in 1865, when, hearing his name had
not been mentioned, he saw the private secretary of the then
First Lord, who, with the First Lord, expressed ignorance
of his services !   Sir Charles Wood and others having then
given testimony to his work, it was considered too late
to make any alteration, and that his "seniority" was not
sufficient.   This is one instance out of many which could
be quoted, showing the want of continuity in naval administration, by which an officer's services, however valuable,
may be unknown to the authorities who later have the
bestowal of promotion and rewards.   Sulivan thought this
record quite sufficient, when again in 1867 further promotions in the Order of the Bath were made, which called
forth the criticism of the *Times* and other papers.   His
"want of seniority" made his name again omitted.   At
length, in some measure owing to the representations of
Admirals Sir James Hope, Sir A. C. Key, Sir Spencer
Robinson, and others, his "turn" was supposed to have

come, and he was made a K.C.B. in 1869, fourteen years after the war.

That there was no feeling against him personally, and that his treatment was caused, as the Hydrographer expressed it, "by overstrained ideas respecting seniority," is proved by the unusual consideration shown Captain Sulivan in other respects. He was asked after the war if there was any appointment he would prefer; and it was intimated to him that, if he wished it, he might have one of the first dockyards vacant, though he was not of the usual standing for such an appointment.

On explaining to the Senior Naval Lord that as the Cape command as commodore would soon be vacant, he would prefer it to a home appointment, Sir M. Berkeley very kindly said he believed every one at the Board wished him to have an appointment that he preferred, and he would mention the wish to the First Lord. Privately he heard that he might make pretty sure of going; but, shortly before the vacancy occurred, Admiral Beechey's death made a vacancy for the appointment of naval officer to the Board of Trade, and the First Lord offered it to Sulivan.

At first he refused it, not wishing to give up active service, and particularly the Cape command; but the permanency of the civil appointment and the apparent advantage to his family induced him to accept it.

It is difficult to understand how the same men, who could so desire to give him an unusually good appointment on account of his Baltic services, without any interest to aid him, could yet refuse him all honorary reward for such special services, though they showered honours so freely on others with, in some cases, very trifling claims to them, and even on some who were never within gunshot of an enemy.

Entire ignorance on the subject will alone explain their

refusing the K C.B. to all under the rank of admiral, while
the military authorities were making numerous colonels
of much less standing both major-generals and K.C.B.'s
It was really for the sake of the principle involved that
Captain Sulivan pushed his claims. His pamphlet on
"Honours" clearly shows how these should be bestowed
to maintain the value of the distinctions.

Two years after Sweaborg, when every officer senior to
him who had the slightest claim had received either a
G.S.P. or an A.D.C, one was given to a captain who was
a year junior to him. Sir R Dundas then told the First
Lord that he thought it should have been given to Sulivan,
and he received the next vacant " good-service pension."

To return to the winter of 1855. Admiral Sir James
Hope wrote as follows :—

"LONDON, *December 21st*, 1855

" MY DEAR SULIVAN,—Sir C. Wood told me to-day that
he intended to put me on a committee with you and Key,
to report on some sub-marine boat. I told him that we
should be glad in such an inquiry to have the assistance
of a civil engineer of acknowledged reputation, accustomed
to sub-marine operations. He promised anything we
should judge necessary.

" And now, my dear Sulivan, I hope you will forgive me
if I have done wrong, but I could not resist the temptation
the other day, when I first saw Sir C. Wood on my arrival,
and he alluded to the good-service pension I refused, of
telling him how highly I thought you deserved it of the
Admiralty, and how well bestowed I thought it would have
been on you or Watson, and that I felt very sure we all
in the Baltic should have rejoiced at your getting it. He
told me that *he was fully sensible of it all*, that he intended
as soon as he could do so to remember you, but that he
could not as yet get over considerations of seniority. So
I hope as soon as two or three more tumble in, which
must happen soon, that you will not be forgotten. He
offered me an aide-de-camp-ship, but I declined, on the
ground that I had been amply rewarded for all I had ever
had the luck to do. I would rather wait till I felt I had

earned it, of which I hoped there might be a chance next
year.

"Believe me, my dear Sulivan, yours sincerely,
"J. HOPE."

The trial of a sub-marine boat, referred to by Admiral
Hope, took place in Poole Harbour, it being thought the
most private locality for the purpose. Imagine a large
inverted whale-boat of iron, with a chamber at each end
filled with compressed air. The commissioners (Hope,
Sulivan, and Key) were watching the trial from a yacht.
The boat was lowered keel uppermost, the crew being under
the thwarts, as in a diving-bell. When the boat was
allowed to sink nearly to the bottom, the men got down,
and, with their heads in the air-filled boat, pushed it
along as they walked on the ground. The air was supplied
as wanted by taps, and buoys attached to each end of the
boat marked its progress. When the boat was some distance from the yacht, suddenly something like the snout of
a whale appeared above the water, out blew a lot of spray,
and down it went. While the yacht was steaming up to
it, the apparition appeared a second time, with the same
result. Then was heard the tapping of a hammer against
the iron sides of the boat, an agreed-upon signal. The
boat was hauled up, and the engineer and five men found
almost at their last gasp. All had gone well until the
boat was wanted at the surface. To accomplish this, a
heavy weight attached at each end of the boat by a chain
had to be thrown out. On the crew attempting to rise, one
chain caught—consequently the unchecked end rose somewhat perpendicularly, and the air inside escaped. The
engineer's presence of mind saved the party. There was a
smaller hold between the main-hold and one air-chamber.
On the loss of air consequent on the two rises, the men
were got into this. With his hand on the cock, the

engineer waited until he saw the men gasping, when he
would give them a little more air.   In this way he spun out
his small remaining supply until the yacht came to their
rescue, and raised the boat by means of the ropes attached
to buoys, which the forethought of Sulivan had provided.
After this, the commissioners themselves went down in
her, but did not go far from the yacht!   This was the
last, I believe, heard of the invention, which was intended
for use against the boom at Cronstadt, etc.

In confirmation of the statement on page 367, I may
state that, on reading it in the proofs, my father's cousin,
Admiral T. B. M. Sulivan, told me that in 1861 he met
M. Tchesterkoff, commodore of the Russian squadron off the
coast of Syria, who, on learning his relationship to Captain
B. J. Sulivan, stated that, after the war, the Russian Government sent an official to consult the latter on the rebuoying
of their Baltic shores.

Not only after the Parana campaign, but also after the
Baltic war, the French admirals therein engaged recommended the Emperor to confer a high grade of the Legion
of Honour upon Captain Sulivan.   For the Parana expedition no exchange of decorations was allowed by our
Government.   After the Russian war, with the exception
of one for Admiral Dundas, all the French decorations sent
for our navy were taken by Admiral Lyons for his officers.
Yet, so far as regarded service with the French fleet, other
Baltic officers besides Captain Sulivan had claims prior to
many Black Sea recipients   Admiral Penaud, in talking
to some of our officers of the power which their naval
authorities possessed of promoting a captain to the rank of
admiral for special service, as Tréhouart had been advanced,
said that, if Sulivan had been in the French navy, he would
certainly have been thus rewarded.

CHAPTER XVI.

THE BOARD OF TRADE.

1857-65.

CAPTAIN SULIVAN joined the Board of Trade in 1857, with the title of "Professional Officer," his chief duties being connected with the Lights Boards of the United Kingdom. He had the departments of Lights, Pilotage, and Life-boats, and, conjointly with Captain Walker, inquiries into losses of ships and the conduct of master-mariners. Later on he undertook also the work of engineer of the Harbour Department, this saving the Board the salary of an engineer, £800 per annum. I have no record of his work under the Board, but we learn his views on important questions connected with it from the evidence he gave at the royal commissions of inquiry before which he appeared. The list of these will show how much labour was thrown upon him. He was a most valuable and interesting witness, as he brought his great and varied experience to bear upon the subjects in question. There is, however, no space in this volume to give more than extracts from the reports of his evidence. These show that he was made the most of by the commissioners, his examinations extending over two and sometimes three days. A summary is given in the Appendices.

The reforms needed in the royal and mercantile navies are stated in his evidence so clearly, and illustrated by such striking examples, that the reports well repay perusal.

His ability for seeing the weak points of any system, and his power of originating remedies, evidently impressed the commissioners, for his ideas were in almost every case recommended for adoption in the reports. If we regret that he did not continue to serve afloat, and so lost the opportunity of showing what he could do in command of a fleet, we have instead the fruit of his plans for naval reform, etc., which have proved of great benefit to the service and to the country.

For the first four years of his official life Captain Sulivan resided at Spring Grove, Isleworth. Both he and his wife preferred living out of London, and he was too tired after his day's work to return to town for dinners and entertainments, which he disliked. He could not have stood the strain of his work so long had he not lived quietly. He kept riding-horses, and often rode to and from London with his wife or one of his daughters. He usually spent Sunday afternoons in the neighbouring poorer districts, taking generally copies of *The British Workman*, which he distributed ; and sometimes he would read aloud a tale from it to a group of working-men. One day, when he was visiting the brick-fields, a woman said to him, " It is all very well for you to tell us not to drink beer, and then to go home to your glass of wine " ; so henceforth he dropped the one glass he sometimes had taken by the doctor's orders. Though he often lunched at his club, the United Service, he was never a club man, and did not keep as much in touch with his brother-officers as he might have done. He was somewhat lax in attention to official and social formalities, disliking " full uniform " work, though occasionally he attended a levée.

The six weeks' summer vacation was usually spent with the whole family at Flushing, Falmouth, where his mother still lived after the death of his father in 1857. He was never so happy as when afloat again in any kind of sailing craft. We boys were trained in the handling of all sorts of rigs. He himself was the biggest boy of the party. Whoever was with him reaped the benefit of his wealth of practical knowledge and fund of interesting anecdote. His beloved *Philomel* was at one time moored as a hulk in the harbour, and on her deck we heard the story of Obligado retold. One of our regular picnics was to a farm on the banks of the river Fal, where lived Nancy, his old nurse. She was so beautiful as a girl that friends used to remonstrate with my grandparents for sending her out with the children in Plymouth. So my grandfather gave her as escort a blue-jacket, an old coxswain of his.

In 1861 Captain Sulivan, desiring to be within easier riding distance of his office, built from his own plans a house at Roehampton, overlooking Wimbledon Common, where the volunteer work, both at the ranges and at the annual summer gathering, was a source of great interest to him. The gipsies encamped on the common were frequently visited by him.

About the year 1863, being desirous to serve a little more time at sea, so as to qualify for the active list of admirals, he applied for and was promised another post as commodore, but it was eventually given to an officer much his junior. This was a great disappointment to him. He came on the reserved list of admirals in 1863.

Had he gone on quietly with only the regular work of the Board of Trade, he might have retained his post much longer than he did. But one occupation led to another, and his active mind was always at work on some scheme of naval reform, which he would press upon the attention of Government. All this told upon his somewhat excitable brain, which had undoubtedly already felt the strain of the two Baltic campaigns. He was nervous about himself, for he sometimes suffered from severe headaches, the result of suppressed gout. In the spring of 1864 he and my mother took a trip to Italy and Switzerland for the benefit of his health.* But in 1865, being perhaps unduly anxious about himself, he resigned his appointment, and took up his residence at Bournemouth. The Board of Trade were very liberal to him, and gave him the highest pension in their power—£320 a year— taking into consideration the fact of his having saved them the salary of an engineer. Mr. Milner Gibson, the President of the Board, wrote to him as follows :—

"LONDON, *April 25th*, 1865.

"We shall not find it so easy to replace you, because you possessed a combination of knowledge on both nautical and engineering subjects, which rendered your advice on the subjects which came before the Board of Trade most useful. Speaking for myself, so long as I am at the Board of Trade, I am sure I shall feel your loss very much, and I am confident, whoever may be your successor, the public will not be better served than they have been by you.

"Yours very faithfully,
"THOMAS MILNER GIBSON."

* The day before returning home from the Grand Châlet, Rossinière, they went out for a walk with an old lady-friend. While searching in a wood for a wild flower, my father heard cries from the friend, who had lingered in a field below. Hastening to her, he found she had been attacked by two ruffians. Having fortunately a stout stick, he disabled for some time the bigger of the two with a blow, and then began a desperate struggle with the second, in which, rolling on the ground, each tried to choke the other. Happily my father prevailed. When the three were struggling for possession of the stick, my mother, coming up, used her Nice parasol on the fingers of one until she made him let go. Owing to his having to return home, my father could not prosecute the men, who were strangers to the neighbourhood. It was the only assault on visitors ever known in the district.

REMINISCENCES OF THE LATE ADMIRAL SIR B. J. SULIVAN, BY LORD FARRER.

" I am sorry to say that I have kept no written record of our intercourse, so that anything I say must be taken with all the drawbacks due to 'slippery memory.' Facts and dates become indistinct, and without these impressions of character, however vivid—and they are very vivid with me in this case—are apt to be vague and uninteresting.

" My first knowledge of Sir B. J. Sulivan was when he joined the Board of Trade in 1857, as one of the two nautical advisers who had been appointed to assist the President in administering the Acts relating to merchant shipping.   His   immediate   predecessor   was   Admiral Beechey, who, like himself, had been a distinguished officer in the Surveying Department of the navy.   The chief busi ness of these officers was to advise the Board on matters connected with lighthouses, pilotage, harbours, and other matters connected with navigation, with respect to which large functions had recently been thrown on the Board of Trade.   It is difficult to describe the actual work which Sulivan did in this department ; he had much to do with the Trinity House, and it is to his credit as well as theirs that the somewhat delicate relations (the Board of Trade had the control of the purse) was not strained.   On the position, character, etc., of lighthouses at home and in some of the colonies he had a potential voice.   He took an active part in the harbour of refuge questions, he was a stout opponent of compulsory pilotage, and a genuine free-trader and upholder of individual responsibility in nautical as well as in other matters.   A marine depart· ment of the Board had been created in 1850 by Mr. Labouchere, and much enlarged by Mr. Cardwell in

1853-54, and it kept on constantly growing for years, till it became the largest department in the Board of Trade.

"I was originally assistant secretary to this department, and in that capacity had much to do with Captain Sulivan, as he then was. We were generally in accord, but often also at variance. I was a civilian, and took the civilian's less arbitrary view, whilst he would naturally take the more decided and thorough-going view of the naval officer. But he was essentially a good man to differ from as well as to agree with. Impetuous, keen, and sometimes hasty, he never bore malice, and was one of the most generous of men. We would have a great fight in the morning, when he would denounce my views as fatal, absurd, etc., etc., and in the afternoon we were always as good friends as ever. I remember one curious instance of the instinct of the naval officer, coupled with the frankness and non-egotistic generosity of the man. There was a question going on in the office whether I was to have the title of secretary or assistant secretary. I did not care about it, but was surprised to find Captain Sulivan taking the warmest part in advocating the cause of the higher title for me. I expressed my gratitude to him, saying I did not care about it. 'Oh,' he said, 'you have nothing to be grateful for. We often differ, and your advice is sometimes taken. Now I don't like being overruled by an assistant secretary, but I don't mind being overruled by a secretary.'

"He was one of the quickest men in seeing a point I ever came across; his *aperçu* of a situation was a sort of inspiration; but no reasoning moved him if he did not see the thing at once. He was essentially a man of action— αὐτοσχεδιάζειν τὰ δέοντα, as Thucydides said of Themistocles: 'To see intuitively what the moment requires.' I never saw him in command, but he was a man whom beyond all others I have known I would have followed in a row. The excitement seemed to sharpen his wits and his perception : he made me understand the sort of stuff our Nelsons, and Napiers, and Outrams are made of. I have no doubt his courage was equal to his perception. I always understood that whatever was done in the Baltic was his doing, and I feel sure that whether it was winds, waves and shoals, or men and guns, that were to be contended with, Sulivan would have been at his best when danger was greatest.

"His relations to his old chief, Admiral FitzRoy, were interesting. When he came to the Board of Trade, FitzRoy was at the head of the Meteorological Office, and it was the duty of the officer in the place to which Sulivan was appointed to superintend FitzRoy's doings. But Sulivan made it the condition of his appointment that he should not be obliged to direct FitzRoy—a sagacious condition, considering the previous relations and the individual characters and tempers of these two distinguished men. Sulivan's respect and admiration for FitzRoy as an unrivalled sailor and a devoted public servant were unlimited ; and when FitzRoy died, after having spent a fortune in the public service, Sulivan moved heaven and earth to get his services acknowledged, and, I believe, with success.

"I used to hear much of the voyage of the *Beagle* from Charles Darwin, whose niece I married, and whose son has married my daughter. He and the other partners in that historical cruise had an infinite respect for FitzRoy, whose abilities as a seaman, whose courage as a man, and whose self-sacrifice as a public servant, won the esteem and admiration, if they did not command the affection, of all who served under him. From all I heard, all the officers and men loved Sulivan ; certainly Charles Darwin did. There must have been something very good and strong about those men to keep them together for so many

years, cooped up in that small uncomfortable vessel, doing
first-rate work with very inadequate means.

> "'One equal temper of heroic hearts,
> Not strong in circumstance, but strong in will,
> To seek, to find, to strive, and not to yield.'

"It was a very interesting thing to get Sulivan to relate
his experience of the French. He had acted with them
in the Plata and in the Baltic. He used to begin by
praising their maritime inscription and bewailing the weakness of England at sea, which he used to say could never
compete with the French till we trained our merchant
seamen to arms ; and then he would begin and tell stories,
all showing how far inferior the French were to the
English in all qualities of cool fighting, either with elements
or with men. I remember two or three of them.

"He was engaged, when in command of an English ship,
in carrying on hostilities in the Plata, and had a French
ship for consort. He told with glee how the French
captain, when they anchored for the night in a tide-way,
used to get him to anchor the French ship as well as his
own. Here they had to engage some hostile batteries,
one on the water-level, which the Frenchman took in hand,
the other on a height, which fell to Sulivan's ship. The
Frenchman silenced their battery by hard and close firing,
and then the French captain came on board Sulivan's ship.
He found the English sailors under fire, and suffering from
it, but pitching their shells as coolly and accurately so as
to fall into the elevated battery as if they were on parade.
The French captain was much struck, and said to Sulivan,
'I could get my fellows to march straight into the jaws
of hell, but nothing could make them shoot coolly under
fire as yours do.'

"Another story he used to tell was of the attack on some

of the fortifications in the Baltic. Sulivan had surveyed the ground, and was ready to lead; but the English and French admirals agreed that the leading must be done by both nations, and they asked Sulivan to choose a French colleague ; he chose one of whom he thought well. 'But,' said he, 'the first thing the Frenchman did was to put his ship aground.'

"Another story was of the attack on Bomarsund, which was made by English and French artillery. Each nation took one fort—the French one that was comparatively near, the English one farther off and less accessible. Sulivan was able to get on to a hill between the batteries and the forts, and watch operations. The Frenchmen opened fire and silenced the enemy and took the fort, which was not damaged, but marked all over with shot as with pock-marks; the English artillerymen directed their fire at one embrasure, and for a while made slow progress, whilst they were falling themselves under the Russian fire (?). Sulivan went down to the English artillery officer, and urged him to try to silence the Russian guns ; his reply was, ' I'm d—d if my men shall do anything else till they have knocked down the embrasure.' They did knock it down, made a practicable breach, and the English soldiers marched up it into the fort.

"The generosity of Sulivan's temper was well shown on his retirement from the Board of Trade, when they gave him a special pension. Few men I have known have been contented with such things; Sulivan was not only satisfied, but expressed himself to me as very grateful for what the Government had done for him.

"I have jotted down what occurs to me. I only wish I could do more. It has been my fate, though non-military in all my feelings and prejudices, to be brought in contact with a good many soldiers and sailors. They have been some of the best and most public-spirited men I have ever had to do with, and amongst them no one more admirable, perhaps no one so lovable, as Admiral Sulivan.

"FARRER."

FROM SIR JOHN BRIGGS,

WHO WAS FOR FORTY YEARS AN OFFICIAL AT THE ADMIRALTY, FOR FIVE YEARS "CHIEF CLERK."

"AUSTRIAN TYROL, *October 24th*, 1893.

"Nothing could afford me greater pleasure than to comply with any request made by the son of my old and much-valued friend Sir James Sulivan.

"Amongst my many naval friends, few flag-officers have I held in greater respect than your lamented father. His gallant conduct at Obligado, and the important and valuable services he rendered to the fleet in the Baltic, were fully recognised by the distinguished admirals with whom he served, and were likewise appreciated by the Admiralty.

"It is now more than thirty years ago since I was fortunate enough to be officially associated with him in the formation of the 'dockyard brigades,' when his aptitude for organisation was so forcibly brought under my notice, and I much regret that I was so unwise, on my retirement from office, as to destroy several letters from your respected father.

"Had I still some of his letters in my possession, they would have furnished you with much interesting matter in reference to his views upon the inadequacy of the navy to discharge the various duties assigned to it, as well as upon the utter want of organisation which unfortunately at that period prevailed.

"Sir James was much in advance of the naval opinion of the day, and was strongly impressed with the conviction that our seaport towns and south coast should be entrusted to the supreme command of the navy, instead of to the divided control of the two military services—the mischievous result of which was painfully exhibited in the Walcheren expedition, rendered celebrated by Croker's epigrammatic witticism:

> "'The Earl of Chatham, with his sword half drawn,
> Was waiting for Sir Richard Strachan;
> While Strachan, longing to be at 'em,
> Was waiting for the Earl of Chatham.'

In a word, the admiral was waiting for the general, and the general was waiting for the admiral. The result—delay, ending in failure!

"Your late father entertained particularly sound and practical opinions in reference to national defence, it being a subject of great difficulty and delicacy, and therefore always postponed to a more convenient season. In conversation upon this and other subjects, your father often regretted with me that so little deference was paid to the professional opinions of the naval members of the Board of Admiralty—opinions which the House of Commons, the British public, and the country know nothing of.

"It is to the professional members of the Board of Admiralty that the country looks for the efficiency of the navy; but the First Lord, or the political Secretary, relieve them of their responsibilities, as their opinions, if made known, might prove embarrassing to the party, and would certainly make the Chancellor of the Exchequer furious! Until the professional opinions of the naval advisers of the First Lord of the Admiralty are recorded and laid before the House of Commons, the navy of the country

25

can never be efficient, and consequently is liable to panics and scares ; nor can the country know the real state of affairs, nor get at the exact truth.

"In conclusion, I can only wish you all success in your undertaking, for any one who takes a part in keeping the navy before the eyes of the nation confers a benefit upon the country.

"I could have wished to have written all this letter under my own hand, but I am nearly eighty-six years of age, and my sight fails me, so Lady Briggs has kindly acted as my amanuensis.

"It may be, and no doubt is, very convenient to silence the naval members of the Admiralty, but the period is fast approaching when party and political convenience must give way to national interests.

"The requirements of the navy cannot be too frequently or too forcibly brought under public notice, especially when Russia and France are augmenting their fleets to so great an extent."

FROM THE RIGHT REVEREND DR. STIRLING,

BISHOP OF THE FALKLAND ISLANDS.

"Straits of Magellan, *April* 30th, 1894.

"I have heard with much interest that a memoir of your father is to be published. A life so full of incident, and in touch with the history of our country for more than half a century, cannot fail to arrest the attention of English readers.

"In this position of the southern hemisphere his name is as well known to navigators as that of FitzRoy ; and it has surprised and gratified me much to hear your father spoken of in many an out-of-the-way place by persons who remember him as a smart naval officer engaged in surveying duties. His name in some families lingered long as a household word, and his character, both private and professional, as a bright and generous tradition. In the Falkland Islands, in Patagonia, on the banks of the Rio Negro, up the Rios Parana and Uruguay, as well as in Buenos Ayres and Monte Video, it has been a singular delight to me, in the course of my visitations, to find myself in contact with some of a passing generation who knew and appreciated the services of the then Captain Sulivan.

"It was in the year 1857 that I first came to know him, when he was head of the Marine Department of the Board of Trade. As a distinguished naval officer, and, in particular, as pilot of the Baltic fleet during our recent war with Russia, he had previously excited my admiration. But when he granted me an interview at the Board of Trade, it was to speak on a subject very far from warlike, but in which we had a common interest.

"I wished for information and advice respecting a mission of our Church in Tierra del Fuego. Of his interest in the subject I was well assured, and of the value of his information there could be no doubt. His knowledge of the country and the people was full and direct; his desire to promote the welfare of the Indian tribes there was strong, hopeful, and courageous.

"In my first interview I felt I was talking to a man who inspired confidence. The keen intelligence of his face, and stamp of sincerity upon it, his rich, kindly voice, and manners so frank and genial, made an impression both prompt and pleasant. I had come for information, and I got it straight and full; for advice, and it was generously and considerately given. It is probable that, among the many influences which have placed me where

I am, the conversation I had with your father at the Board of Trade holds no insignificant place.

"In his general conversation he was conspicuous for the frankness and precision of his utterances. Feebleness and obscurity never characterised his speech. He moved in a lucid atmosphere of thought. Within the limits of his natural powers, which were large, his mind worked with remarkable steadiness, and he took care to have material upon which it should work. He was no mere coiner of words. When he spoke, it was as a master of his subject. He had looked at it conscientiously, and reached strong convictions. From these he never flinched, but gave them forcible expression, as men do who think clearly and feel the importance of what they say. He stood to the opinions he had honestly formed as steadily as he ever stood to his guns in the flame and smoke of battle. This naturally aroused, and sometimes irritated, men who differed from him in judgment, but it charmed and excited admiration in all who knew the splendid simplicity of his character, and the steady aim of his heart for righteousness.

"It was my privilege to be drawn yearly closer to him in sympathy by the intelligent and vigorous support which he gave to the work in which I became and am still engaged. His interest in South America, formed when a young officer in Her Majesty's service, seemed never to abate, but rather to deepen and expand as opportunities for doing Christian work there opened before his mind. To his loyal co-operation—and he was ever loyal and true—I owe much.

"Privately I ever think of your father as a most lovable man, genial, kind, a friend and comrade to the core. One could not be dull in his presence. His information was great, and his readiness and skill in imparting it secured ready listeners. Endowed with a tenacious memory, and charged with subjects of the most varied interest, he often surprised and delighted those sharing his hospitality. Whether describing scenes and adventures abroad, or touching on some, perhaps, 'burning subject' in politics, he stirred the hearts and imaginations of his audience in no feeble measure. In regard to political or social questions, you might not agree with him, you might haply be in flat contradiction as to methods ; but what matter ! There was the case before you. There he would leave it—your judgment adverse, your heart entirely one with his !

" It is impossible for me to think of your father without remembering his great kindness and love for children. My daughters from the very first felt the grace and affection which emanated from him. But it was not only that he understood the hearts of the young, and knew how to draw out their confidence and love. There was more than that in his case. Possibly quite unconsciously to himself, yet most naturally and effectively, he appealed to their intelligence, and thereby increased their sources of pleasure. The names and motions of the heavenly bodies, and the glorious vision of the starlit sky, seen through his telescope at Bournemouth, are lessons never to be forgotten by those to whom he imparted them. And the plants and flowers of the garden or the wayside, and the very stones, spoke through his voice to their hearts and understandings. Naturally they liked him, and felt a pride in being the objects of his attention. And now with their father they cherish his memory, and reverence his character, as indeed in a very special way we all hold in loving admiration the character and beauty of Lady Sulivan.

"It was in 1888 that I last saw your father. The

strong, bright-minded, warm-hearted man was then somewhat broken in health ; but with a kindness I shall never
forget, he came to the station at Bournemouth to bid
my wife and myself good-bye, leaving upon our hearts
ineffaceable impressions of friendship and admiration for
a noble life full of years and honours "

CHAPTER XVII.

RETIREMENT.

1865-90.

AFTER the move to Bournemouth, whilst their house was being built, as he suffered still from headaches, he was recommended to try the Turkish-bath treatment at St. Anne's, Blarney, near Cork, where Dr. Barter had been the first to introduce it into the United Kingdom. He pronounced my father to be suffering from suppressed gout. The result of his treatment was an almost entire cure. He was soon almost as well as ever, and he retained all his powers of mind and body until a year or two before his death.

There was plenty to interest and almost to excite in the social, political, and religious life of Bournemouth. Garden and greenhouse enabled the old love for shrubs and flowers to be indulged in by husband and wife. The active, manly figure could be daily seen hurrying along the pine-walks to the club and beach, or on kindly errands to lonely sick ones—and there were many such—who were cheered by the bright talk and lively stories not less than by the flowers and fruit so freely given; whilst the small, fragile-looking lady, with the snow-white hair, more slowly, and in later years with some difficulty, wended her way to cottage hospital or invalid's couch. Thus these two, so like in heart, so unlike in temperament, spent their later years in cheering and brightening the lives of others.

The South American Missionary Society and the Missions to Seamen—in the origin of both of which he had taken a prominent part—always received his lively interest and help. He was an active supporter of the Temperance cause, and advocated it from the platform. All his life he had made it a rule to contribute at least a tenth of his income to charitable purposes.

Original and decided as were his views on most subjects, his opinions on religious questions were as strong. But it would be out of place here to go into controversial questions. Suffice it to say, he was perhaps the first English Churchman to advocate the disestablishment of the Church—even at the cost of disendowment—as the best way of remedying the evils she suffers from, the laity to be given a greater share in the control of the Church's affairs. Though he hit out hard at opinions he thought erroneous, he made friends of the individuals holding them.

Letters to the *Times* and other papers, correspondence with naval friends and to Government officials on service matters, all tended to show that neither the active life of the sailor nor that of the official need have been ended so early. On one occasion, when fears of war were entertained, he was called to London to confer with Admiral Sir G. H. Richards, that the Admiralty might have the benefit of their advice as to a plan of naval campaign. With his usual candour and humility he expressed fear that the alterations in ships and weapons had lessened the value of his experience. But although the details of naval attack and defence may alter, the main principles which should govern strategy must remain the same. I think I am correct in saying that on a previous occasion peace or war almost hung on his answer to the question put to him as to whether with our navy alone we could venture to take part in a Continental quarrel without the help of a military ally. He answered " No."

In 1869 he received the long-deferred honour of the K.C.B. Whilst waiting with others for his turn to be knighted by Her Majesty, a friend said to him, " Sulivan, the soldiers want to know your recipe for keeping your hair brown ! "

In 1873 occurred the sudden death of his second son, Thomas, lieutenant of H.M.S. *Pert*,* which resulted from the after-effect of an attack of malarial fever caught when surveying in the Mediterranean some years before. He was buried in the cemetery at Monte Video, under the windows of the house occupied during the siege by his parents.

In 1882 my father was attacked with scarlet fever, and this prevented his attending the funeral of his old friend Charles Darwin, to which he was specially invited.

Bournemouth possessed the particular merit of being the meeting-place of many old Cornish and Devonshire friends, South American and Falkland Island acquaintances, comrades of old Naval College days, of the *Beagle* and other ships. The sincerity of these old friendships was remarkable.

A friend, writing of the active religious circle in Bournemouth, said :—

" I often look back with thankfulness to having been permitted to know such a band, and especially your noble father, whom to know was to love. Would we had more in our land like him, a typical Englishman, *sans peur et sans reproche* ! "

* The *Pert* had gone on a rock, near Monte Video at Christmas time, and the exertions he underwent for three days and nights in assisting to get her off proved too much for him. He was a promising young officer, and his captain wrote saying he had as much died from his zeal for duty as a man did who was killed in action.

In 1887, the Jubilee year, Sir James and Lady Sulivan celebrated their golden wedding.

His boyishness of disposition and peculiar clearness of speech and power of mind were retained till two years before his death. Then the serious illness of my mother (who had hitherto enjoyed remarkably good health) visibly affected his own constitution ; his power of speech began to fail, though the mind still kept clear. The autobiography at the beginning of this book was written during the last two years of his life.*

After a life so remarkable for activity of body and mind, it was almost well that at its close there should have been a time of evening quiet. My mother recovered, but was so affected by rheumatism as to be almost entirely confined to the sofa, and my father was her constant companion, often reading aloud to her. Thus side by side they spent their last remaining years. One unmarried daughter, assisted by a widowed sister and her daughters, who resided near, was there to tend them and to keep them from the excitement and fatigue of seeing for too lengthened a time the many friends that Bournemouth contained. His other children and grandchildren often visited them, and his youngest brother, Admiral George Lydiard Sulivan, came to Bournemouth to be near him.

At length, after spending a remarkably bright and happy evening, he had a slight seizure. Bronchitis set in ; he

---

* Though during the last year of his life his brain appeared to strangers to be rather clouded, I believe he was really suffering from *aphasia*—"that rare and wonderful disease which seems to attack none but the strongest, which separates the brain from the tongue, and takes away the knowledge and the sense of language" It was the power of *expression* which failed him A few hours before his seizure, his old friend, General Rollo, was speaking to him about some minor battle in the Peninsula, and mentioned the year in which he thought it was fought. My father dissented from this, then brought his " Napier " from the library, and triumphantly showed that he was right and the general wrong.—Ed

recognised and spoke to each member of the family as he arrived ; and, after five days' illness, at the close of New Year's Day 1890, he quietly breathed his last. He was in his eightieth year.

His coffin, covered with the union-jack, was carried to the grave by seamen from the coast-guard station.

Much as he had loved flowers, he requested that none might be sent for his coffin ; he never liked to see them withering on graves, and he wished also to protest against a custom which, in such a place as Bournemouth, was becoming a serious tax on many people. So in death, as in life, simplicity and thoughtfulness for others were inculcated.

My mother bore her loss with the gentle resignation so characteristic of her, comforted by the hope of soon rejoining her husband. Seven months later she too passed peacefully away. She was of the same age.

The Rev. P. F. Eliot, Dean of Windsor, read the funeral service over both their graves. He had been their great friend for many years, being for twenty-three years vicar of Holy Trinity, Bournemouth, in the building of which my father had taken an active part.

No more fitting words could be chosen to end this memoir, or more descriptive of the faith of him of whom I write, than those engraven on the tomb of another Cornish sailor, Lord Exmouth :—

" All human glory ceases in the grave, but far dearer is the memory of that devout faith which led him in deep humility to the Cross of Christ, the Star which guided him to the desired haven, the Anchor of his hope, when on the death-bed of the just he yielded up his soul to his Redeemer."

APPENDICES.

APPENDIX A.

ROYAL DOCKYARD VOLUNTEERS (1848).

In the course of the year or two after his return from the Parana, Captain Sulivan did all he could to get another ship, but without success; so, seeing no immediate prospects of employment afloat, he thought of entering the colonial service, and applied for the governorship of the Falkland Islands, which was thereupon practically promised him. Just at that time, however, he was asked by Captain Hamilton, the Secretary to the Admiralty, to draw up a report as to the working of the volunteer corps composed of the royal dockyard workmen, which had been established the previous year. The plan had been first suggested by Lord Ellenborough (First Lord of the Admiralty), and on his leaving office it was supported by his successor, Lord Auckland. But it received no favour from the Naval Lords. The organisation was so faulty that the scheme had been pronounced in Parliament a failure. Sulivan drew up a plan of organisation, and on being asked by Lord Auckland to put it into practice, and to take up the training of the corps, inquired if the appointment was likely to be a permanent one. He was told it could not be promised him for more than five years, although he might consider it would last longer. So he gave up his ideas of colonial work, and removed with his family to Portsmouth. He was borne on the books of H.M.S. *Victory* as supernumerary captain. Within three months of his taking the corps in hand, he had greatly improved its discipline. On the outbreak of the Chartist riots, every redcoat in Portsmouth was sent to protect London, and Sulivan and his volunteers were left in charge of Portsmouth and its dockyard. This showed the confidence placed in the corps. He was then required to undertake the supervision of the whole of the seven royal dockyard brigades, comprising ten thousand five hundred men, with his headquarters at the Admiralty; so he removed to London. He was made

"Colonel and Chief of the Staff." A naval officer thus had the honour of being the first colonel of volunteers.

An announcement was made in Parliament that the scheme had turned out a complete success. Captain Hamilton had written as follows to Sulivan, soon after the latter had taken charge at Portsmouth :—

"ADMIRALTY, *January 24th*, 1848

"What you have done far exceeds my most sanguine hopes and expectations. Better thanks than mine will be due to you. I certainly looked for something from you, and the result only proves how correct I was in my estimate of the probable result of your appointment "

But the Naval Lords of the Admiralty, unfavourable to the scheme of the Civilian First Lords, excellent as it was, opposed Sulivan's remaining in charge on the grounds of *his having brought the scheme to such perfection that there was no further need of his services*, and the work could now be left to the officers of the yards ! Lord Auckland positively refused to agree to this, saying it was a breach of faith with Sulivan. The reply was, "But we can give him a ship." Lord Auckland, however, refused to sanction his dismissal until at least the drill season for the year had been completed. It seemed as if those who had opposed the scheme from the first bore no good-will to the man who had upset all their prognostications of failure by making it a success, showing that the very efficiency of a servant may displease some whose interests are not identical with those of the institution of which they have the control. In the letter of dismissal (the original of which is now before me), their lordships expressed their entire satisfaction with the zeal and energy he had displayed in the execution of his duty, and with the complete manner in which he had in so short a time carried into effect their views. Lord Auckland very kindly told Sulivan that he was sorry to see him put out of the work, but that it must be a satisfaction to him to know that those most opposed to the plan had allowed how well his work had been done, and he added, "You shall have one of the first appointments I have to give away." A few weeks afterwards, the sudden death of Lord Auckland at his office (half an hour before Sulivan called about an appointment then vacant) prevented his services being remembered. I should add Sulivan gave the credit of much of the success of the scheme to Lord Auckland and to Captain Hamilton, the Secretary On Sulivan's retirement, two majors took over the force, which, however, soon collapsed. By his system of reorganisation Sulivan had reduced the expenses by £20,000 per annum. The following extracts from his evidence before the Royal Commission on Coast Defences (1860) refer to these volunteers :—

" I may say briefly that I did not organise them at first. They were organised in the summer of 1847. They were trying to drill them during that summer. Through the sad blunders made in attempting to organise them, the whole thing gave great dissatisfaction, and was working very badly. The Admiralty sent for me, and told me to go to all the yards, and report on what caused this state of things ; and I saw that the whole thing had been organised in such a way that it could not succeed. More particularly they had made the great blunder of not making the whole force artillery. They had battalions of infantry thirteen hundred strong (thirteen companies of a hundred men each); and in another yard they had a battalion of infantry a hundred strong (fifty men in a company). There was no system of any kind. On my report, the Admiralty told me to draw up a plan for reorganising them on a uniform system, which I did ; and this document contains a copy of the letter sent to the superintendent of Portsmouth yard, which is a duplicate of those sent to the other yards, stating that my plan was to be carried out."

" *Can you state the reason why those battalions were disbanded ?* " —"I cannot. I was very much astonished when I heard of it. The men were paid extra hours, a shilling a night. The thing worked well, but especially so wherever the superintendent was in favour of it and took an interest in it, and, with the officers, urged the men to take a pride in it. It worked well, in spite of the indifference or opposition of the superintendents in one or two yards. I should like to say a few words on what military men said of the wonderful aptitude of these men for rapidly acquiring the necessary organisation, and how effective they became, particularly in the use of great guns. I have never seen anything in the men of the *Excellent*, or in any men, to exceed the beautiful fire of some of these men at marks, both with musket and great gun. This was attributed by military officers who witnessed it to the men being mechanics, and a superior class of men ; but it certainly astonished every one who saw it. The service was compulsory."

" *These men employed in the dockyards had a pension to look to ?* "—"Yes. All apprentices and men were bound to join the force. When I reduced the Portsmouth brigade by two or three hundred old men, who should never have been taken in, I had to talk to these men to persuade them that they were too old. The desire was to serve, and they did not like to be excluded. That applied to both officers and men. There was not the slightest difficulty in getting them to serve ; the men took a pride in it. There is no doubt that they were the cheapest force in the country, for the value which they were to it. The training cost £30,000 for ten thousand five hundred men and officers ; the two thousand two hundred men who could have been put on to the guns at Portsmouth, or trained to work the guns on the fortifications, were the cost to the country of two companies of infantry two hundred strong."

Sir Frederick Abbott: "*How long did it generally take you to make them efficient as gunners ?*"—"In twenty-one or twenty-two days' drill they were so efficient that artillery officers said that they might be put alongside any gunners."

Chairman : "*Who were their instructors ?*"—"Sergeant-majors of marines and marine artillery were made adjutants of each brigade, and non-commissioned officers were selected for the companies. Some opponents of the system endeavoured to show that it interfered with the men's work ; but except in some instances at first, where men who had to drill in the evening left the yard a little earlier, this was not the case. Had I remained another season, I intended to propose devoting Saturday afternoons during summer entirely to drill, and charging half a day's pay to the military instead of the civil branch. That would have removed all chance of saying that it interfered with work. On the contrary, I doubt if the half-day's pay is ever earned by work on Saturday afternoons. I believe that the Admiralty had proof that the additional order and regularity caused by the organisation and drill were really useful in other than military respects, and particularly so in the case of an alarm of fire, when the men fell in by companies or sections as required, each with its non-commissioned officer, and were more quickly available than under the old system."

APPENDIX B.

FALKLAND ISLANDS (1848-51).

After his appointment had ended, the promised command of a ship was not forthcoming, and Sulivan saw no chance of employment afloat, in spite of his conspicuous services, although several captains, young in age and in sea experience, were being at this time, through interest, given ships. He began to suffer in health, doubtless owing to his disappointed hopes (only those who have been subjected to similar unjust treatment can understand the effects of it). His medical adviser wished him to go to the south of France ; but he said, "If I go anywhere out of England, it shall be to the Falklands." He went to the Admiralty and obtained leave to go abroad for three years. This was on a Monday. Going home, he surprised his wife by saying, "Can you be ready to start for the Falklands on Thursday ?" She replied,

" No, but I will by Monday next." The departure, however, was
delayed a little longer. He chartered a sailing-ship, and took out
some good stock animals. A friend, Captain Philip Hamond,
suffering in his chest, proposed to accompany him. There were
five Sulivan children, the eldest being eleven. Besides, there were
a governess, a man-servant and his wife, and a maid-servant. The
news being conveyed to the Falklands that there was an unmarried
servant coming out, the bachelors of the islands were much
interested in the arrival of the party. One rather elderly one
considered his chance would be increased at any rate if he were
the first to propose, so on the arrival of the ship he lay in waiting
near the place of debarkation. He saw a woman leading the
children. "She is older than I thought," he reflected. "Never
mind, here goes," and he rushed up to her and made his
proposal. He had made the mistake of addressing the married
woman! It was not long before the girl made her own choice,
so my mother was without a servant for some months. After
the piano had been landed, the governess, who had been engaged
in a hurry before starting, suggested that it would require tuning
after its voyage, and said she could manage it herself. My father
interrupted her when she had purposely broken six strings, thinking that thereby the schoolroom practising would be avoided!
She took her departure not long after to England, so my mother
had her hands full. In the course of the year I appeared to add
to her cares. A nurse was sought for me. There was an Indian
princess, descended from a royal South American line, a Diana
of the chase, who in one of her expeditions saved the lives of a
surveying party, a captain and eleven men, who after the loss of
their boat were soon on the verge of starvation in a place teeming
with game. She was to be relied upon so long as she kept from
the bottle. When I was nine days old, she went to the town,
was overcome by her besetting sin, and being ashamed of herself,
did not return, so my mother was left to manage me herself.
During the three years spent in the island, my father was
occupied in stock-raising, my mother with her domestic cares,
unassisted for part of the time, save by her young children.
One day H.M.S. *Rattlesnake* from Australia put into the Falklands to refit. My mother, hearing that there was a lady on
board, invited her to the house during the repairing of the ship.
She was the widow of the captain, a brother of the late Dean
Stanley. Thirty years afterwards, she met us at Bournemouth,
and told us of her recollections of seeing my mother working so
hard. Of the farming operations I have not space to speak. Certainly the life was a healthy one. Captain Hamond recovered so
quickly that in six weeks after his arrival he was camping out
with the other men. His death happening only a few years ago,
speaks well for the Falklands as a "health resort." One story
in connection with him I must relate. One day a cow broke

loose and charged him. He climbed up on a wall and lay on
the top, but forgot to tuck up his leg. This the cow charged,
but the large horns coming against the wall, saved the leg from
the blows. The situation was ludicrous—he calling for help to
his man-servant and to my father, who were so convulsed with
laughter that they could only cry out, " Tuck your leg up." The
dulness of social life was occasionally relieved by the visits of
men-of-war, both British and French, and by the riding-parties
that ensued. The then Marquis of Hastings having heard
through Mr. Robert Hamond of the intended trip to the
Falklands, and of my father's desire to improve the breed of horses
and sheep there, had given him a nearly thorough-bred young
stallion Mrs. Hamond had given my mother a thorough-bred
mare, and my father bought a good cart-horse. The two latter
died during or just after the voyage out, but the young stallion
" Hastings " was turned out amongst a small drove of mares.
His descendants are now celebrated in the island as combining
the strength and fire of the English horse with the endurance
of the South American. The great improvement in the breed
of the sheep owing to Sulivan's importations has led to others,
which have resulted in the Falkland Island sheep now taking
a high place. When the three years' leave was about up, my
father returned home in the autumn of 1851. There was no
choice but to take passage in a ship heavily laden, or to wait
three months for the packet My father chose the former.
Prolonged calms led to the provisions and water running low,
so all were put on short allowances The sailors, led by two
men who had been dismissed from the navy, demanded their full
allowance, and on the captain refusing, mutinied and went below.
The hatches were then fastened down upon them ; the cabin
was barricaded ; whilst the captain, the mate, and my father went
aloft and reduced the sails of the barque one by one, in case
of the wind rising The refractory crew were soon starved into
submission, and all returned to duty but the two ringleaders,
who were put in irons After a protracted voyage of ninety
days, the barque arrived in Liverpool. Captain Sulivan then
took his family to Guildford.

APPENDIX C.

HARBOUR OF REFUGE AT FILEY (1859).

Admiral Sulivan served as the Board of Trade representative
on the Royal Commission of 1859 relating to Harbours of
Refuge.

The want had long been felt of a harbour of refuge and a

strategic harbour on our east coast. The loss of life on that coast, especially in the old sailing-ship days, was enormous, and even now it is very great. There is no really safe harbour on the whole coast from the Thames to the Forth into which large ships can run *at any time of tide, in any weather,* for shelter, or into which our men-or-war could run for coals. The importance of this, were we at war and needing to maintain a fleet in the North Sea, would be very great. I believe there have been as many as five commissions on this very subject, and that the report of every commission, like that of the first, has been to the effect that a harbour should be made at Filey.

This commission was the first of the series. Among the commissioners was the late Sir John Coode, the celebrated engineer, who had just completed Portland Harbour. He was a distant cousin of my father.

The reasons why the commissioners fixed on Filey were the following : the favourable locality, being about the centre of the east coast ; the fact of Filey Brigg forming in itself one of the two great piers needed, which practically would save a million in the cost of constructing a harbour ; the deep water close to the shore ; the good quality of the local stone for building ; the impossibility of its silting up ; accessibility to the railways from the northern or Welsh coal-fields, which could bring down the coals on to the Brigg, alongside which steamers could be moored ; convict labour could be employed. The cost was very carefully gone into, and an estimate given for the construction of the harbour. But the Board pronounced against it, and on this opinion Parliament rejected the proposal.

Admiral Sulivan wrote a letter, which appeared in the *Times* of April 7th, 1871, after his retirement, when the question of harbours of refuge again came up. He stated that, as the representative of the Board of Trade on the commission of 1859, he had at the time prepared a minute to the President on the question.

It was said that the estimates were not to be depended upon, as they were not founded on any reliable basis. Verbally and in his minute he had fully explained that the estimates of the commissioners were carefully based on the actual cost of Portland Harbour, which one of the commissioners had himself constructed. It was therefore unfair to compare the estimates with the actual cost of certain other harbours, where errors had been made and additions to the original plans had been permitted by which the original estimates were exceeded. He had been assured by one of the most experienced harbour contractors, who had gone into the Filey estimates, that he would undertake to construct the harbour on the figures of the estimates, and to give guarantees for its completion. He thought the report of six responsible commissioners, who had given six months' careful consideration to the work, 'should not be condemned without the estimates being gone into by competent authorities.

APPENDIX D.

COAST DEFENCES OF THE UNITED KINGDOM, AND VERTICAL FIRE (1859)

Not long after his return from the Parana in 1846, with the experience there gained of earthen batteries, he visited the battery then in course of construction at Bovisand, Plymouth Harbour. He found ten guns were to be placed in it close together. The fort had stone embrasures, calculated to conduct the enemy's shot on to the guns and men. A high masonry barrack, close in the rear of the guns, would form a trap for shells missing the parapet. He considered it was the form of battery best calculated to assist an enemy. Further, though the guns would bear upon the channel generally used by our ships, the fact had been overlooked that there was a second good channel, by which large ships could enter the harbour *exposed only to about three of the ten guns.* Sulivan at once reported the case to the Admiralty, and recommended a fort with earthen parapets and guns *en barbette.* Admiral Berkeley confirmed his objections, and stated that at Acre they soon silenced the guns in embrasures, but not those *en barbette.* The Admiralty requested the Ordnance Board to suspend operations on the works, but this the Board refused to do, and the fort was completed at great cost. Sulivan then found another battery on the same faulty plan was being commenced on Devil's Point. He again remonstrated, but the influence of the designer was too strong. Tenders were advertised for relating to a third fort on an island on the same plan, with stone casemates in addition Sulivan made a third protest, this and the last being supported by eminent engineers and artillery officers who had written to him on the subject.

Some years after Mr. James Ferguson asked him if it was true that he had urged the use of earth-works for sea defences long before his own work on the subject was published; and the papers and plans being shown him, he very liberally offered to publish a statement of what had occurred in his next edition; but the documents being semi-official, Sulivan did not think it right to take advantage of his offer.

The moral of this is that the naval authorities should be consulted on questions relating to coast defences.

DEFENCE COMMISSION, 1859.—The members of the commission

were General Sir Harry Jones (who had been at Bomarsund), Admiral George Elliot, General Sir F. Abbott, Captain A. C. Key, R.N. (who had served at Obligado and in the Baltic), Colonel Lefroy, R.A., and Mr. James Ferguson (whose book has been referred to above). In the report the commissioners recommended the adoption of several of the suggestions Captain Sulivan made, and especially drew attention to the importance of vertical fire. But it is strange how little this subject seems to have been taken up by our own gunnery men in recent years. The report showed that the then defences of our dock-yards were insufficient.

Much of the evidence referred to the actions of Obligado, Bomarsund, and Sweaborg. As I have incorporated this in the chapters treating of those events, I will not again repeat it.

Being asked by Captain Key if he thought the forts at " Horse-sand" and " No Man's Land " would protect Spithead from an enemy's fleet in the absence of our own, Sulivan gave a decided opinion that they would not. He pointed out that there was great difficulty in hitting a rapidly advancing ship, changing her range every minute, and that no system of fortification at the entrance to a port which, if passed, allows ships to bring up out of range inside is of any use unless combined with a boom. The great defect of the fortifications of all our ports was that they guarded only the entrance. There were no inside forts to protect our arsenals and shipping. The proposed forts at Spit-head themselves would mark the channels for ships entering at night. He said he had never known an instance of a ship being sunk passing a battery. " However small the vessel, and however slow the speed, it would be almost impossible to stop a ship passing batteries, even at close range."

" *On the other hand, it would appear that the ships can do so little harm to earthen batteries, that, if it came to a regular stand-up fight between them, the batteries must in the long-run destroy the ships before they would be destroyed themselves?*"—" Most certainly with wooden ships and properly constructed batteries, and still more so if the ships are not able to close within five or six hundred yards ; but if the batteries are constructed as some even of our earthen batteries are, and the ships can get close, I believe that the batteries can be silenced in a few minutes."

Sir F. Abbott: " *What do you consider to be a well-constructed earthen battery, which would make a good fight against ships?*"— " A battery with raised traversing platforms, and barbette guns over a seven-feet earthen parapet, where the guns would be exposed to direct fire. I do not think that guns at long range will be nearly so dangerous as mortars are. But we shall always have a power-ful means of defence to aid our batteries in iron-cased floating batteries. We ought to be able at Portsmouth to place as many in aid of our forts as could possibly be brought against us, and, with those and the forts I have named, we ought to be secure. But having first secured our inner line of defence, without which no advanced batteries would avail us, we could proceed with the outer batteries on the shoals, which would, I think, ensure us even against any attempt on Portsmouth by sea."

He thought circular forts the weakest kind, as so few of their guns can be concentrated on one spot.

" At one fort at Cronstadt, which ought to have been a principal one, if we had attacked it, we could have placed eight floating batteries, and all the force of the squadron to back those floating batteries, gun-boats and all, with only three guns in each tier which could have borne upon them, and four guns *en barbette* above—that is to say, ten guns. The fort was oval; it had a long face with circular ends, and the circular ends were the weak points "*

He described the barrier built at Cronstadt, which was to be made like a breakwater. This was the only secure barrier for shallow water. Turning to the Needles passage, he again showed that the forts there would not prevent ships passing, and the stronger tide would aid them. (I have in late years passed through this channel with my father, and he said that he believed that the present-day forts could not prevent present-day ships, with their greater speed, from passing) But by protecting Spithead with strong inner defences, no large force would care to risk passing the outer defences, as there would be no object but Portsmouth worth the risk.

133. " Not only will iron-plated ships pass batteries easily, but we have especially to fear them, as bombarding vessels, both with guns and mortars. I believe from direct fire they will be safe at a thousand yards' range, if not less; but I doubt if anything will make them safe from vertical fire. I only feared the effect of vertical fire when we attacked Cronstadt; and knowing that a large number of heavy mortars were placed in all the batteries there before the spring of 1856, I thought it very likely the floating batteries might be sunk by them, and consequently endeavoured, in drawing up a plan for the attack, to place the batteries in such shallow water that, if sunk, their ports might be above water. It would therefore chiefly depend on vertical fire against iron-cased vessels: even at long range many shells would fall on them. At Sweaborg the three-decked ship was at extreme range (nearly four thousand yards from our heavy mortars) in the line of fire of a few only of the mortars, yet twenty-five shells fell through her decks the first day, and nearly destroyed her, killing and wounding above a hundred and fifty men, and obliging them to remove her; yet two Lancaster guns and two sixty-eight-pounders during the same time failed to make

---

* In spite of this evidence the forts built at Spithead are circular.

any impression on her, only striking her two or three times, and at much closer ranges too, but they were not stationary. I would therefore, on all our sea defences intended to prevent vessels anchoring within range, have nearly as many mortars as guns. In all the casemated forts I would have thirteen-inch mortars only on the upper tiers (well protected by traverses), and between the earthen batteries on the shore I would have separate mortar batteries, in order to divide the fire of ships between as many points as possible. When ships could come very close, the mortar batteries should be thrown back a little.

"*Mortars would be of no use against moving bodies?*"—"None, I think, excepting a chance fire. All vessels bombarding must take up their position to get their range accurately, or they will not do you much harm. At that extreme range it would be very difficult to throw a shot into the dockyard."

He continued to dwell upon the importance of vertical fire, illustrating his views by reference to Sweaborg He then described the kind of boom he would recommend—formed of old ships, *with batteries of heavy guns in the bows of each.* Such a boom would be a very serious obstacle—*a boom of batteries.* The general impression of all at Obligado was that, if the vessels forming the boom had been armed, the passage could not have been forced.

"My original plan, when I had the dockyard battalions at Portsmouth Harbour, and seeing how weak it was, was this: I could have run a paddle-wheel steamer even into Portsmouth Harbour then; and it struck me the only chance of closing the entrance, if we were ever surprised by the enemy with our fleet away, or if we lost command of the sea, would be by mooring a couple of ships across the entrance, or putting chains across,* so as to be able to lower them for our own trade. For such a place as Spithead twenty or thirty ships would be required. This kind of boom would not do for the Thames below Gravesend. The Medway would be a more difficult place, on account of the strong tide there. Sheerness would be a very difficult place to block up by a boom, and it is the most exposed to a bombardment. It wants defences in front of it to make it secure against a couple of ships with mortars."

A casemated battery should be put only where no earthen battery can be built. If the embrasures were reversed, it would increase the power of the battery over the guns tenfold.

The Chairman : "*You have had a great deal of experience in navigating in intricate channels and open coasts and all sorts of navigation. Supposing the buoys removed from Spithead, and there were a clear sea there, should you think that it would be very easy*

---

* Wire hawsers have this year (1895) been prepared for closing this very entrance against torpedo-boats, and boom defences added to those of Spithead and the Medway.

for an enemy's fleet to go right into Spithead, as a mere question of navigation?"—" I think that they ought to be able to do it if they had any one fit to lead them in."

He instanced how he had run into the far more intricate channel of Sweaborg for the first time at full speed

" Once the French had sufficient command of the sea to induce them to venture to attack such a place as Sheerness, they could soon destroy it by means of mortar-boats and a few protecting vessels."

Captain Sulivan gave the following evidence, which will be regarded with interest if, as I believe, it is the first suggestion of the use of the ram in naval warfare. Admiral Sartorius, who usually has had the credit of the idea, was later in the field :—

" I believe all vessels ought to be used as rams. I proposed the first day I ever joined Admiral Napier in the Baltic that, if there was a chance of meeting the Russian ships at anchor outside, they should be attacked by cutting off the cutwaters of our ships, taking their bowsprits off and securing their lower masts, and by running down without firing a shot they would run in on their (the Russians') broadsides, and I believe that that would destroy with perfect impunity any line of ships which were at anchor under any fire which they could pour into you."

For the opposite reason he condemned the straight bows of merchant steamers, the projecting old figure head taking the blow of a colliding steamer on the upper structure of a vessel, and thus lessening the force of a collision.*

Being questioned as to the defence of Portsmouth Dockyard, " I have so little confidence in the result of bombarding at very long ranges with guns, compared to the shorter range of the mortars, that I think that the great thing is to protect the place against the heavy mortar range first. If guns are fired at a mortar elevation, then I should consider it vertical fire."

Being asked as to the best foundation for a work on the sand, " That is quite an engineering question, upon which I should not like to give an opinion. The danger of bombarding on the land side of Portsmouth is probably as great as by sea. I have always had an idea that, wherever there are those chalk hills, by scarping

---

* A few years ago my father told me he thought that our officers should be trained in the use of the modern ram. He said that the Russians alone put their officers through a course of ramming. Before a captain was given a command he was exercised in a gun-boat, properly protected The practice took place in shoal water. Two gun-vessels were set at one another ; and in these tactics, although some circles were first described, in the end one vessel always made a hit It was generally found that the most skilful fencer came off the victor, showing it was largely a question of skill He said it was a great pity that our officers were not put through a similar course, to give them experience in ramming or in avoiding a ram. I believe that, if such practice were given, the experience gained would at least come in useful in peace time for the avoidance of collisions.—ED.

down the hill you can make it almost inaccessible in a very cheap way. I have been very much interested in that question in connection with the chalk ridges for the defence of London on the south. I believe that that is a very important question, and that it bears indirectly upon the defences of our ports, because if you make Portsmouth impregnable, and an invading army ever land, it makes it more certain that they will go to London, and, if so, the defence of London becomes very much connected with the defence of Portsmouth."

The Armstrong gun then having come into notice, he pointed out that the greater the range of guns, the greater the need of having advancing forts to guard against bombardment He referred to plans he had sent in some time before for protecting Sheerness by forts on the spits, and spoke of the folly of having placed a dockyard in such a place, it being well known to be the result of a political job to sell the land of a man there.

"Then there is a very serious point in all these isolated forts—namely, that the more detached you make them, the more you make them liable to the attacks of heavy ships; and if it were the object to destroy a place, and mortar-ships could be brought within range by destroying one of these outlying forts, I do not doubt that any fleet would risk a number of ships for the purpose of doing it. For instance, if at Cronstadt, by destroying the two outer casemated forts, the place had been at our mercy, the thing would have been done, with a certain loss of ships and men. And so any fort placed in advance, which is not well supported by the cross fire of other forts, is liable to be attacked as a single fort, and the place would be open to a bombardment. That is a very difficult point in deciding on this question, because, with iron ships especially, I have no doubt that no stone fort which has ever been built will stand against them."

He suggested a fort on Bembridge Point, and wound up with the reiterated statement that no fort of any description would stop the passage of an iron ship.

As years went on he held more and more to the opinion that vertical fire would be the fire of the future. But whilst other nations seem now to be recognising its importance we have neglected it. There are howitzers at Ceuta and at Paris.

In vol. xxix. of the *Century Magazine*, 1884-85, is described the work of the Federal navy on the Mississippi. There is an illustration of the mortar-vessels, forming part of the western flotilla, concealed behind a wooded point, engaging the batteries on island No. 10. The writer says,—

"The gun-boats fired a few shots now and then, but doing no harm. The mortar-boats, however, were daily throwing thirteen-inch bombs, and so effectually that at times the Confederates were driven from their batteries, and compelled to seek refuge in caves and other places of safety."

Further on the same writer describes the passage of the lower Mississippi and the attack on Fort Jackson and St. Philip. To divert the enemy during the passage of the ships past the fort, mortar-schooners were placed some distance off, behind wooded banks, their masts disguised with branches. The reduction of Fort Jackson was almost entirely due to the vertical shell-fire from these mortars, which so completely demoralised the defenders that, although none of their guns were dismantled by the fire of the ships, the Confederates were unable to deliver an effectual fire against them, which therefore passed the forts without damage. It is stated the men were driven from the open barbette batteries into the casemates. At a range of two thousand eight hundred and fifty yards nearly every shell out of the sixteen thousand fired fell inside the fort.

It is interesting to note that the work of selecting the position of the mortar-vessels, furnishing the commanders with proper charts, calculating the ranges for each mortar, was, as at Sweaborg, executed by the surveying officers.

The following extract from an article on "New Weapons of the United States Army," in the *Century Magazine* for February 1895, shows that the experience gained in the above actions has not been lost on American artillerists :—

"SEA-COAST MORTARS.—Not less important in the defence of the United States, nor less successful in the results obtained, are the modern high-power sea-coast twelve-inch breech-loading mortars. Sea-coast mortars are used for the destruction of ships-of-war threatening our coasts, and fire projectiles designed to strike the deck—the most vulnerable part of a ship. . . . Sixteen mortars capable of simultaneous fire will be grouped in sunken batteries, or pits, united under the control of one officer. . . . They will be fired in volley or otherwise. . . . *The knowledge of the extreme accuracy of fire of which these mortars are capable* will render it very hazardous indeed for a vessel to approach within range—*six miles*" (Compare paragraph 133 of the above evidence.)

In a recent speech Viscount Wolseley lamented that our army was, unlike foreign armies, *without guns for vertical fire.* It is to be hoped our naval and military authorities will awake to the importance of this subject I believe we have no naval gun capable of being used for vertical fire, whilst some other nations have. The great range of guns in the present day only adds to the importance of the question.

APPENDIX E.

NAVIGATING AND SURVEYING OFFICERS (1846-63)

We have seen that Captain Sulivan's paper of 1857 led to the committees from which arose the Naval Reserve   In December 1858 he wrote another paper, entitled " Proposals for improving the Lists of Naval Officers and System of Promotion."   Sir John Packington had this printed at the Admiralty, and it led to the House of Commons' Committee of 1860-61, which recommended portions to be carried out.   Mr. Childers, however, later on adopted more of the ideas.   It will be interesting to see how many have been adopted and how many remain yet to be taken up.

1. Cadets to be trained in sea-going training-ships instead of ordinary men-of-war.

2. Abolition of the master line (adopted).

3. Abolition of the distinction of the red, white, and blue, and use of white ensign as the royal naval flag (adopted).

4. Change of titles of naval officers, so as to show relative rank with officers of the army.

5. A certain length of service in each rank, except for service in action, before qualifying for promotion to the next rank.

6. Reduction of lieutenants' and increase of sub-lieutenants' lists.

7. Formation of a reserve of junior officers from the mercantile marine (adopted).

8. Various suggestions (several of which have been adopted) to govern promotion by seniority and selection.

ABOLITION OF THE MASTER LINE.—So early as the year 1841, and again in 1846 and 1847, Sulivan published in a naval paper proposals for doing away with the rank of master without in-justice to the class, and he never ceased taking every opportunity of urging this both publicly and privately, believing that the then existing system prevented young officers properly qualifying themselves for navigating and piloting their ships when they obtained commands.   He felt strongly that, while masters were becoming more and more dissatisfied with their rank and position, higher executive rank could never be given them without gross injustice to the most valuable class of officers—commanders of large ships and first lieutenants of small ships.   All the attempts made to alter their rank and satisfy the masters had failed, as the best masters allowed.   All the masters he consulted approved of Sulivan's proposals.

He also about the same time (1846) urged an improvement in the pay and position of seamen in the royal navy, and specially of petty officers, in order that the service might be made so desirable to seamen as to do away with the necessity of corporal punishment.

His evidence before the commission of 1860 greatly conduced to the abolition of the separate navigating line. He explained that, though he had not commanded large ships, he had had much experience in handling them. In the old war time young executive officers obtained practice in navigation through being sent away in charge of prizes. These opportunities no longer existed. The following incident first drew his attention to the necessity of reform :—

"A twelve-gun brig was lying at Spithead. About noon a signal was made to her to proceed to sea, for the relief of a vessel ashore near St. Catherine's. The signal of inability was made. 'The master is on shore.' 'Are the other officers on board?' 'Yes.' 'Proceed to sea immediately.' The inability signal was again hoisted, the commander refusing to start his anchor till the master or a pilot was sent to take the vessel out of Spithead "

He felt such an incident to be a disgrace to the service, but it was the result of continuance of the old custom, when sailors only navigated ships and soldiers fought them.

At Spithead, on another occasion, the master being ill below, the captain of a ship anchored out of line, and had to get the master of the nearest ship to come and move his, under steam, a cable's length or two, there being no one else on board competent to do so.

"Owing to the bad system, although the work was well done in the higher branches, it was allowed by the masters themselves to be not well done in the junior ranks of their line."

For the second master, instead of being on deck assisting the master, was generally below attending to the holds. After the first year in the Baltic, Sulivan, who had seen how unjust this was to the juniors, got a minute passed remedying this abuse.

"I could mention instances of the utter incompetency of our junior masters in the Baltic, beyond what any man who knows anything of navigation and pilotage would conceive possible. The blunders of the youngest midshipman who had been two years at sea would hardly be greater. Many of those young masters, when put in charge of ships, rapidly learned their work, as captains chose the best of them, and these rose to the higher positions, whilst many were weeded out in some way or other.

"However well the senior masters may have done their duty, it has always been at the expense of the thorough efficiency of our young officers, and consequently of the commanders and captains of our ships.

"I have had experience of young lieutenants being put into command of gun-boats with no one to help them. It was remarkable how well they handled the vessels, even in very intricate pilotage waters, and how rapidly they learned the work."

Although executive officers were supposed to keep up the study of navigation, practically very few did so after passing.

" Every one knows that an ordinary day's work in a ship is a farce. Some captains encourage a better system amongst the youngsters, and a few young men here and there take a pleasure in navigation, and do attend to it from choice. Occasionally a young lieutenant or two may show a taste for it.

" In large ships there are always some one or two officers who like navigation, and who encourage it amongst the juniors. I happened to be in a small frigate as midshipman, for a passage home, in which the captain navigated the ship without a master for nearly three years, and it was done by two midshipmen, and after I joined her by three. Instead of sending in their day's work as a matter of form, they knew that they were navigating the ship, and they took a pride in it, and their observations (not only ordinary ones) were taken separately. Every day every observation that could be taken was taken by those midshipmen (for instance, night or day lunars); and once now and then they were checked by the captain, but he relied on their observations. On one occasion, having relied greatly on a very good chronometer, a very great error in that chronometer, after firing at a mark, was detected by their observations.

" Out of those who began navigating work you could select the pick for the large ships as a reward for their services. When these men came to the higher ranks, they would furnish commanders and captains more efficient as navigators.

" If the Admiralty looked to that position as one giving officers a claim for advancement, just as gunnery lieutenants and first lieutenants ought to look to theirs, then surely many a young officer would gladly take that line.

" I wish to keep perfectly clear of alluding in any way to the surveying service, or to men brought up in that service, because it is not the case that the surveyors are always the best for pilotage duties. They may be very good men for a survey, and they may make a beautiful survey and drawing of a place, but it is a totally different qualification from *the work of handling ships in intricate pilotage waters*, and I have known surveyors under my own command whom I could not trust in that work. Where only one master out of five or six could do it, or could be taught to do it, I have seen a young lieutenant here and another there who rapidly became excellent hands for it, and were able to take charge in places where perhaps two or three months before they would never have dreamt of being able to take a ship."

" *Still, at present you do consider that the masters of our large ships are really useful men in the position that they now hold?*"— " Yes, for the ordinary pilotage and navigation of the ships in known pilotage waters; but to go into any new place, and do work, for instance, on a new and unknown coast, up an unknown river, or on an enemy's coast—in short, where you have no charts [or yet where there are charts], and all the buoys and lights and marks are removed, they are not a bit more so than any other class of officers, and I think we want very much to keep in view in any reorganisation *the wants of a fleet and squadron on an enemy's coast in war.* We have had a few surveying officers accidentally on the stations surveying when expeditions have occurred or war has broken out, and they have supplied a certain want that could not otherwise have been supplied. They are fast wearing out, our foreign surveys, which alone made them efficient, are almost coming to an end.

"In one very intricate place, some twenty miles long, in the Baltic, after I had taken a squadron of line-of-battle ships through the place and put a buoy on every single danger, and a few ships had gone up under masters, the admiral sent for me, and told me that the masters complained that they could not find the channel ; and though I had buoyed out the numerous passages and channels, they did not know which to take. In many cases, before they were satisfied to take their ships up and down, I had to go and whitewash every single point and spot that had to be left on one side all the way up. That was for want of their experience in that practical work. But in a very short time, here and there, you would find a master coming out and becoming as perfect a pilot as any man could be ; but so would you have had in any other class in the squadron had they been given the same opportunities and the same experience." (N.B.—The masters doubtless had a chart as well)

"*In substituting the navigating officer for the master, do you think that that will throw more work in the navigation of the ship upon the captain ?*"—"Not the slightest, because I believe that, however competent a captain might be to navigate his ship, he would not take much part in it himself [the responsibility, however, resting on him]. I hardly ever took an observation when in command at sea; I trusted to two well-known officers, of whom the master was one

PILOTAGE.—"The captain should see to the observation of the officers, and see the position of the ship on the chart. But directly the ship gets into pilotage waters, I think it would be very desirable that the captain should more generally attend to the pilotage of his own ship, or at least be competent to do so, and to see that those under him were doing the work well.

"In intricate waters the captain should be as perfect a pilot as any one. The more competent he is, whoever is under him, the safer the ship is.

"If you call sailing in line through a channel, led by another ship, pilotage, that is no pilotage. All the fleet follow the leader, and the captain's attention may be directed merely to keeping his rank, the same as in the open sea; but where, as occurred once in the Baltic, the whole fleet were in the midst of rocks and shoals, with hardly any anchoring ground, in a strong breeze, overtaken by a dense fog, and the captain is left to his own resources for hours and hours, then is the time when the captain's ability to pilot and handle a ship is everything; and those cases will always occur in important services, particularly on an enemy's coast.

"The French found the want of a class of officers accustomed to pilotage work in new and intricate channels; but that did not bear upon the masters. Our surveying officers took their ships through intricate navigation, the same as they took our ships. The French admiral asked me to try and train some of his officers to that duty, and he told me that he would pick an officer from each ship, and select a small vessel with a commander that he thought most competent, and put all the officers on board, if I would teach them the pilotage, and take his ship up and down the channels, and point them out to them."

When first he argued that young officers would accept command without a master or navigating officer, the First Lord said to him that none would do so. One man was tried, and he said, "*If I am not fit to navigate the ship, I am not fit to command her.*" Sulivan thought the confidence of such officers had been acquired by commanding gun-boats in the Russian and Chinese wars.

"*Do you consider that the competency of young officers to navigate their ships, which has been noticed lately, arises from their source of education at the Naval College?*"—"No, I think not. I think it arises from more of them having been put in positions where they found it necessary to learn the duty, and to do it."

He instanced the case "of a young lieutenant of little experience, put in command of a small brig in the Parana, with no one under him but a boatswain's mate and a party of men. He was taken directly into some of the most intricate river and river-entrance navigation in the world   He felt so nervous and anxious at first he thought his hair would turn grey.   In a week or two he became an unusually good officer.   He alone did a great deal of pilotage and convoy work up and down the river He brought two large sailing-ships as well as his own up five hundred miles without touching the ground, and was soon a better pilot than many surveying officers after years of experience of the work.   This is the class of men I would pick out from the whole service, not only for the navigating class, but with the view of bringing as many of them forward to the head of the service as I could."   (The officer alluded to was the late Admiral Sir Astley Cooper Key.)

THE SURVEYING SERVICE, 1863, COMMISSION.—"*With regard to the surveying officers, is there a permanent staff of surveying officers in the royal navy?*"—"The surveying officers have been all along in a peculiar position; they have never had a recognised position in the service; they have only held certain positions, when, by chance of war, their service has thrown them into the fleet, and their qualifications have led them to perform certain duties, but all of them have been literally on sufferance. The admiral, if he found their value, might employ them, but he need not; nor need he recognise their position if he chose not to do so. The surveying service is quite new. for in the old war we had nothing of the kind. Sir George Cockburn and Lord Melville paid great attention to it some years after the Peace, and it was owing to them that surveys were commenced in different parts of the world In the first China war, in the war in South America, in the second China war, in the Black Sea during the Russian war, there were surveying officers employed on the station who were at once taken by the admirals under their command away from their surveying duties to perform duties which we ought to provide officers for with every fleet.

"If you could refer to the reports of Sir William Parker, Lord Lyons, Sir Michael Seymour, and Admiral Hope, you would see that they specially dwelt on the necessity and value of surveying officers in those expeditions. There is no young class of officer now coming forward. Without them, until you train them in war, disasters will occur for want of them; it is exactly the same as the want of an engineers' force would be with an army on an expedition—as in the Peninsula and in the Crimea. There, for want of sufficient engineers, our operations suffered, and loss of life occurred, until officers were trained to add to the engineers' staff* And so it must be in a naval war. To go in and conduct operations on an enemy's coast, you must have officers who have been trained for the work, just in the same way as you must have engineers for an army in the field. Basque Roads in 1809 is a case in point Had there been an officer of this class there, his duty would have been to settle the question of depth of water and distance from the batteries the first night. All the doubt on this point being officially removed, the fleet must have gone in, and the French squadron would have been destroyed."

"*I see in the Navy List that there are eleven officers, consisting of captains, commanders, and lieutenants, and ten masters in the surveying list*"—" The twenty-one officers in the list are borne on the ships' books for home service; they are a particular class of surveying officers. Some few of them have served on the class of foreign service which I have alluded to, but they are nearly all employed on home service, and the home duties are of a special kind. They are not performed upon unexplored and dangerous coasts, which give the practice that is necessary for officers to enable them to perform the duties which we may anticipate they would have to perform in case of war. They are merely employed in

* Lord Wolseley was detached from a line regiment for such duties.—ED.

carrying out details in connection with the ordnance surveys. It is a totally different class of duty, and it must be looked upon as not meeting the wants that I have mentioned.*

" The great fault of the present day is the absence of advantages to surveying officers sufficient to induce young officers who are fit for it to go into the surveying-vessels.

" It is no advantage putting youngsters, as youngsters, into surveying-ships. They would only learn a little sounding."

PIONEER OFFICERS —In 1858 he wrote " A Proposal for organising a Scientific Corps of Naval Officers," showing the necessity of holding out inducements to officers to take up surveying, so as to maintain a staff of surveyors for war-time. Some of the opinions expressed have been mentioned above. I will therefore merely give the following points :—

It will be seen he meant a superior class of surveying officer, embracing the quality of " pioneer," for doing the kind of work he did in the Baltic. He thought there should be special advantages in pay and promotion held out, so as to make the corps an object of ambition to the best young officers, to be gained by well-tested superiority in seamanship and all the necessary scientific branches. The selection to be made when passing for lieutenants. A more practical examination in navigation, to test ability as an observer, and a certain proficiency in surveying would be required, as well as ability as an officer and sailor (difficult to test). Therefore all offering for this higher examination should be first recommended by their captains as *the pick of the youngsters.* Twice as many as would be required should be put through a year's special training. The half not attaining to the selected posts would be made more valuable officers by the course. A special sea-going ship to be provided for the training, so that practical pilotage, gunnery, and seamanship could be tested in addition to scientific studies. Gunnery—a most important subject, as the planning of attacks would be dealt with by these officers. All admirals and senior officers to have one or more "pioneer" officers attached to their command.

Thanks mainly to Sulivan's exertions the navy is now reaping the benefit of the improved scheme. All officers know something of navigation, although perhaps not as much as could be wished. They all undergo a practical as well as theoretical college course, embracing pilotage, so as to work by the chart anywhere ; but navigators themselves consider this course could with advantage be lengthened. The surveying service is receiving more attention, although a surveying-ship is not a necessary part of every fleet, as it should be. There still, however, seems to be wanting the special class of "pioneer" officer.

Navigators have only recently had the same chance of advance-

* There are now thirty-two executive officers in the surveying service, employed on foreign surveys for the most part.—ED.

ment as officers in other special branches, and there must be no
retrogression in this respect, or the best men will avoid that line.
There should, if anything, be greater inducements, to compensate
for the very great responsibility and risk to his career incurred
by the navigator, which the gunnery and other men are exempt
from.

APPENDIX F.

THE NAVAL RESERVE (1846-60).

As far back as 1846 Sulivan had endeavoured to call the attention
of the authorities and of the public to the necessity of a reserve
of trained seamen, so as to enable us to man a *war fleet* in time of
emergency.

Soon after his appointment to the Board of Trade in 1857
he laid a paper on the subject before the President, who consented to its being brought to the attention of the First Lord
of the Admiralty, who had it printed. This led to the "Manning
Committee" of 1858. The scheme of reserve which resulted
from this committee was almost identical with Sulivan's scheme,
except that it omitted the chief aids to its success—*the pension
fund* * *and school-ships*—and did not provide enough men.

His plan was first to provide from seamen's contributions
a pension fund giving officers £20, men £10, at the age of
fifty, so as to attach them to their country; then to establish
a compulsory service system, by which every young man joining
the mercantile marine should serve a year in a man-of-war for
training, and further in time of emergency. *Failing the adoption
of this plan, a voluntary service system,* going to the merchant
service for forty thousand volunteers to serve in a similar manner :
in either case giving a return in the shape of a pension of £20
at the age of fifty, which, with that from the seamen's fund, would
amount to £30 per annum This would provide an adequate
reserve, and induce a better class of men to join the merchant
service. In addition to either system the establishment of
school training-ships in all our harbours, in which Government
would give a training to seamen's sons and picked boys from the
day schools, on condition of their afterwards serving like the other
reserve men, and on the same terms as to pension, etc. He
thought that the cost to the country would not be greater than
the present system, inasmuch as fewer permanent men-of-war's
men need be maintained if we had a proper reserve.

It will thus be seen that the establishment of the present

* In recent years a small pension of £12 has been granted to reserve men
attaining the age of sixty.

reserve—inadequate though it be—is due to the exertions of my father. The subject is too important in the present day to dismiss in the limits of an appendix, so that I must reserve for another occasion a review of the convincing evidence given as to the need of an effectual reserve. At the present time the French have at their command a hundred and eighty-five thousand sailors and fishermen, all of whom have served at least three years on board a man-of-war, whilst we can muster only ninety-five thousand men, including fifteen thousand marines and twenty-three thousand reserve men, who have not been adequately trained alongside our blue-jackets, so as to acquire the discipline needed for service in action. It is found difficult in the present day even to man our peace navy.

APPENDIX G.

THE BOARD OF ADMIRALTY (1861).

Sir James Sulivan gave evidence before the committee appointed in 1861 *"to inquire into the constitution of the Board of Admiralty, and the various duties devolving thereon, also as to the general effect of such system on the navy."* Here his love for straightforward speaking was strongly evinced. Before a committee comprised of the First Lord and three ex-First Lords, two Secretaries to the Admiralty, a Junior Lord, and six civilian M.P.'s, he boldly pointed out how in his opinion the very construction of the Board of Admiralty prevented adequate reform in the navy and justice to the officers of that service. He, as usual, illustrated his arguments with case after case from his own knowledge.

At the outset of this examination, and publicly in later years, he distinctly stated that the whole system of promotion had changed for the better, and that officers now were advanced in turn and according to merit. In his opinion the great want of the navy was a permanent head, responsible to the country for its administration and for providing an efficient defence. Any one in such a position, in certain times of recent history, would have been able to carry his point with the Government when some alteration was necessary, or by his resignation have called public attention to the matter. Under such a system the unprepared state of the navy as regards the manning question could not have continued. The same applied to the question of discipline. There had of late years been too much interference on the part of the Press and of the House of Commons with the discipline of the navy. Through ignorance of the circumstances evil was often done.

There should be one man whom the country could hold responsible. Sulivan gave instances to show the Admiralty had sometimes given way to public clamour instead of supporting officers whose firmness should have been commended.

There was a general feeling throughout the service that it had suffered greatly from the effects of political and family interest, still more from the constant changes caused by the political character of the administration. The claims of officers might be known to one First Lord, but on he and his colleagues going out of office the man's claims were unknown to their successors.

A PERMANENT NAVAL COMMANDER-IN-CHIEF.—The greatest satisfaction to the navy would result from its administration being assimilated to that of the army, whose head does not change nor his chief of department, he having the promotions and appointments irrespective of changes of government.

"*First of all establish the best system*, which would be more a governmental or parliamentary move ; and when that system was established, it should be handed over to heads of departments, who would be responsible for the working of it. There are two points on which men who agree in principle might differ,—whether the Minister of Marine should be the head of the great departments under him ; or whether the Minister of Marine should be separate, with a commander-in-chief over the executive department of the navy. The affairs of the navy in that case might be divided into three great departments,—the one *the fleet in commission* , the other *the providing that fleet for commission* ; third, *the accountant-general of the navy* "

The plan Sulivan suggested was as follows ·—

"I. COMMANDER-IN-CHIEF OF THE FLEET IN COMMISSION — Branches . 1. The manning and distribution of the ships, and the inspection and discipline of the ships in commission, with a naval officer entirely devoted to this as his assistant , courts-martial. 2. *Coast-guard*: coast guard ships and stations ; naval reserve. 3. *Hydrographer* · the harbour branch, the surveys of the world, etc. 4. *Marines* 5. *Medical.* 6. *Victualling.* All these branches bear directly on the fleet in commission, and therefore should be under one head.

"II. COMPTROLLER.—Branches : 1. *A naval assistant comptroller*, to assist comptroller in inspection of the yards and all works relating to the naval branch and gunnery (fittings of guns and carriages). 2 *Chief constructor.* 3. *Steam director.* 4. *Director of works.·* 5 *Storekeeper.*

"III. ACCOUNTANT-GENERAL, WITH THREE ASSISTANT ACCOUNTANTS.—Branches : 1. Fleet in commission. 2. Dockyards. 3. Civil branch and pensions.

"*The Minister of Marine* to be a member of the Cabinet, changeable with the Government; he might be a civilian.

"The chiefs of departments to be permanent, so long as no

special reason existed for a change. These chiefs not to meet
as a board. Each man should have the nomination of the men
who were to act as his assistants, as on them in a great measure
would depend the credit of his administration.

"In addition, there must be *a council*. Some men might
be admirable for carrying out a known system, but might not be
the ones fitted for suggesting new measures. Very often young
officers would be required to give their opinions, they not being
so wedded to old routine. The council to be formed of officers
of different ranks from the best service men. If this were done,
there should be no jealousy between them and the heads of
departments, who should be glad to join in council with men
fresh from the service."

A council formed so as to include some junior officers would
be less likely to pass over valuable inventions.

He referred to the delays that had sometimes occurred
in adopting evident improvements which were urged on the
Admiralty. He instanced the need of having junior men on
the council, because of the prejudice among older officers to
improvements, by stating that one of our most celebrated generals,
as capable a commander as ever existed, had been long opposed
to replacing the old " Brown Bess " by the rifle !

A civilian would soon become as capable as a naval man for
the post of sole minister.

"*But taking such a system as you have just sketched out, wherein
would be the check upon the abuse of patronage ?*"—" In the sole
responsibility, in the first place, being upon the Minister of
Marine, not a joint responsibility with a board ; but there
would also be the responsibility of the permanent head, or
commander-in-chief of the navy, in picking out and recommending to the Minister of Marine the officer whom, in his experience
as commander-in-chief of the fleet, he had found deserving of
the appointment or promotion, in which he would be very much
assisted by the head of the discipline and inspection branch, who
ought to see every ship before she leaves England and on her
return, and also see every report of the state of the ship abroad, so
that all the facts of the state of each ship might be known before
officers were either promoted or recommended for promotion on
the one hand, or blamed on the other hand, perhaps sometimes
unjustly.

"The evils of the present system, so affecting the promotion
of the officers, particularly of late years, are caused by the
changes more than by the political patronage of any First Lord
whilst he is in power. I believe there has scarcely been a First
Lord at the Admiralty for the last thirty years who, if he could
have remained permanent head of the navy, after once ascertaining the relative merits of the officers, would not have given
more satisfaction to the service officers than has been the case.

"Although a man may have been a good captain, yet, when he comes to be wanted for the higher commands, totally different qualifications are necessary; not one man in twenty, perhaps, would have the qualifications which would make him fit to be picked out for important command in case of war."

"*Is it your opinion that the defect is a want of clear and well-defined responsibility in the First Lord, and in the various heads of departments?*"—"I think so, the navy being administered by a board responsible jointly, instead of under individual responsibility. It has been said that the First Lord is solely responsible, but certainly it is quite a new idea to those who only know the service from the outside.

"I know that the feeling is very strong amongst officers in the army against the suggested assimilation of the system of the army to the system of the navy, because, they say, they have been comparatively free hitherto from the evils which existed in the navy of a changeable head of the fleet."

"*You have looked to the case of the army. Do you think that birth goes for nothing, and that pre-eminent service stands for everything, in the choice of the commander-in-chief of the army?*"—"I think there is a great advantage in having a man who, like the commander-in-chief of the army, has served, and is also free from political bias; and though it is not always so that the commander-in-chief is a member of the royal family, I think the navy would be very well satisfied if their own patronage was in the control of a similar person, if he had served in the navy and had the necessary qualifications."

Reference being made to complaints of recent selections for army commands—"I suppose that under any administration, however good, those cases of unjust selections will occasionally occur; but I think it would be found that they do so through pressure put upon the commander-in-chief by a higher power, and nothing, perhaps, but a man so independent and so determined to stand his ground, and say, 'If you insist upon that being done I resign,' would put a stop to it We have been pretty plainly told that the commander-in-chief of the army has resisted it in some few cases, till he has been told that he must do it.

"The strong impression in the navy is that a great deal of injustice done to the navy in the way which I have stated (in the curtailment of necessary outlays) is owing to the Treasury pressure brought to bear upon the First Lord and Secretary to the Admiralty at times of political change."

In the course of his three days' examination Sulivan, by quoting a number of cases, showed that meritorious officers without influence had formerly had little prospects in the service. There was an attempt in certain quarters to suppress this evidence. The room was once cleared for the commissioners to consider whether testimony he was desirous of giving should be allowed. Whilst outside, from among the large number of officers present, an old gentleman—a stranger to him—came up to Sulivan and said, "We have been saying how good it is for the navy that these things should be exposed; but I understand that you have two sons in the navy. Would it not be well for their sakes that you did not say so much?" Sulivan replied, "If it does good to the service, it will do good to my sons; but, anyhow, I must consider the interest of the service before that of my sons."

The commission terminated with his vigorous denial of the accusation that naval officers entertained jealous feelings when men of real merit were passed over their heads—*i.e.* when the selections were not governed by favouritism.

APPENDIX H.

NAVY (PROMOTION AND RETIREMENT), 1863.

TITLES OF OFFICERS.—When examined before the Select Committee on the Navy in 1863, he suggested that the titles of naval officers should be altered, as great confusion was caused, to their prejudice, when serving in the field with army officers, as well as in civil life, by the existing system. The following are the changes he suggested :—

Present Naval Titles.	Proposed Naval Titles.	Corresponding Army Rank.
Admiral	Admiral	General
Captain	Commodore	Colonel
Commander	Commander	Major
Lieutenant	Captain	Captain
Mate, or Sub-Lieutenant	First Lieutenant	First Lieutenant
Senior Midshipman	Second Lieutenant	Second Lieutenant or Ensign

Junior Mids and Cadets to be confined to training-ships.

FLAG RANK.—"Selection should be one of the means of filling the admirals' list, but it should be selection exclusively for service in action, in order to test the qualifications of a captain for command. I could prove to the committee by cases, if necessary, that officers who have done well and behaved gallantly in the junior ranks have failed through unfitness for command of a squadron during war. For selection to the rank of admiral, without waiting for seniority, distinguished service before the enemy should be requisite. During peace, without the means of ascertaining so well the qualifications of officers, it would be better not to have selection. Officers who, during a time of war, had not only shown gallantry upon ordinary service, which of course they would do, but real superior ability, showing them fit for command, or who had distinguished themselves in any superior way, should be eligible for promotion to the flag list, exactly as there have been men in the army promoted from the rank of colonel, very often of small standing, to that of major-general, both in the Crimea and India, for special service. Some officers who, when that war broke out, were junior to captains in the navy have been promoted not only to the rank of major-general, but to that of lieutenant-general, while a naval officer, going through the same service, must have remained on the captains' list till this time without any promotion for his service, and, if he happened to be a C.B. before, without the slightest honorary reward of any kind."

APPENDIX I.

MERCHANT SHIPPING (1860).

COAST LIGHTS.—The following opinions, it must be remembered, are those of one who was for nine years head of the Lights and Pilotage Department of the Board of Trade :—

"*Have you considered the point as to the desirability of charging the lights upon the shipowners, as compared with charging them upon the Consolidated Fund?* "—"Yes, I think that generally the principle that vessels should pay for what is of use to them is a right one to a certain extent; and, on the other hand, that the safety of vessels and of their crews is partly a State question, and I think that the decision come to by the Harbour of Refuge Committee of the House of Commons is a very fair one, dividing the expense in the case of proposed harbours of refuge into half being paid by the shipping in the shape of a passing toll, and half being paid by the Government for the State benefit derived from those harbours. I would apply the same principle to lights. I think that, in addition to the lives and property in which the State is interested to a certain extent, we have also a large navy interested in the lights, and I think it has been unfair that the State should not have paid towards the lights for the men-of-war that used them. Now if we apply the exact measure of half the payment being made by the State and half by those using the lights, and if we shut out for the present the question of other governments giving our ships their lights free, I think it will be found that the State would really have to take nearly the whole payment of the lights in future to make up its fair share ; for this reason— the whole of the lights have been built and maintained hitherto by dues on merchant shipping. A very large sum has been paid for the material and buildings in connection with the lights, and, very roughly, I have estimated that the value of the lights which the merchant shipping have paid for must now amount to at least £4,000,000. Supposing this to be the case, the interest on that money would very nearly amount to the whole sum now paid for the annual maintenance of the lights ; and if we deduct a proportion for what the navy should pay to the lights, if we allow £4,000,000 at 4 per cent., it is £160,000 a year, which really is due to the merchant shipping ; and as the lights cost something over £200,000 per annum, if the country were now to take the whole of them, it would not be paying much more than the merchant shipping would be paying in having provided the lights and handed them over in the complete state in which they now are."

In answer to further questions he said : " I think there would be no injustice if the lights were charged to the Consolidated Fund. In reality the country would benefit to a large amount by the difference which would be saved in the freights. The coasters pay a very large proportion of the light dues. The competition, particularly with railways, is very great, and I have no doubt that everything taken off lights, in the coasting trade at least, and probably in the foreign trade, would be taken off freights, and in that way the public would indirectly regain a great proportion of what it paid. But then there is another consideration—that is, that the Americans, who are the only nation, perhaps, on a sufficiently large scale to compare with our own, give our ships their lights free to a large extent, and, that being the case, it seems hard that American ships should be charged as they are in our ports. I exclude France from the comparison, because they really charge a tonnage due more than equivalent to what we charge them for lights. I have heard it stated that at the time when our own steamers of the Cunard line were getting the use of the American lights free those of the American line were paying £3,000 a year to the English lights."

PILOTAGE.—The report of the commissioners, amongst other things, mentioned " the various anomalies as to pilotage, described with so much professional acuteness by Captain Sulivan and others, are so glaring that no time should be lost in removing them."

The commissioners seem to have adopted his view that " where the system of voluntary pilotage prevails, the supply of pilots is more abundant, their efficiency in no way inferior."

APPENDIX J.

THE ARMY VOLUNTEERS (1852).

In December 1851, at the late Professor Darwin's dinner-table, Captain Sulivan pointed out to a party of country gentlemen the defenceless state of the country, and how easily a small invading force might overrun our south-eastern counties—that nothing but the establishment of volunteer corps, in addition to a regular militia force, would ensure safety. Those present urged him to write to the papers on the subject. In the issues of the *Naval and Military Gazette* for January 10th and 31st, 1852, his letters appeared, advocating also mounted rifle corps, and proposing certain details as to equipment, etc. A little later in the *Times* Colonel Napier proposed a plan almost similar to that of Sulivan, who then wrote to the *Naval and Military Gazette* supporting Sir C. Napier's "column" plan against the military critics, and illustrating the advantage of it from his own experience in active service in the river Plata, etc. The *Naval and Military Gazette* stated later, "It appears from documents before us on this subject (Volunteer Fox-hunters), as well as that of the equipment of foot soldiers in irregular warfare, that Colonel Napier and Captain Sulivan have suggested nearly the same thing, and without pirating each other's ideas."

The letter of January 10th, 1852, to the *Naval and Military Gazette* pointed out the danger of an enemy's force landing on the Kentish coast and marching on London. It would be of the utmost importance that the defensive positions taken up on the Sussex hills should be *connected by good roads*, either along the heights or to their rear. Further, Sulivan urged the need of light-armed troops to assist our cavalry and artillery. The militia regiments should be armed with the best weapons, *and the formation of volunteer rifle companies should also be encouraged.*

His letter of January 31st—evidently following other correspondence—laid claims to his having been the first to suggest volunteers. He further suggests that in every hunting district troops of well-mounted young men should be formed, armed with sword and light rifle. These would make a most useful force. Further, he showed the need of mounting long guns in martello-towers on our south coast, to protect the towns from the attacks of small squadrons or single ships advocated by the Prince de Joinville. These should be manned by *artillery volunteers.*

The outcome of the correspondence in the two papers was the offer of several volunteer corps to the Government, the first accepted being the South Devon one, doubtless that of Dr. Bucknill, who recently received the honour of knighthood on this account.

Thus it appears that the credit of being the first to propose the formation of volunteer corps in the three arms is due to my father, but he always admitted that Colonel Napier put forward the idea of volunteer rifles somewhere about the same time.

APPENDIX K.

FLEET ACTIONS, ETC (1860).

In his paper to the Admiralty of 1860, besides drawing attention to the manning question, Sulivan pointed out that future actions would be decided more by skilful manœuvring of ships or fleets. In the case of two fleets meeting, success would chiefly depend on bringing a superior force more rapidly to bear on the leading ships of the enemy. This would depend on the order and peculiar arrangements of the ships, so as to facilitate a rapid change of direction, and to the handiness of the leading ships. Short ships, therefore, are better than long ships where speed in chase is not required. The most important duty of a commander-in-chief will be to *manœuvre*, and upon his skill will probably depend the result of the engagement. Therefore we must abandon the old idea of the admiral merely doing the duty of a commander of a brigade by going in the biggest ship into the thickest of the fray, so putting himself into the worst position for observation, and perhaps throwing away his valuable life in doing what a junior could equally do. As well might Wellington have led a brigade in action, leaving his army without a head. Future naval actions will depend as much on the admiral and his captain-of-the-fleet as a land action on the general-in-command and his chief-of-staff. These officers, therefore, should be the picked men of the service. It would be madness to risk the fleet, and perhaps the country, by needlessly exposing the men on whom so much depended. But old custom will be hard to break, and few men would have the moral courage to do so without a positive order from headquarters. The admiral's flag, therefore, should not even in time of peace be in a large ship, for he could not well leave her in time of danger, but it should be hoisted in a frigate [or cruiser ?] abreast of a single or between a double line, with every ship clearly in view, and from whence his signals could be seen by all. If the admiral were the right man, success or failure might depend on this seemingly trifling arrangement. If he were not the best man for the post, we should probably suffer defeat, when so much depends on the chief; for the French especially study these matters, and select their best men for commands, regardless of other considerations.

Sulivan also suggested one very important strategical device in connection with gunnery. I think modern improvements in ships and in guns have made these two suggestions of still greater moment

In the same year Sulivan urged on the Admiralty the necessity of casing some of our wooden ships with iron and providing them with rifled guns, as well as the importance of mortars for coast defence.

LARGE OR SMALL GUNS.—The following letter, dated January 1878, written by Admiral W. A. B. Hamilton to Sir J. Sulivan, may be of interest.—

" . . . I quite agree with you as to actions never being decided at long range, nor am I a great believer in turret-ships In my opinion we go too far in quality and leave out quantity. I had in *Achilles* thirteen 7-in. guns on a broadside—*Hercules* had seven 10 in. and 9 in.; but I have no hesitation in saying, had I got within five hundred yards (as I would have fired three shots to her one, I should really have had thirty-nine to seven), I would have made it too hot for them to return a shot. No naval action ever was decisive at long range. History repeats itself. None, in my opinion, ever will be between ironclads. The American war showed that the greatest number of guns generally won the day. At the first attack on Charlestown the northerners were sixty-five guns to a hundred and thirty; and although they had several monitors and the ironsides, they were licked—and again in the James River against a fort (Darling, I think). But at Wilmington, Savannah and Porte in the Mississippi, also at Mobile with Farragut, where they had the greatest number of guns, they won. I was at Boston in '63. Corvettes were sent to Farragut armed with six 11-in. guns. He took out four, replacing them by eight 9-in. guns Experience had shown him that it was only by an overwhelming fire he could shut up forts."

APPENDIX L.

ADMIRAL SULIVAN'S REMARKS ON MR. G. BUTLER EARP'S WORK.

As the only published work on the campaign of 1854 is that written by Mr. G. Butler Earp, "from materials furnished by Admiral Sir Charles Napier," it may be interesting to naval readers to give certain remarks and criticisms annotated by Sir James Sulivan in the margins of his copy. The figures refer to the pages of the work on

which the notes occur. Some others I have already referred to in the course of the journals.

Page 161. *Removing the piles before Cronstadt.*—"The
'engineering' plan was feasible. *Not* diving-bells, but
diving-dresses and gunpowder, would have been the means
employed against the barrier, had the war gone on, after
the enemy's flotilla had been driven from it."

Page 161. *Russian gun-boats.*—"Admiral Corry's weak
point was ' gun-boats.' He actually shut his ports at night
for fear of being boarded, yet there were only a few gun-
boats near him at Sweaborg, twenty miles off."

Page 165.—"The others were nearly all at Cronstadt,
a hundred and fifty miles off."

Page 97.—Referring to the signal made by Napier on the
announcement of the declaration of war, " Sharpen your
cutlasses, and the day is your own," Mr. Earp says it was
the admiral's intention, had he met the Russian fleet outside, to attempt to board the enemy's ships. Sulivan's note
says :—

"Had he attempted it, he must have been mad. It
would have been throwing away the power his screw-ships
gave him of attacking one end of the line and crushing it."

Reviewing the blockade of the Baltic, Sulivan says :—

" I am convinced that the blockade in the Baltic was
of little importance, except to the poor coast fishermen,
who suffered for want of salt. So long as the trade
through Prussia is open, and a regular trade can be
carried on at Tornea, across the Swedish frontier, a blockade is really nominal. There were lines of vessels established on the Finnish lakes, and from Tornea and other
northern Bothnia ports to Viborg the route was chiefly
by water. The roads from the Prussian frontier were so
improved that a ton of goods to St. Petersburg, which
cost £45 for carriage the first year, cost only £15 the
second. The extra cost of Russian produce fell entirely
on the purchasers. Only articles like salt and coals were
entirely shut out by the blockade, and they got twenty-one
cargoes of coals from Sweden the first winter, after our
blockading squadron left."

On page 467 reference is made to the desire of General
Jones, in September, to know the intentions of the admiral
as to any future operations during the season. He also
asked for a steamer to take him to Cronstadt, so that
he might form some opinion about the place. But the

admiral seemed to consider he was assuming more power
than he was entitled to.   My father makes the following
note ·—

"General Jones ought to have had the steamer. He
asked me if there was any difficulty.   I told him we
could go up with two of the good screw-frigates and
see all in two or three days ; but the admiral refused,
saying this would weaken his force.   With an engineer
officer of so much experience so near Cronstadt, he was
certainly entitled on public grounds to any assistance
for the purpose of seeing the enemy's defences.   The ships
would have been going *nearer*, not away from, the enemy,
and any man less nervous about the safety of the ships
would have sent them."

On page 246 reference is made to the controversy between Napier and the Admiralty.   The MS. note says :—

"These private letters of a First Lord to a commander-
in-chief are really semi-official, and often his only instructions on some points.   If a dispute arises on these points,
I think it quite fair to use the letters."

Again, page 246 :—

"I do not think Admiral Berkeley ever said Sweaborg
or Cronstadt ought to have been attacked with the large
ships—that was Sir James Graham.   Admiral B. said,
'If mortars had been asked for in June' (a month before
their use had been suggested), 'they might have been
sent out in time to have bombarded Sweaborg that year',
and in this he was quite right."

A good deal of discussion and criticism of Napier's proceedings followed the return of the fleet, and a sad controversy is carried on in Napier's book.   It may be right here
to add that the return of the fleet was made too soon, from
Napier's nervousness as to the safety of his ships.   Both
Admirals Chads and Seymour, as well as Captain Sulivan,
when he was in the *Duke of Wellington*, constantly urged
Napier to remain, and told him it was safe for screw-
ships for another month.   Next year they remained until
November, and one squadron was off Cronstadt till late
in October.   Admiral Berkeley (p. 482) also showed
nervousness on this point, but he did not really know
what the risk was.   The notes are as follows :—

"The account of the dangers had been much exaggerated.
After proving the safety of the Nargen anchorage in the
September gales, there ought to have been no fear about

remaining. The admiral was broken down by anxiety, and worried by the attacks made on him by the Press, and was not then in a fit state to judge of the risk. He had been from the first so prejudiced against Nargen, that he never would really believe in it."

" He was too weak and ill to bear the charge of such a fleet."

" He was right in sending the sailing-ships home when he did, as the screw-ships left were sufficient for the blockade."

" He was so broken down by anxiety about the anchorage, safety of the ships, etc., that it was really distressing to witness it. While thinking only of attacking Bomarsund, and knowing the ships were in safety, he was a different man. He became stout and strong during the three weeks there, and showed no signs of nervousness. But directly it was over, and the care of the fleet returned, he broke down rapidly."

In his evidence on "manning the navy," 1860, Captain Sulivan stated :—

" With regard to the Russian navy, there has been too much tendency to call the Baltic fleet a paper and patch-work fleet. Even when it was a sailing fleet, I believe, from what we have heard, that our fleet might have taken a lesson from the regularity in their movements every summer in the Baltic. We were told by Swedish officers that the Russians handled their ships like clock-work, keeping their stations well, and manœuvring in a manner that could not be excelled ; and if the officer commanding a ship was the least inferior to others, he was taken away, and a picked man taken from some other ship put in his place. However inferior those men may be as sailors, if the officers can handle a fleet like that, and if the men are the gunners which they proved to be at Sevastopol, they are very good. When so many men were killed in the first year, six thousand seamen were sent from the Baltic fleet to reinforce the batteries at Sevastopol."

INDEX.

ABERDEEN, Lord, 113
Abo, 171, 238, 256
Acorn, 65
Acre referred to, 159, 160, 404
Admiral to direct, not to fight, 427
Admiralty, Board of, 385 ; consult Sulivan, 392; oppose dockyard volunteers, 398, 399; construction of, 419
Admiralty plans, 122, 182
Adventure, 34, 35
Aland Islands, 122, 139, 140; visited by Buckle, 143 ; surveyed by Sulivan, 163 *et seq.*, 177, 208
Alanders, 247, 258
Alban, 181, 208; ashore, 256, 257; 367
Alecto, 105; rapid descent of Parana, 107, 108 ; 110
Algiers, siege of, quoted, 160, 259
Americans adopt coast mortars, 409, 410
Anapa, 265
Andrews, G., clerk, killed at Obligado, 87, 88
Ango channel, 171, 175, 209
Anson, wreck of, 2, 3
Apollon shoal, 149, 356
Argentine Republic, 52
Army, advantages over navy, x, 369
Army volunteers, origin of, 426
Arrogant, 148, 150, 157, 160
Arrow, 49, 50
Astronomer Royal, reception of, on the *Beagle*, 45
Auckland, Lord, and dockyard volunteers, 397
Aurora, 16
Autobiography of Admiral Sir B. J. Sulivan, vi, 1-35

BAKER, Captain (*Gorgon*), 99, 151
Baltic campaign, xxv, xxvi, 258, 259: 1855—plan of, 272
Baltic fleet, condition of, 128; strength of, 131, 139, 181; sailing qualities, 132, 133, 136; 138; in danger, 146; duties of, 183, 241; handling of, 241; home, 262: 1855—277, 278; deficient in small craft, 280; ships grounding, 363, 364
Baltic, rebuoying, 367, 374
Banda Oriental, 106
Baro Sound, 197, 346, 363
Barons, Russian, 309 *et seq.*, 348, 349, 362
Barratry, case of, 110
Basque Roads, case of, 416
Bastia, 204
Batteries, construction of Obligado, 73, 88 ; San Lorenzo, 108; Hango, 158; 405 *et seq.*
Baugh, R.N., 9, 15, 24
Baxada de Santa Fé, 102, 109
Beagle, 13, 28, 33 ; recommissioned, 36, 37, 39; boat expeditions, 40-45 ; Lord Farrer on cruise of, 381
Beagle's ghost, 33; tenders, 39, 40
Beaufort, Admiral Sir Francis, 65, 114, 119; instructions *re* Baltic, 123 ; 139 ; letters, 144, 199, 253
Berkeley, Admiral Sir Maurice, 122, 404, 430
Bingham, Captain A. Batt, 24-29
Bingham, Captain (*Acorn*), 65
Björkö, 197, 346, 363
Bishop made by a captain, 14
Bishop Stirling's reminiscences of Sulivan, 386, 390

Blockade, effects of, on Russia, 312, 319, 429
Board of Trade, Sulivan at the, xxvii, 375-384
Boating expeditions, 40-44
Boats' sails, 39
Bomarsund, 122, 135, 144 ; surveyed, 163, 166 *et seq.* ; forts, 174, 183 ; report on, 177, 178 ; governor of, 186 ; secret of, 201 ; fall of, 208 *et seq.* ; new forts, 238 ; war-chest, 238 ; blown up, 246 *et seq.* ; strength of, 248, 253-256 ; refused by Sweden, 254
Botany, 39, 51
Bournemouth, life at, 391-395
Bovisand, defective fort at, 204, 404
Brazilian war, 27 ; crimping in, 29
Brickdale, Lieutenant, 72, 87, 88
Brierley, Sir O. W., 209, 234
Briggs, Sir John, on Sulivan, 384.
Brown, Amirante, captures Spanish squadron, 27, 28 ; blockades Buenos Ayres, 53 ; scene with Commodore Purvis, 58, 59 ; 78 ; son of, 79, 85
Buckle, Admiral Sir Claude, K.C.B., 139, 141 ; visits Aland Islands, 143, 171, 178 ; *Valorous* aground, 209 ; 214, 226, 241
Buenos Ayrean squadron, 27 ; army, 71, 77 ; bravery of, 82, 84-86, 92

CAFFIN, Admiral Sir J. Crauford, K.C.B., 176, 212, 226, 344
Calvi, Nelson at, 204
Casualties at Obligado, 83
Cecil, Lord D., 309 *et seq.*
Chacabuco, 94
Chads, Admiral Sir H. D., G.C.B., 131 ; gunnery expert, 138 ; 158, 163, 182, 201 ; at Bomarsund, 208, 209, 212, 216 ; Presto channel, 225 ; 235, 249 ; plan for Sweaborg, 267, 268
Chaplain made acting-bishop, 14
Chartist riots, 397
Chartres, Surgeon, R.N., 67, 104
Childers, the Right Hon., 411
Chilian silver merchants, 4 (note)
Chiloe survey, 40, 43
China war, surveyors in, 416, 417
Cholera among French troops, 225, 247, 252 ; mortality, 251, 252, 257

Cholera in Baltic ships, 174, 191, 195-198 ; in steamers only, 199 ; Sulivan on, 251
Christmas at Chiloe, 43
Cleanliness, necessity of, 179, 251
Coast defence, 88, 385, 404-410
Cochrane, Admiral the Hon. Sir A. A., on Sulivan, 164 ; survey of Bomarsund, 166 *et seq.* ; despatch *re*, 177 ; 219 ; at the baron's, 349, 350
" Cockney Sam," 55
Collegians, R.N., 9, 11, 15, 24, 73
Collisions, 408
Colonia, 64, 67
Commander-in-chief of army, 422
Commander-in-chief of navy needed, 420
Commerell, Admiral of the Fleet, Sir J. E., G.C.B., V.C., at Obligado, 79
Comus in Parana, 71, 77, 83
Convoy in Parana, attack on, 102, 103, 112
Coode, Sir John, C.E., 403
Copenhagen, 29 ; compared to Cronstadt, 203
Corrientes, 55, 95, 105
Corrientinos, 98-100, 105
Corry, Admiral Armar L., 152 ; *re* Russian gun-boats, 429
Cossack's boats fired on, 294, 299
Cotesworth, Lieutenant William, R.N., 11 *et seq.*
Cowell, General Sir John, R.E., K.C.M.G., 165, 166
Creyke, Captain R. B., R.N. (*Merlin*), 276, 304, 309, 338, 339, 341, 347, 348
Cronstadt, survey of, 185 *et seq.*, 287 *et seq.* ; compared with Copenhagen, 203 ; strength of, 204, 205, 255, 262, 265, 281 ; weak side, 273 ; plans *re*, 273 ; 279 ; new defences, 274 ; infernals, 301 ; our means against, 305 ; Ignatieff on, 367 ; lessons from, 406-409 ; 429
Cudlip, Commander F. A., R.N., 127, 220, 224 ; at Bomarsund, 231, 257

DAGO Island, 147, 308, 309, 350, 352
Darwin, Charles, 40, 41, 381, 382

Dauntless, 148

Degerby, intercourse with peasants at, 168, 175, 209, 210, 212, 258

Despatches, Hotham's, 113, 115, 116; Napier's, 240, 263, criticised, 252; Dundas's, 341; Pénaud's, 341; windy, 354, 359; Wellington's on the Press, 361, 362

Desperate and *Lightning,* 147

Dinghy, expedition in, 102

Dirt and disease, 250

Discipline, in *Philomel,* xxiii, 58, 111, 112; in *Merlin,* 126, interference of Parliament and Press with, 419, 420

Disestablishment question, the (Ch. of Eng.), 392

Distilled water, use of, 252

Dolphin, 67, 71, at Obligado, 76-79; casualties, 83, 87; at San Lorenzo, 102, 103

Doyle, Commander, 64, wounded, 76, 84, 88, 94; death of, 104

Dragon attacks Hango fort, 155

Drew, Admiral, 11

Duchesne, Admiral Parseval. See French admiral, 1854

Dundas, Admiral Sir R. A., K.C.B., characteristics, 280; 284; at Cronstadt, 287, 289, 291, 299; divided authority of, 300; Cronstadt, 304, 306; Sweaborg, 323 *et seq.*; congratulates Sulivan, 327, 331; inspects effects, 337; despatch, 341, 344; on Sulivan, 356; humanity of, 362, 363; re Cronstadt, 366; on honours, 370

Dutch loan, Sulivan's proposal *re,* 239

Dyer, Captain R. C., R.N., on Sulivan, 124; 276, 350

EARP, G. Butler, "History of Baltic Campaign of 1854," 428-431

Edmonstone, Admiral Sir William, K.C.B., 11

Ekness, 157, 160, 311

Eliot, the Rev. P. F., Dean of Windsor, 395

Ellenborough, Lord, 397

Engineers, lack of, in Peninsula and Crimea, 416

Ensign, British, similar to Russian, 187

Ensign, red, white, and blue, 411

Erskine, Admiral J. E, 147, 286, 346

Esquina, 97

Evans, Captain Sir Fred T. O. (Hydrographer), joins *Lightning,* 127; pilots Admiral Plumridge, 130, 139, 150, 162; at Bomarsund, 209, 210; pilots French at Bomarsund, 220, 226; despatch *re,* 240

Expéditive, 71, 87

Explosion of infernals, 291 *et seq.,* 300 *et seq.*

Fairley, H.E.I.C.S., mistaken for French ship, 25

Falkland Islands, xxv; survey of, 48-51; tussac, 51; 116; Sulivan farming at, 400-402

Fanny, 71; at Obligado, 75-83; 99; at San Lorenzo, 102, 103; 106

Fanshaw, Admiral E. G., 294

Fantôme, 59

Faro Sound, 130, 279, 282

Farragut, Admiral, U.S., *re* small guns, 428

Farrer, Lord, on Sulivan, 379-384

Fegan, Lieutenant, 57

Ferguson, James, 404

Filey, proposed harbour at, 402-404

Finns, 162, 163, 179, 186; at Biörkö, 195; 312, need of salt, 346, 356; sufferings of, 360, 364

Firebrand, 65; at Obligado, 71, 79, 83; 95; San Lorenzo, 103, 108

First Lord, disadvantage of a changeable, 421

FitzRoy, Admiral R. O'B, Goldmedallist, 12; in *Thetis,* 24, 29; in *Beagle,* 33, 36-46; on Sulivan, 46, 49

Flag captured at Obligado returned, 91

Flag-of-truce, Sweaborg, 199, 243, 298, 299; fired on at Hango, 294, 295

Flag rank, promotion to, 423

Flag-ship should not be a battle-ship, 427

Fleet actions, 427

Fleet. See Baltic fleet

Floating batteries, 241, 273, 274, 366

Flogging for drunkenness, 32

Flores, Colonel, 63, 105

Fog, fleet in a, 146, 147, 282

Foote, Lieutenant, drowned, 140, 143
Forts, shelling of, 152, 157; Cronstadt, 190 *et seq.*; defective at Bovisand, 404. See Batteries and Ships *v* forts
Francia, Dr, *re* Paraguayans, 95, 98
French admiral : 1854—Bomarsund, 182, 209, 214, 216 1855—supports Sulivan, 275; Cronstadt, 306, *re* Helsingfors, 307
French captains taught by Sulivan, 291, as pilots, 415, 416
French general (D'Hilliers) at Bomarsund, 216, 217, 220, 228 (note), 247; *re* Abo, 237, 238; (Niel), *re* Sweaborg, 270
French gunnery proverb, 265
French impetuosity, 382
French in Parana, system of drill, 55, 56; rewards, 112
French, knowledge of language useful, 249
French mortars, 320
French officer's remarks on Sulivan, 196, 214, *re* Bomarsund, 217, 218, 232, 242, 291, 297, 374
French ships in Baltic, well manned, 121; 137, 139, 143, piloted, 137, 209, 415, return home, 249 1855 —at Cronstadt, 289
French ships in Parana, 65, 71, gallantry at Obligado, 77, 80, 82, casualties, 83, 86, 90, 103, ascending Parana, 104, 108, 383. See *San Martin, Fulton,* and Tréhouart
French troops in Baltic, 201, arrive, 212, at Bomarsund, 215, 219, 223, 225, 227, 228 (note), 230; blow up forts, 247, cholera among, 250-252
Fulton (P S), 71; at Obligado, 78, 79, 83; damage to, 89; up Parana, 97, 106; in Baltic, 219

GAMLA Carleby disaster, 180, 199, 295
Ganges, 12
Gardiner, Captain Allen, R.N., xxviii
Garibaldi, red shirts of, 55; in the Uruguay, 66, 67
Ghost, the *Beagle's,* 33
Gibraltar, salvage work at, 17-20

Glasse, Admiral F. H H, 143
Gorgon ashore, 63, 65, 71; at Obligado, 79, 83, 90; up the Parana, 99, 101, 102
Goss, Thomas, Master, R.N., 65
Gothland, 131
Gowdy, William, Master, R.N., 24
Goya, 97, 100
Graham, Sir James, 144; *re* Cronstadt, 272, 430
Grey, Admiral Sir George, 10, 20
Grey, Admiral the Hon. Sir Frederick, 31
Grivel, Lieutenant Richild, on vertical fire, 343 (note)
Gun-boats, at Sweaborg, 328; 333, 359; new type, 366; Russian. See Russian gun-boats
Gunnery, 417
Guns at Obligado, 81, 82, 86, 90
Guns, large and small, 428

HALL, Admiral Sir W. H., K.C B, 148, 157, at Ekness, 161, at Bomarsund, 190, 214, 216; 241, 303
Hamilton, Admiral W. A. B., 120; letter on retirement, 316; dockyard volunteers, 397; on small or big guns, 428
Hamond, Philip, Captain, R N, at Falklands, 401, 402
Hamond, Robert N., Captain, R.N., 20, 202, 402
Hango, 141, 148, Sulivan inspects and reports on, 152-160, 246; attacked by *Dragon,* 156, French admiral at, 243; destroyed by Russians, 246; calamity to *Cossack's* boats, 294, 295
Hapsal, 308; scare at, 311, 313, 356
Harbour needed on east coast, 402, 404
Harston, Captain, R.N., 64
Hastings, Marquis of, 402
Hecla. See Hall
Helsingfors, 133, 152; the *Times* on, 263, 282, French designs on, 307; Sulivan helps to save, 318; 337, gratitude of inhabitants, 360
Hewett, Commander William, joins *Merlin,* 276; 309, 349
Hewlett, Admiral R, 191, 334

Hogland, 185, health of, 282, 283, 300

Honorary rewards, 114, 368

Hooker, Sir William and Sir Joseph, 39

Hope, Admiral Sir James, G C.B., 70, 73; cuts chains at Obligado, 79, 80, 114; 81, 83, 93, at San Lorenzo, 103, in Baltic, 126, 151, 346; refuses G.C.B., 369; at submarine trial, 372

Hotham, Captain C., saves *Gorgon*, 63, commands Parana squadron, 65; at Obligado, 73-80, decision of, 81, 84; on *Philomel's* men, 86; ascends Parana, 95, 97, 101, 114; on Sulivan, 116, 119

Hurdle, General, R.M, at Obligado, 72, 81

IGNATIEFF, Colonel Count, 238; re Cronstadt, 367

Illustrated London News, artists, 209, 234, 292, 295, 350

"Infernal machines," 187, 288, 291 *et seq*, 295, 296; drawing and description of, 301 *et seq*.; 306, 308, 319

Inglefield, Admiral Sir, 55, 73

Inman, Rev. Professor James, 9 *et seq*.

Instructions to Napier, 122; to Sulivan, 123, 137, 138

Irish sailors, 31

Iron bottoms for ships, 241

Ironclads, 428

Italians at Monte Video, 55, 66

JAMES, Admiral Bartholomew, vii, 1, 2

Jellicoe, Lieutenant Henry, R.N, 13

Johnson, J. F, Surgeon, R.N, joins *Lightning*, 127; on cholera, 251; *Merlin*, 276

Jones, General Sir H., R.E., 204, at Bomarsund, 215, 216, 219, 220, 224, 233; at Abo, 238; at Revel, 242; 248, 259, 262; Defence Commissioner, 405; request to see Cronstadt refused, 429

KALBADEN Shoal, 282

Key, Admiral Sir A. Cooper, K.C.B., on Sulivan, xi, xxiv, 116; 35; at Obligado, 73, 76; lands a company, 81, 82, 88; at San Lorenzo, 103, 104; in Baltic, 126, 212, 356, 357; at Bomarsund, 223, 224, 228; saves his ship, 241; 291, 315; watches Sweaborg, 357, 358, humanity of, 358, 359; sub-marine trial, 373, 405, as navigator, 415

King, Philip Gedley, R N, 42, 45, 46, on Sulivan, 47, 48

Koivasto, 192, 285

LAINÉ, Admiral, 55

Lawrence, Colonel, R M., 98, 329

Led Sound, 167; anchorage, 253

Legion of Honour, Sulivan recommended for the, 218, 374

Leiningen, H S.H Admiral Prince Ernest of, G.C.B., in Baltic, 351-355

"Letters from the Baltic," by Lady Eastlake, 284

Letters, official's private, fair evidence, 430

Letters, Sulivan's, how to be treated, 127

Levinge, Commander R, 71, 72; at Obligado, 75-78; losses in *Dolphin*, etc, 83-89; at San Lorenzo, 103

Lighthouse at Cronstadt, 189, 190

Lightning commissioned, 122, 129, sandwiched, 133; takes *Desperate* for enemy, 147; leads French fleet, 178; at Cronstadt, 187 *et seq*.; takes officers to Cronstadt, 192; takes masters to Bomarsund, 209; French officers ditto, 216; supplies rocket battery and men, 210, 231, 257; behaviour of men, 236; immunity from cholera, 251, 252

Lights, coast, 375, 378, 424

Lindley, Professor, 38, 51

Lovisa, 311

Lucas, Admiral C D, V.C, 190

Luckraft, Captain Charles M, 132, 140

Lydiard, Captain, in wreck of *Anson*, 1-3

MACKINNON, Captain, 94, rides with

mails, 105; describes descent of *Alecto*, 107; with rocket battery, 112

Maderiaga, General, 55, 105

Mandeville, W., 53

Manning the navy, deficiency of men for Baltic fleet, 120, 121; Sulivan's scheme, 418, 419

Mansell, Captain, 258

Marines at Obligado, 82

Martin, Admiral H. B., K.C.B., 196, 208

Martin, Captain G. B., 57

Martin Garcia, 64, 67, 69

Master of Baltic fleet: 1854—135, 142, 151; places *Dragon* against Hango, 156, 157, 212; with *Penelope*, 226; at Bomarsund, 227

Master line, abolition of, 411 *et seq.*

Masters, R.N., 151; at Bomarsund, 209, 212, 237; at Sweaborg, 266; junior, inexperienced, 412; as pilots, 414

Matheson, Sir J., 51

Mazères, Lieutenant, 74

Mechanics good gunners, 400

Medals, 114

Mellersh, Admiral A., C.B., on Sulivan, 46, 47

Merchant Shipping Bill, 424

Merchants in Parana, 100, 104

Merchants of Chili, 4 (note)

Merlin, Captain Dyer on, 124; commissioned, 276; explodes infernals, 291, 292; at Sweaborg, 320; ashore, 336, 339, 347; officers recommended, 338; home, 365; leads line at review, 367.

Midshipmen, education of, 23; as navigators, 413

Milner Gibson, T., on Sulivan, 378

Missions to Seamen Society, 392

Money, Captain, R.N., 3, 5, 6

Monte Video, 28; siege of, 54, 57, 62; Colonel Flores shot, 105; 110

Moresby, Captain, 173

Moriarty, Master of *Duke of Wellington*, 213

Mortars, Sulivan suggests, 268, 274, 430; ranges, 275; for Cronstadt, 299; at Sweaborg, 320 *et seq.*; French, 328, 334, 335; bursting, 339, 340; Wemyss on, 342; for coast defence, 406 *et seq.*

Mosquitoes in Parana, 72, 97, 98

Mundy, Admiral Sir R., K.C.B., 215, 224, 291

NAPIER, Admiral Sir Charles, K.C.B., 120; commands Baltic fleet, 122, 135; his anxiety, 123, 158, 430, 431; 138, 145; his advisers, 150, 151; plan *re* Bomarsund, 181-184; Cronstadt, 191, 192, 195; Sulivan defends, 202-207; attack on Bomarsund, 213, 216, 221; divided responsibility, 237; wishes to attack Abo, 238; despatch *re* surveyors, 240; 243; Beaufort on despatches, 252; orders home sailing-ships, 253; character of, 254; firmness of, 259; coolness of, 261; attacked by Press, 263; goes home, 266; kindness to Finns, 365; "Sharpen your cutlasses," 429

Napier, Colonel, *re* army volunteers, 426

Napoleon Bonaparte on army in relation to navy, x

Nargen, Sulivan urges its safety, 150; visits peasants at, 284, 300; fleet at, 344; 347; gale at, 362, 363

Nash, Charles, Lieutenant, 15

Naval reserve, origin of, 120, 121, 411, 418, 419

Naval review at Spithead, 1856, 126

Navigating officers, 411-418

Navy in relation to army, x

Navy, reforms in, 375; administration of, 385, 419 *et seq.*; commander-in-chief needed, 420

Nelson, tactics of, 118, 151, 203, 207; blockading, 265

Newspaper Press and correspondents, 123; officers' letters to, 201, 214, 237; as war critics, 255, 256, 259; Wellington on, 361; interfering with discipline, 419

Nicholson, Lieutenant, at Obligado, 79

Niddrie, Surgeon, R.N., gallantry of, 90

Niel, General, plan *re* Sweaborg, 270

Nugent, Colonel Sir C. B., R.E.,

K.C.B., at Hango, 155, 156; *re* Bomarsund plan, 182

Nystad, 311

OBLIGADO, battle of, 55, 73 ; action, 75-92; French at, 382

Obligado, schooner, 76, 97

Odin's boats attacked, 180, 240

Oribe, General, 58-60

Osborne, Captain Sherard, on Obligado and Sevastopol, 90

Otter, Admiral H. C., C.B., pilots French, 137 ; 176; destroys telegraph, 181 ; 212, 218, 223 ; at Bomarsund, surveys landing-place, 224, 227, 240 ; ship on shore, 256 ; 257, 277, 286; explodes an infernal, 292 ; 338, fired on, 345, 346 ; leads line at review, 367

Ozel, 308, 309, 312

PACKINGTON, Sir John, 411

Paisley, Admiral Sir Thomas, 64

Palmerston, Lord, interview with, 112

Pandour, 71, 77, 83

Paraguay, 95 ; commerce of, 96 ; manifesto, 98, 99

Parana campaign, xxiv, xxx ; cause of, 52 ; 65, 95, 101

Parana, navigation of the, 106, 113, 115

Parker, Admiral Sir W., 124, 416

Patuxent, expedition, the, 4

Paysandu, 66

Paz, General, 71, 98; generalship, 100, 105

Peace, 318 ; Sulivan's desire for, 319, 361

Peel, Sir R., on Napier, 202, 203

Pelham, Admiral the Hon. F., at Bomarsund, 223, 229 ; 291, 304

Pénaud, Admiral, despatches, 341 ; at Revel, 344 ; 348, 356

Penelope on shore at Presto, 226

Pension, Sulivan's, 378, 383

Phillimore, Admiral Sir John, Bart., 11, 12, 14-24

Philomel, commissioned, 56 ; smartness of, 57, 63, 86; at Obligado, 71 *et seq.*; casualties in, 84; passes batteries San Lorenzo, 108 ; discipline of, 111, 112; home, 112.

Pilots, in Parana, 107 ; Baltic, 134, 135, 136, 139, 413 *et seq.*; compulsory, 379, 425

Pincher, loss of, 48-50

Pioneer officers needed, 416

Plumridge, Admiral Sir J. B., K.C.B., 128 ; at Aland Islands, 130-135 ; 139 ; burns vessels, 171 ; 185 ; at Bomarsund, 218, 220, 224 ; handling of ships, 241 ; 243; goes to Kiel, 262 ; destroys Russian property, 295

Political patronage, 422

Ponsonby, Lord and Lady, 20, 21, 31, 33

Port Baltic, 206, 207, 347

Preedy, Admiral G. W., 223, 239

Press. See Newspaper Press

Prisoners, treatment of Monte Videan, 63 and note ; Russian, 161

Procida, 71, 83

Promotions, Obligado, 113 ; Bomarsund, 256 ; Sweaborg, 359; by interest, 419

Punishments, 58

Punta Gorda, 95

Purvis, Admiral, 53, 58 ; scene with Amirante Brown, 59, 60

RAM, the, suggested by Sulivan, 408 ; Russians practise the use of, 408 (note)

Ramsay, Admiral G. (*Euryalus*), 282, 283, 304

Ramsay, Admiral Sir W., K.C.B. (*Hogue*), at Bomarsund, 223, 229 and note, 231, 232

Ramsay battery, the, Russian astonishment at, 234 ; scanty promotion for, 239, 248 ; behaviour of "Lightnings" in, 236

Range of Russian guns, 289, 306

Reforms checked by older men, 421

Republicano, the, 77-79

Reserve. See Naval reserve

Revel, question of attacking, 243, 259, 360-362 ; new defences at, 281, 284, 308 ; 311 ; Grand Dukes at, 314

Review at Spithead 1856, 366

Richards, Admiral Sir G. H., K.C.B., F.R.S., vi ; reminiscences of Sulivan, xxi-xxxii ; in *Philomel*, 56, 58, 68, 73 *et seq.*; lands at Obli-

gado, 81; 93, takes temporary command of *Philomel*, 100; promoted, 113, 392
Rincon Gallinos, the, 65
Risking lives, 93
Riviera, General, 53, 110
Road, military, needed on Surrey hills, 426
Rodriguez, Colonel, gallantry of, at Obligado, 79, 92, 93
Rosas, General, stories of, 52, 69; policy of, 95, 98-100, strategy of, 102-104
Rossinière, Suisse, fight at, 378 (note)
Rouse, Lieutenant J. Wood, 9
Royal commissions See list of Appendices, xix, xx
Royal Naval College, 8, 73
Royse, Rev. N., R.N., acts as bishop, 15
Russian charts, 274
Russian compliment to Sulivan, 367, 474
Russian cutting-out plan, 357
Russian fleet in Baltic, 121; strength of, 132, 139, 152, 159, 253; position of, at Cronstadt, 187-189, 281, 284, 286; good handling of, 431
Russian frigate, a, 245
Russian gun-boats, 142, 289, 295, 304, 305, how built, 317; 357
Russian gunners, at Ekness, 160, Sevastopol, 431
Russian heating apparatus, 352 and note
Russian peasants, at Hango, 162, 163; Aland Islands, 168, 172, 173, 176, 209, 287; sufferings of, 301. See also Finns
Russian police officer, 209, 211
Russian prisoners 161, 257; killed at Hango, 295
Russian tactics, 152
Ryder, Admiral Sir A. P, K C.B, 148-150

SALT trade, Russian, 312, 346
San Lorenzo batteries, the convoy passing, 103, 108, 112; *Philomel* passing, xxxi, 109
San Martin at Obligado, 71, 77, 79, 83, damage to, 88; 95

Saumarez, Admiral Sir J., tactics of, 206; 261
School-ships, 418
Scurvy, 97
Seaman's letter, a, 111
Seamen, drink and, 32; at play, 44; when trusted, 56, 58; drilling, 72, 73; *Philomel's* behaviour, 111; *Merlin's*, 126; improvement in, xxix, 411
Seamen-battalions, 72, 120, 145; at Bomarsund, 181
Seamen, qualities required in, xxii
Selection for service, 221, 280, 315, for flag rank, 423
Seniority *v* service, 370
Seskar, 185, 186, 192, 354
Sevastopol compared, 90, 263, 266, 340; effects on Russian spirit, 297, 318, 319, 361
Seymour, M, Vice-Admiral of the U. K., G C.B., captain of Napier's fleet, 144, 151; on Bomarsund plan, 182; at Bomarsund, 220, 231, 250; in praise of, 247; 260, 262, 269; at Cronstadt, 287, 299; accident to, 303, 306, 307, 345
Sheerness defences, 407
Ships' merits in Baltic, 132
Ships *v.* forts, Obligado, 88-90; Sulivan's warning, 118; Hango, 152-158; Cronstadt, 190; policy of Russians, 202-204, Nelson's tactics, 262-265; coast defence, 405
Shot and shell, effects of, at Obligado, 84-90
Sibbo Fiord, 356
Small-pox in Baltic, 179, 197, 282, 285
Somerset (Lieutenant), L E H., at Bomarsund, 239
Somnambulism, case of, 37
Spaniards oppose salvage of wrecks, 17
Spithead defences, 405-410
St John's, rescue of schooner party, 67-69
St. Michaels, bishop of, 14
Stag, 4
Stakleberg, Baron, 349
Stanley, Mrs, at Falkland Islands, 401
Sternberg, Baron, 309 *et seq.*, 348, 349

Steveley,(?), R N , at Obligado,74,75
Stirling, Bishop, reminiscences of Sulivan, 386-390
Stokes, Admiral, 39
Sub-marine boat, a, 373
Sulivan, Admiral George Lydiard, vii, 6, at wreck of *Jasper*, 274, 304, 394
Sulivan, Admiral Thomas Baker M , 374
Sulivan, Admiral Thomas Ball, C B , vi, vii, career of, 1-6, 51, with Nelson in Baltic, 151, 165
Sulivan, Commander James, 3-8
Sulivan, Commander William S , R N , at Obligado, 80, 87, 148
Sulivan, Commander J Y. F S , vii (note), 51
Sulivan, Lady (B James), vii, viii, Richards on, xxxii, 37, collects flora of Falklands, 51; during siege of Monte Video, 61, 62, 65, at Bournemouth, 391, 394, 395
Sulivan, Lieutenant Daniel Hunt, 3-8
Sulivan, Lieutenant Samuel Hood, 3-8
Sulivan, Lieutenant Thomas E, death of, 393
Sulivan, Mrs. (Thomas Ball), character of, vii
Sunday services and work, ix, xxx, xxxi, 137, 181, 228, in fleet, 291, 297
Surveying, in *Beagle*, 40-42, in Parana, 107, 108, 115, Baltic, 120, instructions re, 123, Napier's opinion re, 128, 134, 136, 262; his despatch re surveyors, 240, a unique cruise, 351, service, Sulivan on the, 415-417, work, Sulivan's, x, xii, xxii; official recognition of service, xxvii, 418
Sweaborg, delay in examining, 135, 136, 150, 151, flag-of-truce to, 199, 298; 203, 204, French admiral at, 244, party under Sulivan nearly netted at, 259, 261, plans of attack on, 266 et seq, defences of, 270; Sulivan's scheme against, 270 et seq; Dundas's hesitancy, 275; preparations against, 279, 280, the admiral's view, 281, detached forts attacked, 304, 309,

bombardment of, 318 et seq, buglers, 323-325, opening fire, 329, effects of mortar fire, 335, 345, 358, 406, batteries uninjured, 340, despatches re, 341, 342, losses at, 361, effects on peace, 367, honours for, 367, 368, rapid mortar fire at, 368
Sweden, attitude of, 130, 131, refuses Bomarsund, 254
Swedish pilots, 134, 139

Tchesterkoff, Commodore, re Sulivan, 374
Tea v grog-drinking, 12
Theorell, Lieutenant, 133, 166
Thetis, 11-30, song re, 16, nearly fires into *Furley*, 25
Thorn, Colonel, at Obligado, 79
Tierra del Fuego, mission to, xxviii, 387
Titles of naval officers, 411, 423
Tonnelero batteries, 110
Townshend, Marquis of, on Napier, 202
Trave, 3
Trehouart, Admiral, xxiv, 74, gallantry at Obligado, 77, 78, 80, 88, 91, ascends Parana, 91, 97, 101, made admiral, 91, 103, 374
Tucker, Admiral Jervis E, 14, 15, 20
Tupper, W. L M (23rd R. W. F) 17, 18

Urquiza, General, 55, 100, 105
Uruguay river, expedition up the, 64
Usborne, Admiral Alexander Burns, 22, 45

Vansittart, Captain N, 350, 353
Vertical fire, at Obligado, 88, at Sweaborg, 329 et seq, Colonel Wemyss on, 342, Lieutenant Grivel (French) on, 343, Sulivan advocates, 406 et seq, foreign countries using, 408, 410, Lord Wolseley on, 410
Viborg, 285
Volunteers, royal dockyard, xxi, 397, 400, army, origin of, 420
Vulture, disaster to boats of, 14, 180

WAR appliances, lack of, in Parana, 69, in Baltic, 296, Admiral Hamilton on, 316
War declared, 1854, 129
War, effects on Russian transit, 362, 429
War, horrors of, 284, 360
War, how to conduct, 160, 194, 197, 337-339, 353 *et seq.*
War policy, the best, 297, 318, 319
Warren, Miss, 51
Warren, R., wounded at Obligado, 88
Washington, Captain (Hydrographer), letters from, 139, 140, 242, 317; on Sweaborg, 347
Washington, capture of, 4
Watson, Captain R B, at Cronstadt, 187 *et seq*, 192, 241, 243-245, 260, 279, 346
Wave, sixty-five feet high, 23
Wellington on intuition of survey, x; on the Press in war, 361, 362
Wemyss, Colonel Sir T H, K C B,
275, 329 *et seq*, 336, 342; promoted, 368
Weser, 3
Wolseley, Viscount, on vertical fire, 410, as engineer, 416
Wodehouse, Admiral George, 15, 21, 24, 245
Wood, Sir C, 272, 365, 370
Wood *v.* iron, ships' bottoms, 241
Woolwich, 3
Wormso, 149, 308, 348
Wrottesley, Lieutenant the Hon. C, killed at Bomarsund, 231, 236

YELVERTON, Admiral the Hon. Sir Hastings, G.C B, at Hango, 148, 150; action at Ekness, 157, 160, 212, seamanship, 241; at Hogland, 300, forced (?) guests, 301, protects Lovisa and Ekness, 311, Russian boats, 353; humanity of, 358
Young, Admirals: James, Sir William, James; Secretary, xii

Milton Keynes UK
Ingram Content Group UK Ltd.
UKHW020711061024
2026UKWH00032B/243